The Decline of Iranshahr

The Decline of Iranshahr

Irrigation and Environments in the History of
the Middle East, 500 B.C. to A.D. 1500

Peter Christensen

Translated from Danish by Steven Sampson

MUSEUM TUSCULANUM PRESS
University of Copenhagen 1993

© 1993 Museum Tusculanum Press & the Author
Printed in Denmark by AiO Tryk a/s, Odense
Cover design: Kim Broström
AiO Print Ltd., Odense, Denmark

ISBN 87 7289 259 5

On the front cover: Ruins of Sultaniyeh. Drawing by Préaux (c. 1840).
On the back cover: Qanat, underground water channel. Photo: Roger-Viollet

Published with the support of
The Danish Research Council for the Humanities
C. L. Davids Fond og Samling
Landsdommer V. Gieses Legat

Denne afhandling er den 5. marts 1991 af Det humanistiske Fakultet ved København Universitet antaget til offentligt at forsvares for den filosofiske doktorgrad.

Jan Riis Flor, h.a. decanus

Forsvaret finder sted fredag den 10. december 1993 kl. 14 i Auditorium A, Studiestræde 6, København K.

Acknowledgments

Historical research is a collective endeavour. This is especially true of long term or macro-history. Working in this field you are obviously dependent on the research and scholarship of specialists. The notes at the end of the book indicate particularly influential authors. Yet the notes show only in part the extent of my debts. In the more than ten years since I began research for *The Decline of Iranshahr*, I have received support from a number of sources. Thus my thanks goes to Professor Jens Erik Skydsgaard and Professor Niels Steensgaard for their advice and timely encouragement. Niels Finn Christiansen, Bernard Eric Jensen, and Peder Mortensen spent time in reading early drafts and discussing some of the issues. They may have forgotten by now, yet I wish to take the occasion to thank them all. I am also much indebted to Jens Rahbek Rasmussen who read the entire manuscript and made many useful suggestions. Needless to say, the errors, oversights, and infelicities that remain are my very own.

This book, in spite of all imperfections, is for Ulla (who is not imperfect).

Copenhagen, October 1993   *Peter Christensen*

A Note on Transliteration and Measures

I make no philological arguments; therefore rigorous transliteration has not been attempted. Place-names are generally given in the common English versions. For other Arabic and Persian names and terms I have largely followed the system used in the *Encyclopaedia of Islam* and the Cambridge histories with the following exceptions:

- Persian *ezafeh* is represented by é or yé
- Persian "silent *h*" is written -eh
- the Arabic definite article is always *al-* (i.e. even when it precedes the "sun letters").

Finally, I have dispensed with the flood of diacritic marks.

The varying measures found in ancient and medieval sources are notoriously difficult (if not impossible) to convert into the metric system. In Iranshahr, as elsewhere, small measures of length were based on the human body: finger's breadth, arm's length, i.e. ell (*zira'*), pace (*gam*), etc. During the Middle Ages several attempts were made to standardize these measurements, but considerable variations remained.[1] Moreover, the small measures are difficult to bring into agreement with the larger measures such as the *farsakh* (in theory the distance covered in one hour) and the *marhaleh* (or *manzil*), i.e. one day's march. On the western Plateau, in the 9th and 10th centuries, one *farsakh* equalled 12.000 *zira'*.[2] Malik Shah (11th century), in an attempt at standardizing, decided that one *farsakh* should be equal to 6.000 paces (*gam*); but in the 13th century Yaqut was told that the *farsakh* in fact was equal to 7.000 paces.[3] I use the following rough equivalents:

1 *farsakh* = 6 km
1 *gam* (pace) = 1 m
1 *marhaleh* (day's march) = 6 *farsakh*[4]
1 *mil* = 1/3 *farsakh* = 2 km
1 *schoinos* = 4.5 to 5.5 km
1 *stadion* = 180 m
1 *zira'* (*dhira, zar'*) = 0.55 to 0.65 m

NOTES

1. See Hinz (1955).
2. Ibn Rusteh (tr.: 186).
3. Mustawfi (*Nuzhat* tr.: 160f); Yaqut (Jwaideh tr.: 54f).
4. Cf. al-Muqaddasi (tr.: 106).

List of Tables

Abbreviations used in Notes and Bibliography

AMI   *Archaeologische Mitteilungen aus Iran*
BGA   *Bibliotheca Geographorum Arabicorum*
BSOAS   *Bulletin of the School of Oriental and African Studies*
BSOS   *Bulletin of the School of Oriental Studies*
CAH   *Cambridge Ancient History*, 3rd ed., London 1970–
CAJ   *Central Asiatic Journal*
CHIr   *Cambridge History of Iran*, London 1968–
CHIs   *Cambridge History of Islam*, I–II, London 1970
CSSH   *Comparative Studies in Society and History*
EI/1   *Encyclopaedia of Islam*, 1st ed., Leyden 1913–1938
EI/2   *Encyclopaedia of Islam*, 2nd ed., Leyden 1954–
GMS   *E.W.J. Gibb Memorial Series*
IC   *Islamic Culture*
IJMES   *International Journal of Middle East Studies*
JAOS   *Journal of the American Oriental Society*
JESHO   *Journal of the Economic and Social History of the Orient*
JNES   *Journal of Near Eastern Studies*
JRAS   *Journal of the Royal Asiatic Society*
JCRAS   *Journal of the Royal Central Asian Society*
JRGS   *Journal of the Royal Geographical Society*
PW   G. Wissowa (ed.): *Paulys Realencyclopädie der Classischen Altertumswissen-schaft.* Neue Bearbeitung, Stuttgart 1894–
REI   *Revue des études islamiques*
RGTC   *Répertoire géographique des textes cunéiformes*
RSJB   *Recueils de la société Jean Bodin*
SHA   *Scriptores Historia Augusta*
SKZ   *Res Gesta Divi Saporis*
TAVO   *Tübinger Atlas des Vorderen Orients (Beihefte)*
TP   *Tabula Peutingeriana*
TS   *Tarikh-é Sistan*
ZA   *Zeitschrift für Assyriologie*
ZDMG   *Zeitschrift der Deutschen Morgenländischen Gesellschaft*

Contents

INTRODUCTION

Universal history, the Middle East, and the Environmental Perspective

According to the Western view of world history the Middle East, in contrast to Europe, has suffered a prolonged decline. Long ago it had flourished economically and culturally, to be sure, and had made an important contribution to the general advance of civilization; but after that Golden Age, which is usually dated back to the early Abbasid period, things had begun to change: populations decreased, ancient cities declined or were even deserted, and barbaric nomadism spread at the expense of civilized agriculture. In a parallel process intellectual creativity was stifled and artistic originality dried up. Thus even before the capitalist world economy made its influence felt, the once dynamic civilizations of the Middle East were turning into stagnate "proto-developing countries": impoverished, disease-ridden, and techno-logically backward.[1]

The present study asks a few simple questions about this notion of decline. How extensive and how general was the contraction of agriculture and the de-urban-ization? What kinds of explanations can we offer? For practical as well as method-ological reasons the inquiry is limited to the lands between the Euphrates in the west and the Amu Darya (Oxus) in the east. The geopolitical unit which we today call "the Middle East" is a rather unwieldy object of study; it is too large and too vaguely defined. In pre-modern times, however, the lands between these two rivers made up a distinct unit, ruled by Persians and marked by Persian civilization; the ancient name of this unit was *Iranshahr*. What forged Iranshahr into a unit will be discussed below. First, however, I shall explain why I have taken up the question of the decline of the Middle East, and how I have tackled it.

The goal of academic history is to explain how the world has come to be as it is. While it may have other tasks and functions as well, this is the primary one, that which makes history a science. Today global problems and conflicts are becoming increasingly visible; the antagonisms between the industrial and the developing countries, the accelerating environmental changes are two obvious examples. So academic history has in recent decades begun to view its issues in more universal, long-term perspectives.[2] However, the effort to obtain new knowledge (as opposed to simply more knowledge) by working in a more synthesizing and comparative manner runs into methodological problems because the data from the various parts of the world are unequal in quantity and quality. Our knowledge of non-European history remains significantly poorer than our knowledge of European history. Outside Europe the data are often insufficient or not reliable, and they have been far less systematized and classified through theories and hypotheses. We cannot be certain that phenomena and processes observed within broad comparative categories such as "pre-modern Eurasian agrarian societies" are really as analogous as they seem on first sight. What world history lacks, therefore, are theories dealing with specific areas and periods outside Europe.

As concerns the Middle East, this lack is especially unfortunate. Regardless of how it is defined and delimited the Middle East includes areas that have always occupied a unique position in the European world view. South and east of the Mediterranean lie those foreign countries with which the Europeans have had the longest continual contact and of which they quite early on formed a systematized (and largely negative) image. Orientals and Muslims, more than all other peoples, have been the others, the aliens, in relation to whom the Europeans could contrast and define themselves.

As early as the 15th and 16th centuries, long before history had become an academic discipline, Orientalism was established as a separate field at the universities of Europe. This early institutional separation, together with the practical difficulties in mastering foreign languages and writing systems, made the study of Middle Eastern cultures and societies an esoteric field for specialists trained in philology. They worked according to their own methods, traditions, and priorities, and gradually formed a set of postulates and generalizations about what made precisely their object of study something unique.[3]

One of these postulates is that the religion of Islam is so heavily imprinted on the societies of the Middle East that it can ultimately explain everything which has occurred or, more to the point, failed to occur. A popular explanation of the decline of the Middle East is that Islam was essentially conservative, irrational, and obscurantist. Thus it constituted an obstacle to development and progress. However, to make such use of Islam as a historical constant is clearly unreasonable, and in recent years this practice has generated several bitter attacks on the Orientalist tradition. Orientalism has been accused of harbouring racist and Social Darwinist ideas and of serving as both an ideological and practical tool of imperialism.[4]

Seen from an impartial perspective these attacks seem not wholly unfounded. But all scholarship operates in a social context, and Orientalism is hardly unique in being an expression of its time; similar accusations of racism and of legitimatizing imperialism could be directed at history, anthropology, geography, biology and other academic disciplines. What *is* peculiar to Orientalism, however, is its academic isolation and its ballast of postulates and generalizations, and these have left the discipline with a restricted thematic perspective. Thus *The Cambridge History of Islam*, presented in 1970 as "an authoritative guide to the state of knowledge at the present day," gives overwhelming emphasis to the history of thought and to political events in the most narrow sense. Social and economic conditions are cursorily treated in a separate chapter with little relation to the rest of the book.

Partly, this is due to the nature of the extant sources. We have masses of legal, literary, and philosophical texts, but little quantitative information about material conditions. Yet it is not the nature, amount, or content of the sources which determine what questions should be asked. The sources can only influence the character of the answers. The priority accorded to the history of thought and elite cultural phenomena is primarily rooted in the professional traditions and methods of Orientalism which emphasize the study of literary and legal texts. These texts reflect the attitudes and preoccupations of small and hardly representative groups. For instance, scholars have thoroughly analysed how, during the Middle Ages, the Middle East transmitted and refined the medical knowledge and theories of the classical world; but few have broadened the perspective to ask from what diseases people actually died and to discover what role disease played in the societies which carried out this theoretical refining. It may be that the conventional priorities within Middle East research are legitimate; but they are also highly selective. This means that whenever the Middle East is included in comparative studies, it will be on the basis of information that has rarely been classified and presented in a way that accords with the issues of world history.

Recently attempts have been made to align Middle East history with mainstream history, chiefly by taking up new research topics and applying techniques that have brought good results in other contexts. Some fine studies have come from this.[5] Yet I am not convinced that this has really shaken the basic framework of research, the deep-seated assumptions and the scheme of priorities. The role of Islam, the progressive decline, even the Mongol disaster, still figure as fixed points in the history of the Middle East. Moreover, some of the techniques, such as quantification, may be of little value because of the nature of extant sources. The new specialized techniques and approaches may even further split up Middle East history into extremely small fields of limited interest.

One way of establishing a framework productive of new insights would be to focus on precisely those phenomena and processes which in the conventional scheme of priorities have been disregarded. Thus the present study does not define the pre-modern societies of Iranshahr as "Muslim societies." They were so only part of the time, anyway. Rather, the point of departure is that they were always agrarian societies. The elite culture and the intellectual life which so dominate the Orientalist tradition had, after all, their material basis in agriculture. So had the political institutions and structures whose fate is often taken as evidence of crisis or decline in society as a whole.

Agriculture in Iranshahr was practiced under severe environmental conditions, qualitatively different from those found in pre-modern Europe, India, and East Asia. This is obvious, but the implications for historical analysis have been largely ignored. Moreover, environmental conditions in Iranshahr were not an unchanging backdrop for the historical processes, including the alleged decline. On the contrary I shall argue that the continual efforts to coerce and modify the environment constituted a dynamic field of change.

Europeans have long considered society and nature (or in less emotional terms, the environment), as two distinct and essentially different entities. Each is governed by its own set of laws; the first by cultural regularities, the second by natural laws. Thus each has become the object of separate, specialized sciences.[6] Belonging to the sciences of society and culture, history has tended to view nature precisely as something apart from society. Nature is a passive stock of resources or a set of obstacles which the human species must overcome to improve its condition. Indeed, key concepts such as development and progress are often defined as man's ever increasing control over nature. Seen in the context of the Western World's success in freeing itself from hunger, in controlling epidemic diseases, and in raising the level of material wellbeing, such definitions seem quite self-evident. Applying broader perspectives, however, it could be argued that developments have in fact gone in the opposite direction: toward less control of the environment and toward increasing impoverishment of the human species in general.

If we have learned anything from the environmental changes in our own era, it is that the two great abstractions of the European tradition – society and nature – must be viewed as a whole. We are locked in one interacting system in which changes in one place inevitably generate changes in the rest of the system. Human agency itself continuously transforms the natural foundations of society; therefore the environment cannot be treated as a constant or a backdrop. This insight applies to the analysis of past as well as contemporary societies. In the millennia before the industrial revolutions man cleared forests, drained swamps, built dikes, dammed rivers, bred animals and plants, and in other ways manipulated nature, often with unintended and destructive results, ranging from soil erosion to the creation of ecological niches for diseaseproducing microorganisms. In fact the rise of the great epidemic killer diseases clearly shows why we cannot separate cultural from biological (including genetic) variables in historical analysis; in a less dramatic way the same point is illustrated in any grain field.

In the arid lands of Iranshahr *irrigation* was the most drastic form of coercion and manipulation of nature. Changes in the extent and character of irrigation were essential features of the historical process encapsulated in the concept of decline. However, irigation was not a necessary precondition for human habitation in Iranshahr, nor even for agriculture. The forms it took were the result of specific historical processes, as we shall see. Irrigation, therefore, constitute a focus in which we can observe the interaction between demographic, geographic, political and other factors. Of course, only closer investigation can reveal the relative importance of these factors in the process of decline. As used here, the environmental perspective is a simple heuristic device, a program of research; it says nothing about causal hierarchies or specific causal relationships; it implies no geographical or biological determinism.[7] The environmental perspective merely serves to highlight some conditions which have gone unrecognized in the past but which we now realize are essential to any analysis of long-term change.

In the present study of decline in Iranshahr I have combined the environmental perspective with a comparative approach. Within the boundaries of Iranshahr regions differed widely in water resources and irrigation techniques. It is the basic assumption of this study that a comparison of the history of the various regions can shed light on the character and extent of the decline and point to the key influences.

Iranshahr's division into environmental regions will be described in greater detail below in part one, as will the sources used for this study. Parts two and three deal with aspects of the historical sequence in the two principal regions: Mesopotamia-Khuzistan and the Iranian Plateau. The analysis covers the period from the 6th century B.C. to around A.D. 1500. The broad chronological perspective is given to distinguish simple fluctuations from more profound, even irreversible, changes. Some emphasis is given to the dating of the changes in irrigation technology and settlement structure, as establishing a fairly precise chronology is a first step toward setting these changes in the proper historical context. In fact, several current theories about Iranshahr and the rest of the Middle East do not fit at all with the chronology of the long-term development. Part four discusses the region of Sistan and compares it to the two larger regions. Finally, a concluding chapter outlines the main patterns in Iranshahr's history and argues that the actual historical changes cannot be defined simply as decline. Therefore the conventional image of Middle Eastern history needs revision.

Part 1
Starting Points:
Themes and Sources

Chapter 1

A Melancholy Prospect

In the winter of 1834–1835 James Baillie Fraser, Scottish landowner, man-of-letters, and sometime political agent, made a journey to the Mesopotamian flood-plain. Once this had been the center of great empires and the heartland of brilliant classical Muslim civilization. Now Fraser found a dreary wasteland studded with the crumbling remains of ancient towns and irrigation works. In the shadow of the *Taq-é Kisra*, the ruin of the palace of the Sassanian kings, wandering Arabs grazed their herds. Altogether it was "really a melancholy prospect," Fraser thought.[1]

Yet it was hardly an unexpected one. As early as the 17th century, when the Ottoman military machine showed the first signs of weakness, the Europeans had convinced themselves that the Middle East had entered a phase of decadence and progressive decline. Within the Ottoman Empire the defeats did cause some critical introspection, but the observers thought that the situation could be salvaged by adjusting and by returning to the virtues of the past. The Europeans, however, saw the Ottoman decline as inevitable and irreversible.[2]

They did so because the Ottoman decline fitted well with other ideas emerging in early modern Europe. History was now thought of in terms of *progress*: Europe's history, despite all temporary setbacks, was characterized by *progress*, understood as cumulative change for the better in material as well as in moral terms. As mentioned, the Europeans were used to think of Islam, i.e. the Middle East, as the absolute opposite of Europe, the inverted reflection of Europe. So it followed logically that the opposite of progress, *decline*, must characterize the history of Middle East.[3] With such a premise, it was not difficult to find confirming evidence.

At close quarters the Europeans could see how military defeats and creeping decadence in the state and the civil society transformed the dreaded Ottoman Empire. Eventually it became the "sick man" who survived only because his European neighbors could not agree on how to divide his estate. In the remoter parts of the Middle East conditions were even worse. Fraser is but one example of how European diplomats, spies, advisers, antiquarians, and other travellers could report back to the European public that the Middle East was indeed in a state of material and moral decline. Few doubted that this sad condition should be ascribed, ultimately, to defects inherent in Middle Eastern society. The Europeans had come to see progress as a virtually natural process. If a society had not evolved in the same positive way as had Europe, there had to be something wrong with it. The defects or obstacles could be several: superstition, ignorance, tyranny, absence of private property, unfavorable environments, or barbarian invasions. The Middle East, which had experienced a veritable slide down the evolutionary ladder, apparently had such defects in plenty.

The defects most frequently emphasized by the Europeans in explaining the plight of the Middle East can be listed roughly under four headings. First, *climatic changes*. According to this theory decrease in rainfall and gradual dessication had led to the desertification of large areas formerly cultivated. At the same time pastures disappeared, a process which contributed to the recurrent invasions of Central Asian nomads. The theory was widely popularized by the American geologist Ellsworth Huntington. As member of the Pumpelly Expedition to Turkistan (1904), Huntington had observed the countless sand-buried remains of ancient towns and this led him to the conclusion that in the past climatic conditions had been more favorable.[4]

Second, *nomadic invasions*. In its simplest form this explanation states that the incursions of the Middle Ages, and especially the Mongol onslaught of the 13th century, caused such extensive material and demographic losses that the Middle East was unable to recover. This is really a paraphrase of the medieval horror stories of Mongol savagery and rests on the assumption that nomadism and settled agriculture are antagonistic ways of life. In the continual struggle between the two, the nomads allegedly enjoy the advantage of an inherent military superiority: they are born to fight on horseback, and their way of life breeds in them endurance and discipline.

Similar assumptions lie behind more recent theories of nomad destructiveness. However, emphasis is put not so much on the individual attacks as on the cumulative effect of nomadic pressure. A constant birth surplus forces the nomads to expand; this leads to bedouinization of areas under cultivation and thus to a reduction of the material basis for civilized life.[5]

Third, there is *Islam*. Ever since the 12th century, when church propagandists first drew a distorted picture of Islam as the perverted reflection of Christianity, Europeans have defined the societies of the Middle East as *Muslim* societies. In these, all aspects of life are completely dominated by religion. Islam therefore attained a central position within the field of Orientalism. By definition it was "the great synthesizing agent," as *The Cambridge History of Islam* puts it, the all-embracing religion which ultimately caused the decline of Middle Eastern civilization.[6]

A modern exponent for this deeply rooted idea was Gustav von Grunebaum, and since he organized oriental studies in the United States after World War II, his opinions came to exert considerable influence on the direction of research. His argument can be summarized as follows: Islam does not duly distinguish between that which belongs to God and that which belongs to Caesar. Therefore it has stipulated norms for all aspects of social life. Unfortunately Islam is, or in any event very quickly became, obscurantist, fatalistic, irrational, and several other unpleasant things. This is evident from its rejection of the "Hellenistic legacy." Islam has therefore retarded economic development and contributed to political violence and the establishing of totalitarian, reactionary regimes.[7]

Finally, there is the *Oriental Despotism*. This is the oldest and yet still the most current theory of why the Middle East and the rest of Asia stagnated and declined. Like the images of Islam sketched out above, Oriental Despotism rests on the assumption of an essential difference between Europe and Asia. However, the distinction is geographical and political rather than religious. Even in antiquity authors like Herodotus and Aristotle had argued that on the endless plains of Asia there had evolved a particular form of political organization: it was arbitrary and centralized and very different from the European states which were governed by law. We need not follow the evolution of this idea in detail. By the 18th century the Europeans, while observing the Ottoman military retreat and the chaotic conditions of Mughal India, had associated despotism with decline. From here the argumentation went as follows:

In the Asian empires political power is centralized and unrestricted. This may be because the empires were originally founded on conquest, or because their very size makes centralization a necessity if they are to be administered in an efficient manner. In any case the basic security of life and property known to Europe is lacking. In Asia all people live in constant peril of losing everything, including their lives, without warning. Hence, no one will produce any more than is necessary for the maintenance of life and the paying of taxes. The subjects have no incentives to carry out long-term investments in technological improvements or innovations. As for the rulers, they are usually more interested in elephants and dancing girls than in economic development. Therefore the state's iron grip on social life leads to stagnation or decline.[8]

Despotism also became associated with irrigation. Adam Smith suggested that despotism had originated from the need for large-scale irrigation, and this idea was later elaborated within the Marxist tradition. The key argument is that it takes a large labor force to construct and maintain large irrigation works. To mobilize and discipline this labor force Asian societies had to evolve strong, centralized political leadership. However, once in control of the distribution of water resources, this leadership (and its extensive bureaucracy) assumed control over all other aspects of social life. As the subjects were forced into permanent and total submission, the "hydraulic trap" closed and put a stop to further development.

The first of these four explanatory themes, climatic change, can be dismissed. Admittedly our knowledge of past climatic conditions in the Middle East leaves much to be desired. However, most specialists agree that no significant overall changes have occurred over the last millennia. This has nothing to do with climatic fluctuations: i.e. recurring variations in relation to a statistical average. Such fluctuations have always posed a threat to agriculture in Iranshahr.[9]

The invasion theories have also been criticized in recent decades. Nomadism and settled agriculture are not as distinct and antagonistic as the theories would have it. Rather, the two ways of life might as soon be viewed as end points in a continuum of methods of subsistence. In Iranshahr, it is certainly difficult to find empirical evidence to support the theory of progressive bedouinization. It has even been argued that Iranshahr was in fact understocked with nomads and that the immigrations of the Middle Ages were an economic advantage because they opened up environmental zones hitherto unexploited.[10]

If our view of nomads has become more differentiated, the idea persists that the Mongols and Timur-é Lenk did inflicted serious damage on the Middle East. Western scholarship may now have acknowledged that the reports from the Middle Ages are exaggerated. Certainly the destructions were much more localized than previously assumed. Nevertheless, while nomadic invasions are no longer considered the only factor, they are still brought in to explain the decline.[11] We shall discuss later whether this is justified.

As noted, the idea that Islam has determined historical developments in the Middle East has been subjected to severe and emotional criticism.[12] Further discussion of this idea would be redundant because the basic premise, that Islam is a historical constant, cannot be taken seriously. No doubt Islam contains several constant elements, and as an ideological system it has certainly had great influence on the societies of the Middle East. Yet to elevate religion into something which stands above society and history is clearly absurd. Like other ideological systems Islam has been affected by circumstances external to its specific doctrines. The recent transformation of Shi'ism from political passivity to militant activism illustrates how Islam changes together with the societies in which it exists. This holds true even though the people, who make the new interpretations, claim that they are simply returning to the unchanging essence of Islam.

The debates over the Oriental Despotism offer more perspectives. As mentioned, the ideas concerning despotism rested largely on the empirical knowledge which the Europeans had of the great Asian empires in the late 18th and early 19th centuries. More knowledge has since come to light and has shaken several of the key elements of the concept.

Private property, or something which in practice must have been almost the same, was much more widespread than assumed. Moreover, in spite of their extravagant titles and brilliant courts, the sultans, caliphs, and padishahs of the Orient were not as powerful, neither in theory nor in practice, as the idea of despotism supposes. Geography, technology, and political realities set limits on how centralized the exercise of power and control over the surplus could become.

Perhaps the kings of Europe never became as absolute as they might have wished. Yet within their smaller states they probably exercised more effective control than did their Middle Eastern counterparts. J.M. Steadman may be putting it rather strong when he says that "the Oriental Despot (...) reigns with foremost authority in the realms of fiction."[13] Nevertheless we must be far more specific about time and place, if a category such as "the despotic" state is to have any meaning at all in a Middle Eastern context.

It is precisely lack of historical precision and context that has discredited the hydraulic version of the theory. Of course nobody denies that irrigation and water management were of vital importance in many pre-modern societies; but the ardent advocate of the hydraulic theory, Karl Wittfogel, ignored that irrigation in fact covers a wide range of different practices. By subsuming, for instance, Sung China and pre-colonial Hawaii under a single category, he weakened the geographical determinism that formed the core of the theory. These two societies were in fact very different in terms of technologies, resource bases, political structures, and social organizations.[14] To make matters worse, Wittfogel insisted that Czarist Russia and the Soviet Union also were oriental despotisms. Since neither of them depended on large-scale irrigation, this served only to further weaken his theory. Moreover, Wittfogel's critics have had little difficulty in showing that, contrary to the theory, large-scale irrigation and the development of centralized states did not always coincide.

Yet despite the conceptual and empirical objections, variations on the Oriental Despotism theme remain a popular way of explaining the historical differences between Europe and the rest of the world.[15] Of course this might simply be because no other general explanation has offered a serious alternative; but the theory of despotism does in fact highlight some variables relevant for long-term and comparative analysis. These include the environmental conditions for production, the size of political units, and the way in which the surplus is extracted and redistributed. The problem lies with the speculative causal hierarchies embedded in the theory. As we have seen, the environmental perspective focus on the same phenomena as the theory of despotism, but does so without assuming from the outset any fixed causal relationships between them.

Chapter 2

The Middle East, Iranshahr, and the Persian Empires

As a historical term, the *Middle East* is less than satisfactory. It is rich in connotations, but lacking in precision. In modern usage it refers broadly to the arid lands east and south of the Mediterranean. While that region today may in some sense be considered a single geopolitical unit, this has not always been the case. When we speak of the Middle East as a historical entity parallel to Europe (another vaguely defined term), we assume that the ancient societies of the region shared some basic geographical, cultural, and historical characteristics. Yet these are difficult to find. Instead we tend to project back into time modern structures and contexts.[1]

The arid climate and extensive use of irrigation are characteristic traits, of course. Yet they are not particular to the Middle East. More convincingly one could point to the widespread nomadism, existing in symbiosis with settled communities, as something that distinguishes the region. Today, however, this characteristic becomes less significant, as nomads are increasingly sedentarized. The conventional view of the Middle East as something created and defined by Islam is certainly misleading, since the Middle East would then include Muslim countries like Bangladesh and Indonesia. This would completely rob the term of any geographical meaning. In the long view, then, the Middle East seems to lack any distinctive unifying feature. The area was, and still is, heterogenous in geographic, ethnic, and economic terms. Nor has any state succeeded in dominating the entire area for any length of time.

Yet if we apply a political perspective, a certain structure to the area can in fact be discerned. Until the 16th century, when the Ottoman Empire emerged as a great power, the Middle East roughly consisted of two spheres centered upon Egypt and Mesopotamia respectively. These two river valleys formed the largest agricultural enclaves of the region, and each was dominated by successive hegemonic states. Both before and after the spread of Islam the border between the two political spheres ran along the Euphrates. The areas east of the Euphrates and up to the Amu Darya (Oxus), including the modern states of Iraq and Iran as well as parts of Afghanistan and Turkistan, were called in the Persian literary and administrative tradition *Iranshahr* (or *Iranzamin* or simply *Iran*) because Persian domination was a principal characteristic.[2]

For two thousand years, from Cyrus' conquest of Babylon in 539 B.C. until

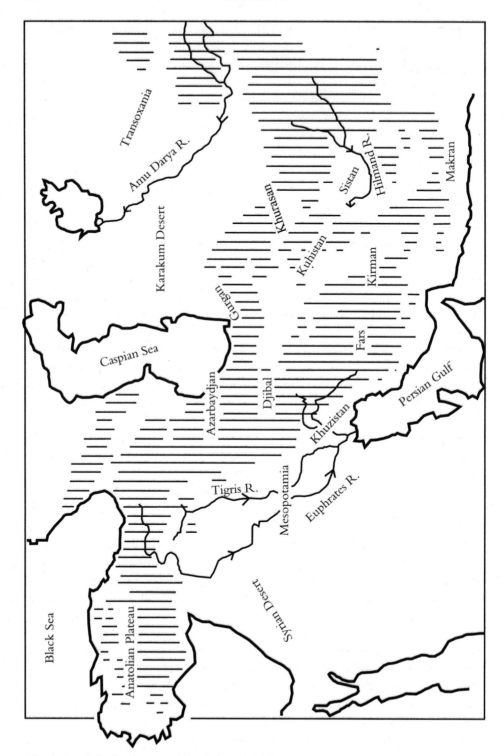

Fig. 1. Iranshahr (hatchings mark land above 1.000 m).

Sulayman Qanuni took Baghdad in A.D. 1534, the Mesopotamian floodplain and the Iranian Plateau were united, formally at least, under successive hegemonic states. Together these may be referred to as the "Persian Empires." The use of such a common designation serves to emphasize that these states, despite their often dramatic history, had considerable territorial and institutional continuity. New conquerors knew very well that Iranshahr could not be ruled from horseback; therefore they usually took over the administrators and the bureaucratic practises of their predecessors with few changes. When the Muslim Arabs conquered Meso-potamia in the 7th century they took over the Sassanian officials, archives, taxation practices, and institutions. Only as late as 697 did the new masters succeed in having the registers written in Arabic instead of Persian.[3]

Other examples could be given of this continuity. Richard Frye even asserts that it was the original Achaemenid bureaucracy that continued in existence, seemingly undisturbed by all the upheavals.[4] That is perhaps an exaggeration. Yet if Iranshahr's history appears on first sight to be nothing but a chaotic series of wars of succession, harem intrigues, and barbarian invasions, the successive empires in fact had a certain institutionalized, impersonal structure. V.G. Kiernan's quip that in the East empires were "ten a dinar" is not a fair appraisal of the Persian Empires. Government may not have been as organized as in the later Roman Empire and some medieval and early modern European state; still the administration of Iranshahr was clearly more than just a ruler's arbitrary exercise of power. Taking the long view, then, we may think of Iranshahr as a historical entity roughly comparable to the Roman Empire. This is not to say that Iranshahr resembled that empire or any other pre-modern "bureaucratic" empire in detail.

In the first place, Iranshahr lacked uniformity. The lands under Persian dom-ination differed from each other in their ethnic composition, geographic features, and patterns of subsistence. In Mesopotamia the mass of population spoke Syriac as late as the 10th century. In Khuzistan the inhabitants retained their own language, *Khuzi*, though they usually spoke Arabic or Persian as well.[5] On the Plateau, where Arabic never seriously achieved a foothold, people spoke different languages and dialects. Their conversion to Islam and to the use of Standard Persian were prolonged processes; in fact the latter is not yet completed. Thus in pre-modern times the uniform and unifying "Persian-Muslim culture" was largely confined to a small elite.

Geographically Iranshahr was divided into countless larger and smaller enclaves and oases, separated by deserts and rugged mountains. In contrast to the Roman Empire, where the chief regions were linked by the Mediterranean, Iranshahr possessed no natural infrastructure. Though the Persian Gulf had from prehistoric times served as a thoroughfare for long-distance trade, it was of little use for internal communication and transport. The larger enclaves and oases were all situated far from the coast and, moreover, were separated from it by mountain ranges.

Beyond Mesopotamia and Khuzistan the normal means of communication and transport were therefore camels, mules, or horses. They were slow and expensive. The imperial courier service, of course, could cover long distances over a short time. In the 10th century, it took seven days to send a message from Shiraz to Baghdad, and this was through difficult terrain. Ordinary travellers, using easier routes along the edge of the great deserts, could cover about 50 km per day. In the mid-11th century Nasir-é Khusraw, travelling as part of a military escort, covered the 400 km from Nishapur to Damghan in a week, and he even had time left over to visit the holy shrine at Bistam on the way. That this speed was not extraordinary can be seen from the reports left by the Polos and later European travellers.[6]

Caravans with goods moved much slower. In spite of the camel's undisputed qualities as a pack-animal and the efforts made by empires and private persons to ease traffic by building bridges, tanks, sarays, and by marking routes through the deserts, caravans rarely covered more than 30 km per day. Yet if caravan transport was slow and dangerous, so was pre-modern seatravel. Sandstorms and high-waymen were hardly worse than hurricanes and pirates. The difference was that the caravans did not have the capacity to transport subsistence goods such as grain across the distances separating the enclaves of Iranshahr. We find nothing in Iranshahr which can compare with the large quantities of grain shipped from Egypt to Rome and Byzantium or, in Muslim times, to the holy cities in Arabia; nor with the grain trade between the Baltic areas and Western Europe.[7] In the 6th century the Byzantines annually shipped 175.000 tons of grain from Egypt. In Iranshahr a similar transport would have required the efforts of 750.000 camels. The regional division of labor and specialization within the production of basic goods, a typical feature of Europe's history, was simply impossible in Iranshahr. In the absence of railways and other cheap, mechanized means of transport the geographic and topographic conditions precluded any close economic integration of the regions under the control of the Persian Empires.

The same conditions which excluded economic integration also set natural limits on the effectiveness of centralized government. In titles, epigraphs, and official history writing the rulers of Iranshahr certainly boasted of their extensive powers. However, if we take the ability to control the extraction and redistribution of the surplus as a criterion, it is easy to prove that their power was in fact quite restricted. None of the successive hegemonic states was ever able to establish permanent administrative control over the surplus from the entire territory they claimed to rule. Of course, under normal circumstances the Empire may not have been prepared to sacrifice considerable resources just to bring remote and poor lands such as Kirman under tighter control.

In some periods the hegemonic states in fact enjoyed authority and prestige extending beyond the range of their effective power. As a rule, however, the farther away one moved from the physical centers of the Empire, the more prominently the local powers, nobles and patricians, figured. The central government had to take them into account and cooperate with them to hold the Empire together.[8] Before the arrival of the telegraph (and the machine gun), centralized administration of the immense, fragmented area was unthinkable. Seen pragmatically the Persian Empires consisted of the imperial core-areas and a surrounding fringe of principalities and enclaves that acknowledged the suzerainty of the "king of kings."

The basic strength of the Empire lay of course in its core-area tax-payers. If the empire wanted to increase the resources at its command, it could either try to conquer more taxpayers or increase production in those territories already under its control. The latter option, however, implied an extension or intensification of irrigation.

1. The Irrigation of Iranshahr: an Overview

Besides the somewhat fragile political unity the lands of Iranshahr had something else in common: the widespread use of irrigation. Everywhere human activity has worn down the landscape, making it difficult to reconstruct the details of past environments. However, the climate itself, i.e. temperature, precipitation, length of the growing season, has not changed significantly over the last millennia. We can therefore assume that agriculture in the past was practiced under roughly the same severe physical conditions as today.[9]

The principal characteristic of the climate is lack of precipitation. Usually the limit for rain-fed farming in the Middle East is set at 250 mm annual rainfall. Large parts of Iranshahr (Djibal, Fars, Azarbaydjan) in fact lie within this limit which, however, is a theoretical one. Since the normal climate is characterized by considerable variations from year to year, averages will tell us little. In recent decades Shiraz' yearly average of 380 mm has masked interannual variations from 114 to 501 mm. In Kirman the variations are from 70 mm to 300 mm, and in the Baghdad area from 72 to 336 mm.[10] Besides, most of the rain falls between November and April when cold in many places has stopped or slowed plant growth, thus preventing full use of the moisture. Conditions other than rainfall affect agriculture as well, e.g. soil composition, dewfall, and local winds. Taken together these conditions point to an annual average precipitation of about 400 mm as the safety limit for rain-fed agriculture, and even within this limit irrigation is frequently practiced to stabilize production and raise the level of yields.[11] On the Iranian Plateau an irrigated field will yield three to six times more than a field watered solely by rainfall.[12]

This reliance on irrigation applies primarily to settled agriculture. Semi-nomads can extend rain-fed farming far into arid zones where average annual precipitation is below 150 mm, because they combine different methods of subsistence and are therefore less dependent on the size of the harvest. Until recently, when the states in the area at last obtained the means to pacify nomads, semi-nomads, mountain peoples, and others with politically suspect ways of life, a broad spectrum of subsistence patterns thus existed in Iranshahr. In other words, large-scale irrigation and the hard work it requires is not the inevitable result of environmental pressures. It is not a necessary precondition for human survival in Iranshahr. Of course, in the arid climate water has always been a vital resource, but there are many ways of putting it to use. Large-scale, labor-demanding irrigation is just one of them. Seen from an evolutionary perspective, irrigated agriculture may seem to represent a higher stage of development than extensive, semi-nomadic forms of agriculture. Therefore it is assumed to be better and more civilized, and a change from intensive to extensive types of agriculture must be a step backwards on the path of human advancement. This is correct in the sense that intensive, irrigated agriculture will yield more per area unit and thus be capable of feeding more people, including non-producers. What is usually ignored, however, is that irrigation is also labor-demanding as well as in many ways risky and unhealthy. The peasants did not necessarily reap the rewards of the construction of large irrigation systems. It would seem that the decision to expand irrigated agriculture was made by those who laid claim to the surplus. At least, they stood to gain most.

In any case the extent and character of irrigation had to be adapted to the specific environmental conditions. If we consider the nature of available water resources, and if we for the sake of argument disregard the existence of innumerable ecological niches and micro-environments, Iranshahr can be roughly divided into three main regions, each with distinct irrigation technologies and agricultural traditions.

The first includes the lowlands to the west: i.e. Mesopotamia and Khuzistan, watered by the Euphrates, Tigris, and Karun, and their tributaries. In the past, exploitation of these rivers was based on extremely labor-demanding technologies, involving construction and maintenance of embankments, weirs, and canals.

The second region consists of the highland Iranian Plateau, including the intermontane basins of the Zagros. Here surface water is dispersed and scarce, and irrigation has to a large extent been practiced by a special device, the *qanat*, that taps the groundwater. Strictly speaking the Sistan Basin to the east is part of the Plateau. Yet in irrigation technology and environment it resembled Mesopotamia, as settlement was also dependent on a large river, the Hilmand. Sistan will therefore be considered separately.

The third region lies along the southern coast of the Caspian Sea. It consists of two deltas, Gilan and Mazandaran (or Tabaristan), connected by a narrow strip of land and separated from the Plateau by the high Alburz Mountains. Because of ample rainfall, environmental conditions here differ radically from the two other regions. Annual precipitation ranges from 1000 mm to 2000 mm (highest in Gilan, to the west). Tehran, just 150 km to the south but on the other side of the mountains, receives 200 mm per year. Even Ibn Isfandiyar (13th century) from Tabaristan, who like other Iranian local historians was convinced that his homeland had the greatest wealth, the bravest heroes, the most learned scholars, and the most beautiful and virtuous women, had to admit that it simply rained too much.[13]

With its swamps and dense forests (now largely gone), the Caspian region offered a unique environment. Irrigation was practiced here too, but chiefly for rice cultivation, something quite different from the irrigation agriculture of the two other regions. The environmental conditions also insured the region a high degree of genuine independence from central control. The Persian Empires might spend considerable resources to establish bases in Amul and other settlements on the coastal plains and attempt to extract tribute; but in the wild, forest-covered mountains the local rulers were virtually untouchable, even when preoccupied with their internal feuds. In this zone Islam penetrated only slowly and the inhabitants continued to speak their own dialects.[14]

In political, cultural, and environmental terms the Caspian zone thus formed a world unto itself; perhaps not completely isolated, but peripheral and in any case clearly distinct from the other regions of Iranshahr. For this reason I have chosen to exclude it from this study. Thus the comparative analysis will include only the first two regions: the floodzones in the west and the Iranian Plateau.

Chapter 3

Sources

The historical information on Iranshahr is unevenly distributed in time and space. Thus we have only two general descriptions of the region in pre-modern times. The first of these, quite brief, dates from the 4th to the 2nd centuries B.C. The second was written more than a thousand years later, in the 9th and 10th centuries. Of some periods, primarily the Parthian, we know virtually nothing for lack of written records, and all periods are characterized by the almost complete absence of quantitative data. In spite of all such lacunae the sources taken together still form a considerable body, written in very different languages and in equally different writing systems. Any attempt to survey long-term developments must of necessity rely on the philological and paleographic expertise of other scholars. Also a selection from the mass of materials is required. The present study largely draws information from the "standard sources," i.e. sources which have been published and in most cases also translated. Since their origin and transmission is generally well-known, it is unnecessary to evaluate each of them here.[1] However, we must briefly examine how reliable or representative the information of the key sources is in relation to the issue of decline.

1. The Image of Persia in the Classical Sources

For the period up to the beginning of the 3rd century the main source for the history of the Iranian Plateau is what survives of the information which circulated in the classical world. There certainly exist contempory Middle Eastern sources such as the accounts of the Assyrian kings about their campaigns in the Zagros in the 9th to 7th centuries B.C.[2] Also there are the Urartu royal inscriptions in Azarbaydjan, the Achaemenid inscriptions,[3] and thousands of clay tablets found among the ruins of Persepolis, containing information about aspects of daily administration in Achaemenid times.[4] Similar information can be derived from the Parthian ostraca discovered by Soviet archaeologists at Nisa, near Ashkhabad.[5] However, all of these texts are difficult to decipher. Brief and providing only details, they are poor substitutes for the overall picture found in the classical sources. It is the historical, geographical, and anthropological information in the classical sources which enables us to sketch out, however tentatively, the main features of Iranshahr's history in pre-Sassanian times.

Precisely for that reason we must keep in mind the limitations of these sources.

Often they have been accorded great authority, as if their every word was well thought out and every single detail carefully checked. In fact the authors were not especially well-informed and inflated their accounts with rumors and various stereotypes. When Plutarch states that Alexander taught the Arachosians (in what is today the Kandahar region) to cultivate the land, this runs counter to all archaeological evidence, and the statement is simply a reflection of the Greek feeling of superiority to the barbarians.[6]

The authors' exaggeration and their Hellenocentric selection of data are not the only difficulties. The way in which the image of Persia was put together also raises methodological problems. The classical world regularly got information about Mesopotamia until the 7th century, including information from participants in various campaigns.[7] The image of the floodplain was therefore largely kept up-to-date. In contrast, nearly all the information about the Plateau was collected over a short time, between 330 B.C. and 100 B.C. Later it was processed and edited, but without any essentially new information being added, until it attained the form in which it was passed down.

Especially in Ionia there must early have been many rumors and bits of information circulating about the Persian Empire, brought back by Greek mercenaries and craftsmen who had worked for the Achaemenids. During the 6th and 5th centuries B.C. Hecataeus, Herodotus, and Ctesias assembled this second-hand knowledge into rather fanciful descriptions of the Iranian Plateau and the lands further east. Apparently the classical world first received reliable information about the lands beyond the Tigris during Alexander's campaign. None of the original reports from the campaign have survived. They are known today only from later biographies of Alexander (Arrian, Quintus Curtius, Plutarch), from historical accounts (Diodorus, Cassius Dio, Justin, etc.), and from geographical compilations (Strabo, Pliny, Ptolemy).[8] In the next two centuries some new information, gathered in the Seleucid campaigns, was added. Strabo thus made use of the report of Patroclus' expedition on the Caspian Sea, while Pliny could cite the general Demodamas on Transoxania. Various information from other campaigns has been preserved in Polybius and Diodorus Siculus.[9]

Strabo did not consider the reports of Alexander's campaign altogether trustworthy. He thought that they had been exaggerated to enhance Alexander's reputation and the farther away from Greece the events took place, the more blatant the exaggerations. Fortunately more reliable sources were becoming available in his own time, he said, thanks to Roman and Parthian domination. He was referring to the historical and geographical works of the Oriental Greek authors such as Apollodorus of Artemita who, around 100 B.C., had written histories of the Parthians and of Bactria; Dionysius of Charax had written a description of the Parthian Empire and this was later used by Pliny. Another Greek from Charax, Isidore, wrote a roadbook of the Parthian Empire, perhaps based on an older

Parthian source from the 1st century B.C.. In contrast to other Greek-Meso-
potamian works this small book has survived.[10]

Strabo's optimism, however, was misplaced. After the establishing of Roman
control over Syria in the middle of the 1st century B.C. the flow of new information from the east gradually dried up. So when describing the countries
beyond the Tigris, Strabo still had to rely on the older reports from Alexander's
time (Aristobulus, Nearchus, and others). It can hardly have been the frequent wars
between Rome and the Parthians that caused the flow of information to stop,
because long-distance trade went on relatively undisturbed. In spite of the wars
caravans continued to bring silk and pepper across the Plateau to the Mesopotamian
cities, from where the goods were transported onward to Syria.[11] Yet the extant
sources indicate that no new information came through this channel. Perhaps the
Parthians and later the Sassanians kept a watchful eye on the traffic, refusing Roman
and Syrian traders to come any farther than the Mesopotamian caravan towns. But
there is evidence that Palmyrene merchants in fact travelled as far east as Marv,
though it is not clear whether this traffic was regular.[12] Perhaps the persons who
wrote the sources extant today did not have contact with the caravan milieu where
new information would be circulating, preferring instead to gather their information from the scholarly literature. Yet Pliny expressly cites merchants as sources for
some of his information on Mesopotamia.[13]

Regardless of what the explanation might be, Roman campaigns came to be the
most important source for new information on Iranshahr. Strabo thus cites Dellius,
one of Marcus Antonius' friends who had participated in the abortive invasion of
Azarbaydjan in 36 B.C., and Pliny sought to keep abreast of developments by
collecting information from participants in Domitius Corbulo's campaign in Armenia (A.D. 54–59).[14] However, the Roman armies never reached the Plateau itself.
When Ammianus Marcellinus, in the 4th century, wrote his account of Julian's
Mesopotamian campaign, he had to put together the description of the Persian
Empire from pieces of centuries-old information without being able to add any-
thing new.[15]

One of the authorities used by Ammianus was Claudius Ptolemy who in the 2nd
century had assembled and systematized the geographical knowledge of the classical
world. Ptolemy's work illustrates how inadequate this knowledge was about Iranshahr. Ptolemy states, for instance, that the Amu Darya (Oxus) flowed into the
Caspian Sea and that the Arghandab emptied into the Indian Ocean. Also he made
the Murghab flow into the Oxus and the Hilmand into the Persian Gulf (via Arbis,
Nearchus' Arabis, in Gedrosia). It is obvious that neither Ptolemy nor his fellow
geographers and cartographers had any clear knowledge of the structure of the
Iranian Plateau, including its drainage pattern.[16]

Nevertheless Ptolemy and a later itinerary, the *Tabula Peutingeriana* (hereafter
referred to as *TP*) have been frequently cited in the attempts to reconstruct the

historical geography of Iranshahr. No doubt this is because they contain many more placenames than can be found in Strabo and Pliny.[17] These names are of little use, however. In his brief description of Kirman Ptolemy says that the interior contained the following towns and villages (*poleis* and *kumai*): Portospania, Carmana Metropolis, Thaspis, Nipista, Chodda, Taruana, Alexandria, Sabis, Throasca, Ora, and Cophanta. With the possible exception of Carmana Metropolis, none of these can be identified with any known settlements, and we cannot determine which were towns and which were villages. Ptolemy then does not allow us to say much about the settlement pattern in pre-Sassanian Kirman. We can only conclude that classical Europe knew of a country called Kirman (Carmania), which contained, not surprisingly, settlements of varying size.[18]

TP is no better. Here, too, it is impossible to determine whether the placenames listed refer to towns, villages, caravanserais, or fortified resting places. Like Isidore's itinerary (which perhaps served as one of the sources) the map shows routes. It is not a systematic geographical description. This perhaps explains why *TP* and Isidore fail to include, respectively, Isfahan and Kumis/Hecatompylus, two large settlements which lay on or near the indicated routes.[19]

With perseverance and no small degree of creative effort scholars have sought to identify nearly all the names which appear in the classical descriptions of Persia. They have compared them with names of known localities and have compared the distances given with those in the Muslim geographical literature. In this way Gabae, in the region of Paraetacene, can be identified as Isfahan. The descriptions of Paraetacene's location fit the Isfahan region, and the name Gabae clearly resembles Djay, the Muslim geographers' name for the old urban center (the *shahr-é Isfahan*) of the Isfahan enclave. In the same way Ecbatana can be identified with Hamadan, Raga (Rhaghes) with Ray, Antioch Margiana with Marv, etc. In all these cases the sources describe the location and character of the settlement in such detail that the identification is unproblematic.[20] But often we are given only vague distances referring to an unclear starting point and rather superficial similarities of names. Identifications made on such a basis, and there have been many, easily become very tentative and of little use.[21]

The French Near Eastern archaeologist Daniel Schlumberger, frustrated with the classical authors' obvious ignorance and the fragmentary nature of their data, proposed several years ago that scholars should to disregard the classical sources. Instead Iran's history in Hellenistic times should be reconstructed solely on the basis of archaeological data.[22] His proposal has never been taken seriously, nor does it deserve to be. The archaeological record is both too scanty and too unrepresentative to constitute an alternative to the classical sources, however defective and chronologically vague these turn out to be on closer examination. We must simply keep in mind that beyond the Tigris we enter a zone where the classical sources are notably less credible than for other regions. Nevertheless we will probably never be able to completely de-Hellenize the image of Achaemenid and Parthian Iranshahr.[23]

2. Khuda-nameh: "The Good King" as a Theme in the Persian Tradition

After the Greek description of Iranshahr the next set of structured, coherent information consists of the accounts of the lives and exploits of the Sassanian kings, recorded in the 9th and 10th centuries by Muslim historians such as Tabari, Dinawari, Hamza Isfahani, Mas'udi, and Tha'alibi.[24] The amount of information varies somewhat from one author to another, and there are several contradictions stemming from confusing kings with similar names (especially Shapur I and Shapur II). In general, however, the structure of the accounts and the character of their data is markedly uniform.

In part, this is because the younger historians used their predecessors as sources. Both Mas'udi and Tha'alibi cite Tabari (Tha'alibi also cites Hamza Isfahani). Yet they were not simply plagiarizing. Tha'alibi also has information not found in Tabari and both he and Mas'udi expressly state that they had acquainted themselves with the "Persian sources."[25] The accounts are uniform chiefly because they all were based on a set of common sources. Tabari, whose account is the most extensive, hardly names his sources, but on the basis of information in Hamza Isfahani, Mas'udi, Tha'alibi, and Ibn al-Nadim's *Kitab al-fihrist* we can roughly identify these common sources.[26]

In the first place, there was the *Khuda-nameh*, i.e. "The Book of Kings," the Sassanian chronicle on Iranshahr's history from the creation of the world up to and including the reign of Khusraw II Parviz (591–628). Secondly, the *Ayin-nameh*, a kind of handbook of administration, was used by the Muslim historians. Thirdly, there was the *Tadj-nameh*, a collection of royal regulations dealing with court etiquette. Also used were various *andarz*– or *pandnameh* writings, i.e. brief treatises with practical rules for living, guidance in statecraft, etc. The good advice here was often ascribed to kings such as Ardashir I, Khusraw I, or wise counselors like the legendary vizier Burudjmihr.[27]

Finally, the Muslim historians made use of short romances relating the adventures of both mythical heroes (such as Rustam and Isfandiyar) and historical figures. Mas'udi had seen stories about Ardashir I and Bahram Chubin; the *Tarikh-é Sistan* refers to the *Bakhtiyar-nameh*, a romance about a local Sistani hero, while the *Kitab al-fihrist* mentions accounts of Bahram Gur, Khusraw I, the religious agitator Mazdak, Khusraw II, and the famous commander Shahrbaraz.[28]

Thus the extant account of the Sassanian kings was put together like a mosaic. The most important piece was the *Khuda-nameh*, the Sassanian chronicle which apparently obtained its final form in the 7th century, immediately before the fall of the Sassanian Empire.[29] The chronicle was then translated into Arabic in the 8th century, with material from the other cited sources added. Most famous was the translation by the Persian official Ibn al-Muqaffa.[30] Both the original(s) and the various translations have been lost, and the purpose and content of *Khuda-nameh* must be discussed using the brief summaries found in the works of the later Muslim historians.

The intention of the *Khuda-nameh* was clearly to glorify the Sassanians as good, competent and just rulers. The writing down or final editing took place following the death of Khusraw II, in 628, when war and rebellion threatened the existence of the Empire. This was also a time when disastrous plague epidemics must have raised doubts whether the luck of the kings still held and whether the Sassanians still enjoyed favorable divine attention. Hence, the glorification obviously was intended to legitimatize the dynasty and mobilize loyalty. We do not know who did the actual writing or editing, but the authors probably were scribes and bureaucrats with access to the royal archives and annals.[31]

The *Khuda-nameh* was composed around several themes which together furnish a definition of the "good king." One of these themes is that the king must be more than a just ruler and a great warrior who can maintain the social order and defend society against external enemies. He should also found cities, build irrigation systems, and protect and promote agriculture. In a typical passage in the *Tansar-nameh*, a Sassanian *andarz* treatise, it is said of Ardashir I that

"…with his diplomatic skill, his strength and his efficiency he has made the water flow in all the deserts and has founded towns and created villages, where there before him had been nothing equal to it for 4000 years. He has found master builders and attracted people to populate towns and villages…"

The summaries of the *Khuda-nameh* provide long, quite uniform lists of the cities said to have been founded and populated by the Sassanian kings, leaving the impression that the Sassanians were exceptional colonizers. The question is whether this is correct or whether we are dealing with a fiction intended to stress the subjects' moral debt to the rulers. To have effect a theme must somehow reflect reality. So the *Khuda-nameh* does not assert that the Sassanians had founded all sorts of towns. It consistently distinguishes between new and old towns. The latter had been founded by mythical kings far back in time. In this group Hamza Isfahani includes Marv, Ctesiphon, Fasa, Darabgird, and others.[32] As concerns the new towns, detailed accounts of their founding are often given, and in these accounts mass deportation and forced settlement figure as key elements alongside the construction of irrigation works. Some of the information can be confirmed by sources independent of the *Khuda-nameh*-tradition. Ammianus Marcellinus, for instance, tells of Shapur II's deportations of people from Syria to Khuzistan. Procopius and John of Ephesus confirm Khusraw I's founding of Veh-Antioch and his deportations of Greek-Syrian prisoners to this place. Kavadh I's deportations from Anatolia and Djazirah are confirmed by Armenian and Syriac sources (e.g. Ps. Joshua Stylites).[33]

The colonization accounts can also be verified archaeologically. Many remains of structures, traditionally said to be Sassanian, and of such size and complexity that only the kings could have commanded the resources to build them, date in fact from the Sassanian era. They include the massive weirs at Dizful and Shushtar, the Nahrawan Canal, the defensive fortifications in Gurgan, and towns such as Djunday-Shapur, Gur (Firuzabad), Veh-Shapur (Fars), Veh-Ardashir (Mesopotamia), and others. Thus the account of the *Khuda-nameh* seems reliable, though not every bit of it should be taken at face value. Sometimes Sassanian foundations just consisted in the re-naming of existing settlements, possibly combined with repairs or the construction of new fortifications. Moreover, in the process of transmission there have occurred mix-ups and confusions. Also, later historians have sought to add to the lists of foundations by etymological inferences sometimes verging on the ridiculous.[34] The important point, however, is that the tradition reflects a real historical process that must have left visible marks on the settlement pattern in Iranshahr.

Long after the fall of the Sassanians, writers reproduced this tradition. They did so partly because knowledge of history was seen as an important part of being cultured. Instructive tales about the great kings of the past, like tales of the Prophet and the first caliphs, provided guidelines for political and administrative practice. Yet there was more to it than that. Both the authors (often theologians, jurists, or administrators) and their readers (who were to be found especially among the educated elite groups staffing the imperial and local bureaucracies) were mostly Persians, ethnic or assimilated. They were clearly conscious of their own role as bearers of Persian culture and the imperial tradition, and to them the Sassanian Empire was the quintessence of a well-ordered state.[35] So the themes of the *Khuda-nameh* continued to determine whether a ruler was to be seen as a "Good King." At the end of the 11th century the vizier Nizam al-Mulk thus explained to his Saldjuq master, Malik Shah, that the ruler's task was not only to defend society against internal and external enemies. He must also promote civilization by digging *qanats* and canals, building bridges and sarays, repopulating villages, and founding towns.[36]

At the same time the rulers sought legitimacy and authority by projecting images of themselves as just kings and as promoters of civilization, for example through official historiography. When, in the 10th century, Adud al-Dawleh instructed Ibrahim al-Sabi' to write the *Kitab al-tadji*, the history of the Buyid Dynasty, he issued precise instructions how to do it and made sure that Ibrahim adhered to them. The result, in the view of many contemporaries, was a work full of lies.[37] Yet despite this and his barbarian origins and his tolerance of the Shi'ites Adud al-

Table 1. Foundation lists in the *Khuda-nameh*.

Tabari	*Hamza Isfahani*
Ardashir 1	Ardashir 1
Ardashir-Khurreh	Ardashir-Khurreh
Ram-Ardashir	Veh-Ardashir
Rev-Ardashir	Veh-Ardashir (Kirman)
Hormizd-Ardashir	Ram-Ardashir
Veh-Ardashir	Hormuz-Ardashir
Astarabad-Ardashir	Insha-Ardashir
Pasa-Ardashir	Batn-Ardashir
Budh-Ardashir	Budh-Ardashir
	Bahman-Ardashir
	Rev-Ardashir
	Vehesht-Ardashir
Shapur 1	Shapur 1
Shad-Shapur	Nishapur
Djunday-Shapur	Bishapur
	Shad-Shapur
	Djunday-Shapur
	Shapurkhwast
	Valash-Shapur
	Firuz-Shapur
Hormizd	
Ram Hormuz	
Shapur 2	Shapur 2
Buzurg-Shapur	Buzurg-Shapur
Firuz-Shapur	Khurreh-Shapur "and another town nearby"
Iran-Khurreh-Shapur	
Iranshahr-Shapur	
Giba-Shapur	
Nishapur	
Bahram 4	
"a town in Kirman"	
Firuz	Firuz
Ram-Firuz	"Many towns in India, Ray, Gurgan and Azarbaydjan." Only
Rawshan-Firuz	two are named, Ram-Firuz and Rawshi-Firuz, "both in India."
Shahram-Firuz	Balash
	Balashabad
	Balashazz
Kavadh 1	Kavadh 1
Ram-Kavadh	Iranshad-Kavadh
Hulwan	Shahrabad-Kavadh
Kavadh-Khurreh	Arradjan
	Hambu-Shapur
	Balashgird
	Shapur-Kavadh
	Yazd-Kavadh
Khusraw 1	Khusraw 1
Veh-Andew-Khusraw	Veh-Andew-Khusraw
	Khusraw-Shapur

Dawleh became numbered among the "good kings." He appears as such in the works of Nizam al-Mulk and Ibn al-Balkhi, both writing long after the Buyids had been eliminated as a political factor. The reason is that Adud al-Dawleh in fact had lived up to some of the ideals. for instance by building the famous Band-é Amir weir on the Marvdasht plain and improving canals around Baghdad.[38]

Thus actual deeds played an important role in accepting a ruler into Persian historiography's cumulative list of "good kings." Nizam al-Mulk and others cite 'Amr b. Layth among the exemplary rulers of the past.[39] 'Amr and his brother Ya'qub had begun their amazing careers of conquest as lower- class leaders in Sistan, and most sources are hostile to them, because their social background disqualified them as rulers. Yet the same sources admit that the brothers were in fact very competent and just administrators. If the idea of the "good king" was to maintain credibility and continue to serve as a means of creating authority and loyalty, the Persian historians had to recognize the qualities of the Layth brothers.[40]

On the other hand the historians got into difficulties when the kings whom they were supposed to glorify failed in their allotted role, as was the case with Mahmud of Ghazna. Mahmud's reputation as a just king and untiring fighter for the Faith suffered because of his heavy-handed and illegal (i.e. canonically unacceptable) taxation of the territories under his control. To salvage Mahmud's reputation his biographer, al-'Utbi, tried to put the blame for the exhorbitant taxation on greedy and faithless officials such as the vizier Abu al-Abbas b. Fazl.[41] However, since the "good king's" task was also to appoint the proper officials and to keep an eye on them, this was not a convincing excuse. In any case it could not prevent the erosion of the enclaves' loyalty to the Ghaznavide state and this eventually helped the Saldjuqs conquer Iranshahr from Mahmud's successors.

As a source of legitimacy the *Khuda-nameh*-tradition thus came to color Persian historiography. When the victorious rulers posed as founders and protectors of civilization, they simultaneously sought to smear and to delegitimatize their rivals as destroyers. Too often scholars have accepted at face value the accounts of good times under strong, just rulers and of bad times under weak, unjust ones. The accounts of war, destruction and misrule, like the praises of the "good kings," served to legitimatize and delegitimatize power. They must not be used uncritically as if they were objective reflections of reality.

3. Iranshahr in the 10th Century

The accounts of the deeds of the great kings, despite much information on foundations and constructions, does not provide a systematic description of Iran-shahr. After the formation of the classic image of Persia, including some later revisions and additions,[42] the next general description does not appear until the 9th and 10th centuries. It is found in a body of administrative handbooks, didactic writings, and travel descriptions, often with such titles as "The Book of the Lands" or "The Book of Roads and Provinces." Later compilations and updated entries dating from the 12th to 15th centuries were added to this body.

The writings can be divided into three groups or genres, each reflecting the different intentions of their authors.[43] The first includes the administrative–fiscal handbooks written by officials as practical guides for other officials. Apparently the proto-type was Ibn Khurdadhbih's *Kitab al-masalik wa'l-mamalik* ("The Book of Roads and Provinces") from the second half of the 9th century. Also included in this genre are Ya'qubi's *Kitab al-buldan* (*c.* 890) and the *Kitab al-kharadj* by Qudama (*c.* 930).

The second group consists of the *adab* literature, transmitting that which gentlemen of refinement and culture were required to know about the lands of Iranshahr, their characteristics and wonders. This group of works includes Ibn al-Faqih's *Kitab al-buldan*, dating from around 900, and preserved only in an abridged version. The *Kitab al-a'laq al-nafisa* by Ibn Rusteh, from the early 10th century, is also incomplete. The *Hudud al-'alam*, an anonymous compilation from about 980, can be included in the genre as well. So can the geographical sections of Mas'udi's *Kitab al-murudj al-dhahab wa ma'adin al-djawhar* and of the abridged and revised version, *Kitab al-tanbih wa'l-ishraf*. Both were written in the middle of the 10th century.

A third genre is made up of three "ethnographic" descriptions of Iranshahr (and of other parts of the Muslim world as well), dating from the middle and late 10th century: al-Istakhri's *Kitab al-masalik wa'l-mamalik*, Ibn Hawqal's *Kitab surat al-'ard*, and the *Ahsan al-taqasim fi ma'rifat al-aqalim* by al-Muqaddasi. Much of the information collected by these three authors consists of personal observations made on long journeys. Very little is known about al-Istakhri. The two others were presumably merchants and perhaps also Fatimid agents. However, for whom they were writing is not clear. In any case we may consider their books as a single body. The three authors relied on each other and on common earlier sources. Ibn Hawqal, for example, says that he carried Ibn Khurdadhbih's work with him everywhere on his travels. Among his other sources he names Qudama and Djayhani.[44]

During the 9th and 10th centuries a fund of information and themes about the lands of Iranshahr was cumulatively assembled. This fund was then used in later centuries by authors writing in the *adab* genre, for example Yaqut who wrote his geographic encyclopedia, *Mu'djam al-buldan*, in the early 13th century. In the mid-14th century Mustawfi al-Kazwini wrote the *Nuzhat al-qulub*, and around 1415 Hafiz-é Abru made a similar geographical compilation. The latter work apparently had no title and is generally referred to as the "*Djughrafiya*."

Because of the cumulative manner in which the Muslim description of Iranshahr was assembled, it has some methodological problems in common with the description provided by the classical authors. First, it was composed from a mixture of out-of-date themes and up-to-date information. This is especially noticeable in the later writings. Second, the authors' intentions and the cultural ideals of the time influenced what they regarded as relevant information to be included in the texts. Hence, while enlarging upon the importance of long-distance trade, they offer little information on agriculture. Further problems revolve around the quantitative information, primarily about taxation. This will be discussed below.

Yet, let us first look at the problem that arises when the often vague statements in the medieval sources are compared with similarly subjective impressions of later European travellers. Without a quantitative index of measurement comparisons of this kind tend to say a lot about the different world views of medieval Arab merchants and 19th-century British officers, but they tell us little about actual changes in material conditions. That Ibn Hawqal characterizes a city as "large and prosperous," while the same city in the eyes of a later European traveller was a stagnating provincial hole, is not in itself proof of decline.

An example can explain this elementary problem of perspectives. In 1347 the Moroccan traveller Ibn Battuta visited Shiraz, the capital city in the country of Fars. He gave the following favorable, but also vague and subjective description (in H.A.R. Gibb's translation):

"Shiraz (...) is a city of solid construction and wide range, famous in repute and high in esteem; it has elegant gardens and gushing streams, sumptuous bazaars and handsome thoroughfares, and is densely populated, substantial in its buildings and admirable in its disposition."[45]

A British diplomat, William Ouseley, who visited Shiraz in 1810, was not so impressed:

"The city of Shiraz seems rapidly hastening to decay, and most of its public structures, once very numerous, are in a state of ruin or neglect (...) Many parts of the city are scantily inhabited, and I passed one day through the southern quarter which seemed to be in a state of absolute depopulation."[46]

The difference between the two descriptions is striking and would seem to indicate a distinct decline. However, the lack of quantitative reference points prevents us from determining the actual extent and character of change. Perhaps it was only temporary. Many Iranian cities had suffered during the prolonged wars in the 18th century. However, Shiraz had in fact enjoyed particular political favor as capital of Karim Khan Zand, and other British descriptions are not so negative as Ouseley's. We may also note that public buildings could fall into disrepair for several reasons, some of them not directly linked with the community's general economic condition. In fact, the reason that Shiraz' *madresehs* were in such a pitiful state was that their income from *auqaf* had been usurped.[47] If a ruler decided to build a new palace or citadel, he often took bricks and other materials from buildings constructed by his predecessors. The populace would then purloin remaining materials, and so the original buildings were eventually left as ruins.[48] Moreover, the usual construction material, both in the countryside and in the towns, was sunbaked mud-bricks. The lifetime of these rarely exceeded 40 years and their gradual erosion by wind and weather tended to give Iranshahr's towns an permanent aura of decay.[49]

Apparent decay also had something to do with the unstable water-supplies. If a *qanat* ran dry, the village or urban quarter had to be moved, and the original settlement was then allowed to decay. It is therefore misleading simply to count inhabited and abandoned houses (or villages) in a given area, compare the figures, and then conclude that the total settlement had declined by a given percentage. Europeans have often failed to realize that many ruins in Iranshahr in fact represent *successive* settlements. They cannot be taken as an index of general decline in the population and the economy.

Scott Waring, another British traveller who visited Shiraz just before Ouseley, gives us some clues as to why the European descriptions tend to be so negative. He came "with a determination to be pleased (...) but whether my expectations were originally too high I cannot determine; I was, however, disappointed."[50] Likewise the prospect of visiting "Persia, that imaginary seat of Oriental splendour! that land of poets and roses! that cradle of mankind!" had filled James Morier with joyful expectations. Yet Morier was disappointed as well. In the preface to *Hajji Baba* (1823) he concluded: "perhaps no country in the world less comes up to one's expectations than Persia, whether in the beauties of nature, or in the riches and magnificense of its inhabitants."[51] The European travellers certainly expected to see signs of decay, but on an imposing scale. What really disappointed them was the unimpressive, even mean appearance of an Iranian reality remote from the romantic and exotic imagery conveyed by the *Arabian Nights*. In any case, the travellers' disappointment can hardly be accepted as proof of long-term decline. Yet the scholarly literature is full of subjective evaluations and impressions being used in heavy-handed comparisons without regard to the fact that they were created and processed in contexts so different as to make comparison extremely problematic, if not misleading.

4. The Fiscal Assessments of Iranshahr: a Summary of the Quantitative Information

Lack of quantitative data makes it difficult to answer the key question: how comprehensive was the actual decline? It is only with the census of 1956 that we get any reliable information about the number of people living within the current borders of the Iranian state. In the sources we can certainly find some dispersed quantitative information, typically dealing with such topics as large and well-known towns, their area and circumference, the number of houses, mosques and public baths. Sometimes figures are given on prices and wages, the size of armies, casualities during campaigns, and deaths during epidemics. Some of the figures are absurd, either because of copying errors or because the authors exaggerate, and cannot be used in any serious analysis. For example, Sayf al-Harawi's statement that the Mongols, in the spring of 1221, killed 1.7 million people in Nishapur cannot be used to calculate the city's population. It is nothing but an arbitrary estimate. Considering local hydrological conditions and the extent of the city's remains, Nishapur, even in its heyday, could at most have had a population between 100.000 and 200.000.[52]

Other figures appear probable enough, but are hardly representative. They may in fact have been recorded precisely because they were unusual. In any case they are so dispersed in time and space that a systematic comparison is difficult. An example will explain the problem. According to Ibn al-Faqih the Hamadan enclave in the 10th century contained 765 villages. In the early 13th century Yaqut listed their number at 660, but a hundred years later, according to Mustawfi al-Kazwini, there were only 212. Russian scholars especially have used statistics of this kind as proof of the large-scale destructions wrought by the Mongols in Iran. Nevertheless this type of statistical documentation is misleading, for the enclave was periodically subjected to administrative reorganizations. Ibn al-Faqih thus listed 24 districts in Hamadan, Mustawfi only five.[53] Moreover, in some cases we are dealing with enumerations not of agrarian settlements but of fiscal units.[54] In Bayhaq (Sabzavar) in the time of 'Abdullah b. Tahir (9th century) there was said to be 395 villages. Hafiz-é Abru, in the early 14th century, counted only 60, but adds that the mazra'eh, a term which refers to small settlements or to settlements which did not constitute fiscal units by themselves, were not included in his count.[55]

In some places, changes in the settlement pattern can be quantified by archaeological survey data. The method consists of recording all the remains found on a given site and dating them from sherds and other surface debris. This should give a rough outline of the chronology of the settlement. However, when using the results of these surveys, we must bear in mind the limitations of the method. First, ceramic dating is seldom so precise that it can provide precise links between changes or trends in a settlement pattern and specific historical events such as the Arab conquest. Much of the pottery data remains unpublished anyway.[56] Second, how representative are these surveys? Can we make statements about the entire Mesopotamian floodplain using data only from the central parts and the Diyala plain? On the Iranian Plateau the problem is even greater, because the size of the Plateau alone excludes systematic archaeological surveys. In addition, the survey method is obviously best suited to deserted wastelands where continous cultivation and habitation have not disturbed or hidden the remains of earlier settlements. In spite

Table 2. Tribute payments from Iranshahr, *c.* 500 B.C. (according to Herodotus II. 89–94)

	Babylonian silver talents
Mesopotamia	1.000
Khuzistan (Susa and Cissia)	300
Djibal (Media)	450
Sistan (incl. Kirman and Kuhistan)[a]	600
Khurasan (incl. Bactria, Transoxania and Khwarizm)[b]	300
The Caspian lands and Gurgan[c]	450
Azarbaydjan (Matiene)	200

Further east more puzzling names appear, but they have not been convincingly identified. *Fars*, the Achaemenid homeland, was according to Herodotus exempt from tribute.
Tribute from outside Iranshahr proper comprised over 2.000 talents from Asia Minor and Syria, 700 talents from Egypt (incl. Libya) and 360 *Euboean* talents of gold dust from India (Sind).

[a] "Sarangians, Sagartians, Thamaneans, Utians, Myci." The Sarangians must relate to Zranka (Sistan). The Sagartians are more difficult. If they are to be identified with the Asagarta of the Achaemenid inscriptions, then they resided in Media/Djibal (Frye, 1962: 70). Of course, this does not make sense in an administrative context; so, failing anything better, it has been suggested that they migrated. The Thamaneans perhaps relate to the Farah region (Frye, 1962: 49), while the Utians could be identical with the Yautiya of the Persian inscriptions, who apparently should be sought somewhere in Kirman (Frye, 1962: 50). Finally, the Myci may relate to Maka (Makran or 'Uman).
[b] "Parthians, Chorasmeans, Sogdians, Arians, Bactrians."
[c] "Caspians, Pausicai, Pantimathi, Daritae": 200 talents; further down the list the Caspians are mentioned together with the Sacae paying 250 talents. This may be a reference to Gurgan (Varkana). Formerly it was believed that the Paricanians – another of the "nations" mentioned by Herodotus – represented Gurgan. This identification is no longer accepted (cf. *CHIr*, II: 258). Instead it has been suggested that the Paricanians were natives of Media. However, Frye (1962: 46, 50) believes that they might have resided in either Kirman or Ferghana (!) as well, which shows how speculative these identifications really are.

of its dreary appearance the Plateau is not a wasteland, however. Ancient settlement enclaves such as Isfahan, Hamadan, Kirman, and many others are currently inhabited and cultivated and are thus difficult to investigate by archaeological methods. Surveys have tended, therefore, to focus on abandoned or marginal zones which by definition are not representative.

We must finally look at a group of quantitative data which scholars have often used without asking whether they were in fact representative. As part of their routine administration the Persian Empires regularly recorded the amount of land under cultivation and the kinds of land taxes imposed. These data were then collected in archives and used whenever the Empire needed an overall view of its resources. Since they always employed professional soldiers rather than citizen armies, the Persian Empires did not count heads, as did Republican Rome. They just registered income and expenses.[57] Most of these archival data an lost, but fragments and paraphrases of resource surveys have been preserved in other sources. From the period before 1500 we have four such surveys:

1. Herodotus' satrapy list which records tribute from the territories ruled by Darius (around 500 B.C.).

2. Fragments of a Sassanian survey, presumably from the first half of the 6th century.

3. Several uniform lists written between the 8th and 10th centuries and transmitted in administrative handbooks such as the *Kitab al-masalik wa'l-mamalik* and *Kitab al-kharadj*. These books were compiled by officials in the central administation and can be supplemented by data derived from the geographical literature of the 10th century.

4. The survey found in Mustawfi al-Kazwini's description of Iranshahr around 1340. Mustawfi is supplemented by some contemporary guides for officials in the fiscal administration.

The origins and transmission of these surveys raise several questions. Herodotus' list in particular seems suspect. Did he have an official Achaemenid survey as his source or did he simply record some fanciful tales of the wealth and power of the great kings. In the 5th century B.C. many such tales were circulating in Ionia, and Herodotus could easily have picked them up here. Suspicion has been raised because his satrapy list, which allegedly reproduced Darius' administrative reorganization, does not agree with Darius' own *dahyava* lists. Moreover, the Achaemenid epigraphic sources list several satrapies not mentioned by Herodotus. It may be, however, that the *dahyava* lists count ethnic groups, or "nations," and have nothing to do with the administrative division of the Empire.

Herodotus' information that Mesopotamia was the fiscal heavyweight is no doubt correct, as it is confirmed by other sources. He was in fact reasonably well-informed about the Empire's western territories, but it appears that he had only vague ideas about the lands east of the Tigris. The bits of genuine knowledge he did have are therefore mixed with stories of gold-digging ants and with the popular stereotypes about barbarians: they shared their women, did not know ordered social relations, etc. Some of Herodotus' tribute statistics for eastern territories such as Sistan and Kirman are equally improbable, and they hint that he had no access to official Achaemenid documents. It is in fact difficult to see how he could have got such access. All things considered, Herodotus' list should not be taken too literally.[58]

The information on the Sassanian survey rests on a somewhat more solid foundation. The lists are preserved in later Muslim *Kitab al-masalik wa'l-mamalik*, most exhaustively in the book by Ibn Khurdadhbih, leader of the *barid*, the caliphal communication and intelligence service. The uniform nature of the data indicates that the various Muslim authors all used a common source (or group of sources). The differences are often due to simple copying errors or to the fact that the authors have forgotten to distinguish between *mithqal* and dirham. The figures are said to date from the time of Kavadh and Khusraw I, i.e. the first half of the 6th century. No doubt the common source was ultimately based on a cadastral survey carried out in connection with these two kings' reorganization of the fiscal administration.

Table 3. The Sassanian assessment of Iranshahr, 6th Century. (According to Ibn Khurdadhbih).

	Dirhams
Mesopotamia	214.000.000[a]
Khuzistan	50.000.000[b]
Fars	57.000.000[c]
Kirman	60.000.000[d]
Djibal (incl. Azarbaydjan, Kumis, Tabaristan)	30.000.000[e]

To this assessment Muslim historians add a number of stories demonstrating the immense wealth of the Sassanian kings: of Khusraw II it is said that in the 18th year of his reign (i.e. in 608, *before* the short-lived conquest of Egypt and Syria) he collected a total *kharadj* of not less than 420 million *mithqal*, equivalent to 600 million dirhams. Moreover, his treasuries allegedly held a fabulous wealth of 1.600.000.000 *mithqal* (i.e. 2.285.700.000 dirhams), approximately 7.000 tons (Tabari, Noeldeke tr.: 353ff, 376; Hamza, tr.: 45).

[a] Ibn Khurdadhbih (tr.: 11); the exact figure is 150.000.000 *mithqal*-dirhams (1 dirham equals 7/10 *mithqal*); Mas'udi (*Tanbih*, tr.: 62) states the figure in dirhams only; Ibn al-Faqih (tr.: 249) has 123 million dirhams; see also Ibn Hawqal (tr., I: 227).
[b] Ibn Khurdadhbih (tr.: 31).
[c] Ibn Khurdadhbih (tr.: 34) gives the figure as 40 million *mithqal*-dirhams, whereas Ibn al-Faqih (tr.: 249) just says 40 million dirhams; Ibn al-Balkhi (tr.: 83) gives a figure of 36 million dirhams, equivalent to 3.000.000 dinars, in the time of Khusraw I.
[d] Ibn Khurdadhbih (tr.: 25); this figure is incredibly high and must be due to an error in a common earlier source as it also appears by Ibn al-Faqih (tr.: 249). A more plausible figure would be 5–6 million, as in Ibn Khurdadhbih's own time.
[e] Ibn Khurdadhbih (tr.: 15f); the figure does not represent all of Djibal, only the following districts are specifically named: Ray, Hamadan, the two Mahs (i.e. Nihawand and Dinawar), Demavand, Masabadhan, Mihridjankadhak and Hulwan).

How many links the data have passed through is impossible to determine, but the Sassanian archives remained largely intact until 812/13 when most of the fiscal administration's archives were burned during the fighting in Baghdad between al-Amin and al-Ma'mun. Some local archives survived even longer. Thus in Isfahan one could still see the Sassanian *kharadj*-registers as late as the 10th century.[59]

Fiscal administration during Sassanian times was probably characterized by considerable local variations, and the little we know chiefly refers to Mesopotamia-Khuzistan. According to the Babylonian Talmud the Sassanians levied a general poll-tax (*kraga* or *krg'*), based on assets, and two forms of agricultural tax. One was the *tasqa* (*tsq'*), apparently a fixed rent from the crown estates; from all other categories of land was demanded the *mantha da malkha* ("kings' share") which consisted of a fixed proportion of the produce, varying from 1/6 to 1/3.[60] It seems that the reform of Kavadh and Khusraw I aimed at generalizing the principle of *tasqa* taxation: all land was surveyed and registered according to the quality of the land, the nature of the crops raised, the type of farming practiced, and the water supply; taxes were then assessed as a fixed rent to be paid in three yearly installments.[61] Though Mas'udi states that the reform applied only to the Sawad, it seems that at least some of the major enclaves on the Plateau were in fact included as well.[62] The purpose must have been to make the revenue of the Empire predictable and thus to help planning long-term redistribution. That the Empire had growing needs for this can be linked with the military reorganization which also took place in late Sassanian times.[63]

Muslim taxation was at the outset rather complicated for two reasons. First, the new conquerors could not see why they should pay the same taxes as the conquered infidels. Second, during the conquests several territories had made local tribute agreements that had legal consequences for later assessments. The result was that land was divided into many legal categories, each having its own rate of taxation. In the reign of 'Umar II (717–20) and later, in al-Mahdi's reign (775–85), several standardizations and systematizations were carried out that essentially aimed at perpetuating late-Sassanian taxation practices. At the local level many special rules still applied, but in principle there now existed only three legal forms of taxation:

1. *Kharadj*, etymologically derived from *kraga*, but semantically equivalent to *tasqa* and *mantha*, i.e. a general land-tax. Certain types of landed property were exempt and assessed at lower rates. According to local traditions *kharadj* was assessed either as a fixed rent (the *muqata'eh* principle) or as a fixed proportion of the harvest (the *muqasameh* principle), as a rule between 1/5 and 1/2.

2. *Djizya* (*djawali*) was a poll- or tolerance-tax imposed by the Empire on non-Muslims.

3. *Zakat* (*'ushr*, *sadaqa*), i.e. a sort of tithe which formed the legal basis for taxation of *kharadj*-free land and nonagricultural occupations.

In practice the Empire levied several special and irregular taxes, fees, and requisitions which were all difficult to bring into agreement with the Holy Law. They especially affected trade and industry.[64]

On the basis of the registers in the *Diwan al-kharadj* the Abbasid administration routinely drew up summaries of the Empire's resources, especially of the *kharadj*, the largest as well as the most predictable source of revenue. These summaries served as basis for budgets and presumably also for setting the prices on tax-farming.[65] Five such relatively detailed summaries have been preserved from the 8th to the 10th centuries:[66]

The first dates from the reign of Harun al-Rashid (786–809). It was drawn up by Ibn al-Mutarrif, a prominent official within the *kharadj* administration, and addressed to Yahya b. Khalid b. Barmak, al-Rashid's vizier. It survives in al-Djahshiyari's collection of vizier and bureaucrat biographies. A slightly different version is given by Ibn Khaldun.

The second summary, from the beginning of Harun al-Rashid's reign, is preserved in Khalifah b. Khayyat's *Kitab al-ta'rikh*. It is also addressed to Yahya b. Khalid and must be a variant of the list mentioned above.

Third, there is Qudama b. Djafar's list in his *Kitab al-kharadj*. The figures refer to 819/20 and to the 830s.

Table 4. The Abbasid assessment of Iranshahr (in dirhams).

	788	819/20	c. 840	840–73	918/19
Mesopotamia	114.120.000	114.457.000		94.035.000	31.000.000
Khuzistan	25.000.000	23.000.000		30.000.000	25.000.000
Djibal	52.600.000	54.878.000	44.600.000	34.000.000	50.000.000
Fars	27.000.000	24.000.000		34.000.000	38.000.000
Kirman	4.500.000	6.000.000		5.000.000	7.000.000
Azarbaydjan	4.700.000	4.500.000	4.000.000	2.000.000	4.500.000
Tabaristan	6.000.000	4.280.700[a]	4.000.000		
Gurgan	12.000.000	4.000.000	10.000.000		
Kumis	1.500.000	1.150.000	1.500.000	2.196.000	
Khurasan	28.000.000[b]			12.000.000[c]	
Sistan	4.150.000	1.000.000	10.000.000	6.776.000	
Makran	400.000	1.000.000			

Sources:
Ibn al-Mutarrif (788).
Qudama (819/20).
Ya'qubi (c. 840).
Ibn Khurdadhbih (840–873).
'Ali b. 'Isa (918/19). Note: these figures are given in dinars. Here they are converted at the rate of 1:20.

[a] Qudama also gives the figure 1.163.070.
[b] "besides 1.000 *ratl* of silver," i.e. between 400 and 1.500 kilograms depending on the *ratl* used.
[c] Cf. the detailed assessment of Khurasan on p. 223.

Ibn Khurdadhbih's list in *Kitab al-masalik wa'l-mamalik* refers chiefly to the years between 840 and 870.

Finally we have the vizier 'Ali b. 'Isa's estimate from 918/19, preserved in a Hilal b. Sabi' fragment.

Additional figures can be found in other sources such as Ya'qubi (*Kitab al-buldan*, the time before 840), Miskawayh (early 10th century), and in the geographical literature. Ibn Hawqal, for instance, provides several figures for the period around 960, including figures on tax-farming.

Around the middle of the 14th century a former Ilkhanid official, Mustawfi al-Kazwini, wrote a description of Iranshahr entitled *Nuzhat al-qulub*. He got his data largely from older sources (e.g. Ibn al-Balkhi's *Fars-nameh*) and he did not always bring them up to date. However, he did add some figures from two tax assessments carried out in 1335 and 1341. These figures, collected by Mustawfi when he served in the fiscal administrations in Kazwin and Baghdad, are expressed in "currency dinars" of silver, *dinar-é rayidj*, an Ilkhanid accounting unit equal to six small or new dirhams.[67]

The question is whether the quantitative differences between the various assessments can be used to measure the alleged decline in Iranshahr. Comparing the figures is tricky, however, because the conversion rate between currencies is uncertain. The relation between the (golden) dinar and the (silver) dirham was constantly fluctuating. There was a canonically set rate of 1:14 2/7, but that was unrealistically low,[68] and the actual rules for currency conversion were extremely complicated, allowing all kinds of manipulation. (In the hope of arriving at a rough average I have used the rate 1:20.) Also the length of the intervening period makes it difficult to establish the actual value of Mustawfi's *dinar-é rayidj* in relation to the Abbasid dirham.[69]

The picture is also distorted because the size of the fiscal units was frequently changed in the administrative reorganizations. In Abbasid times Yazd was included in Fars, but in the Ilkhanid period it was part of Djibal. We have already seen that Hamadan in the 9th century was something quite different from Hamadan in the 14th century. This partly explains the marked deviations in the assessments.

Third, the figures do not tell us how much wealth the Empire in fact had at its disposal. They were estimates, not statements of the total amount of silver which actually passed through the State Treasury in a given year. Ibn Khurdadhbih, for example, informs us that the tax in Khuzistan, set to 30.000.000 dirhams, was in fact farmed for not less than 49.000.000.[70] On the other hand, both he and Qudama faithfully list taxes from Sistan and Khurasan, though these territories had long ago ceased paying tribute to Baghdad.[71]

To sum up, it would seem that the Abbasid lists were composed of two elements. First, there was an estimate of how large an income the Empire could expect from the core-territories. As this estimate was of practical political significance, it had to be reasonably realistic and detailed and kept up to date (though Miskawayh gives examples of how, in the early 10th century when the Empire had fallen into serious economic difficulties, the viziers for tactical reasons began to draw up completely unrealistic revenue estimates).[72] Second, there was a more or less arbitrary assessment of remote territories like Sistan, Kirman, etc. These areas were put on the lists because they belonged formally to the Empire. However, since they did not pay regularly, if at all, their *kharadj* was simply given in round, undifferentiated numbers. Thus the figures cannot be used to measure which country was richest or most densely populated.[73] Qudama, for example, states that Sistan was assessed at just one million dirhams, no more than the amount stipulated in the original tributary agreements from the 7th century. This does not mean that the country was poor or thinly populated, only that the Empire had little control over it. The geographical literature in fact describes Sistan as exceptionally prosperous and fertile.[74] As an index of qualitative change, the first of the two elements in the Abbasid lists, the estimate of the core-territories, is of greatest interest.

In spite of the uncertainty about conversion rates there can be no doubt that the drastic reduction in the Abbasid Empire's revenue, as revealed by a comparison of the lists, was real. Other contempory sources give vivid impressions of the caliphate's economic difficulties from the end of the 9th century and onwards (the earlier and generally ignored decline in assessments between Sassanian and Muslim times

Table 5. The assessment of Iranshahr, 1335–1341 (according to Mustawfi al-Kazwini).

	Dinar-é rayidj
Mesopotamia...	3.000.000
Khuzistan..	325.000
Djibal	c. 2.900.000
Fars (incl. Shabankareh)	3.137.300
Kirman (incl. Makran)[a]......................................	676.000
Azarbaydjan (incl. Mughan and Arran)	c. 2.500.000

Khurasan (including Kuhistan, Kumis, Gurgan, and Mazandaran) formed a separate fiscal unit, and taxes from here seem to have been beyond the control of the central government. Mustawfi (*Nuzhat*, tr. : 147) offers no figures, stating only that large sums were held back on the pretext that they were to used for paying the soldiers.

[a] Also including Hormuz which alone paid 60.000 *dinar-é rayidj*.

will be discussed later). David Waines, who has most recently analyzed the Abbasid figures, estimates that from the year 800 up to the beginning of the 10th century the total revenue, including taxes and tribute from Egypt, Syria, and the Arabian Peninsula, fell by more than half, from 520.000.000 to 217.000.000 dirhams.[75]

Of course part of the explanation must be that the Empire in this period lost control over productive areas outside Iranshahr, for instance Egypt. However, Egypt was not of vital fiscal importance.[76] It was only assessed at *c.* 54.000.000 dirhams in the reign of Harun al-Rashid. At the same time Mesopotamia and Khuzistan were assessed at 139.000.000 dirhams and Djibal and Fars at nearly 80.000.000. Incidentally these figures also show the great fiscal importance of the western Plateau to the Empire. As Waines points out, and as Table 4 confirms, the decline was chiefly caused by a disastrous reduction in the Mesopotamian revenue: the assessment dropped from 114.000.000 to about 31.000.000 dirhams. In marked contrast to this, assessments in Djibal and Fars remained stable.

Compared with the Abbasid lists, Mustawfi al-Kazwini's figures would seem to show that by the 14th century the total revenue (measured in silver) had fallen further and that the contribution of agriculture had been reduced severely. However, these conclusions are based on the assumption that Mustawfi was recording the same things as his Abbasid predecessors. But was he? In the *Nuzhat al-qulub* Mustawfi primarily registers *huquq-é divani* and *tamgha*. *Huquq* is a vague term which from the context would appear to correspond to *kharadj*, the basic land-tax, while *tamgha* seems to include taxes on trade and industry (this is also indicated by other sources).[77] What is remarkable is that the latter source of revenue occupies such a prominent place by Mustawfi. As mentioned, the Abbasid lists recorded for all practical purposes only *kharadj*. In 'Ali b. 'Isa's detailed estimate from 918/19 Mesopotamia was thus assessed at a total 1.5 million dinars. Of these, only 10% (166.139 dinars) would come from non-agrarian sources such as the poll-tax in Baghdad, customs duties, market fees, etc. According to an another (undated) statement, which al-Muqaddasi had seen in a book in the library of Adud al-Dawleh in Baghdad, the *kharadj* from the Sawad ran to 86.780.000 dirhams. To this should be added 8.500.000 from the Kuwar Didjla (the Basrah region). Other taxes collected in the Sawad amounted to only 4.000.000.[78] Of course, non-agrarian activities were in fact taxed more heavily than these figures indicate, but the point is that in Abbasid times agriculture was considered by far the most important object of taxation. Apparently this had changed by Ilkhanid times.

In his description of several large cities and their regions – Tabriz, Baghdad, Shiraz, Isfahan, Hamadan, Sultaniyeh, Kazwin, Wasit (but not Basrah) – Mustawfi records what should be paid in *huquq* and in *tamgha*. This would indicate that taxing of the towns, and of the towns of Djibal and Azarbaydjan in particular, had now become vitally important. The impression is confirmed by examples from some of the accounting handbooks intended for officials in the fiscal administration from the same period (i.e. the first half of the 14th century).[79] Several scholars have asserted that the importance of *tamgha* taxation reflects that agricultural production all over Iranshahr had declined drastically in Ilkhanid times. As supporting evidence they cite Rashid al-Din's description of how terrible the situation was until Ghazan Khan came to the throne (and Rashid himself became vizier).[80] This conclusion appears too rash, however. Rashid had an obvious interest in exaggerating the administrative chaos and the extortionate taxation of Ghazan Khan's predecessors, the Ilkhans Ahmad (Tegüder), Arghun, and Gaykhatu. Ghazan Khan had won the throne in 1295 in a civil war, and to make legitimate Ghazan's rule (and his own position) Rashid cast his master as the "good king" who after decades of chaos and destruction brought order and renewed attention to agriculture. Further it should be noted that Mustawfi tends to lump together *huquq* and *tamgha*, making it difficult to determine their relative size (which is why we use here only the total amounts).[81] Moreover, Mustawfi did not register all the taxes, fees, and labor services imposed on agriculture. He fails, for instance, to mention the *qubchur* (Persian: *mawashi*), a poll-tax which weighed heavily on the peasants. It was, of course, uncanonical, which may explain why it went unmentioned.[82] In brief, Mustawfi's figures are not clear enough to enable us to draw far-reaching conclusions about the declining fiscal importance of agriculture.

We must conclude that, with certain reservations, the Abbasid lists can be compared among themselves. They originated within a relatively short period, within the same departments, and employed largely the same methods of calculation. Mustawfi's figures not only appear five hundred years later, they also represent something different. Methodologically it is unsound to compare his figures with the Abbasid lists and then work out the decline in percentages. What is remarkable about the picture drawn by Mustawfi is not so much the size of the figures as the way in which they are distributed geographically. In the five hundred years between Harun al-Rashid and Ghazan Khan the resource base of the Empire had clearly shifted: Djibal and Fars, already noted for their stability, largely retained their position, but the old heartland of Mesopotamia-Khuzistan had lost its predominance. In contrast, once peripheral Azarbaydjan had become important. In this same period the capital of Iranshahr was transferred from Mesopotamia, first to Djibal (Isfahan) and later, in Ilkhanid times, to Azarbaydjan (Maragheh, Udjan and Tabriz). *If* this shift ultimately had something to do with changes in agricultural production, then significant decline in the lands of Iranshahr must have been a local rather than a general phenomenon, which means that local conditions must have been decisive.

Part 2
"The Heart of Iranshahr": Mesopotamia and Khuzistan

Introduction

In Sassanian times, when the Persian Empire was a genuine world power, the rulers used to say that Iranshahr was to the world like the breast to the human body and Suristan, i.e. Mesopotamia, was to Iranshahr like the heart within the breast. Hence, Mesopotamia came to be called *Dil-Iranshahr*, "the heart of Iranshahr."[1] It continued to enjoy this reputation for a long time. Even the geographical literature of the 10th century is overflowing with superlatives describing the floodplain as the center of the civilized world, though the brilliant facade had by then begun to crack.[2]

The enthusiasm of the Persian rulers had its straightforward explanation. In a drought-stricken world of dispersed oases Mesopotamia held the largest cultivated area and the largest population cluster. These advantages, however, were not given naturally. They were the result of the continuous toil of building and maintaining large-scale irrigation systems. The common people who carried out this work and who, unlike the rulers, could not escape the stifling heat of the summer with its swarms of flies, understandably took a more sober view of the land, calling it "the place for poverty."[3]

In pre-historic times the Mesopotamian floodplain consisted of various landscapes – swamps, steppes, river oases – which were exploited in different ways. For instance, extensive agriculture could be combined with fishing or nomadism. Intensive agriculture demanded more drastic manipulation of the environment in the form of irrigation, but this could again take different forms. The gigantic canal systems described by the 10th century sources were only one of many ways in which resources could be used. But before looking further into when and how these systems were constructed, we must briefly describe the environment they were intended to modify.[4]

Chapter 4

The Twin Rivers.

Any idea of what the floodplain looked like in the past must be based on projections from the present. But existing conditions are the product of millennia of human activity. Even the number and location of the river channels have changed considerably since pre-historic times as a result, in part at least, of irrigation.[5]

As stated, the climate has probably not changed greatly over the last millennia. We may therefore consider as constant the amount of precipitation, the length of the growing season, the temperature, the evaporation levels, and other such factors. The climate of Mesopotamia is primarily characterized by sparse rainfall. The annual average for the Baghdad area is 151 mm, far below all theoretical limits for dry farming, even considering that the rain does fall during the winter, i.e. in the grain-growing season. Grain has always been sown in October-November and harvested in April-June; but to complete its growth before the summer heat and drought sets in, it must receive extra water, in other words it must be irrigated. This is done by flooding the fields, usually once a month until the harvest.[6]

Water for irrigation is carried to the floodplain by the Tigris and Euphrates. However, the discharge pattern of the two rivers, does not fit in with the agricultural cycle. Maximum flows occur in April (Tigris) and May (Euphrates), when the grain is ready for harvesting and there is no need for irrigation; in fact, flooding will cause serious damage to the standing grain. Conversely the minimum flow occurs in August–September, when sowing is prepared and the need to irrigate is greatest. The low flow in the autumn and early winter thus limits the amount of land which can be irrigated.

It is estimated that the Euphrates will irrigate between 8.000 and 12.000 sq km.[7] On its long journey across the north Syrian steppe the river is fed by only one large tributary, the Khabur, and therefore its flow rarely exhibits dramatic fluctuations. The Tigris, while carrying considerably more water, is more unpredictable and therefore less attractive as an irrigation resource. It has four major tributaries: the Greater and Lesser Zabs, the Azaym, and the Diyala, all rising in the Zagros mountains. Because of the large catchment area a sudden rainstorm in the mountains may rapidly increase the flow of the Tigris and cause floods. The problem has worsened because of the clearing of the forest in the Zagros.[8]

The danger of sudden, uncontrollable flooding is further increased because of the weak slope of the land. As one travels south towards the Persian Gulf, the velocity of the water flow decreases, causing an increase in the rate of sediment deposition. During the flood season, the coarser particles settle immediately next to the channel, building up natural levees which will normally keep the river in its bed. The finer particles are deposited on lower-lying areas farther away and forms a hard, impermeable surface often covered with standing water.[9] If a strong flood washes the levees away, the river can change its course completely, as happened to the lower part of the Tigris at the end of the 5th century A.D.

In the Mesopotamian floodplain large-scale irrigation thus requires two principal tasks. First, the construction and maintenance of weirs and canals to raise and transport the water for irrigation in times of low flow. Second, the construction of dikes, embankments, and reservoirs to protect the fields against uncontrolled and destructive flooding in the spring.

Large-scale irrigation involves certain environmental risks, however. The first is siltation. The more water diverted for irrigation, the slower the speed of the flow in the rivers and canals, and the greater the rate of sediment deposition. So canals and other irrigation works must be regularly cleaned out to remain functional. Incidentally wind erosion of the cleaned-out silt has contributed to the formation of extensive sand or rather clay dunes, another sign of how the Mesopotamian landscape has been shaped by human activity.[10] During irrigation, sediments are also deposited on the fields, and the fine particles will degrade the soil structure and impede drainage. This increases the second major risk associated with irrigation, namely, salination.[11]

Salination, i.e. the accumulation of soluble salts in the surface layers of the soil, results from the evaporation of water brought into the fields by irrigation and from the rising of the water-table. If, as a result of regular irrigation and seepage from the canals, the water-table rises to 1–2 meters below ground level, the capillary movement will draw the water up to the surface. Here the water evaporates, leaving its salt content in the soil. As a rule increased irrigation will lead to a rise in the water-table and thus to salinity build-up. As soil salinity increases, the ability of the plants to germinate is impeded, their growth is crippled, and their yield decreases. In the end only particularly salt-resistant plants can survive.

The process can be counteracted in various ways. One method is to apply extra irrigation water and literally flush the soil clean in the rooting zone. Unfortunately the soil nutrients will be washed away as well. The method requires effective drainage and cannot be employed in situations where all water resources are already allotted to expand the area under cultivation. In any case, frequent flushings may eventually lead to a permanent rise of the water-table and thereby worsen the salinity hazard.

Another and perhaps more effective countermeasure is to let the land lie fallow regularly and thus give the water-table time to sink. This can be speeded up by having certain hardy plants with deep roots grow on the fallowed fields and dry them out. Obviously this solution is only possible where agriculture is not under constant pressure to increase production.

Regardless of countermeasures, salinity build-up through irrigation is virtually unavoidable in arid areas, though the actual extent of course will depend on local geomorphological conditions, cultivation techniques, and the nature of soluble salts. Egypt, for instance, with its unique geomorphological and hydrological features has sustained irrigated agriculture for millennia without significant damage to the soil, at least until the building of the new Aswan Dam. In contrast, the Mesopotamian floodplain is practically predisposed to salination because of its soil structure and the gentle slope of the land which even without irrigation makes water-tables high and drainage poor. To what extent salination actually contributed to turning the floodplain into the wasteland seen by Fraser and other European travellers is not clear. Information found in the sources is sparse and ambiguous. An argument for salination as the decisive factor must therefore rest on indirect indicators and on comparisons with present-day conditions.[12]

Large-scale reclamation began in Iraq at the end of the last century and was intensified after World War II. Almost instantly it led to salinity build-up. Though salination is rarely so serious that cultivation must be given up, it certainly contributes to the low yields characteristic of modern Iraqi agriculture.[13] Recent expansions of irrigation has caused severe salinity problems in other arid regions as well.

In the second half of the 19th century the British, after their initial successes in the Gangetic plains, began constructing irrigation systems in the Indus River Valley. Huge perennial canals such as the Upper Bari Doab Canal (completed in 1859), the Sirhind Canal (1882), and the Lower Chenab Canal (1892) replaced traditional inundation canals. By the early 20th century all the major rivers of Pandjab (except the Beas) had been tapped for extensive irrigation works, and the area under intensive cultivation had been greatly expanded. However, from the beginning the canals and the increased irrigation caused widespread waterlogging and salinity problems. The Rechna Doab, the land between the Ravi and the Chenab, in particular developed into a bad case of salination.[14]

In Sindh, i.e. the southern part of the Indus River Valley, the British long confined themselves to repairing and extending existing inundation canals. Not until 1932 did they introduce large-scale perennial irrigation with the construction of the barrage at Sukkur-Rohri. After independence irrigation was further extended, chiefly through the construction of the huge barrages at Kotri and Kashmor. But in the south the alluvial plains have less slope than in Pandjab, water-tables are high, and the monsoon brings little rainfall. Consequently the great barrages, especially the Ghulam Muhammad Barrage at Kotri with its 2.500 km of distributing canals, precipitated salinity disaster. By the early 1960s between 20% and 25% of the total irrigated area in West Pakistan were severely affected, and American experts were called in to help relieve the waterlogging and growing salinity. So far, countermeasures such as lowering the water-table by power-driven tubewells and the extensive use of chemical fertilizer have proved costly and not altogether effective. The southwestern United States, the Central Asian republics of the former Soviet Union, and Australia provide other examples of how irrigation in arid lands leads to nearly insuperable salinity problems.[15]

It is certain, therefore, that irrigation in Mesopotamia has always involved environmental risks and that the extent of these risks has been largely proportional to the extent of irrigation. Hence, the construction of the huge and complex canal system described in the 10th-century sources must have aggravated environmental hazards. However, this drastic modification of the Mesopotamian environment occurred relatively late in the floodplain's long history.[16]

2. Irrigation Patterns in the Past

Any outline of the hydrological conditions and the development of irrigation technology in pre-Persian times is bound to be tentative since we have no extant descriptions of the floodplain as a whole. For some localities such as Uruk and Nippur the cuneiform sources do provide information on the courses of canals and rivers in certain periods; but this information is too dispersed in time and space to allow any general long-term trends to be brought out. We must therefore rely on archaeological reconstructions that trace the remains of canals and dikes (using satellite photographs) and then date the settlement remains along the ancient watercourses.[17]

For several millennia after the earliest agrarian colonization (c. 5000 B.C.) settlement and cultivation remained concentrated along the channels of the Euphrates. The Tigris region appears to have remained thinly populated.[18] Irrigation was based mainly on parallel diversions from the Euphrates channels, though the scale and complexity of these diversions changed over time. While the early settlements had been evenly located along the channels and had practiced a technically uncomplicated inundation irrigation of the back slopes of the natural levees, the rise of cities and states around 3000 B.C. brought significant change. Settlement became increasingly concentrated in enclaves, and within these the area of irrigated land expanded.[19]

Eventually the political and demographic center of the floodplain shifted toward the north, away from the old city states in the south. Some assyriologists have argued that progressive salination of the low-lying southern plains was the ultimate cause of this process. The evidence is not convincing, however. The salination hypothesis assumes that in the middle of the 3rd millennium B.C. yields were as high as 1:30 or even 1:76. For reasons of plant physiology alone this is impossible. Besides, the soil of the floodplain, then as now, was generally infertile, being poor

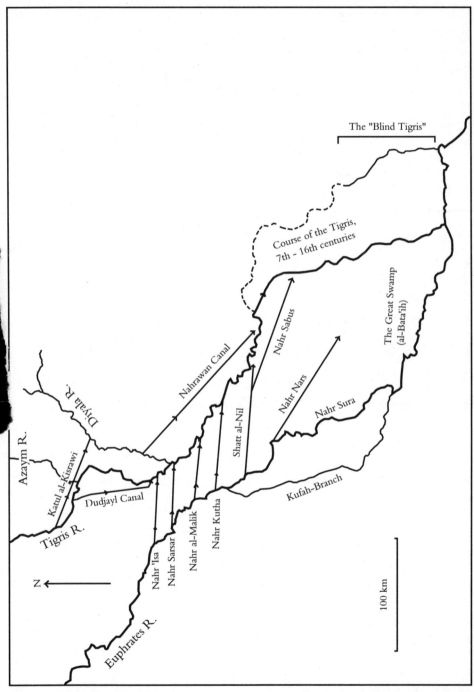

The "Blind Tigris"

Course of the Tigris, 7th – 16th centuries

Nahr Sabus

Nahr Nars

Nahr Sura

The Great Swamp (al-Bata'ih)

Nahrawan Canal

Shatt al-Nil

Diyala R.

Azaym R.

Kātul al-Kisrawi

Dudjayl Canal

Tigris R.

Nahr 'Isa

Nahr Sarsar

Nahr al-Malik

Nahr Kutha

Kufah-Branch

N ←

Euphrates R.

100 km

Fig. 2. Mesopotamia. Plan of the transverse canal system (according to Ibn Sarabiyun, 10th century)

in both organic materials and essential nutrients like nitrogen and phosphorous. Certain favorable areas under intensive cultivation may have produced seed-yield ratios between 1:20 and 1:10. However, from what we know of past and present productivity under similar conditions the normal yield from average fields can hardly have exceeded 1:10. This remains, incidentally, a high level of productivity for non-industrialized agriculture.[20] Another argument against the salination hypothesis is that summer cultivation, to the extent it was practiced at all, was probably restricted to intensive horticulture on top of the well-drained levees and along the river banks. Ordinary fields were fallowed.[21]

Although there can be no doubt that salination was a problem, especially in the south, it had apparently not reached disastrous levels. The shifting from south to north can be adequately explained by the political conflicts, including the recurring bitter wars between enclaves for control over the Euphrates. Here the northern settlements obviously had the upper hand because they could disturb or interrupt the flow of water to the downstream settlements. In any case, the increased irrigation carried out by the northern settlements even in peacetime must have inevitably reduced the water supply to the south.[22]

Irrigation caused another important change in the hydrological system: the displacement of the Euphrates' channels. As late as the beginning of the 2nd millennium the river still flowed in three large channels down the central floodplain. Then, because of sedimentation, which was greatly increased by irrigation, the river began moving westward. By the 1st millennium B.C. it had established its new main channel in a position close to that of the present-day Hillah branch. The old settlements on the central floodplain thereby lost much of their water supply.[23]

This shifting of the Euphrates can explain the construction, in the Babylon area, of several eastward-flowing canals mentioned in Assyrian and Neo-Babylonian sources from the 7th century B.C. One such canal seems to have reached Kish, but whether it continued further in the direction of Nippur is not known.[24] In any case, neither this nor any of the other eastward-flowing canals were connected to the Tigris (the position of which at this time is not precisely established).[25] Yet we may consider these canals as harbingers of the drastic changes in irrigation strategy and hydrological conditions which were to take place in the period of Persian domination.

The first clear description of the canal system in the Mesopotamian floodplain as a whole is found in the geographical writings from the 9th and 10th centuries, and the picture drawn here differs markedly from that which has been reconstructed for previous epochs. The most striking aspect is that the old system of parallel diversions was now replaced by several gigantic transverse feeder canals which carried water from the Euphrates across the central floodplain. Here they supplied an extensive network of distributory canals before they emptied into the Tigris. According to the most detailed description, given by Ibn Sarabiyun (early 10th century), this new system included (from north to south):

1. The *Nahr 'Isa* (also *al-Rufayl*), with intake at al-Anbar (Firuz-Shapur) a few km from the present-day Falludjah, flowed into the Tigris at Baghdad. The canal was named after an Abbasid prince who is said to have repaired it. There also existed a canal further north, the *Dudjayl*, "the Little Tigris," a parallel diversion which carried water from the Tigris at Kadisiyah to Baghdad's northern suburbs. It was 50 m wide and a 100 km long.[26]

2. The *Nahr Sarsar* with its intake three *farsakh* (*c.* 18 km) south of the village of Dimmima, also somewhere near Falludjah. It flowed into the Tigris 20 km south of Baghdad.

3. The *Nahr al-Malik*, the "Royal Canal," which left the Euphrates *c.* 30 km south of the *Nahr Sarsar* and entered the Tigris 20 km below al-Mada'in, i.e. the old Seleucia-Ctesiphon.

4. The *Nahr Kutha*, originating three *farsakh* south of the *Nahr al-Malik* and flowing into the Tigris 10 *farsakh* below al-Mada'in.

South of the *Nahr Kutha* the Euphrates bifurcated. The eastern channel which corresponded roughly to the current Hillah branch was called the *Nahr Sura* and was considered the main arm. The western branch passed by Kufah and corresponded to what is today the main channel of the river. From the Nahr Sura were diverted:

5. The *Sarat-Nil-Zabi* complex, originating just north of ancient Babylon and flowing out into the Tigris north of al-Kut (Kut al-Imara). Parts of the complex seem to have consisted of old Euphrates channels. The same applied to:

6. The *Nahr Nars* which left the river south of Hillah. The canal passed by Nippur and emptied into the southern swamps.

Furthermore, the region east of the Tigris was by now under large-scale irrigation. This had been achieved through the construction of:

7. The huge *Nahrawan* complex which tapped the Tigris. The complex consisted of two sections: the first was the *Katul al-Kisrawi*, which had its main intake at Dur (Dawr) north of Samarra. Here, in the mid-19th century, British officers of the Indian Navy saw the remains of what they believed was a massive stone weir that once had raised the waters of the Tigris into the intake. The *Katul* had another intake at Kadisiyah and here must have been a weir as well. The canal then crossed the Azaym River and emptied into the Diyala. The increased water flow in the Diyala was carried south by the second section, the *Nahrawan Canal* proper, which ran down to al-Kut where it rejoined the Tigris. The scale of the system was impressive by any standards. The total length was more than 300 km, the width of the canal bed was between 40 and 120 m, the depth between 5 and 10 m. At intervals are the remains of large masonry regulators, marking the intakes of major secondary canals.[27]

The transverse system made possible a much more extensive use of water resources, and the construction of the canals was in fact accompanied by a major expansion of settlement and cultivation which turned Mesopotamia into the chief resource base of the successive empires. It was not enough to dig canals, however. The canals had also to be provided with increased amounts of water, and to do so it was necessary to construct weirs across (or at least into) the rivers to raise the water up into the canal intakes in the low flow period. Unfortunately the history of weir construction in Mesopotamia remains obscure. From the 3rd millennium B.C. sources refer to weirs, but these seem to have been regulators: i.e. devices placed in the levees to regulate the flow into the canals.[28] Until the 1st millennium B.C., Mesopotamian engineers apparently lacked the capability of building permanent weirs across the main river channels. Perhaps they lacked the incentive as well. In any case the construction of large weirs across the rivers must have begun together with the digging of the large new canals. At its zenith Mesopotamian irrigation cannot have been based solely on the seasonal level of the rivers. It must somehow have been weir-controlled, because large-scale cultivation of basic foodgrains in winter would have required some kind of water-raising structures at the intakes of the main feeder canals. Such structures cannot have been beyond the technical competence of the Persian engineers who, after all, had built the weirs across the Karun in Khuzistan. In fact, classical authors refer to structures across both the Eu

he new system involved a drastic modification of the hydrology of the flood-plain. The transverse canals cut across the natural lines of drainage, dividing the central floodplain into many small closed basins with poor or even no drainage. This cannot but have increased the danger of salinity build-up and environmental instability.[32]

Chapter 5

The Construction of the Transverse Canals

It is not possible to determine exactly when each particular component of the new canal system was constructed. In outline, however, the pattern of development is reasonably clear. If we are correct in assuming that transverse canals did not exist in Neo-Babylonian times, construction must have begun immediately afterwards, during Achaemenid rule. Visiting the floodplain in the middle of the 5th century B.C., Herodotus remarked that here, as in Egypt, the countryside was traversed by canals. He then added: "the greatest of these canals is navigable, flows toward the southeast and goes from the Euphrates to another river, the Tigris." This is the first unequivocal mention we have of a transverse canal.[1] Through the 4th century B.C., more Greeks, many serving as mercenaries, were able to observe the Persian Empire from within. One of them, the Athenian Xenophon, writes of four transverse canals, "each 1 *plethron* wide" (i.e. *c.* 30 m).[2]

The descriptions do not make clear whether these transverse canals were part of the irrigation system. They are mainly mentioned as means of inland navigation. But then the Greeks knew little of local irrigation practices. Herodotus correctly says that, unlike Egypt, Mesopotamia cannot be irrigated by the natural flooding of the rivers. However, he then goes on to state, erroneously, that all irrigation must be done by manpowered water-lifting devices.[3] Water-lifting devices of the *shaduf* type, i.e. a swinging beam with a bucket and a counterweight, had certainly been known and used as early as the 3rd millennium B.C., but their capacity was limited. They could be used for irrigating gardens and palm orchards. Regular grain fields were irrigated by gravity-flow inundation, as the Mesopotamian sources clearly state.[4]

1. The Royal Canal

The transverse canal seen by Herodotus was no doubt a forerunner of either the Nahr 'Isa, the Nahr Sarsar, or the Nahr al-Malik. The various historical traditions ascribed great age to the northern canals and especially to the Nahr al-Malik, the "Royal Canal." The Muslim historians thus accorded Solomon, Alexander, and the Parthian king Shapur b. Ashk the honor of having constructed the latter.[5]

The Royal Canal is first mentioned by Polybius in his account of the civil war between Antiochus II and Molon (221 B.C.). From the context it appears to have been a transverse canal, since Molon, in Babylon, regarded it as a line of defense against the king who came from the north, along the Tigris. Its location is given as 6 days' march south of Libba (which, however, has not been located).[6] Pliny is more precise. He informs us that a canal with the name "Naarmalchas," a distortion of Aramaic *Nahar Malkha* (i.e. the Royal Canal), had its intake at Massice (Misikhe, later Firuz-Shapur) and flowed into the Tigris at Seleucia. He adds, probably with the Oriental Greek authors as his source, that it was originally constructed by the governor Gobares. This official may be identified as an Achaemenid viceroy, Gaubaruva, (535/34 – ?525/24 B.C.).[7] Ammianus Marcellinus, who in A.D. 363 had marched along the canal during Julian's campaign in Mesopotamia, also says that the Royal Canal originated at Firuz-Shapur and flowed into the Tigris at Seleucia-Ctesiphon. However, this Royal Canal cannot be identical with the Nahr al-Malik of the 10th century. The topographical clues provided by Pliny and the other classical authors in fact point to the Nahr 'Isa or the Nahr Sarsar.[8] The explanation may simply be that in the intervening period floods, repair work, and expansion had considerably altered the canal system and that canals had subsequently changed their names or obtained new ones.

In any case, classical sources clearly show that the foundation of the transverse system was laid no later than in Achaemenid times. Pliny's remark about the governor Gobares further indicates that the construction in fact was begun by the new rulers, no doubt to increase production. But other information about Achaemenid rule in Mesopotamia, especially in the early and later phases, is fragmentary, making it difficult to form an overall picture of the period.

There exist local cuneiform sources such as the temple archives from Sippar and Uruk and the family or "firm" archives, chiefly the Murashu archives from Nippur. But given their local character they may not be representative. The Murashu archives suggest strong state regulation of economic life and systematic intervention into daily production, including the maintenance and expansion of irrigation systems. Especially for the Nippur region there are in fact signs of considerable state-controlled expansion.[9] Nippur, however, enjoyed a special position under Achaemenid rule. The city had apparently been made capital, temporarily at least, following a revolt in Babylon in 482 B.C. and seems consequently to have been favored. Hence, developments in this region may not be representative of the floodplain as a whole. It seems, for instance, that the southern areas around Ur actually saw a decline.[10]

On the other hand, according to the archaeological surveys the Achaemenid period was characterized by a general settlement expansion over the entire central floodplain, especially towards east, in the direction of the Tigris.[11] This indicates that the transverse canals had been constructed not only to ease transport and communication, but also to deliver water to new settlements and to make possible an expansion of the cultivated area. Even some sizable diversions from the Tigris are documented. On their retreat from Cunaxa, Prince Cyrus' Greek mercenaries crossed two large canals on the west bank, presumably in the area opposite the mouth of the Diyala, and Xenophon noted how these canals branched into a network of distributaries, "big ones at first and then smaller ones, until in the end they are just little channels like we have in Greece for the millet fields."[12]

Like their predecessors the Achaemenids carried out deportations and forced resettlement. The survivors from Miletus were deported to Susa and later settled in Ampe, at the mouth of the Tigris. Prisoners of war from Euboea and Boeotia were deported, respectively, to Khuzistan and Mesopotamia, and in 345 B.C. prisoners from Sidon and Phoenicia were moved to Babylon and Susa on the way to an unknown destination. The "Carian villages" in the Sittacene district, on the east bank of the Tigris, were presumably also a product of deportations after the suppression of the Ionian revolt.[13]

It has been widely held that Achaemenid rule brought stagnation and decline to Mesopotamia. The evidence for this was found in the allegedly heavy tax-burden, the concentration of landed property in the hands of the royal family (as occurred in Nippur), and the concomitant deterioration of the conditions of the peasants.[14] Recent research has challenged this conventional wisdom. Living conditions may well have been diffcult for the common people, but we have no evidence that they were more difficult than in other periods. In any case, Achaemenid rule, far from bringing stagnation, initiated dynamic changes in the floodplain, above all by constructing the first elements of the transverse canal system.

2. The "Hellenized Orient" (1): Greek and Arsacid Foundings in Mesopotamia

In spite of the emergence of the first transverse canals, the political and economic center was still located in the old cultivated lands on the Euphrates when Alexander, in 331 B.C., conquered the floodplain. Babylon had apparently long ago recovered from the revolt in 482 B.C. The city dazzled the Macedonians by its size, its cosmopolitan atmosphere, and the immense system of dikes and reservoirs which protected it against natural disasters. As might be expected, Alexander planned to make Babylon the capital of his new empire.[15] Yet this plan was never realized. The dust had hardly settled after the fighting between the Macedonian generals over who should succeed Alexander before Seleucus, the new master of Mesopotamia and the eastern satrapies, founded an entirely new capital, Seleucia, on the banks of the Tigris.

This founding was the most spectacular element in a process of colonization and urbanization carried out by the Seleucids in Mesopotamia. So impressive was this process that Pliny introduces his description of Mesopotamia by stating that the inhabitants had lived dispersed in villages until the Macedonians arrived and gathered them into towns.[16] This is sheer nonsense of course. The floodplain had been home to urban settlement for nearly 3000 years, and Pliny's remark reveals that the classical authors whose works have survived knew little about the Orient – or else they disregarded what they knew to show that the Hellenic culture was superior and had a unique civilizing mission. The Seleucids in fact became famous for having spread this Hellenic culture and long after, in the 4th century, Libanius of Antioch still praised Seleucus I for having founded so many towns that the barbarian world had been "Hellenized."[17]

This theme came to figure prominently in the European view of the East: Alexander's campaign was a turning point in world history, the beginning of a distinct age, the age of "Hellenism," when the superior and dynamic Greek culture was spread in the more or less stagnant East. A natural extension of this view is that the decline of the Middle East was ultimately caused by the Hellenic legacy being rejected (or misinterpreted) during the Middle Ages.[18] It is not, however, my intention to discuss the degree or results of Greek cultural influence in the Middle East. Suffice it to note that Mesopotamia's subjugation to Greek domination did not entail a break with the past. Recent research, making more systematic use of contempory local material, has shown that the Seleucids largely continued Achaemenid political and administrative practices. The process of Hellenization, understood as the assimilation of Greek customs, norms, and institutions, affected only a minority in the towns, and even here only superficially.[19] It is significant that Greek, unlike Arabic later, did not spread as the language of everyday usage; apparently it was not even the first administrative language. When a theatre was built in Babylon, it was for the benefit of the Greek colony and not because the Aramaic-speaking population had taken to attending tragedies in their spare time.[20]

In a way, however, Pliny was correct. Throughout their farflung empire the Seleucids did found towns and military colonies or settled colonists – for the most part Greeks or Macedonians – in existing settlements such as Babylon. Yet the purpose of this colonization activity was hardly to "Hellenize" the natives but, rather, to secure political and military control over the productive enclaves and important lines of communication. The scope varied from one place to another, and precisely in Mesopotamia, the Seleucid core-land, economic considerations also played a role.[21]

The classical sources, i.e. primarily Strabo and Pliny, together mention about a dozen "Greek" towns in Mesopotamia: Seleucia, Artemita, Laodicia, two Antiochs, two Apamias, Apollonia, Alexandria(?)-on-the-Pallaconta (Pallacopas), and Sittace.[22] Some of these names no doubt refer to ancient towns. In Syria and Asia Minor there are several examples of the Seleucids giving old towns new dynastic names when they placed colonies there or made treaties with them. We know that Greek colonies were established in Babylon and Uruk and something similar probably occurred in towns such as Nippur, Kutha, Borsippa, etc. To mark the arrival of the Greek colonists these towns too may have been given new official names.[23]

The sources, however, are explicit that half the Greek towns in Mesopotamia in fact were newly founded. The best known of these is *Seleucia-on-the Tigris*, the new capital of the floodplain. As noted it had been Alexander's plan to follow Achaemenid practice and make Babylon one of his capitals. Nevertheless as soon as Seleucus I had achieved effective control over Mesopotamia, he chose to build an entirely new city. Why? Babylon's inhabitants are unlikely to have been exceptionally unruly or hostile to the new conquerors. Part of the explanation undoubtedly is that Seleucus wished to make a symbolic statement of his position as sovereign ruler. Yet why did he not place the town in the old cultivated lands along the Euphrates?[24] What is most remarkable about Seleucia is precisely its location. For millennia settlement in Mesopotamia had gravitated around the Euphrates, and Babylon was but the last of several large political and economic centers here. Seleucia, however, was situated on the west bank of the Tigris. From the very outset it was more than just a barracks-cum-palace complex. It was genuine urban settlement laid out in a gridiron street pattern and may have housed up to 100.000 inhabitants.[25] Even though classical sources insist on calling Seleucia a "Greek city,"[26] most of the inhabitants must have been of local origin. The Seleucids certainly attracted many Greek-Macedonian colonists to the area, but they also populated the city by more or less forcible transfers of local populations. Thus, in 275 B.C., Antiochus I deported part of Babylon's inhabitants to Seleucia. The classical authors saw this as a conscious attempt to suppress the ancient barbarian capital.[27] They were hardly correct, since Babylon remained a significant urban and local administrative center. Moreover, the Seleucid kings maintained the tradition of repairing the city's temples and, as stated, also established a Greek colony there.[28] Shortly after 130 B.C. the Parthians burned part of Babylon and deported some of the inhabitants, and this may explain the decline mentioned by Strabo. However, it is only with Trajan's Mesopotamian campaign in 116 that we have information about the ancient city being definitively abandoned.[29]

The founding of Seleucia was perhaps a drastic step, but not inexplicable when seen in the context of the eastward expansion already begun in Neo-Babylonian and Achaemenid times. A major reason behind the transferring of the political center of the floodplain must have been a desire to promote colonization of the thinly populated, but productive Tigris region. Prolonged and intensive cultivation must inevitably have caused salinity build-up and decreasing yields in the Babylon region and this might have stimulated the interest in expanding towards the east. The hypothesis is supported by the information about the other Greek towns in Mesopotamia.

Artemita stood 500 *stadia* east of Seleucia on the river "Silla" (the Diyala or a diversion from it) in the midst of an extensive agricultural area. It is classified as Greek, but Isidore adds that it was colloquially called Chalasar.[30] Apparently, the Aramaic-speaking population did not care for the Greek names. Artemita has been identified with the Karastel site on the Diyala plain, near Ba'quba. Covering 150 ha, Artemita-Chalasar was a fair-sized town with perhaps 20.000 inhabitants.[31] Surface debris and sherds in the area fail to show any settlement before Seleucid-Parthian times, making credible Pliny's statement that Artemita was a Greek foundation.

It is less certain whether Sittace was also an original Greek founding. The district of Sittacene proper, i.e. the east bank of the Tigris immediately south of the Diyala, was an ancient agricultural zone, but archaeological surveys in the area have not revealed any traces of larger settlements (over 10 ha) before Seleucid-Parthian times. The possibility exists, however, that Achaemenid ruins are hidden beneath the remains of later constructions. In Seleucid times the district was also called Apolloniatis, apparently after the Greek town of Apollonia which is perhaps identical with Sittace. If so, the latter was an old settlement re-named when Greek colonists arrived.[32]

Of the two Antiochs, one was the same as Charax (see below); the other was located by Pliny "between the Tigris and the Tornadotus," i.e. in the Diyala area.[33] As to the Apamias, Pliny states that one was "surrounded by the Tigris" with the "Archous" (unidentified) flowing through it. The second was situated near the confluence of the Euphrates and the Tigris and may have been identical with an old settlement named Digba.[34] East of the Tigris lie several Seleucid-Parthian sites of the same size as Artemita; among these one should probably look for the remains of at least some of the towns named here.

In the southernmost part of Mesopotamia, known by the Greeks as Mesene (Syriac: Mayshan), where the Eulaios (Karkheh) flowed into the Tigris, Alexander founded Alexandria. In this town he settled Macedonian war invalids and natives deported from the nearby settlement of Durine. This Alexandria was later damaged by floods, and when Antiochus IV, around 165 B.C., repaired the damage, he re-named it Antioch. Later in the 2nd century B.C. the town was again destroyed by floods. This time it was a local ruler, Hyspaosines, who rebuilt it, and to prevent new destructions he surrounded it with huge embankments. The city's Aramaic name was distorted by the Greeks to *Charax Spasinou*, from which they then derived Characene, another name for Mesene/Mayshan. The purpose of this founding was primarily to ensure control of the trade in the Persian Gulf, and in Seleucid and Parthian times the town did serve as an entrepot both for trade up the Tigris to Seleucia-Ctesiphon and for the caravans going to Palmyra and Petra.[35]

Although our information about Greek foundings and re-namings in Mesopotamia remains scarce and imprecise, we can nevertheless draw two general conclusions: first, a considerable effort at colonization was directed towards the Tigris region; second, the activity was not restricted to stationing Greek garrisons

and colonies in strategically important places. We cannot determine how many
Greeks and Macedonians came to Mesopotamia during Seleucid rule. A large
founding like Antioch-on-the Orontes (Syria) may have received between 17.000
and 25.000 colonists.[36] As an imperial center, Seleucia-on-the Tigris must have
received at least that number. However, even though immigration, especially from
Greek towns in Asia Minor, apparently continued through the 3rd and early 2nd
century B.C., the colonists can only have been a small minority within the Aramaic
population. Moreover, many of them no doubt quickly succumbed to the Mesopotamian infections. In any case, the Greeks formed a privileged group of surplus-
extractors, not an addition to the labor force.[37] The labor force was increased or,
rather, strategically relocated by moving local populations around. We have direct
evidence for this in the cases of Seleucia and Charax, but it must have occurred
frequently. If a Greek town or colony had been established in a hitherto uncultivated or thinly populated area, the Seleucids would have had to supply it with some
kind of labor force. Thus, regardless of their purpose, the colonization schemes in
the Tigris region must have led to the establishing of new productive enclaves or
the expansion of existing ones.

This must obviously have had hydrological consequences. In Mesopotamia
colonization and the founding of towns could not take place without modifying
and expanding the irrigation system. After his return from India Alexander, whose
interests focused on Babylon and the Euphrates region, put 10.000 men to work for
three months cleaning out and improving the Pallacopas, a long southward flowing
diversion on the Euphrates' west side. His intention was probably to improve the
supply of water to some of the old towns in the south.[38] With the founding of
Seleucia the focus, however, shifted to the transverse canal system. Though classical
sources say nothing of Seleucid canal construction, the founding of the new capital
most likely involved an enlargement of the forerunner to the Nahr 'Isa/Nahr Sarsar
(and a corresponding reduction of the water reaching Babylon). In the 2nd century
B.C. Polybius was aware that the Euphrates did not in fact empty into the Persian
Gulf; the canals which traversed the floodplain simply drained the river of water,
before it reached the sea.[39] Finally, the foundings and colonization in the Tigris area
must also have involved the construction of canals, primarily from Diyala, pre-
cursors of the great Nahrawan system.

3. Arsacid Rule and the Founding of Ctesiphon

The end of Greek rule in the middle of the 2nd century B.C. caused no noticeable
discontinuity in Mesopotamia's history. Neither the prolonged wars between the
Seleucids and the Parthians, the recurring Arsacid wars of succession, nor the
destructive Roman invasions of 116, 165, and 198, seem to have halted settlement
expansion. Evidence is chiefly provided by the archaeological record. There is

broad agreement that the surface debris and sherds point to a considerable expansion in Parthian times, especially in the areas east of the Tigris. However, these are only rough indicators. Over the 400 years of Parthian rule fluctuations must certainly have taken place. Seleucia, for instance, suffered decline.[40]

The actual circumstances of the expansion, i.e. the extent of state planning and initiative, are almost impossible to detail further, because the sources are so weak. The Sassanians deliberately sought to push their Arsacid predecessors out of recorded history, and this is one reason why later Oriental historical traditions, the Armenian excepted, have very little specific to say about the Parthians.[41] The sporadic references in the classical sources are virtually all we have at our disposal.

Nevertheless the Arsacid kings carried out at least two major foundings in Mesopotamia: *Ctesiphon* and *Valashgird*, both in the Tigris region. Ctesiphon was founded on the east bank of the Tigris directly opposite the existing capital Seleucia, no later than the 1st century B.C. It originally served as garrison town, but later the Arsacids began using it as a winter residence. Afterwards it eventually evolved into a genuine city.[42]

A few kilometers west of Seleucia King Valash I (*c.* 176/80) founded Valashgird, a name which classical authors rendered as Vologesocerta or Vologesias. The king's intention probably was to create a commerical center for the entire Seleucia-Ctesiphon complex and thereby force long-distance trade from the semi-independent Charax to pass through Parthian-controlled territory. His strategy apparently succeeded, because Palmyrene inscriptions indicate that Valashgird rapidly developed into an important entrepot for caravan traffic towards the west.[43]

On the basis of information in Pliny and Tacitus the founding of Ctesiphon and Valashgird have been explained as an attempt to stifle rebellious Seleucia. The Arsacids frequently had problems with Seleucia and other major towns such as Susa, which rebelled or supported the host of pretenders that seem so characteristic of Parthian history.[44] Some scholars see these conflicts as a reflection of the resistance of the urban upper classes to Arsacid attempts to reduce the *polis* autonomy which the Seleucids are said to have given the towns. The idea is that autonomy assured the ethnically defined upper classes their high status and privileges.[45] Yet it is hardly correct that the Seleucids accorded the Greek towns *polis* status in the accepted sense. Seleucia was in fact controlled by a special royal official called the *epistates* (or *strategos*), and as to the other Greek towns, their privileges, including a degree of autonomy, were hardly different from those enjoyed by towns generally.[46] McDowell has suggested that the conflicts between Seleucia and Susa and the Arsacids originated from strong social tensions within the urban society rather than from opposition to Arsacid power.[47]

So it is unlikely that the founding of Ctesiphon and Valashgird was an attempt to undermine Seleucia or draw inhabitants away. More likely the foundings were part of the expansion of the imperial center on the Tigris. The two new towns gradually coalesced with Seleucia into a single, large complex, colloquially known as *Mahoze* (Arabic: *al-Mada'in*), that is, "the cities." Some Muslim sources say that Shapur b. Ashk, traditionally considered the third Arsacid king, built the Nahr al-Malik.[48] As already stated, this cannot refer to the canal which bore that name in the 10th century, and perhaps the information is of mythical character. On the other hand it may well reflect historical fact, because the urbanization of the Tigris region must have involved an expansion of the transverse system.

To sum up, the sources do not contradict the archaeologically-based hypothesis of a considerable expansion in Parthian times. Admittedly the Arsacids did not always have control of the entire floodplain. Thus in the south, Characene retained, somewhat precariously, its semi-independence. But in the core-lands the Arsacid kings had both the power and the resources to launch large-scale projects such as city-foundings and, probably, extension of canals.

Chapter 6

The Climax of Irrigation:
Mesopotamia under Sassanian Rule

On the basis of the archaeological surveys Robert Adams concludes that the expansion of settlement and cultivation that had begun in Neo-Babylonian times reached its high point under Sassanian rule, i.e. from the 3rd to 7th centuries.[1] There is considerable evidence in the written sources to support this conclusion; the evidence even allows us to form a rough idea of how this was achieved.

The Sassanians, another powerful family from the Iranian highlands, had conquered Mesopotamia and most of Iranshahr from the Arsacids in the 220s. At first this brought no major political or administrative changes. Nonetheless, the Sassanian conquest is a turning-point in the history of Iranshahr, because it marks a change in the nature of the sources: where the classical sources provide only disconnected bits of information about the Parthian era, we now have the (admittedly abridged) versions of the *Khuda-nameh*, the "Book of the Kings," i.e. the offical acccount of the deeds of the Sassanian kings. In the *Khuda-nameh* the kings presented themselves as great colonizers: builders of cities and irrigation-works. This of course served legitimatizing purposes, but, as stated before, the *Khuda-nameh* in fact is reasonably credible, at least as regards the colonization theme.

In the *Khuda-nameh* Sassanian colonization is not represented as a smooth, continuous process. The activity clearly peaked in two periods: in the 3rd century, the "founding and consolidation phase," and in the 6th century, the "centralization phase." The founder of the dynasty, Ardashir I, began the first phase immediately after conquering Mesopotamia. Wishing no doubt to show that he was now the master of the plain, he built next to Seleucia a circular town, *Veh-Ardashir*.[2] A few years earlier he had founded another circular city, Firuzabad, to emphasize his position as sole ruler of Fars.

The founding of Veh-Ardashir was not simply a re-naming of an old settlement. Seleucia had long been in decline, either because of the sack by Avidius Cassius' army in A.D. 165 or because of changes in the course of the Tigris. In any case, Italian excavations in the al-Mada'in area clearly show that Veh-Ardashir, known colloquially in Syriac as Koché, was a new town, laid out on top of the ancient necropolis of Seleucia. The excavations also confirm the sources' description of the town as circular.[3] Later Sassanian kings further enlarged the imperial center of Mahoze/al-Mada'in, i.e. the Seleucia/Ctesiphon/Valashgird complex, and tradition has it that it eventually came to comprise no less than seven cities. Though this figure should perhaps not be taken literally, the capital certainly became the object of a comprehensive urbanization program. Thus Kavadh I built the suburb of *Djanbu-Shapur* (or Hanbu-Shapur), presumably on the east bank of the Tigris.[4] Also on the east bank, 6 or 7 km south of Ctesiphon, Khusraw I constructed the famous *Veh-Antiokh* in which he settled prisoners from his campaigns in Byzantine territory. Of course not all of Mahoze was made up of residential and commercial areas. The conglomerate city also contained extensive palace-cum-park complexes such as *Asbanpur* just south of Ctesiphon.[5]

Military considerations played a key role in the first phase of colonization. Commemorating his victory over the Romans in 243/44, Shapur I renamed the village Misikhe on the Euphrates (north of Falludjah) *Firuz-Shapur*, "Shapur-Is-Victorious," and here he settled Arab military colonists and built the Nahr Shayla Canal.[6] The town was later enlarged to become the cornerstone in the defence of Mesopotamia as is indicated by its Arabic name al-Anbar: i.e. "the Storehouses," "the Depot." In the 4th century Firuz-Shapur served as base for Sassanian attacks into Syria, and Zosimus describes it as Mesopotamia's largest town (after Ctesiphon): it was surrounded by double walls and further protected by a huge citadel, that surrendered to Julian in 363 only after heavy fighting.[7]

According to some versions of the Persian historical tradition Shapur I also founded al-Hira on the west bank of the Euphrates. This town, seat of the Arab vassal princes of the Lakhmid family, was the center of the defence of the middle Euphrates region against desert nomads and the Ghassanids, the Roman-Byzantine vassal princes in Syria.[8] The defence of the Euphrates was further strengthened by Shapur II who constructed *Khandaq Shapur*, "Shapur's Trench," a line of forts and trenches extending from Hit in the north to Ubulla (Apologos) in the south.[9] After Julian's unsuccessful invasion of Mesopotamia Shapur II pushed his line of defence forward to the Khabur. Here he settled 12.000 Persians from Isfahan and Istakhr in the strategically important fortified town of Nisibis (Nusaybin) which the Romans had been forced to cede.[10]

Colonization in the early phase, however, comprised more than just the enlargement of the imperial center on the Tigris and the construction of various fortifications. In the south, Ardashir eliminated the Characene principality and re-named two of its towns, Charax and Furat (near the later Basrah), respectively, to *Astarabad-Ardashir* and *Bahman-Ardashir*. No doubt the intention was to demonstrate that Mayshan now had new masters.[11]

Shapur I is noted for founding two towns in the south: *Shad-Shapur* in Mayshan and *Hasar-Shapur* in Kaskar (the Shatt al-Hayy region). In the latter he settled "people from the East."[12] The exact location of these towns is not known. Frye suggests that Shad-Shapur was simply a renaming of the third Characene city, Apologos/Ubulla.[13] Hasar-Shapur, and perhaps also other towns said to have been founded by Shapur, must be sought among the unidentified Sassanian sites in the southern plain, for instance fortified Ruqbat Mada'in and Djidr; from from the size of the site the latter appears to have been one of the largest towns in Mesopotamia in Sassanian times.[14] The Muslim accounts of conquest mention yet another large town, Zandaward (another name for Hasar-Shapur?) in the south. This may be identical with the Djidr site, but also with the Persian town which stood where, in the early 8th century, al-Hadjdjadj founded Wasit.[15] Even though these towns cannot be located, the archaeological data and written records all point to the southern floodplain as the scene of large-scale Sassanian colonization. This must have involved a reactivation or extension of the southward flowing canal which in the 10th century bore the name Nahr Nars.[16]

In the north, some 50 km above Baghdad, Shapur I (or Shapur II according to other versions of the *Khuda-nameh* tradition) founded the town *Buzurg-Shapur*, i.e. 'Ukbara. Aerial photos show the remains of a large canal system which presumably was built or enlarged in connection with the founding of the town.[17] Further to the north, Shah Firuz is said to have built the town of *Karkh-Firuz*. This may be identical with the remains of a small, fortified settlement within the later Samarra complex.[18]

As was noticed above, the Sassanians revived the deportations and forcible resettlements practiced by their predecessors. We have no reliable figures, but the *Khuda-nameh* and western sources give the impression that large-scale population transfers were integral parts of the colonization schemes. The "people from the East" settled in Hasar-Shapur by Shapur were no doubt ethnic Persians entrusted with insuring political and military control. The same was true of the 12.000 Persians whom Shapur II later brought to Nisibis. While these resettlements no doubt took place peacefully, deportations were also used as punishment of rebellious tribal groups, for instance in Kirman.[19] Above all, however, the Sassanians systematically deported prisoners of war. In his inscription at Naqsh-é Rustam Shapur I boasts that he had the prisoners from the Roman Empire and "Non-Iran" brought to Fars, Parthia, Khuzistan, and Mesopotamia and settled in areas under direct royal administration. Shapur II did the same with the prisoners he captured during his campaigns in Syria and Arabia.[20]

The second phase of expansion, beginning at the end of the 5th century, coincided with a fiscal reorganization which has been briefly outlined above (p. 38). It is generally believed that this reorganization also involved a territorial extension of direct royal administration with the underlying intention of eliminating the old powerful nobility, replacing it with a loyal "aristocracy of service."[21] This seems unlikely, however. The reorganization was apparently limited to Mesopotamia, and all traditions agree that the great nobles had their bases outside the floodplain. Considering that the reorganization took place at the very time when the Sassanian kings were carrying out a renewed colonization, it is more likely to have been part of a wider scheme for increasing revenue from the heartland of the Empire. The sources refer repeatedly to the Sassanians using legislation to pressure landowners and peasants into expanding production, for instance by imposing tax on land left uncultivated.[22] The change to a fixed fee, as an extra benefit, must have had a similar effect: the larger the area under cultivation, the better chance one stood of being able meet the tax demands.[23]

The greatest project during the second phase of colonization was begun on the Tigris' east bank and included canal construction as well as city foundings and deportations. The key element was the enlargement of the Katul al-Kisrawi-Nahrawan complex which ran from Samarra, across the Azaym and the Diyala, down to al-Kut. Diversions from Diyala must have existed by Seleucid-Parthian times, but the linking together of the various elements into a single gigantic system cutting through the considerable topographic barriers, must have been planned and executed as a single operation. Apparently this was done in late-Sassanian times, and later Muslim traditions may be correct in naming Khusraw I as the builder.[24] Yet at least the Nahrawan part may have been in operation earlier: this is indicated, for instance, by Kavadh I's settlement of cavalry soldiers in the Nahrawan district where their maintenance was no doubt secured by the expanding cultivation. Their descendants still lived there in the 9th century.[25]

Large-scale deportation was used when Khusraw I founded a new suburb 5 or 6 km south of Ctesiphon. Its official name was *Veh-Antiokh* (Veh-az-Andew-Khus-raw), i.e. "Khusraw's-(City-Which-Is)-Better-Than-Antioch," because the prison-ers from Antioch, conquered in 542, were settled here. Later arrivals to Veh-Antiokh included prisoners from the 573 campaign in which the Persians, accord-ing to John of Ephesus, deported no fewer than 292.000 persons from Dara, Apamia, and other Syrian towns. John also cites a letter stating that "we are more than 30.000 prisoners here," i.e. in Veh-Antiokh. While the figures may not be taken literally, they nevertheless reflect the impression which Khusraw's deporta-tions made on his contemporaries. Colloquially the new town was naturally called *Rumagan* (Arabic: al-Rumiyah), "Greek town."[26]

Together with the founding of Veh-Antiokh, Khusraw I also carried out an administrative reorganization of the region along the Nahrawan Canal. Similar reorganizations had taken place in connection with the founding of Veh-Ardashir, Buzurg-Shapur ('Ukbara), and Djunday-Shapur (in Khuzistan). Considering this, Kavadh I's establishment of the Veh-Kavadh district (between the Nahr Sura and the Sarat Canal) may reflect colonization schemes such as the enlargement of the Sarat complex and the founding of the large but unidentified site known today as Zibliyat.[27]

East of the Tigris, Sassanian colonization reached far into the Zagros foothills. According to Ibn al-Faqih the foundings extended all the way from al-Mada'in to Asadabad (near Hamadan). Kavadh I is thus said to have founded the fortified town of Hulwan on the transition from the floodplain to the mountains (near present-day Sar-é Pul); the nearby town of Valash'azz is ascribed to his predecessor, Valash (484–488). The laying out of villages, parks, and palaces – including Khusraw II's residence, the famed Dastkarat al-Malik – in the climatically more tolerable foothills is further mentioned.[28] Finally, numerous ruins of bridges in this area testify to the Sassanians' efforts to ease and control traffic and communication along the strategically important Khurasan road.

Works such as the Katul al-Kisrawi-Nahrawan canal obviously made it possible to expand the area with winter crops (wheat and barley). Yet increased control of Tigris water must have made possible an expansion of perennial irrigation as well. The technological prerequisites for raising summer crops certainly existed in the form of weirs and flood-gates. This does not mean that two crops were now raised on the same piece of land each year; without modern chemical fertilizers most land in Mesopotamia would not have been fertile enough for that. The real advantage of perennial irrigation was that it could prolong the growing season and thus make possible the cultivation of heat- and water-demanding long-season crops. The notable urbanization must have increased demands for such luxury and industrial crops.

But were the summer crops described in the 10th and 11th century sources already being cultivated in Sassanian times? A.M. Watson has argued that the medieval agricultural system in the Middle East only took form in the centuries *after* the spread of Islam: it was the Arab conquests and the creation of a single Muslim world which, together with navigation on the Indian Ocean, created a unique opportunity for crop diffusion. This was seized upon by both the rulers and more anonymous historical actors such as seamen and peasants to bring acclimatized tropical plants westward and to spread knowledge about various water-lifting devices.[29]

This theory of a Muslim "green revolution" may well be valid for the Levant, North Africa, and Spain. Yet it does not hold for Iranshahr. There had been ample opportunity long before the Arab expansion for the diffusion of exotic plants from India and Southeast Asia. Even in Parthian and Sassanian times the Persians had regularly sailed with the monsoon to India and Ceylon (and perhaps all the way to China).[30] Besides, there is evidence of acclimatized tropical plants being cultivated in Iranshahr in pre-Muslim times.

In the 10th and 11th centuries summer cultivation involved primarily rice, sugar cane, and cotton. Now rice was certainly known and cultivated in both Mesopotamia and Khuzistan several centuries B.C. In the cadastral surveys carried out in connection with the fiscal reorganization of late-Sassanian times, rice appears an important crop after wheat, barley, dates, olives, wine, and alfalfa.[31]

The dating of the diffusion of sugar cane is more difficult. When Chinese sources mention "crystal honey" from pre-Muslim Iran, they are no doubt referring to sugar, but we do not know if the sugar had actually been produced in Iran. Persian merchants and envoys may have brought sugar with them as a transit commodity.[32] The same may be true of the sugar which Heraclius' troops found during the sack of Daskarat al-Malik in January 628.[33] Moreover, it is remarkable that sugar is not mentioned in the late-Sassanian surveys of Mesopotamia. On the other hand, sugar may already have been cultivated in Khuzistan; in the 10th century sugar production there was far more important than in Mesopotamia. In any case, a later cadastral survey in Mesopotamia, carried out in the reign of 'Umar b. al-Khattab (634–44), refers to sugar as one of the important crops next to wheat, barley, dates, and wine.[34] It is unlikely that the Arabs, only a few years after conquering the floodplain and long before reaching the Indus Valley, could have managed to introduce sugar cane on a large scale. More likely, sugar cane was widespread even in Sassanian times.

A similar uncertainty applies to cotton. Early references, from the middle of the 1st millennium B.C., are to the cotton tree (*Gossypium arboreum*), not the cotton plant (*Gossypium herbaceum*). The Babylonian Talmud (4th-5th centuries) mentions oil of cottonseed, but this does not prove that the plant was being cultivated for its fibres.[35] From cadastral surveys made in the time of 'Umar b. al-Khattab and of 'Ali it is clear that cotton was cultivated in several places in Mesopotamia, including Veh-Ardashir, Nahr al-Malik, Kutha, and Veh-Kavadh. Again the indications are that diffusion had in fact occurred in Sassanian times at the latest.

In short, the diffusion of tropical plants in Iranshahr must have long predated the Arab conquests. Some of these plants were apparently used as summer crops on a large scale by late Sassanian times, if not earlier. Also the idea that the early Muslim period saw a wider and more systematic application of various technical devices for irrigation can be dismissed. As an example Watson cites the *qanat* which the Arabs brought with them to North Africa and Spain. However, this says nothing of qualitative changes in Mesopotamia where the *qanat* was of marginal importance.

It would thus seem that Adams is right in assuming that Mesopotamian agriculture reached its zenith in Sassanian times and that the expansion involved increased cultivation of water-demanding summer crops. The Arab conquest brought with it no technological advances (including knowledge of new plants) which could expand production or increase productivity and thus justify a hypothesis of an "agrarian revolution." In any event, the notion of an agrarian heyday in the first centuries following the establishing of Muslim rule in Mesopotamia is misleading: precisely during this period the floodplain in fact saw a dramatic decline in both settlement and cultivation.

Chapter 7

The Crisis of the Seventh Century:
Environmental and Demographic Disaster

Shortly after the completing of the great Nahrawan system, Mesopotamia was ravaged by a series of disasters: civil wars, invasions, floods, and epidemics. The combined effect was devastating and by late Sassanian times the southern part of the floodplain disappears from the archaeological record.[1] Thus the Arab conquest did not usher in an era of growth and prosperity, but one of contraction and decline.

While the course of the wars and the establishing of the Muslim Empire is reasonably well-known, the natural disasters need closer examination. Their impact was decisive, as we shall see; yet in the conventional presentation of Middle Eastern history they hardly figure at all.

Judging from modern conditions, we must assume that the expansion of irrigation and summer cultivation had put a heavy strain on the Mesopotamian environment. Heavy-feeding crops such as cotton will drain the soil of nutrients, and increased waterings will raise water-tables. We know very little about fallowing practices, but a general intensification of agriculture, together with the interruption of the lines of natural drainage by the transverse canals, must have caused waterlogging, salinity build-up, and decreasing yields. Yet such problems are not mentioned in the sources. Perhaps the processes were too gradual to attract attention; more likely, the chroniclers were simply not aware of the importance of these things. However, they did record some dramatic hydrological changes which reflect the increasing strain on the environment.

Until the reign of Bahram V Gur (421–439) the Tigris had largely followed the line of its present channel, i.e. from Baghdad to al-Kut and onward to al-'Amarah and al-Qurna. In the second half of the 5th century, however, it began to change its course south of Fahm al-Silh (near al-Kut), moving to a position close to that of the present Shatt al-Hadr. It now merged with the Euphrates in the Great Swamp in the south (al-Bata'ih), and from there the two rivers flowed in a single channel out to the Persian Gulf. In the lowest section of the old Tigris bed, up to Madhar (four days' journey north of Basrah), some water remained because of the pressure from the tide in the Gulf. This channel was known as the "Blind Tigris."[2]

The shift had two immediate consequences. First, parts of Mayshan, between Madhar and Fahm al-Silh, lost their water supply and had to be abandoned as farmland. Second, the low-lying areas along the new channel were submerged.

Through the 6th century the Sassanians built dikes along the river to bring the waters under control; the reports of Kavadh's and Khusraw I's administrative reorganizations in the south may reflect the extent of the disturbances and the efforts to restore the situation.

All was to no avail. In 628 a flood breached the dikes, and despite desperate efforts made under the king's personal supervision, the workers were unable to stop the waters. The permanent swamps grew and swallowed up the entire al-Tharthur district in Kaskar; in the following years they expanded even further. According to al-Baladhuri this was because the *dihqans* were preoccupied with fighting the Arabs and therefore did not have time to oversee the dikes and repair the breaches.[3] They also lacked both labor and a stable administrative framework, as Mesopotamia was at the same time hit by recurrent outbreaks of plague. Though overshadowed in later historiography by the expansion of Islam, the plague was a terrible disaster that left an indelible mark on Mesopotamian society.

Seen from the perspective of world history, plague is rare. Ordinarily the disease-producing parasite lives quietly in fleas carried by wild rodents; only under extraordinary circumstances will it infect humans. As far as we know, it has happened only three times on a large scale: in the 6th, 14th, and 19th centuries. Each time the result were widespread pandemics: i.e. linked series of epidemics that strike in a cyclic fashion. In each pandemic the plague was characterized by extreme virulence, though death-rates varied depending on the form which the disease took; while the most common strain, bubonic plague, has a case mortality between 50% and 60%, pneumonic plague is almost always fatal.[4]

Also the course and consequences of plague epidemics may differ from one society to another. During the second pandemic, from the 14th century onward, Western Europe, in spite of enormous death-rates, achieved a fairly rapid demographic recovery. By the mid-16th century pre-plague population levels had been regained, and by the mid-17th century the disease had disappeared, except for the occasional isolated outbreak. In Egypt and Syria, however, plague epidemics still appeared, and here the demographic decline continued unabated until the end of the 18th century. In part, this difference owed to the fact that medical thinking in Europe had begun to question traditional ideas of disease and contagion. More important, observation and experience had made the European states introduce effective quarantine measures to check the spread of the disease. No doubt any satisfactory explanation must take account of other factors as well. The point to be made is that the course of the plague, its dissemination, and its consequences do not simply reflect biological and environmental variables. The plague cannot be understood outside the proper historical context in which it appeared.[5] The proper context incidentally includes other diseases. Because of its terrifying properties, plague has tended to obscure the presence of other infectious diseases. Though separately less virulent than the plague, these diseases together contributed heavily to the general morbidity.

1. The Mesopotamian Disease-Pool

Infectious diseases originate from a combination of three factors: the host, the parasite, and the environment. Since none of these are constant, the level of infection among humans cannot be constant either. In prehistoric times disease-patterns presumably changed at a slow pace. Humans lived with several infections specific to them; owing to prolonged reciprocal adaptations, the relationship between the human host and the parasites must have been reasonably stable: i.e. infections must have been largely chronic and only mildly debilitating. (We are, of course, not counting infections due to lesions and alimentary causes.) Populations were too dispersed to allow the rise of epidemics, and if the prehistoric disease-pattern eventually did change, this would primarily have been because of changes in the environment.[6]

This stable situation was fundamentally altered by the Neolithic Revolution when, in a relatively short time, some groups of humans created new environments and, hence, new risks of infections. The domestication of animals brought humans into contact with a wide range of disease-producing microorganisms, among them the remote ancestors of smallpox and measles. Settled ways of life and irrigation favored the dissemination of waterborne infections. Eventually in some places there arose population clusters large enough to sustain acute epidemic infections on a permanent basis. While chronic infections can survive in small and dispersed populations, acute infections need a constant supply of susceptible hosts; otherwise they will simply die out as soon as everyone has been infected and acquired immunity – or has died. The necessary size of such a community will vary from one infection to another; measles, for instance, cannot be propagated continuously in communities of less than half a million.

This knowledge is derived from modern observations; but the conditions for the rise and spread of acute infections in the past must have been basically the same. By the 3rd millennium B.C. (if not before) these conditions were present in Mesopotamia. Although precise quantitative data are lacking, the number, location, and size of city states indicate that the total population of the floodplain by the Ur III period was between a half and one million. Other communities of adequate size were at the same time emerging in Egypt and the Indus River Valley. Of course this does not prove that acute epidemic infections were in fact present. Positive evidence of their existence must be sought in the written records (acute infections leave no trace on skeletal remains).[7] Such evidence exist from the beginning of the 2nd millennium B.C. Besides various medical texts – i.e. collections of brief examples of diagnosis and prognosis – there are incantations as well as divinatory and prophetic texts which frequently refer to diseases, including acute epidemic ones.[8] Official and private letters from the 2nd millennium also mention epidemics.[9]

Thus there is no doubt that epidemics were well-known, recurring phenomena; but we lack the necessary data to discuss the frequency and nature of the diseases involved. Most of them cannot be identified with any certainty, and we must therefore be cautious when drawing conclusions about the past from modern epidemics. The descriptions of symptoms tend to be brief and may refer to diseases which have disappeared or greatly changed long before the advent of modern medical science. Owing to the constant variations and changes of the disease-producing organism, no disease will remain the same over millennia or even centuries; this makes it difficult to compare diseases over a long time.

Moreover, the Mesopotamian disease-terminology and the entire world view behind it is difficult to understand. The medical texts thus describe several diseases as the "blow," "grip," "touch," or "hand" of some deity. Not only do the descriptions of symptoms indicate that diseases placed in the same category were in fact quite different; the classification includes all kind of accidents and disasters besides disease. This means that diseases are sometimes classified according to an assumed common origin, for instance an offence against the deity, and not according to their symptoms or course.[10] In other cases, however, where the evil demons are involved, certain types of diseases, including some acute and contagious infections, are indeed classified according to symptoms.[11] Especially feared in this category was the "baby killer," the female demon Lamashtu, who "snatches the newborn babes from the mother's arm." It has been suggested that she personified enteric infections such as typhoid fever, dysentery, and the like.[12]

No doubt the opaque terminology and the vague descriptions of symptoms also conceal several of the degenerative, chronic infections which must have been present at an early date, e.g. schistosomiasis, malaria, and tuberculosis. Traces of schistosomiasis (bilharziasis) are found in Egyptian mummies from the 12th century B.C., thus attesting to the antiquity of the disease. In Mesopotamia its presence can only be documented directly in modern times, but there is some circumstantial evidence for early diffusion. Shells of the Bulinus snail (*Bulinus Truncatus*), which serves as intermediary host for the disease-producing parasite, have been found in the bricks of several ruins, including the temple-tower in Dur-Kurigalzu (built *c.* 1400 B.C.); mention of hematuria in the sources may be considered a further indication.[13]

Malaria, primarily the *plasmodium falciparum* strain, was already present throughout the eastern Mediterranean in the middle of the 1st millennium B.C. Frequent mention by Mesopotamian sources of both jaundice – malaria affects the liver – and "cold and warm fevers" indicates that the disease had been established in the floodplain perhaps as early as the 2nd millennium.[14]

Tubercular infections were apparently widespread in the Middle East as early as the Neolithic and can be documented in Egypt from about 3000 B.C. It is unlikely that tuberculosis should not also have existed in Mesopotamia. The medical texts in fact furnish several descriptions of what looks like tubercular symptoms (e.g. coughing and blood-spitting).[15]

In brief, it seems that by the end of the 3rd millennium B.C. Mesopotamia had become an important disease-pool: i.e. the focus of several acute and chronic infections. From here and from Egypt, where the situation must have been largely the same, infections were spread by armies and caravans. We know that about 1350 B.C. Egyptian prisoners of war carried a lethal infection to the land of Hatti in Anatolia, apparently with fateful consequences.[16]

Sketching the world history of disease in broad strokes, William McNeill argues that classical civilization in the Mediterranean area was largely disease-free (apart from malaria). This situation remained stable until the "Plague of the Antonines" and "Cyprian's Plague" in the 2nd and 3rd centuries burst onto the Roman Empire from the east and allegedly decimated the population. In McNeill's view these outbreaks marked an epidemiological breakthrough, comparable to the transmission of the Eurasian infections to the New World in the 16th century.[17] This is certainly misleading. First, the epidemics of the 2nd and 3rd centuries were not so serious as later sources would have it. They were not as virulent as one would expect of genuine virgin soil epidemics.[18] Secondly, the population of the Roman Empire, especially that of the eastern provinces, could not possibly have been as susceptible to infections as were the pre-Columbian Americans. Greek colonists had settled in Syria (al-Mina) and Egypt (Naucratis) as early as 600 B.C., and at that time the Egyptians also hired Greek and Carian mercenaries in great numbers. Thus the entire eastern Mediterranean Basin must have been in close, regular contact with the Middle Eastern disease-pools. In his description of the "plague" of Athens in 430/29 B.C., Thucydides says expressly that the disease came from Egypt, another indication that the eastern Mediterranean formed a single unified zone of infection. The infection of Xerxes' troops in Thessaly and the frequent epidemics on Sicily and in North Africa in the 5th and 4th centuries B.C. further show that military movements could transmit infections around the entire Mediterranean.[19] Very early, then, the special relationship which had evolved between humans and microparasites in the densely populated river-oases became a factor affecting the history of the entire Middle East and the Levant.

It is often assumed that pre-modern populations were especially susceptible to disease, because they were chronically malnourished; their resistance is said to have been weakened by inadequate diets containing too few and too poor proteins and vitamins. The situation was aggravated in times of famine when the general debility of the population caused endemic diseases to assume epidemic proportions. As tradition has it, pestilence inevitably follows famine.[20]

Yet from the high levels of infection we cannot infer that the material conditions of life were generally miserable for the common people in Mesopotamia. It is not certain that they actually suffered malnutrition. Apparently the basic diet consisted at all times of barley and dates. In themselves these were inefficient sources of protein, to be sure, but under normal circumstances they would be supplemented with fish, pulse, vegetables and, at times, a little meat. On the basis of Ur III documents referring to deliveries of food rations, one scholar concludes that the adult population at least was relatively well-nourished at that time (c. 2000 B.C.). But even if this is correct, it still says little about conditions in other periods.[21]

In any evaluation we would also have to consider the fact that the early, "primitive" varieties of grain generally had a higher protein content than do modern varieties.[22] Moreover, the yardstick for what constitutes an adequate diet has changed in recent decades. The standards of FAO and WHO are frequently used as a basis for evaluating nutritional conditions in the past; but in these standards the recommended daily minimum intake of proteins has been consistently reduced. At the same time the notion that plant proteins are generally poorer than animal protein has been revised. Thus the amount of fresh meat in the diet is no longer the decisive index of the quality of nutrition. (The recommended number of calories has not been changed, however.)[23] Finally, the link between diet and disease is less clear than most historians seem to think. Nutritional inadequacy may certainly help the spread or worsen the effect of diseases such as tuberculosis and (perhaps) schistosomiasis.[24] Yet for acute infections such as smallpox and plague the nutritional state of the host is not an important factor. The rich and well-fed are as likely to be infected and die as are the poor and undernourished. Thus there is no causal link between famine and the outbreak of plague epidemics.[25]

A factor of greater importance in spreading infection is housing conditions. If an entire family lives together in a single room, the risk of spreading airborne infections increases simply because each individual is exposed to large and frequent doses of infection.[26] Excavations of residential quarters in Nippur indicate that the inhabitants indeed lived very close together at the beginning of the 2nd millennium B.C.. Logically they must have been subject to a high risk of infection; but we do not know whether the population density in the Mesopotamian cities was constant through history. As to conditions in the villages, we know even less.[27]

We can be quite certain, however, that water-borne infections were a constant threat. Hydrological conditions on the floodplain made it extremely difficult to keep drinking-water separate from sewage-water (if indeed people realized that this was important). Medical texts mentioning vomiting and diarrhoea among children, often with a pessimistic prognosis, give the impression of a heavy infant mortality caused by enteric infections. So do the many exorcisms of Lamashtu, the "baby killer," and the prayers to Nergal, the God of pestilence, to let the children go free.[28] Obviously the adult population must have acquired immunity to the common acute infections, excepting those that do not confer any lasting immunity (e.g. dysentery and influenzas). Instead adults suffered from several chronic diseases: malaria, schistosomiasis, tuberculosis, various intestinal worms, etc. Though not immediately fatal, such diseases certainly had debilitating effects.

We do not have the data to estimate the average lifespan in Mesopotamia before the 19th century, nor indeed in any other comparable pre-industrial society. Probably the best figures are from Imperial Rome. Here, it is assumed, life expectancy at birth in the first centuries A.D. was as low as between 20 and 30 years. The data are even defective in a way that tends to exaggerate life expectancy, because they say little about infant mortality and ignore the lower classes. In any case it seems that the low life expectancy was not simply due to heavy infant mortality; mortality was high among other age groups as well, though the causes are in dispute. The most obvious explanation would be high and constant levels of infection.[29]

There is no reason to believe that the demographic situation was worse in the Roman Empire than in Mesopotamia; on the contrary, the Roman level of infection was probably lower. Though we know nothing about fertility, we must therefore assume that the demographic balance in Mesopotamia was at least as fragile as in the Roman Empire. Of course, under normal conditions population growth was possible. The expansion of settlement in Parthian-Sassanian times must obviously have been accompanied by such growth. But owing to constantly high mortality, increases must have been slow, and this may explain the Mesopotamian rulers' forcible deportations. Among the colonists, however, mortality must have been especially high because they were both biologically and culturally unprepared for the encounter with the local microparasites. The fate of Alexander the Great may serve as an example of the perils awaiting foreigners coming to Mesopotamia.

In view of its fragile demographic balance Mesopotamia must have been extremely vulnerable to new infections of foreign origin. In cases of severe mortality even a society with high fertility rates would find it difficult to recover from the loss of life, as the local infections would continue to decimate both children and women of child-bearing age. However, until the first plague pandemic Mesopotamia seems to have been spared demographic disasters of this kind.[30]

The lethal, unidentified epidemic which struck besieged Athens in 430/29 B.C. was almost certainly a new, hitherto unknown infection. According to Thucydides it originally had come from Ethiopia to Egypt; from there the disease spread to Athens, North Africa, and the Persian Empire. However, no local sources suggest that an epidemic of extraordinary virulence occurred in Mesopotamia at that time.[31]

The "Plague of the Antonines," one or several unidentified epidemic diseases striking the Roman Empire in the middle of the 160s, may in fact have originated in the Mesopotamian disease-pool. Later sources (Ammianus Marcellinus and the Historia Augusta) tell how Avidius Cassius' troops were infected as punishment for sacrileges committed during the sack of Seleucia in A.D. 165–166; then they go on to describe how the pestilence ravaged the entire Roman Empire.[32] These later descriptions are behind the theory that a new infection (smallpox has been suggested), emanating from India, either caused or strongly contributed to the demise of classical civilization.[33]

But had the "Plague of the Antonines" been a completely new disease from the east, it ought to have had catastrophic results in Mesopotamia as well. Yet there is nothing to suggest this. On the contrary, the Parthian era saw a considerable expansion of settlement which could not have occurred in a situation with prolonged and severe mortality. The few contempory classical sources, primarily Cassius Dio, in fact give more restrained accounts.[34] Thus the apocalyptic reports of the later sources seem to be stereotypes rather than factual descriptions of the course of the epidemic. That the disease should have come from India is pure speculation. There is no denying that the "Plague of the Antonines" was a serious epidemic, perhaps of Mesopotamian origin. However, the idea that it was a unique disaster comparable to the later plague epidemics does not stand up to scrutiny.[35]

The same can be said of "Cyprian's Plague," another unidentified epidemic which swept parts of the Roman Empire between A.D. 250 and 270. It is even less known than the "Plague of the Antonines". Two contempory sources describe the outbreak of a severe epidemic in, respectively, Carthage and Alexandria.[36] Both authors may have exaggerated from a desire to praise the Christians and their care for the sick. In any case, it is only in later sources such as the Historia Augusta and Zosimus that the epidemic is described as universal.[37] We do not know if "Cyprian's Plague" ever reached Mesopotamia. In theory the disease could have been disseminated during Shapur I's campaigns in Syria in the 250s, had it indeed spread beyond the borders of North Africa. Yet the sources do not allow us to reach any conclusions. When, for example, the Babylonian Talmud refers to epidemics during Sassanian times in Mesopotamia and Khuzistan, these do not seem to have been unusual in any way.[38]

The same is true of the epidemic which struck northern Syria and the Djazirah in the winter 500–501. This was clearly a malignant disease; a contempory local chronicle, which otherwise gives no description of the symptoms, claims that in a medium-sized town like Edessa burials averaged a hundred a day over a period of several months. Nevertheless the account leaves the impression that the epidemic was of short duration and geographically restricted to the area between Antioch and Nisibis. Thus the demographic consequences cannot have been far-reaching. In Edessa there were in fact enough people left the following year to man the city walls and turn back a Persian attack.[39]

It may be objected that the sources are too meagre to allow for any conclusions about the frequency of epidemics in pre-Muslim times. It is evident, however, that the great settlement expansion during Parthian and Sassanian times must have entailed population growth. This strongly suggests that the Mesopotamian disease-pool had reached an equilibrium of sorts that lasted until the arrival of the plague in the mid-6th century. On the negative side we may note that, as a corollary of the extension of the great irrigation systems, the dissemination of malaria and schistoso-miasis was eased.

2. The First Plague Pandemic

The plague made its first appearance in the Nile Delta at the end of 541. Byzantine chroniclers subsequently added that it had originally come from Ethiopia. Though this may simply be one of many stereotypes borrowed from Thucydides' account of the Plague of Athens, the Ethiopian rodent communities were in fact the most likely reservoir of infection. Yet how and why it was disseminated from here is impossible to say today.[40]

From Egypt the plague spread by sea to Constantinople and overland to Syria and further to Osroene and Armenia. From there Persian armies brought it to Meso-potamia where it raged for three years.[41] In the 10th century Mas'udi cited sources which estimated that a third or even half of the population in Mesopotamia and adjacent countries died. If the first epidemic of the first pandemic is comparable to the better known first epidemic of the second pandemic (i.e. the Black Death), a population loss of about 30% would seem quite probable.[42]

We have very little detailed information, however, of the course of the first pandemic in Iranshahr. Few contemporary accounts have survived. In the 9th century, when the plague had finally disappeared, scholars in Basrah wrote several brief summaries of the history of the disease.[43] Though considered highly authoritative by later Muslim historians, these "Books of Plague" are in fact incomplete. They chiefly record outbreaks occurring in Muslim times and affecting Basrah. On the other hand, there is little doubt that what they recorded was in fact plague (and not other lethal epidemics).[44]

The available evidence suggests that in the two centuries after the first epidemic, major outbreaks of plague occurred at least ten times in or close to Iranshahr (the precise geographical extension is rarely given by the sources):

562 The Djazirah. In Amida alone the death count was said to have reached 30.000.[45]

599 The Djazirah and Mesopotamia.[46]

627/28 "Sheroë's Plague," a severe outbreak in Mesopotamia during the reign of Kavadh II Sheroë.[47]

638/40 Syria and Mesopotamia.[48]
669/70 Kufah (localized outbreak?).[49]
686/87 The Djazirah.[50]
688/89 Mesopotamia. Probably the same outbreak as the one just referred to. Just
      in Basrah 200.000 are said to have died in three days.[51]
  706 The Djazirah and Mesopotamia.[52]
718/19 Mesopotamia.[53]
744/45 Mesopotamia.[54]
  749 Great outbreak throughout the Middle East and the Levant.[55]

Muslim sources claim that the outbreak of 749 was the last. Then the dreaded disease disappeared suddenly, just as the Abbasids seized power. This certainly looks like a piece of heavy political editing aimed at glorifying the new dynasty by showing that it had the favor of God. Christian sources in fact refer to later outbreaks which may well have been plague, e.g. the lethal epidemic which swept the Djazirah in the disastrous year 774/75. According to Dionysius of Tell-Mahré it killed all the priests at the church in Amida. Itinerant laborers then carried the disease eastward to Mosul where, for a time, mortality ran as high as 1000 a day. The description of the symptoms is vague and leaves the impression that several infections, including plague, occurred at the same time.[56] However, the plague did gradually disappear in the second half of the 8th century. A few later outbreaks of *ta'un* reported from Basrah (892) and Baghdad (913/14) can hardly have been plague; in these cases the term probably refers to lethal epidemic disease in general.[57]

This list of plague epidemics lays no claim to be exhaustive. It does show, however, that in Mesopotamia and the Djazirah plague came with terrifying regularity and, apparently, with undiminished virulence for two hundred years. In the Mediterranean region about 15 major outbreaks are recorded for the same period.[58] Any estimate of the first plague pandemic's effects upon Iranshahr must therefore take into consideration the cumulative mortality. Of course we have no definite figures, but by all accounts the death rates were staggering, and J.C. Russell's estimate of an overall population decrease of 40% in the Mediterranean region may therefore be accepted as a rough indication of what happened in Mesopotamia.[59]

Mortality on such a scale must have had far-reaching effects upon the labor-intensive agricultural system in Mesopotamia. The extant tax assessments hint at the magnitude of the disaster. During the reign of Kavadh I (488–531), just *before* the arrival of the plague, the Mesopotamian land-tax was assessed at 150 million mithqals of silver, equivalent to 214 million Muslim dirhams.[60] By Umayyad and early Abbasid times the assessment had fallen to a little more than 100 million dirhams. This drop is too great to be explained solely in terms of administrative changes, or failure to register *kharadj*-free land, or even milder tax demands.[61] On the contrary, the Syriac sources complain that the Arab domination brought grievous extortion and cruelty in collecting the taxes.[62] The tax base had obviously been severely reduced by the ravages of the plague.

In addition, the decimated labor force would not have been able to maintain and operate the huge network of canals, particularly when unstable hydrological conditions in the south made increasing demands for labor. It is said that when al-Hadjdjadj, around 700, repaired the Sarat-al-Nil system, he had the workers chained together to stop them from running away. Though this sounds as just another anti-al-Hadjdjadj anecdote, it may in fact reflect a desperate shortage of manpower for the vital public works. In Egypt, rulers in the 15th century resorted to similar harsh measures.[63] The point is that in Mesopotamia the plague not only caused severe loss of life; acting in combination with the particular environmental conditions, it also destroyed capital equipment such as dykes, weirs, canals, and, ultimately, cultivated land. The lost resources could not be recovered piecemeal by later generations of peasants. The restoration of the decayed irrigation works would have called for overall organization and massive inputs of labor, and the post-plague Empire was not equal to this task. In the long term it was not capable even of stabilizing the situation. In spite of the Muslim rulers' efforts at reparations and city foundings, the decline continued even after the disappearance of the plague.

Something similar happened in Peru when the Eurasian infections arrived with the Spanish conquerors. Between 1500 and 1600 overall mortality from epidemics, aggravated by social and political disruption, claimed an estimated 75% of the Indian population of America, a loss far more severe than even the plague death-toll in the Old World.[64] The coastal lands were obviously struck worse than the *Sierra*. In the clustered populations of the irrigated coastal valleys diseases were more easily transmitted than in the cooler mountain valleys where population was more dispersed, and the *corregimientos* of Piura and Chicama as well as the southern coastal valleys suffered enormous death-rates; Lambayeque and Saña were not struck quite as hard. Obviously the depopulation had fateful consequences for the labor-intensive irrigation agriculture, as it was no longer possible to gather labor for the cleaning-out of canals or the reconstructions of irrigation works after floods. Thus the *el Niño* of 1578 caused widespread destruction that was never repaired again.[65]

Disease-mortality in the *Sierra* was considerably lower than in the coastal lands, yet high enough to affect agriculture. The dry highland valleys had been brought under intensive and permanent cultivation through great efforts in constructing irrigation works and terracing the hillsides. We do not know if this system already had run into environmental difficulties; but now it quickly collapsed as disease killed a large part of the labor force and the Spanish overlords transferred the survivors to work in the mines and in the plantations of the coastal regions. Centuries later, recolonization of the valleys was attempted, but as the skills of the ancient terracing farmers had been lost, this resulted in widespread erosion.[66]

Chapter 8

From Crisis to Continued Decline:
Mesopotamia between Two Plague Pandemics

In spite of demographic losses and environmental instability Mesopotamia remained the Empire's chief resource base. In the two centuries after the crisis of the 7th century, tax assessments of agriculture stabilized at a level of about 100 million dirhams. Though this amount was below the level of Sassanian times, it was still considerably higher than anything contributed by other areas under the Empire's control (see table 4).

This situation lasted until the beginning of the 10th century when assessments dropped sharply to 30–40 million, i.e. below the level of, for instance, Djibal and Fars. By the 14th century they had fallen further to about 13 million.[1] There can be no doubt that the declining tax revenues were correlated with a general material decline in Mesopotamia. Admittedly the geographical literature of the 10th century describes the country as rich and pleasant and as the center of the civilized world;[2] but on closer examination this turns out to be pure convention. Having given such a flowery standard description, al-Muqaddasi adds that while this may have been true in the past, Mesopotamia was now in a state of decline, afflicted with famine, oppression, and excessive taxation. Other contemporary sources, for instance Mas-'udi and Miskawayh, also provide vivid impressions of the Empire's financial troubles, the administrative chaos, and the neglect of agriculture and irrigation works.[3]

The decline was not a uniform phenomenon, however. In the assessment from the 14th century several formerly productive areas had simply disappeared from the fiscal picture, while other areas, primarily in the northern plain, continued under intensive cultivation. Whatever the explanation may be, these differences suggest that developments in Mesopotamia between the two plague pandemics was strongly influenced by local conditions.

1. Reconstruction and Stability in the South: Basrah and Wasit

Around 640, when the Arabs conquered Mesopotamia from the Sassanians, vital parts of the great irrigation systems were in a state of decay. This was partly the result of plague and floods, but the civil wars of the preceding decades and the destructive raids of the Arabs had done their part as well.[4]

After the conquest the Arabs began to fight among themselves over the division of the spoils, and the continued political troubles hindered efforts to repair the damage. The Arab warlords who had conquered Mesopotamia more or less on their own initiative regarded the country as their property and saw no reason to divide its wealth with others. In far-off Medina the leaders of the new Muslim state did not yet have the power to enforce their will in Mesopotamia; so they had to be content with the canonical 1/5 of the spoils and grudgingly recognize the special seniority system by which the remainder was distributed among the conquerors.

In order to remain apart from the rest of the population and to have a clear avenue of retreat in case of a Persian counterattack, the Arab warriors had gathered in two large military encampments on the edge of the floodplain: *Kufah*, on the western edge of the desert near old al-Hira, and *Basrah* in Mayshan. Here their names were recorded on a list, the *diwan*. Each man on the list then received his share of the spoils in the form of a yearly payment, the *al-'ata*, the size of which depended on when the individual warrior had converted to Islam. In 645/46 the Kufah list comprised 40.000 men; twenty years later the number had grown to 60.000. The Basrah list contained no less than 80.000.[5] Even though groups of converted Persian soldiers were also entered in the records, the figures indicate the size of the Arab immigration to the floodplain. However, this could not at all compensate for the demographic losses caused by the plague, especially as the immigrants did not help increase the labor force. On the contrary, they constituted a religiously and ethnically defined group of surplus-receivers.

The immigrants were not a homogenous group, however. The recent arrivals were certainly entered on the lists but received a much smaller payment than did the veterans. In Kufah the *al-'ata* eventually varied from 250 to 3.000 dirhams. In Basrah the differences were somewhat smaller. Inevitably disagreements arose among the privileged and the discontented warrior groups and this, together with the conflicts between the warlords and the Muslim Empire's formal leaders, caused continuous political tensions and several open revolts.[6]

Only toward the end of the 7th century, after having moved its seat from Medina to the strategically better situated Damascus, did the Empire achieve some control over the unruly land. Supplied with sufficient military power from Syria, loyal governors like Ziyad b. Abihi and al-Hadjdjadj ruthlessly subdued the local Arab aristocracy. The recalcitrants were killed or exiled, and the economic basis for their independence reduced by declaring large areas, presumably former Sassanian crown lands, to be state lands. All *kharadj* due from these lands now went directly to the treasury rather than being distributed according to the *al-'ata* system.[7] The dissatisfied common soldiers in Basrah and Kufah were sent east to raid Transoxania, Zabulistan, and Sind, far from the Empire's core-lands.[8]

While ensuring political control, Ziyad and al-Hadjdjadj also began to repair and restructure some of the damaged irrigation works.[9] Though they partly did so for

personal economic benefit, the two governors in fact revived the former practice of
centralized intervention in production. Consequently, in the 8th century Muslim
jurisprudence decided that the state should bear the responsibility for the construction and maintenance of the larger canals, dikes, dams, weirs, floodgates, and other
vital parts of the irrigation system.[10] The state could transfer some of these duties to
private persons, for instance by allowing them to build canals as a status-giving
public charge. The state could also give away abandoned or unused land as qati'a,
i.e. on the condition that the recipients would bring it under cultivation (the
attraction was that qati'a land was not subject to kharadj but only to the lesser sadaqa
taxes).[11]

Much of the construction and investment in the first centuries after the Arab
conquest was concentrated in the south, in the enclaves around the two new towns
Basrah and Wasit. Here the warm climate (and reduced risk of frost) favored the
cultivation of tropical cash crops like rice, cotton, and sugar. As noted before,
Basrah had been founded originally as a military encampment and base for further
attacks into Khuzistan and Fars; but when Ziyad b. Abihi began building the first
mosque of baked brick, the settlement clearly was taking on a more permanent
character. Ziyad also constructed or finished two navigable canals, the Nahr
al-Ubulla and the Nahr al-Ma'qil, which connected Basrah with the Shatt al-Arab.
On these canals Sindbad and his fellow captains set out on their long voyages into
the Gulf and the Indian Ocean. In Abbasid times the less adventurous inland
navigation was made easier through the construction (or extension) of the Abu
al-Asad Canal between the Shatt al-Arab and the Great Swamp.[12]

The irrigation of Basrah was a system unto itself, based on local diversions and
without direct links to the great transverse canals to the north. In the area west of
the Shatt al-Arab the main diversion seems to have been the Nahr al-Mar'ah which,
according to certain traditions, dated back to Sassanian times. It had its intake just
south of the swamps and ran parallel with the Shatt al-Arab down to Basrah.
Between the canal and the river was a branching network of distributory canals,
conducting water to the palm groves and plantations.[13] East of the Shatt al-Arab, Ibn
Sarabiyun lists three larger diversions, of which at least one, the Nahr Bayan, was
connected to the Karun. In all, the Basrah enclave is said to have had more than
100.000 canals.[14]

Irrigation was literally automatic, as the tide in the Gulf regularly pushed the
water up into the canal system. In this way the inhabitants were spared the work of
lifting the water. However, the inflowing tide, together with with the terrain's low
altitude above sea level, made both surface water and groundwater rather saline.[15]
Fresh drinking water, therefore, was scarce. Even when the Abbasid prince and
governor Sulayman b. 'Ali had spent one million dirhams on enlarging the Nahr b.
'Umar, a diversion from the Great Swamp, the problem of lack of fresh water
remained.[16]

Table 6. The assessment of Mesopotamia.

	Dirhams
Kavadh I (488–531)	214.000.000[a]
'Umar b. al-Khattab (634–644)	128.000.000[b]
al-Hadjdjadj (695–714)	18.000.000[c]
'Umar II (717–720)	124.000.000[d]
788	119.880.000[e]
800	120.180.000[f]
819	114.457.650[g]
Middle of 9th century	92.766.840[h]
918	30.955.000[i]
969	42.000.000[j]
1335	13.000.000[k]

[a] More precisely, 150 million *mithqals* of silver, 1 dirham being equal to 7/10 *mithqal* according to al-Baladhuri (tr., II: 262). The amount given is the same in practically all the sources: Ibn Khurdadhbih (tr.: 11); Mas'udi (*Tanbih*, tr.: 62); Ibn Hawqal (tr., I: 227); Ibn Rusteh's 1.550.000 dirhams is clearly due to an error in copying. Only Ibn al-Faqih (tr.: 249) lists a lower figure: 123 million dirhams.

[b] Ibn Khurdadhbih (tr.: 11); Ibn Rusteh (tr.: 117).

[c] Ibn Khurdadhbih (tr.: 11). The figure can not be correct for al-Hadjdjadj's entire term of office. Al-Baladhuri (tr., I: 428) also lists a higher amount: 40 million. The explanation may be that the lower figure dates from one of the troubled years immediately after the war against al-Zubayr, when the tax registers were burned. It is also very likely that it reflects the consequences of the great outbreaks of plague at the close of the 7th century.

[d] Ibn Khurdadhbih (tr.: 11); Ibn Rusteh (tr.: 117).

[e] al-'Ali (1971: 306). In contrast to Waines (1977a: 286, table 2), I have included the taxes from *Kuwar Didjla* ("the Districts of the Tigris," i.e. the unflooded parts of Mayshan); these taxes also include the *sadaqa* payments.

[f] al-'Ali (1971); von Kremer (1889).

[g] Qudama (tr.: 180f). This figure also includes 6 million in *sadaqa* from Basrah.

[h] The figure dates from the period 845–873 and includes 2.375.000 dirhams in *sadaqa* from the *kharadj*-free districts of al-Sibayn and al-Wakuf (south of Wasit): Ibn Khurdadhbih (tr.: 6–10).

[i] von Kremer (1888: 312f). The figure includes *Kuwar Didjla* and is converted from dinars (1.547.734) at the rate of 1:20.

[j] Ibn Hawqal (tr., I: 231, 233, 239f), citing Abu al-Fadl Shirazi as his source. Wasit (Kaskar) and Basrah (Kuwar Didjla) each pay six million dirhams, with 30 million from the rest of the Sawad.

[k] Mustawfi (*Nuzhat*, tr.: 36). The figure is really three million *dinar-é rayidj*, here converted into Abbasid dirhams according to the silver weight.

Basrah was notorious as an extremely unhealthy place, even by Mesopotamian standards. The hydrological conditions were clearly one of the causes. For instance, the inhabitants were in the habit of relieving themselves on the banks of the canals at low tide; when the tide rose, excrement and other refuse was washed up and mixed with the water drawn for drinking. A local proverb said that Basrah's water consisted of equal parts seawater, brackish water and sewage-water. Obviously such a mixture, combined with the warm climate, favored the spread of water-borne infections. Sometimes local outbreaks of disease in the enclave even developed into country-wide epidemics.[17]

Wasit in the territory of Kaskar was founded, in 703, by al-Hadjdjadj on the new lower channel of the Tigris (i.e. approximately the Shatt al-Hadr). On the site there already stood an older town, perhaps identical with the non-located Zandaward which is mentioned in the Muslim accounts of conquest. In any case it is said that al-Hadjdjadj got building materials by demolishing Zandaward and that he deported the inhabitants from here to his new founding.[18] At first Wasit primarily served as garrison for the Syrian troops who had subdued Mesopotamia for al-Hadjdjadj and the Umayyads. Yet it was meant to be more than just a military base, as is clear from the alterations in the canal system on the central floodplain made by al-Hadjdjadj at that time. He repaired and extended the old Sarat/al-Nil-complex in the direction of Wasit, which thereby received water from both the Euphrates and the Tigris. No doubt this reduced the discharge of the Nahr Nars Canal which in Sassanian times had conducted water to the lower part of the Euphrates plain.[19] The story goes that al-Hadjdjadj was not satisfied with simply repairing existing canals because he wanted to punish the *dihqans* in the south for supporting one of the recalcitrant Arab nobles, al-Ash'ath b. Qays. Disruption of the water supply and withholding of investments in maintenance works was a well-known means of exerting political pressure; al-Hadjdjadj might conceivable have used it, as did the caliph Hisham (724–743) on later occasions.[20] Nevertheless we should see al-Hadjdjadj's activities in a broader context.

As mentioned before, the central floodplain south of the Kufah-Nippur line disappears almost completely from the archaeological record by late Sassanian times.[21] It also disappears from the written sources. It does not figure in district-lists or tax assessments from the 9th-10th centuries, if we leave out of account a few smaller localities directly on the banks of the Euphrates. It is hardly mentioned by the geographers of the 10th century. Only the Great Swamp drew some attention because of its unique environment and the lawlessness of its inhabitants. All of this strongly indicate that the depopulation of the south was already advanced in the first centuries following the Arab conquest. It had long been completed when Ibn Battuta, in the first half of the 14th century, journeyed from Huwayzah in Khuzistan to Kufah. The route over the southern plain he describes as five days' march through a deserted wasteland.[22]

Of course, the south was not literally deserted. But all major settlements had disappeared and extensive methods of subsistence had largely replaced intensive cultivation. There remained enclaves of cultivated land along the river banks, where simple diversion irrigation was possible without a large, coordinated labor-effort. In a political sense, too, the land was deserted. It was now home to the Khafadjah and Muntafiq bedouins and other lawless elements, who had no respect for the Empire's authority.[23]

This entire process had not been set in motion by al-Hadjdjadj. It is simply improbable that he would have deliberately turned large cultivated areas into empty wasteland just to punish some recalcitrant nobles. In fact, the Nahr Nars was not

Table 7. The assessment of Mesopotamia, 1335/36 (according to Mustawfi al-Kazwini).

	Dinar-é rayidj
Nahr 'Isa.	876.505
Baghdad	800.000
Wasit.	448.500
Basrah.	441.000
Tariq-é Khurasan	164.000
Bandanidjin/Bayat/Bazar al-Ruz[a]	142.000
Qusan (Nu'maniyah)	94.000
Daquq[b]	78.000
al-Khalis	73.000
Wanah/Harbah (on the Dudjayl)	60.100
Nahr al-Malik	50.000
Radhan	50.000

Certain smaller amounts from al-Anbar and other districts are not included in the list.

[a] The upper Diyala plain and the land up to the Zagros foothills (Mandali-Badrah).
[b] The area south of Kirkuk, *outside* the Mesopotamian floodplain proper.

completely disrupted but continued to carry water down the plain for some time.[24] The rearrangement of canals appears instead to be a well-considered retreat, an attempt to stabilize the situation by using those resources of labor and land which plague, floods, and salination had not destroyed. If this was the plan, it certainly succeeded, owing not least to the *qati'a* assignments to Umayyad princes and officials. One of the largest investments was undertaken by the famous general Maslamah b. 'Abd al-Malik who spent over three million dirhams to repair dikes near the Great Swamp. He also settled colonists in the reclaimed areas and built the Sib Canal (a diversion from the Tigris).[25] The founding of Baghdad, the new imperial center upriver, provided the Wasit enclave with a market for its agricultural produce, further stimulating interest in investment. Thus Harun al-Rashid's mother financed the colonization of the districts of Mubarak and Silh, north of Wasit city.[26]

Ya'qub b. Layth's attack on Mesopotamia, in 869, damaged part of the canal-works around Wasit, and in 878 the city itself was sacked and burned by the Zandj rebels (see below). However, the Wasit enclave had the attention of the Empire because reliable supplies of cheap foodstuffs were essential for keeping Baghdad's populace quiet. When the fighting led to the depopulation of the districts of Mubarak and Silh, the regent al-Muwaffaq therefore invested 30.000 dinars to reclaim them.[27]

In the 10th century Wasit and its hinterland was described as flourishing and, according to Yaqut, it was still prospering in the 13th century, though he adds that the lowest part of the Nahr Sabus was no longer working.[28] Wasit resisted the Mongols in 1258, and as punishment Hulagu's general Buga-Timur allegedly massacred 40.000 inhabitants;[29] but the enclave apparently suffered no lasting damage because of this. New waterworks were constructed in Ilkhanid times, and in the 1335 tax assessment Wasit registered as the floodplain's third largest tax-payer.[30] Ibn Battuta's contempory description confirms the impression of continued prosperity.[31]

Up to the 15th century, then, Wasit must have remained a fairly important town, though suffering under the constant fighting with the Musha'shas in Khuzistan.[32] At some later date, however, both the town and the enclave were abandoned. In 1674 Abbé Carré, one of the few Europeans to visit this part of the floodplain, noted that the territory along the Shatt al-Hayy immediately west of Wasit was deserted.[33] In part, the reason was that the lower course of the Tigris in the 16th and 17th centuries returned to its ancient channel between al-Kut and al-'Amarah.[34] However, Abbé Carré noted that between the Tigris' new course and the Shatt al-Hayy there was yet another river. This must have been the Wasit channel, which then at the end of the 17th century still carried some water.[35]

Since Wasit was linked to the transverse canal system, the enclave must inevitably have suffered when this system collapsed. The general shrinkage of cultivation on the upper plain meant that the flow of water into the Great Swamp increased. In the 13th century the swamps still lay south of Wasit; by the early 19th century they almost reached the Shatt al-Hayy and had thus flooded parts of the old enclave.[36] Both soil salinity and population losses in the second plague pandemic must have accelerated the decline.[37]

Like Wasit, Basrah also profited by the founding of Baghdad. Princes and nobles competed for qati'a allotments and conducted large-scale reclamation works until the reign of Harun al-Rashid (786–809). By then, salinization and increasing expenses for dikes and other protective works against flooding seem to have put a stop to further expansion.[38]

Especially east of the city, around Furat, there existed extensive salinated and abandoned areas. The reclamation work here was done by black slaves (zandj), 15.000 in all, who literally peeled off the upper, sterile soil layers; the plantations were then laid out on the cultivable soil below.[39] This arrangement was unique for Iranshahr where large construction and reclamation works were normally carried out by hired laborers or labor raised by corvée.

The slaves proved to be a source of continuous disturbances. After several minor revolts in the 7th and 8th centuries their discontent culminated in the protracted, savage Zandj revolt (869–883). There is some disagreement whether the uprising was a genuine slave revolt or whether it was part of a broader ethnic-social conflict between mawalis and privileged Muslims of Arab extraction.[40] In any case, the revolt was a political disaster for the Caliphate and brought immense destruction to Mayshan and Khuzistan; Basrah itself was sacked and burned by the rebels in 871. Mas'udi estimates that the revolt and accompanying famines together cost more than one million lives.[41] Though the revolt put a definitive end to large-scale plantation, it is not certain whether it had other permanent, negative consequences for Basrah. Even after a another round of plundering and burning, this time by the Qarmatians in 923, Ibn Hawqal and the other 10th century geographers could still describe the city as large and prosperous.[42]

Just 100 years later, however, Nasir-é Khusraw found it in a state of considerable decline, though he remarked that the surrounding countryside still was densely populated and under intensive cultivation.[43] In 1090 the Qarmatians again sacked Basrah and, in a note to Ibn Hawqal's description, the anonymous copyist who himself had visited the town in 1142 states that there was hardly anything to be seen but ruins. The decline had begun, he adds, with the Zandj revolt and then continued because of tyrannical governors and raids by lawless Khafadjah bedouins. Additional information provided by the copyist, however, indicates that Basrah was not being so much abandoned as transferred to a new location, perhaps in search of fresh water.[44]

In the first half of the 14th century both Mustawfi and Ibn Battuta described the town as large and productive. Yet Ibn Battuta adds that it previously had been even larger.[45] Both he and the anonymous Ibn Hawqal-copyist may have erroneously interpreted the ruins of successive settlements in the area as signs of an absolute decline. Yet Basrah must have in fact become smaller. Not because of the Zandj revolt, but because of the decline in other parts of Mesopotamia. Thus Baghdad's loss of population and political status must have deprived Basrah of some of its traditional markets.

European accounts from the 16th and 17th centuries, when the town had come under Ottoman domination, show that Basrah remained an entrepot for long-distance trade and that it was still surrounded by productive agricultural land.[46] Around 1600 Pedro Teixeira estimated the city to contain 10.000 houses (which would indicate a population between 30.000 and 50.000). He adds that Basrah was rather unimpressive because the houses were built of either sun-dried brick, "which hardly lasts three years", or rush mats. The enclave produced wheat, rice, barley, fruits, and vegetables as well as large quantities of dates which were still exported to Baghdad and the seaports along the Gulf. There was considerable cattle raising, and horses from Basrah were exported as far away as India.[47] On the threshold of the modern era, then, Basrah was no longer the metropolis it had been in Abbasid times; yet seen in a West Asian context it was still a fairly important city with considerable trade and other economic activity. Basrah's location directly on the sea-route between India and the Middle East was certainly part of the explanation for its survival. Another reason was Basrah's independence from the large fragile irrigation systems higher up on the floodplain. When these systems broke down the Basrah enclave was not affected in the same way as was Wasit, but could survive on its own.

2. Contraction in the Tigris Region: Baghdad and the Nahrawan

After the depopulation of the south during and immediately after the crisis of the 7th century, the land east of the Tigris was the next to go out of production. With Yaqut as a reliable and contemporary source we may conclude that the process largely was completed around 1200 when the areas along the Nahrawan Canal was finally abandoned.[48]

Archaeological survey data from the Diyala plain indicate that considerable decline had in fact occurred already in early Muslim times when approximately 1/3 of the settlements were abandoned. This depopulation, occurring primarily in the marginal areas colonized by the Sassanians, obviously was the result of plague and other disasters during the crisis of the 7th century.[49] Apart from the hints furnished by the tax assessments this initial decline is not readily discernible from the documentary evidence. What stands out in these are the large new cities founded at the same time.

With the Abbasid victory in 750 and the revival of the Persian imperial traditions, the political center of the Muslim Empire was moved to Mesopotamia. On the west bank of the Tigris the caliph al-Mansur, in 762, founded a fortified palace and barracks complex – circular after the Persian model – which he called Madina al-Salam, the "City of Peace." Part of the building materials were obtained by demolishing the abandoned sections of nearby al-Mada'in, the old Sassanian capital.[50] Because of its political status the new city, known colloquially as *Baghdad*, rapidly grew into a huge complex of palaces, parks, bazaars, and residential quarters on both sides of the river. In the 9th century it covered 7.000 hectares and may have had 500.000 inhabitants.[51]

In the period 836–892 Baghdad had to compete with another imperial center, *Samarra*, founded by the caliph al-Mu'tasim a bit farther up the Tigris. The caliphs and the Empire's magnates spent enormous sums on construction here, and in a short time the new city had grown into a sprawling settlement on both banks of the river, 35 km long and in places 5 km wide. Al-Mutawakkil (847–861) and his immediate successors are said to have spent no less than 300 million dirhams on palaces and mosques.[52] But when the caliphs and their army and administration returned to Baghdad, Samarra declined nearly as rapidly as it had expanded. In the middle of the 10th century, geographers remarked that one could walk more than one *farsakh* in the city without seeing a single inhabited house. All that remained of the short-lived capital was a small settlement around a Shi'ite shrine.[53]

Abbasid Baghdad was the largest city in the floodplain. Its thousands of soldiers, officials, and servants presented the Empire with a serious supply problem. While foodstuffs were brought by river from Basrah and Wasit in the south and from Mosul in the north, supplies had to come from the city's own hinterland as well.

Consequently the Abbasids made some investments in promoting cultivation here. A notable instance was Harun al-Rashid's construction of the Abu al-Djund Canal between the Katul al-Kisrawi and the Tigris.[54] Nevertheless it appears that investments of this type were quite modest compared to the sums spent on constructions in Baghdad and Samarra. Irrigation and cultivation on the east bank of the Tigris thus largely continued to operate on the basis of the Sassanian works.

The fighting which accompanied the Abbasid caliphate's political dissolution in the first part of the 10th century obviously hit the Baghdad area hard. During the continual maneuverings of the armies, crops were burned, peasants robbed, and canals neglected. The destructions culminated in the autumn of 938 when one of the rival warlords, Ibn Ra'iq, for tactical reasons breached the Nahrawan to increase the water-flow in the Diyala. Deprived of its supplies of water the land south of the Diyala dried up, cultivation ceased, and food prices in Baghdad immediately soared.[55] In 941/42 the caliph al-Muttaqi in vain tried to have his troops repair the breach;[56] but the damage was not repaired until 956/57, after the Buyid warlord Mu'izz al-Dawleh and his wild, semi-pagan highlanders from Daylam had conquered the floodplain and enforced some degree of political order. An anecdote tells that the respected old statesman 'Ali b. 'Isa immediately advised the conquerors to keep a particularly watchful eye on the dikes.[57] Mu'izz al-Dawleh certainly had the breach quickly repaired, to the unmitigated joy of Baghdad's population. The canal again flowed all the way down to the great weir at Uskaf, and Ibn Hawqal and other 10th century geographers could describe the lands along the canal as densely populated and well-cultivated, with flourishing towns.[58]

Of the Buyid warlords who controlled the floodplain up to the middle of the 11th century, 'Adud al-Dawleh (978–983) was particularly famed – even in those sources he had not himself ordered written – for his repair works on the canals, and several stereotyped "good king" anecdotes are told of his rigorous supervision of the responsible officials.[59] At the same time, Adud al-Dawleh had no scruples about increasing the tax load, inventing several new non-canonical taxes and customs fees, confiscating auqaf, and making the state take over the production of luxury goods (for instance silks). These new taxes and confiscations indicate that even an energetic repair and maintenance policy could no longer solve the fiscal problems.[60]

The historian Miskawayh believed that the Buyid rulers themselves had made these problems worse by their generous distribution of iqta's to their Daylami and Turkish officers. As member of the civilian bureaucracy, the kuttabs ("the secretaries"), Miskawayh observed with bitterness that the professional soldiers seized control over the fiscal administration and he accused them of robbing the peasants and neglecting the canals. He further complained that the soldiers not only refused to pay for the water but also hindered the officials from the water department in keeping check on their domains. This resulted in the decay of the irrigation system and, eventually, the flight of the peasantry.[61] So Miskawayh was nostalgic for the time when diligent and loyal tax-farmers had ensured that the central government would receive its rightful income. However, on the basis of his own description of the decades before the Buyid seizure of power it is doubtful whether earlier practices had indeed been advantageous for the peasants. It is also doubtful whether the *iqta'* institution itself was more harmful than the other methods of tax-collecting which the Empire had at its disposal.

After Mu'izz al-Dawleh's repairs the Nahrawan continued to operate for another 200 years, though not as efficiently as before. There are archaeological indications that the flow of water had been reduced, which of course made it more difficult to raise water out of the canal. Yaqut mentions siltation as a growing problem, because the Saldjuq sultans neglected to have the canal-beds cleaned out. Moreover, their armies brought devastation to the lands along the canal during the frequent wars of succession which followed the death of Malik Shah (1092).[62] Saldjuq officials attempted on several occasions to repair some of the damage and increase diversions from the Diyala but without success. Finally another breach in the dikes about 1150 put a stop to the operating of the great canal, at least south of the Diyala, where the last enclaves of intensive cultivation were abandoned. As early as 1184 the Spaniard Ibn Djubayr noted the presence of Khafadjah bedouins encamped near Baghdad, a sign that extensive patterns of subsistence were spreading.[63]

North of the Diyala, along the Katul al-Kisrawi, depopulation and decline had also left clear marks. The areas on the other side of the Tigris, along the Dudjayl Canal, however, are described as well-cultivated, a reminder of the regional differences which characterized the development in Mesopotamia.[64] We may conclude, nevertheless, that after 1200 intensive cultivation had largely contracted to a few enclaves around Baghdad which in the 1335 assessments figures as the second largest source of revenue. Along the Diyala the districts of Khalis and Tariq-é Khurasan remained under cultivation as well, supplying Hulagu's army during the prolonged siege of Baghdad in 1258.[65] In spite of floods and other natural disasters and frequent wars this situation remained stable for several centuries.[66]

When Baghdad in fact lost its status as imperial capital between the 9th and 10th centuries, it ceased being the center for consumption of the surplus which the Empire still managed to collect. This loss of administrative and economic functions inevitably caused population decline. The contraction was clear as early as the 10th century, even after the Buyid rulers had carried out their restoration works. In the late 12th century Ibn Djubayr remarked that the quarters on the Tigris' west bank were completely decayed. The city appeared to him as "the ghost of a statue;" only the name was left. Here he certainly exaggerated for dramatic effect, because his own description shows that the quarters on the other side of the Tigris were thriving and well-populated.[67] Though declining, Baghdad remained the largest and most important town in the floodplain, the regional center for administration and long-distance trade. It also retained an considerable textile industry.[68] Around

1600 Pedro Teixeira thought that the 4.000 weavers in the city were able to use up all the raw materials which the hinterland could produce. According to his estimate the city still had 23.000 inhabited houses of which 20.000 stood on the east bank of the Tigris.[69] On this basis a population of about 70.000 would not seem improbable. In brief, Baghdad retained enough inhabitants and economic activity to keep its hinterland under cultivation.[70]

3. The Collapse of the Transverse Canals

In the long term the transverse canals proved to be the most stable part of the great irrigation systems which the Persian Empires had built in Mesopotamia. However, relatively little archaeological information is available on the northern and central plain. What follows is based, therefore, on the scarce written records and cannot claim to be more than a rough outline of the course of events.[71]

To begin with, we know almost nothing about how the troubles of the 7th century affected the operating of the transverse canals; the repair and expansion work undertaken on the Nahr 'Isa in early Abbasid times can be explained by the fact that this canal was to serve as the main feeder to the new capital of Baghdad.[72] Disturbances in the operating can be seen, however, during the upheavals of the first half of the 10th century. In some cases canals were deliberately damaged as part of military movements. Ibn Ra'iq's breaching of the Nahrawan canal is the most dramatic example, but even before, in 927/28, the caliph's own troops had breached the dikes in the al-Anbar area in a desperate attempt to halt a Qarmatian attack.[73] As we have seen in the case of the Nahrawan, the caliphate during these decades had neither the ability nor the will to allocate sufficient resources for repair work. When, around 940, a flood breached the dikes along the Nahr 'Isa and cut off the water to the Baduraya district (which grew a large part of Baghdad's food supplies), the caliph al-Radi's first thought was to have 1.000 dinars distributed in charity among the inhabitants of the district. Eventually he was persuaded to double the amount and spend it on repairing the breach instead. Even so, that was far from enough.[74] Shortly before Ibn Ra'iq had spent no less than 14.000 dinars to buy a famous singer, which goes to prove that the caliphate had completely lost control over Mesopotamia's dwindling surplus to the military leaders who used it to reward loyal officers and for status consumption.[75] As al-Radi himself despondently remarked: "the treasury is empty, the army insatiable, and the country impoverished."[76]

Baduraya remained out of cultivation until 956/57 when Mu'izz al-Dawleh put his army to the task of repairing the damage. Mui'zz al-Dawleh personally took part in the work, carrying earth in his mantle, and thus made a favorable impression on the people of Baghdad who for nearly ten years had suffered from high prices and food shortages.[77]

The reason that contempory sources draw a generally positive picture of the first Buyid rulers was, in part at least, the incontestable ability of these rulers to mobilize resources and labor for repairing the damage caused by decades of political and social disorder.[78] In spite of their heterodox religious views and barbarian origins – Mu'izz al-Dawleh ruled Mesopotamia for 20 years but never learned Arabic – they did live up to some of the ideals of the "good and just king:" Besides the Nahr 'Isa, Mu'izz al-Dawleh also repaired the Nahrawan, as we have seen, and Adud al-Dawleh undertook extensive repairs of the damage caused by the sectarian fighting in Baghdad. He cleaned out the city's drinking-water canals and after new floods in the mid-970s he resolutely had the damaged dikes and channels repaired by *corvée* labor.[79]

Al-Istakhri and Ibn Hawqal, both writing in Buyid times, in their descriptions and on their maps mention only the names Nahr 'Isa, Nahr Sarsar, and Nahr al-Malik, besides referring vaguely to the numerous diversions from the Nahr Sura. The impression, however, is that the transverse system generally functioned again following the Buyid repair works.[80]

The account of Ibn Djubayr, who in May 1184 travelled from al-Hillah to Baghdad, makes clear that the canals were still working and that the countryside was densely populated and intensively cultivated.[81] When Ibn Battuta travelled the same way 150 years later, conditions had apparently not changed noticeably.[82] A contemporary of his – the geographer 'Abd al-Haqq al-Baghdadi who paraphrased and revised Yaqut – states that the Nahr al-Malik, the Nahr Sarsar, and the Shatt al-Nil were still working at this time.[83] So was the Nahr 'Isa, as the 1335 assessment shows: of the rather more than 3.000.000 *dinar-é rayidj*, which the Ilkhanids theoretically demanded from Mesopotamia, the largest part was to be collected precisely in the Nahr 'Isa district (and in Baghdad's hinterland, see Table 7). Of course, the northern plain may have seen some decline since Buyid times, but at least the key elements of the transverse canal system were still operating at the close of Ilkhanid times. Two hundred years later this was no longer the case.[84]

In 1563 and 1583, respectively, two Europeans, the Venetian Cesare Federico and the Englishman John Eldred, travelled along the same route from Aleppo to Baghdad: first to the village of Bir (Birrah), then in flat-bottomed boats down the Euphrates to Feluchia (al-Falludjah). Here was the intake of the Nahr 'Isa and the beginning of the transverse system. Yet neither of the two sailed any further. The rest of the journey was overland by caravan, most likely because the Nahr 'Isa no longer functioned. Certainly it did not carry water for irrigation, for Eldred noted that the land between al-Falludjah and Baghdad, i.e. the old Nahr 'Isa district which had still been under cultivation in Ilkhanid times, was a desert.[85]

A third European, Pedro Teixeira, travelled across the floodplain twice during the autumn and winter of 1604, first from al-Musayyib to Baghdad, then from Baghdad to 'Anah. The second trip took him past Aqarkuf, the ruins of Dur-

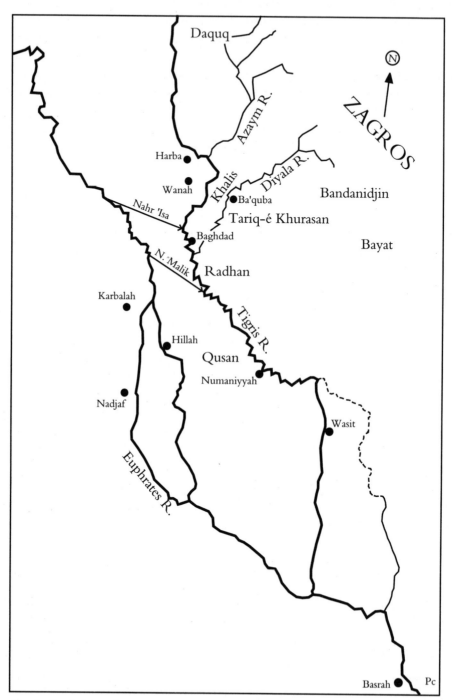

Fig. 3. Sketch-Map of Mesopotamia (early 14th century).

Kurigalzu, 20 km west of Baghdad. Here he saw the remains of canal-works which had formerly irrigated the area. He then followed a dried-up channel westward, perhaps a section of the Nahr 'Isa, and learned that it still carried enough water during flood season to be navigable all the way to Baghdad. Like Eldred, Teixeira observed that the countryside was desert, abandoned to extensive methods of subsistence.[86] Another European, Abbé Carré, travelled in May 1674 from Baghdad, passing Aqarkuf, to Habaniyah. On the way he watered his horses at "one of the Euphrates' channels," i.e. the Nahr 'Isa or a diversion from this.[87] So in one way some of the transverse canals still existed in the 16th and 17th centuries, but they had turned into what amounted to natural water courses, no longer regulated or maintained by human effort. Though some of them still carried enough water in spring to be navigable, they had ceased to feed the irrigation system, and the cultivated areas along them had reverted to wildnerness.[88] In the winter of 1765–1766 the Frisian explorer Carsten Niebuhr travelled from al-Hillah to Baghdad – through the country which Ibn Djubayr had praised – and found but a single newly founded village, Mahmudiyah. The rest of the land, he noted, was completely deserted.[89]

So far the demographic side of the decline has been discussed only in relative terms, and there is really no data with which to quantify it. Still, it is possible hazard a few guesses at the order of magnitude concerned. On the basis of archaeological surveys Adams estimates the total area under cultivation in late Sassanian times to have reached 50.000 sq. km.[90] In other arid areas such as Egypt, Yemen, and the oases on the Arabian peninsula, where irrigation agriculture still takes place by traditional labor-intensive methods, population densities today range from 300 to 700 persons per sq. km.[91] Of course, modern population statistics cannot be applied to ancient or medieval contexts without reservations. The Mesopotamian floodplain was clearly not intensively nor permanently cultivated in all places; large areas must have been fallowed every year and we know little of the population density in the towns (except that it was hardly constant). However, in view of the labor required by the irrigation systems, an estimate of 100 persons per sq. km would not seem entirely unreasonable. This would roughly put the total population at five million in the period before the first plague pandemic. The Ottoman fiscal surveys, which also count some of the nomadic population, indicate that the population in the mid-16th century hardly exceeded one million.[92] Estimates of the extent of cultivated lands around 1800 tend to confirm this picture of a severe demographic decline during the Middle Ages. Not until this century did the size of the population in the floodplain again reach the level of late Sassanian times.

4. The Decline of Mesopotamia: a Hypothesis

Mustawfi al-Kazwini was not in doubt about the reason why Mesopotamia in his time was only a shadow of the richer and far more civilized society he had glimpsed through the ancient tax assessments in the archives of Baghdad: the Mongols and the massacres they had allegedly perpetrated were to blame.[93] This idea was hardly original. Mustawfi simply repeated a myth which had long been imprinted in the world-view of educated Muslims: that the heathen Mongols had dealt Islam an irreversible blow.

Whatever the Mongols may have done to gain their reputation as destroyers of civilization their share in the decline of Mesopotamia was minimal, however. This is evident from the chronology of events: Nahrawan, the largest of the Meso-potamian irrigation-works, had stopped operating a hundred years before Hulagu took Baghdad and murdered the caliph al-Musta'sim. This obvious chronological inconsistency between the presumed cause and the actual course of events has in recent years led scholars to play down the role of the Mongols.[94]

In his study of the development of Mesopotamian settlement patterns Adams argues that the decline was a long-term, complex process which cannot be ex-plained by a single factor. Instead he emphasizes the interaction between the environmental risks involved in large-scale irrigation, the distorted relations be-tween town and country due to Baghdad's excessive growth, the crushing burden of taxation on the peasants, and the political instability starting in the late 9th century. What he presents, however, is a catalogue of key influences rather than a genuine explanatory hypothesis.

Such a hypothesis has been suggested by David Waines who emphasizes the weakness of the Abbasid state itself, its inability to suppress internal struggles for power, and its ruthless and short-sighted fiscal policies. Above all, he says, the state lacked any understanding of how fragile large-scale irrigation agriculture really was.[95]

Obviously the mental and material resources of the central government must play a decisive role in an agrarian system which rests on centrally constructed and maintained irrigation works. Waines' view of the political impotence of the Abba-sids as a key factor in the decline is certainly convincing. Yet it is not an adequate explanation. Land had gone out of cultivation and canals had stopped operating before the Abbasids' time and continued to do so long after they were gone from the scene.

Let us briefly review the course of events. The three important stages in the decline were: first, the abandonment of large parts of the southern plain between the 7th and 9th centuries; second, the destruction of the Nahrawan and the abandonment of most of the land east of the Tigris in the period from the 10th to the mid–12th centuries; finally, the the transverse canals in the central plain were abandoned between 1350 and 1550.

Each phase occurred in a specific historical context and the question is whether they in fact were parts of a single, larger process. I have argued that the decisive factor in the first phase was the plague, although its effect must be seen in the light of several other circumstances such as hydrological instability, salinity build-up, and wartime destruction. After the plague had disappeared, in the 8th century, demographic growth and agrarian regeneration were hindered, as lack of maintenance had caused irreparable damage to the irrigation works. Besides, other epidemic diseases continued to exert pressure on the population. The latter factor is evident from the following outline of major epidemics in the Djazirah/Mesopotamia/ Khuzistan region between the 8th and the early 13th centuries (no attempts have been made to identify the diseases; the sources usually designate them as *waba'*, *'illah*, *mawtan*, and *marad*, terms that all have the connotation of "virulent epidemic disease"):

783/84: Kufah.[96]

855/56: Epidemic reached Mesopotamia and Khuzistan from Sarakhs in East Iran.[97]

892/93: *Waba'* and *ta'un* in Basrah and Kufah.[98]

913/14: *Salima* and *ta'un* in Baghdad. The Harbiya quarter is said to have been depopulated. (*Salima* possibly refers to a benign illness. As for *ta'un*, it can hardly mean plague proper in this case.)[99]

942/43: Baghdad.[100]

957/58: *Waba'* and *'illah* in Mesopotamia and Khuzistan, apparently part of a larger epidemic extending over all of Iranshahr. In Basrah mortality averaged 1.000–1.200 a day for a period. Miskawayh calls this disease *mashara*.[101]

967/68: Djazirah.

1015/16: Epidemic spreads from Basrah to the rest of Mesopotamia.[103]

1031/32: Epidemic spread "from India" across Iran to Baghdad; at the same time 4.000 children died in Mosul. The epidemic, which in 1033/34 reached Baghdad and Basrah from Shiraz, was presumably just another outbreak of the same disease.[104]

1056/57: Mass epidemic throughout the Middle East.[105]

1075/76: *Waba' azim* in Mesopotamia, the Djazirah and Syria.[106]

1123/24[107]

1136/37: Epidemic reached Baghdad from Djibal, killing up to 500 people a day.[108]

The Egyptian historian Ibn al-Furat (*c.* 1400) registered additional Mesopotamian epidemics in the years 1145/46, 1149/50, 1157/58 and 1167/68.[109] Though incomplete, the list above does provide some indication of the level of infection. In addition the population suffered from several debilitating chronic infections which must have had considerable effects on the general state of health. These included malaria, schistosomiasis, trachoma, tuberculosis, leprosy, etc.[110] In the intensively cultivated enclaves, various forms of intestinal worms were also easily spread, thanks to the extensive use of human faeces as fertilizer.[111]

Besides disease, Mesopotamia's population endured droughts, floods, frosts, and attacks by locusts and other pests, all of which caused frequent harvest failures and sometimes even famine. A systematic registration of all known disasters is beyond the scope of this study, but by way of example we can here list some of the crises which occurred in the 10th century:

904/5   : The Tigris flooded Baghdad.[112]
908/9   : Snowfall in Baghdad.[113]
922/23: A snowstorm in the Djazirah caused the death of many people and large numbers of animals.[114]
*c.*940: the Nahr 'Isa dikes were breached, interrupting the water supply to Baduraya: famine in Baghdad.[115]
940/41: Famine in Baghdad and Wasit.[116]
942/43: Locusts and famine in Baghdad.[117]
945/46: Famine throughout Mesopotamia. Many deaths.[118]
958/59: Drought owing to lack of winter rain.[119]
978/79: Floods and breachings of the dikes.[120]
998/99: Frost damaged date palms; several years passed before production returned to normal.[121]

There is no reason to believe that the 10th century was any more beset with disasters than other periods; climatic fluctuations have been a constant feature of Mesopotamia's history. What varied, however, was the political ability and will to alleviate the effects of crop failure and to repair flood damage. As we have seen, ten years passed before the Nahr 'Isa breach of 940 was repaired. Conversely, the damages after the 978/79 floods were repaired immediately, and their consequences were not nearly as serious.[122]

When the records refer to famine, they mean acute shortages. As is the case for previous periods, we know very little about the common people's nutritional level in normal years when no disasters occurred. The question has been explored by comparing data about prices and wages and then calculating how many basic foodstuffs a family could afford to buy. Thus E. Ashtor estimated that the common people in Mesopotamia in the 11th century got less than 2.000 calories per day and that the proteins were both insufficient and substandard. The data, however, are so dispersed in time and space that they are hardly representative or comparable; the procedure endows the hypothesis with a false aura of statistical reliability. Furthermore, the data refer only to the urban population. The peasantry, who constituted the overwhelming majority, are ignored.[123] Had the Mesopotamian population in Muslim times generally been mal- or undernourished, it would have had obvious consequences for morbidity and for the ability to recover from demographic losses. However, whether this was in fact the case cannot be determined.

Let us now return to the question of why the Nahrawan and the Tigris' east bank were abandoned during the second phase of the decline. The sources primarily draw our attention to the political troubles; but, as we have seen, these were only a part of the total pressure on agriculture. Regular cleaning-out of the Nahrawan system must have required great labor, and even though the abandonment occurred in the period between the two plague pandemics, the high frequency of other epidemic diseases may have made it difficult to raise manpower for the repair and maintenance work.

In the third phase, when the transverse canals were abandoned, plague again appears as a key factor. The "Black Death" struck Baghdad in 1349, brought either from Syria or from Azarbaydjan.[124] Another outbreak occurred ten years later. In 1437 another epidemic is said to have killed all the inhabitants of Baghdad and to have left only seven survivors in Haditha; though al-Ghiyati calls it *waba'*, it was probably plague.[125]

Because of inadequate sources it is impossible to determine precisely the frequency of plague in the 14th and 15th centuries. Consequently, it is difficult to make any reliable estimates of cumulative mortality. Later, in the 17th to the 19th centuries, Mesopotamia was regularly afflicted by plague disseminated from the wild rodents in Kurdistan. One such outbreak, in 1773, is said to have cost the lives of 60.000 people in Baghdad. To what extent these later epidemics also involved the very contagious and lethal pneumonic plague is not clear.[126] Citing data from Egypt, where the course of the plague is far better documented, Dols estimates a population loss of 1/3 until the beginning of the 15th century.[127] If pneumonic plague also appeared in Mesopotamia during the first phases of the pandemic – and it probably did, considering that it did so everywhere else – the population loss must have been roughly similar. Thus plague must be a decisive reason for maintenance work on the transverse canals to cease precisely between 1350 and 1550.

The impact of plague and epidemic diseases has been underestimated or even disregarded in historical analysis, at least until recently. However, changing disease patterns did have considerable, if not decisive, influence on the development. This does not mean that epidemic disease should be made a "prime mover" at the cost of other influences. Many other societies, including irrigation societies, were ravaged by plague and recurrent epidemics but did not suffer lasting decline. In Mesopotamia, however, epidemic disease affected a situation characterized by high environmental instability. As has been argued above, the plague, especially during the first pandemic, by decimating the labor force caused so much damage to the irrigation systems that these in fact became irreparable. In this way plague and epidemic diseases in general make visible the inherent environmental instability which I believe was the key factor in the decline of Mesopotamia. The large-scale colonization and expansion in Parthian and Sassanian times had created an ecological system extremely sensitive to the smallest disturbances. In the long term the system may even have been selfdestructive because of the inevitable salinity build-up and siltation. In any case, the effect of wartime destructions, political troubles, administrative incompetence and other factors should be viewed in the specific environmental context. In the next chapters we shall to test this hypothesis of environmental instability as a key factor by tracing the developments in other parts of Iranshahr where physical conditions differed more or less from those in Mesopotamia.

Chapter 9

Khuzistan

Immediately east of Mesopotamia lay another ancient river-irrigated land: Khuzistan.[1] In spite of its location and the fact that it was often ruled by the larger Mesopotamian states, Khuzistan formed a distinct region in both hydrological and ethnic terms; from ancient times it had been politically oriented away from Mesopotamia, toward Anshan and the other states in the Zagros foothills and basins, known collectively in Mesopotamian sources as *Elam*.[2]

Khuzistan is watered by the *Karun* (with the tributary Ab-é Diz) and the *Karkheh*, plus by several smaller rivers such as the Djarrahi. Their discharge patterns resemble that of the Mesopotamian rivers: i.e. maximum flows occur in spring, minimum flows in autumn. Topographic conditions, however, make irrigation in Khuzistan work somewhat differently.

Broadly speaking, Khuzistan is made up of two regions. The first consists of the flat plain south of the Ahwaz Ridge, which in climatic and topographic terms is an extension of the Mesopotamian floodplain: precipitation is scarce, the summer heat extreme, and owing to the weak slope of the terrain and the high water-table there is considerable danger of salination and waterlogging. The second region, the rolling plains between Ahwaz and the Zagros, receive rather more rain (annual averages are between 200 and 400 mm). Dry farming is possible, but again irrigation will raise the level of yields and insure against droughts and variations in rainfall. The problem facing irrigation farmers here is that the rivers have downcut their channels, which means that water for irrigation must be raised up in some way.[3] Furthermore, the landscape is so hilly that irrigation may lead to soil erosion. In the few areas large and flat enough to support large irrigation systems, such as the plains around Susa and Dizful, there is a latent danger of salinization.[4]

The upper plains were colonized by farmers around 5000 B.C. Settlement was dispersed and based largely on extensive dry farming. Irrigation was probably limited to zones immediately around the major centers, primarily Susa, which in the 3rd millennium B.C. reached urban size (50 ha).[5] Apparently the plain south of the Ahwaz ridge was not settled to the same degree in pre-historic times.[6] Perhaps the difference simply reflects that the south has been less thoroughly surveyed, or perhaps the remains of smaller settlements have been destroyed completely by erosion or buried beneath layers of sediment. Be that as it may, the south was probably not very attractive. Sources from Muslim times describe the country as unhealthy, with swarms of biting and stinging insects.[7] A high frequency of infections such as malaria may have discouraged settlement on a larger scale.

We know little of Khuzistan's early history and the frequent wars with the Mesopotamian and Assyrian states. There are archaeological indications that settlement varied in density and size through this long period, and the patterns of political organization presumably underwent concomitant changes. But there is no sign of qualitative changes in the methods of subsistence, including irrigation technology.[8]

1. Khuzistan in the Classical Image of Persia

The classical sources offer only little and imprecise information about Khuzistan. Their descriptions of the river system, for instance, are contradictory. This may of course be attributed to errors in the transmission of the texts or to hydrological changes since ancient times; but it also suggests that the authors were in fact poorly informed about the far-off country.[9]

They knew most about the capital city of Susa and its fertile hinterland. Strabo says that here yield ratios of 100:1 were the norm and 200:1 not uncommon. Obviously these figures are pure fantasy, but they may be taken to indicate that the enclave was under intensive, irrigated cultivation.[10] From the time of Darius I, Susa was treated with considerable favor as one of the capitals of the Achaemenid Empire. The city was enlarged with a special royal quarter, containing palaces and the like, and probably had between 20.000 and 30.000 inhabitants. Its importance is shown by the fact that Alexander, after conquering Babylon, made it his next objective.[11]

Apparently the Achaemenids were also involved in colonization activities elsewhere in the country, including the south. Near the Gulf Darius is said to have settled the survivors from Miletus and farther inland he settled Carians from Pedasos.[12] At the close of the 4th century B.C. Nearchus noted that the country along the Pasitigris (Karun) was both prosperous and densely populated, another sign that settlement expansion in the area south of the Ahwaz ridge must have begun no later than Achaemenid times.[13] The actual extent of the Empire's activities is unclear, however, because effective Achaemenid rule was restricted. They had poor control over the tribal societies in the Zagros valleys to the east and north, and the great kings chose to keep open the routes of communication between Fars and Susiana by paying the highland tribes tribute and giving them gifts.[14]

The Seleucid and Parthian periods are badly documented as well. We know that Greeks settled in Susa, now re-named *Seleucia-on-the Eulaios*, and no doubt in other places as well;[15] but that is not proof of any substantial changes in settlement and subsistence. Pliny lists the following towns:

Seleucia-on-the Hedyphon, originally called Soloké and perhaps identical with the later Dawrak on the river Djarrahi.
Asylum, also located on the Hedyphon (Djarrahi).
Magoa, near Charax.
Seleucia-on-the Red Sea (i.e. the Gulf).

On the upper plains stood, besides Susa, the town *Sostrate* (i.e. Shushtar) and, finally, Diodorus, in his account of Antigonos' campaigns around 317 B.C., mentions the town *Badaké* on the Eulaios.[16] From the context it appears that all of these settlements must go back to Achaemenid times, if not even farther.

There is archaeological evidence, however, for a settlement expansion occurring in Seleucid-Parthian times.[17] But did this involve substantial changes in irrigation practices? On the basis of Strabo's remark that rice was grown in Khuzistan, it has been suggested that the expansion was in fact accompanied by the construction of large canals. However, since rice culture was certainly widespread by Achaemenid times, this argument for qualitative changes in irrigation in Seleucid-Parthian times can be dismissed.[18] Some few references, found in the Parthian epigraphic sources, to repairs of local waterworks around Susa do not justify any far-reaching conclusions about changes in irrigation technology, either.[19] Large-scale constructions would imply that the Seleucids and the Parthians had made their rule effective throughout the country and this was not the case.[20]

In contrast, the sources are clear that the Sassanians carried out large colonization programs, including the construction of huge irrigation-works. Even though some of these works may have had Seleucid-Parthian predecessors, the Sassanians built on a scale that marked a qualitative technological leap forward.

2. Khuzistan in the Khuda-nameh Tradition

As in Mesopotamia, the Sassanian colonization policy in Khuzistan included three elements. First, the construction of large irrigation-systems; owing to the special conditions on the upper plain, this involved building massive weirs to raise the water up to the intake of the canals. Second, the founding of new towns, and finally, forcible deportations and re-settlements. That these three elements were in fact closely linked and that the schemes were centrally planned is clear from the four or five largest Sassanian projects.

The Shushtar complex

The most impressive of all Sassanian works in Khuzistan was the complex of weirs and canals which Shapur I (240–272) built at the old town of Shushtar. It consisted of a great weir across the Karun – the remains are still nearly 600 m long – that

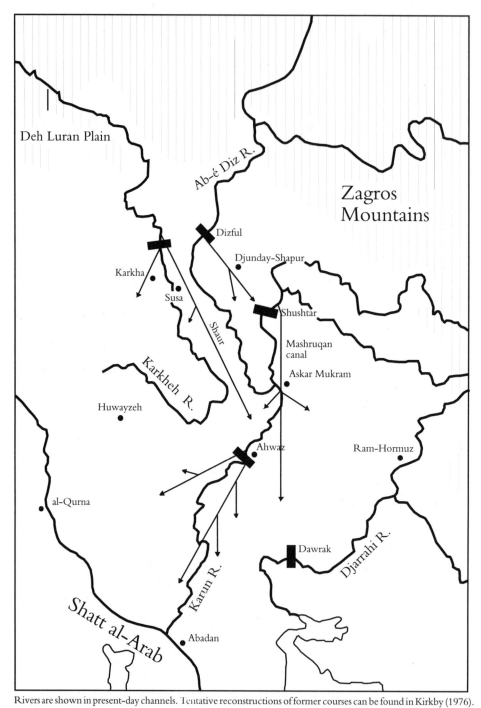

Rivers are shown in present-day channels. Tentative reconstructions of former courses can be found in Kirkby (1976).

Fig. 4. Khuzistan. Sketch-Map of weir-building and city-foundings in Sassanian and early Muslim times.

raised water for the *Mashruqan*, a large feeder canal on the east bank of the Karun. At the intake of the canal stood a great regulator weir.[21] Muslim sources also mention a westward canal, the *Nahr al-Shahidjird*, clearly one of the old canal beds recognizable in aerial photos.[22]

The Mashruqan ran for *c.* 40 km down to Rustam-Kavadh. The site of this town and of its successor settlement, 'Askar Mukram, is known today as Band-é Qir, i.e. "the Bitumen Dike." In the 14th century the canal flowed back into the river at this point and the name may refer to a regulator weir.[23] In the 10th century, however, the canal continued to Ahwaz and perhaps even farther down the plain to the estuary of the Karun. The territories along its banks were famed as the richest and most productive in all of Khuzistan.

This particular project involved no city-founding, but Shapur II later settled some prisoners from the Syrian campaign of 359–360 in Shushtar. Among them were many weavers, and Shapur no doubt had them deported to boost the local textile industries.[24]

In Muslim times the Shushtar complex was considered one of the wonders of the world and made the object of legends and romantic tales. According to one such legend Shapur forced the captured Roman emperor Valerian to build the weirs, and hence they were called such names as Band-é Kaisar and Pul-é Kaisar ("the Emperor's Weir," "the Emperor's Bridge"). Western scholarship has seen these legends as comforting evidence that the Sassanians in fact were dependent on the technology of classical civilization and that the imposing weirs were not really a Persian achievement.[25]

It is conceivable, of course, that Roman prisoners of war were employed in the construction of the weirs, but considering the competence demonstrated by the Sassanians on other occasions, it is improbable that they would have needed the help of Roman engineers to carry out colonization projects. After all, complex irrigation technology had been applied for a long time throughout Mesopotamia, for instance in constructing the transverse canals. Though Roman (and later Byzantine) engineers certainly were skilled at building weirs and dams, they had little experience of the hydrological conditions found in Mesopotamia and Khuzistan. When Trajan, during his invasion of Mesopotamia in 116 A.D., thought of digging a canal from the Euphrates to the Tigris so his supply ships might follow the troops, the plan was abandoned precisely for fear that the waters could not be controlled. Neither Parthian nor Sassanian engineers had such reservations.[26]

The Ab-é Diz/Djunday-Shapur Complex

Shapur I also built a weir, some 400 m long, across the Ab-é Diz, near Dizful. From this weir a network of canals conducted water over the Diz plain to a new town, Djunday-Shapur. Officially it was called *Veh-az-Andew-Shapur* ("Shapur's-town-

better-than-Antioch") because some of the prisoners of war resettled in the town by
Shapur had come from Antioch. Hamza Isfahani says that Veh-az-Andew-Shapur
was laid out like a chessboard, and his account is confirmed by aerial photographs.[27]

The Karkheh Complex

The *Pa-yé pul* weir across the Karkheh was built by Shapur II as part of a larger
project that also involved the founding of a new town, *Iran-Khurreh-Shapur*. Here
Shapur re-settled prisoners deported from Amida (Diyarbakir), Bezabde, and Sin-
gara during the Syrian campaign of 359–360.[28]

The Ahwaz-Complex

A fourth weir, 1.000 m long, was constructed at Ahwaz, on the transition from the
upper to the lower plain. The builder must have been either Ardashir I or, more
likely, Shapur I. The Muslim sources have it that Ardashir I founded Ahwaz,
officially *Hormizd-Ardashir*, but this cannot be entirely correct. At least, Ahwaz was
not a *de novo* foundation. Rather, an existing settlement was re-named. A remark in
the inscription at Naqsh-é Rustam would seem to indicate that it was actually
Shapur I who began the enlargement. The weir was presumably built on this
occasion.[29]

   Hamza Isfahani further says that merchants were settled in a quarter called
Khuzistan-Vadjar. Here, too, traditions differ: some say that this settlement was
made by Ardashir, while others mention Kavadh I. In any case, there is no doubt
that during Sassanian times Ahwaz evolved into a key center for communication
and trade between Fars and Mesopotamia.[30]

   The town was also the center of a large agricultural enclave. Aerial photos clearly
show the remains of a branching canal system which conducted water from the
weir across the southern plain. Some of these remains must be identical with canals
mentioned in later Muslim sources, but the descriptions of the hydrological system
are too vague for precise identifications.[31] This is also true of the *Nahr Tira*, a canal
which Ardashir is said to have constructed west of the Karun, with its intake either
in the Karun itself or in the Karkheh. In the area west of the Karun Muslim sources
cite yet another canal, the *Nahr Dulut*.[32]

The Djarrahi Complex

At Dawrak in the southern plain stand the ruins of a large weir across the Djarrahi
River. Style and construction methods point to Sassanian origins, and medieval
Muslim sources say that Dawrak (Seleucia-on-the Hedyphon?) was in fact founded

by Kavadh I. It is tempting to assume that the weir was built as part of a city-founding project.[33]

Other colonization activities referred to in the Muslim sources were Shapur II's settlement of prisoners from the Arabian campaign in *Ramaliya* (not located) and the founding of *Ram-Hormuz* in eastern Khuzistan. Finally, Mustawfi al-Kazwini states that Shapur II also founded *Huwayzah* (although other sources date it to the 10th century).[34]

The irrigation schemes briefly outlined above would have served primarily to expand the area under irrigated winter cultivation (wheat, barley). However, the great weirs must also have made it possible to use more effectively the reduced flow in summer. In the favorably situated enclaves production must by now have been intensified by cultivating the summer crops known to us from Muslim times, i.e.: sesame, rice, and sugar.

Sesame, used mainly for oil, was an ancient crop which had spread long before Achaemenid times. It requires no further discussion.[35]

Rice was introduced no later than in Achaemenid times, and even though we do not know the details, it was certainly widespread by Sassanian times. In the 10th century rice was the most cultivated crop after wheat and barley, and bread baked from rice flour formed a typical element of the Khuzis' basic diet. The culture was concentrated in the intensively irrigated enclaves around Susa and Djunday-Shapur. In general terms this description presumably holds good for Sassanian times as well.[36]

In the early Muslim era Khuzistan was also famous for its production and export of *sugar*. Sugar cane grew everywhere, but especially around Shushtar, Susa, Ahwaz, and along the Mashruqan. Though conclusive evidence is missing, it is most likely that the crop was already widespread by pre-Muslim times.[37] The same was certainly true of cotton and dye plants such as safflower and indigo.[38]

The great irrigation schemes must partly have aimed at supplying the growing population with foodstuffs and raw materials. The towns founded by the Sassanians were not just administrative or military centers. The size of the sites show that the four largest towns on the upper plain – Susa, Shusthar, Djunday-Shapur, and Iran-Khurreh-Shapur – must have had a total population of about 100.000; many, if not most, of them were nonagriculturalists employed in the textile industry. The production of luxury textiles such as gold brocade, one of the country's specialties in the 10th century, had already been set up in Sassanian times, owing in part to Shapur II's deportations of Syrian weavers.[39] Thus Sassanian colonization in Khuzistan appears as a complex and ambitious project. That it was a success, at least in the short term, is indicated by Khuzistan's fiscal importance in relation to the rest of the Empire (see Table 3).

In the high country to the north and east of Khuzistan there are countless ruins of bridges, cisterns, and fortresses, which on archaeological criteria can be dated to

Sassanian times. They testify to the efforts made by the Empire to protect the productive lowlands and safeguard communications with another of the core-lands, Fars. Large military structures in Saymareh and Idhadj and other places probably served to contain the mountain peoples who had caused the predecessors of the Sassanians so much trouble.[40]

   As a concluding detail, we can briefly mention the results of the archaeological survey of Sassanian Deh Luran. In this small outlying plain, watered by the streams Mehmeh and Dayayridj, canals were enlarged and *qanats* constructed (the latter to capture the water seeping from the streams). Even though part of the population remained semi-nomadic, there is little doubt that permanent settlement and intensive cultivation advanced markedly.[41] This cannot be explained as a result of strategic location, as Deh Luran was situated far from all important caravan routes. Rather, it reflects that in Sassanian times efforts were made to bring ever more peripheral lands under cultivation.

3. The Decline of Khuzistan

In the early 19th century British intelligence reports described the upper plains of Khuzistan as "a forsaken waste." This was somewhat exaggerated, however. It is true that Ahwaz had been reduced to a wretched hole with less than a thousand inhabitants; yet both Dizful and Shushtar were still considerable towns by local standards. Each had perhaps 15.000 inhabitants and was surrounded by intensively cultivated enclaves watered by the still partly functioning weirs and canals.[42] Compared to the 10th century descriptions, however, there is no doubt that settlement had contracted and agricultural technology deteriorated. The cultivation of sugar had thus stopped long before the 19th century.

   The chronology of this decline is rather vague. The few sources give little indication that Khuzistan experienced anything comparable to the Mesopotamian crisis of the 7th century. Yet the first plague pandemic must have struck severely. Tax assessments certainly dropped from 50 million dirhams in Sassanian times to about 25–30 million in early Muslim times, and the widespread destruction caused by the Arab invasion was no doubt also a factor. On the other hand Ibn Khurdadh-bih informs us that in 834 revenue, chiefly collected through tax-farming, in fact ran to no less than 49 million dirhams.[43] Whether this reflected recovery in Khuzistan or whether it simply was the result of increasing rates of taxation is impossible to say.

   It is only from the beginning of the 12th century that we find definite signs of decline. Ibn al-Balkhi observed, for instance, that Bilad Shapur(the Hendidjan region), once densely populated, had fallen to ruin. Likewise, Djunday-Shapur, still an important town in the 10th century, was now apparently abandoned. A similar fate befell ancient Susa in the 13th century.[44]

Table 8. The assessment of Khuzistan.

	Dirhams
6th century (Sassanians)	50.000.000[a]
788	25.000.000[b]
800	25.000.000[c]
819	18.000.000[d]
845–73	30.000.000[e]
918	25.000.000[f]
969	30.000.000[g]
1335	1.423.000[h]

[a] Ibn Khurdadhbih (tr.: 31).
[b] el-'Ali (1971).
[c] el-'Ali (1971); von Kremer (1889).
[d] Qudama (de Goeje tr.: 183f); on p. 190 he gives the figure 23 million, however; al-Tanukhi (VIII/14, tr. in IC 3, 1929: 509) states that the assessment in the first half of the ninth century was 24.000.000, but that the tax-farming in fact ran to 48.000.000.
[e] Ibn Khurdadhbih (tr.: 31).
[f] von Kremer (1888: 313); the original figure is 1.260.922 dinars, here converted at the rate of 1:20.
[g] Ibn Hawqal (tr., II: 257).
[h] Mustawfi (Nuzhat, tr.: 107) gives the figure 325.000 dinar-é rayidj. He adds that in the time of the caliphate taxes amounted to 3.000.000 dinar-é rayidj.

Ahwaz declined as well. The town suffered from an "unhealthy climate" and was notorious for its lethal epidemics. During the reign of al-Ma'mun (813–833) the weir was breached, and it cost 100.000 dinars to repair the damage. Then, in 840, an earthquake hit the town, and on two occasions, in 870 and 873, it was ravaged by the Zandj rebels. The prolonged and savage war against these rebels may have favored the rise of the new town 'Askar Mukram at the expense of Ahwaz.[45]

Around 1300 the Ilkhanid vizier Rashid al-Din invested considerable sums in repair work in the Huwayzah region and in this connection spoke of the decline which had occurred.[46] Ibn Battuta, however, observed that the town of Shushtar was still large and prosperous.[47]

That Shushtar was thriving, while nearby Djunday-Shapur had been abandoned, may indicate that decline was localized and perhaps caused by local topographic, hydrological, or political conditions. This certainly seems to apply to Ahwaz. On the other hand, Benjamin of Tudela remarked in the 1160s that large parts of the country had been deserted.[48] The low tax assessments from Ilkhanid times seem also to reflect a more general decline.

In any case, part of the settlement contraction noted by the 19th-century travellers could not have occurred until post-Mongol times. In the 15th century Huwayzah was still a prosperous town, capital of the Musha'sha movement which had made Khuzistan a de facto independent buffer state between the Ottomans and the Safavids.[49] But in 1604 Pedro Teixeira said of both Huwayzah and Dawrak that they "lie widely waste, not barren, but untilled for fear of the Turks."[50] Huwayzah was finally abandoned at the beginning of the 19th century because a weir was breached. Changes in the course of the Karkheh probably was a contributory factor. In any case the town was replaced by nearby Susangird.[51] Dawrak was apparently abandoned somewhat earlier, in the 18th century, but was also replaced by a new settlement, Fallahiyeh, which according to British intelligence reports had 8.000 inhabitants.[52] The surrounding countryside was at the same time recolonized by the Cha'b Arabs practicing extensive agriculture based on temporary, quickly constructed weirs.[53]

As in Mesopotamia, decline in Khuzistan must have been the result of the interaction of many factors. Yet the sources are so weak that the key influences are difficult to discern. It is fairly clear that hydrological changes, partly caused by human regulation of the rivers, played a role in some places. In other places salinity build-up owing to intensive cultivation must have contributed as well, not because it completely laid waste the land, but because it reduced productivity and thus favored more extensive methods of subsistence.

We must further consider the effect of infectious disease. The Babylonian Talmud refers to several epidemics in Sassanian times,[54] and later the swampy Ahwaz region in particular was known for its "constant fevers" which made the inhabitants "yellow and lean," no doubt a reference to malaria.[55] Schistosomiasis, a common disease today, must also have been widespread as a result of the expansion of irrigation in Sassanian times.

Unfortunately we know next to nothing about the first plague pandemic in Khuzistan. Mas'udi's information that between 1/2 and 1/3 of the population of Iraq and the adjacent countries died must hold true of Khuzistan, but we have no indications of the consequences.[56] We do know, however, that Khuzistan was affected by all great epidemics that broke out in Iranshahr in the time after the plague. Considering the environmental similarities, the disease-pattern must have resembled what we have seen in Mesopotamia, i.e. high levels of both chronic and acute infections. Thus the demographic balance in Khuzistan must have been as fragile as in Mesopotamia and, most likely, the impact of the first plague pandemic was devastating.

Finally the effects of the political fragmentation of the Persian Empire must be noted. Freed from imperial control, local lords could consolidate their power over their respective enclaves. Here they certainly sought to promote agriculture, for instance by making use of the old Sassanian irrigation-works. Shushtar and Dizful thus remained under intensive cultivation. But the dissolution of the Empire spelled the end of overall planning and resource management. As the great feeder canals decayed, large areas reverted to extensive cultivation.[57]

Part 3
The Oases on the
Iranian Plateau

Chapter 10

Environment and Irrigation Technologies

On the Iranian Plateau, i.e. the high country extending from the Zagros to the Hindu Kush, the environment sets conditions completely different from those in Mesopotamia and Khuzistan. These conditions, however, are difficult to describe briefly because they vary considerably over this immense territory: relatively well-watered areas like Azarbaydjan and Gurgan differ from arid Kirman, while the mountain regions contain a broad spectrum of favored micro-environments which can be of great importance to local economies.

In general, however, irrigation is essential for settled and permanent agriculture. Large parts of the Zagros region certainly lie within the theoretical limit for rain-fed agriculture, but it is hazardous, at least in most places, to rely solely on rainfall. First, precipitation varies greatly from year to year; as we have seen, the average annual precipitation of 380mm in the Shiraz area actually masks variations from 114 mm to 501 mm. Second, most of the precipitation falls between November and April when the intense winter cold characteristic of the Plateau has stopped plant growth; i.e. the rains arrive too late for the autumn sown crops and too early for the spring sown.[1] Cold winters are also the reason why the date palm, so important in Mesopotamia, will thrive only along the Gulf coast and in a few other places. On the Plateau wheat and barley have always been the principal crops.

By pre-industrial standards the irrigated agriculture on the Plateau seems to have been quite productive, although medieval or earlier sources provide us with few useful figures. Typically they report only the exceptional. Mustawfi states, for instance, that in fertile Marv wheat yielded no less than 100 times the seed sown; if the field was left untouched after the harvest, the grain not gleaned would next year yield 30 times the original seed; left idle for another season, the field would still yield 10 times the seed.[2] Very high yield ratios may have occurred in favored places, but Mustawfi's information is hardly representative for the entire Marv Oasis and certainly not for the rest of the Plateau. As an indicator of the harvest yields we can instead use the information gathered by the British consul Keith Abbott during his travels in Iran in the mid-19th century. From his observations it appears that the following seed-yield ratios were the norm in Fars, Kirman, and parts of Djibal:[3]

Kashan: 1:5 – 1:15
Yazd: 1:15 (with manuring)
Ardakan (near Yazd): 1:30–60 ("but with great labour")

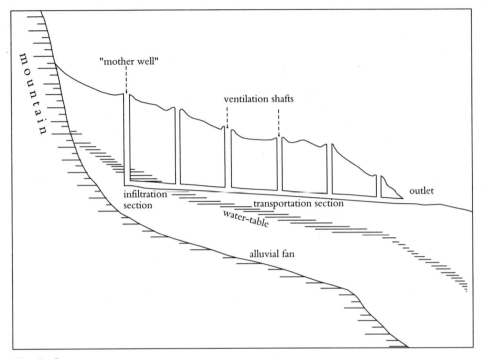

Fig. 5. Qanat.

Firuzabad: 1:3–10 (without manuring)
Fasa: 1:5–12
Farrashband: 1:10–12 (without manuring or use of fallow)
Arradjan (Bihbihan): 1:10 (but in certain places 30–40).
Darabgird: 1:10–50
Kuh-é Payeh (Kirman Basin): 1:5–10
Bam and Narmashir: 1:10–30
Djiruft: 1:5–30
Sistan (Hilmand Delta): 1:25–100

In part, the local variations in yields must have owed to environmental differences, but Abbott's comments show that they primarily reflected the productivity of various methods of farming: the greater the amount of irrigation and manure and the larger the input of peasant labor, the larger and more stable the yield.

When Abbott wrote, Iranian agriculture was in fact changing, largely because the world market now stimulated landowners to increase the production of cash crops. Opium culture, for instance, had expanded in Isfahan and Yazd as early as the first half of the 19th century, and from the 1860s silk and cotton spread out, especially in

Azarbaydjan, the Caspian lowlands, and parts of Khurasan, i.e. in the northern provinces close to the Russian market.[4] A new basic crop, maize, had appeared presumably by the 17th century, though it never came to threaten the primacy of wheat and barley. Nor were these two crops to be challenged by the potato which the British emissary Sir John Malcolm claimed to have introduced in the Bushire area.[5] These changes, however, were not of a technological nature. Apparently no significant innovations occurred in regard to tools, irrigation technologies, sources of energy, crop rotations, etc. Thus, for lack of anything better, Abbott's figures can serve as rough indicators of medieval yields. On this basis we can assume that – provided investments were made in irrigation and the peasants were brought to intensify their labor – agriculture on the Plateau could produce average yields well above those of many parts of medieval Europe.[6] Under normal conditions, i.e. in years without prolonged drought, locusts, or other natural disasters, Iranian agriculture must therefore have been able to feed a relatively high proportion of people not directly involved in agriculture. This does not justify, of course, the extravagant speculations which have sometimes been made about the size of the Iranian population in ancient times.[7] After all, the total area under cultivation was never large: Of present-day Iran's 1.650.000 sq. km only an estimated 17.5 million ha, roughly 10%, are under plow today, and of these almost half lie fallow each year. Moreover, most of the land under crops is actually watered only by rainfall (in Azarbaydjan and Kirmanshah). The irrigated area amounts to no more than 5–6 million ha, though it does produce 80% of the foodstuffs.[8] As we shall see, there is no reason to believe that the cultivated area was any larger in the past or that farming was more intensive; water resources simply were insufficient for that.

Water for irrigation comes from the mountain ranges encircling the Plateau. In April and May snowmelt releases large amounts of surface water. However, since both the Zagros and the Alburz Mountains primarily have outward drainage toward the Persian Gulf and the Caspian Sea, respectively, most of the water literally runs off the Plateau's outer edge. The few rivers flowing toward the interior are small and frequently seasonal, i.e. they tend to run dry in the summer. Even when they do not dry up completely, their salt contents will often increase markedly, making them unsuitable for irrigation during this time of year.[9] The Plateau therefore contains relatively few natural oases.

However, water can be found in other places than on the surface. From the mountains groundwater constantly seeps down toward the lower-lying interior. On its way the groundwater accumulates soluble salts and minerals and when it finally reaches the depressions in the center of the Plateau it forms extensive, sterile salt marshes and salt deserts: the *kavirs*. Close to the *kavirs*, the gradients of the surrounding alluvial plains are weak; water-tables are high, the drainage is poor, and the soil will rapidly grow saline if irrigated. Farther up the plains, however, and on the alluvial fans conditions are more favorable to farming: the groundwater is fairly fresh and steeper slopes and coarser soils make for better drainage, though salination remains a risk even here.

The pre-industrial farmers on the Plateau employed a range of techniques and constructions to collect and exploit the scarce water resources: rain–water was stored in cisterns or captured by embanking fields;[10] melt water, filling the seasonal streams in spring, was stored in reservoirs which then could be tapped later in spring and summer. Small streams were dammed up with temporary constructions of earth and bundles of brushwood, while larger streams were controlled by true storage dams made of stone or brick. As these generally were tapped from the top rather than from the bottom, the reservoirs would accumulate silt until they eventually ceased to be functional. This technical weakness, rather than wartime destruction or natural disasters, explains the large number of ruined dams that can be seen on the Plateau today.[11] In terms of the quantity of water generated the *qanat* (*kariz*) was by far the most important device. Given the extensive literature on the technical aspects of the *qanat*, a brief description will suffice.[12]

The *qanat* is a deceptively simple device for collecting and transporting ground-water in sloping alluvial areas; it consists of two parts (see figure 5):

1. a well, called *pish-é kar* or *madar-é chah* (the "mother well"), which reaches down to the water-table.

2. a gently sloping tunnel, *kar*, which ends farther down the alluvial fan.

Gigantic *qanats* of 30–40 km in length and with wells up to 100 m deep are reported from around Yazd and Kirman. The average *qanat*, however, has far more modest dimensions: the length is about 4 km and the depth of the well between 10 and 50 meters.[13]

In spite of the simplicity of the device, *qanat*– building requires considerable skill. First a suitable location for the "mother well" must be found, and that may require several trial diggings; then the surveyor must carefully determine the course and gradient of the underground tunnel: too great a slope will cause erosion and eventual collapse of the tunnel. The constructing is done by experts, the *muqannis* (*chahkan, karizkan*). They usually begin by digging the "mother well" and then, after selecting the outlet point, they dig the tunnel from there up to the well. Along the path they dig ventilation shafts at regular intervals, using these to haul the spoil to the surface; here the spoil is arranged around the shaft mouth to serve as protection against rainstorm damage. On the surface the *qanat* therefore appears as a line of characteristic spoil craters. If during their diggings the *muqannis* encounter sand or loose soil, they reinforce the tunnel with hoops of baked or sun-dried clay. Eventually the tunnel will reach the water-table and then the tunnel and the well must be connected. This final operation is especially risky; but *qanat*-construction is altogether a hazardous and difficult undertaking; as the Khurasani proverb says: "snake charmers, lion tamers and karez diggers very seldom die in their beds."[14]

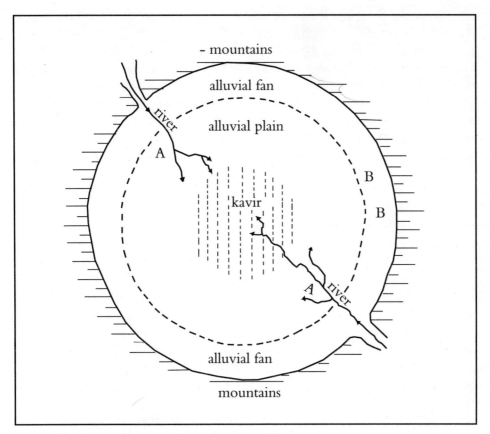

Fig. 6. The Basic Settlement Pattern on the Iranian Plateau.
A. Settlement in natural surface-water oases.
B. Settlement based on groundwater extraction.

The finished *qanat* then operates as follows: the "mother well" and the upper part of the tunnel collect the infiltrating groundwater; the rest of the tunnel serves as the "transportation section," conducting the water to the surface by gravity flow. The *qanat* requires neither constant surveillance nor animal or human labor to work, it must, however, be regularly cleaned out and otherwise maintained.

The *qanats* on the Iranian Plateau yield an average of 15–16 liters per second; but the discharge varies with the season, reaching a maximum in spring and autumn. During the summer discharge is reduced; how much will depend on the depth of the mother-well and the nature of local groundwater resources, but prolonged drought will dry out practically all *qanats*, even the deepest. One obvious disadvantage of the *qanat* is that it also produces water during the winter when irrigation is not needed. The surplus water can be collected and stored in reservoirs, but these make excellent breeding-grounds for mosquitos; in fact there is no doubt that the *qanat* has helped the spread of malaria on the Plateau.[15] Other drawbacks are the loss of water from percolation, especially noticeable in long *qanats*, and the sensitivity of the structure to earthquakes. Finally, in spite of its simplicity, the *qanat* is expensive. The *muqannis* have to execute the entire work by hand and since even a small *qanat* involves the removing of several thousand cubic meters of earth, this is time-consuming: larger *qanats* may take years to build. It is estimated that the construction costs for an ordinary *qanat* in the Kirman region around 1950 ran to about $10,000 per kilometer.[16] Since the average *qanat* will normally water but a few hectares, a long time can pass before the outlay is recuperated.

In recent decades deep wells with motor-driven pumps have begun to replace *qanats*. These wells are much cheaper to build, but literally dry up the surrounding *qanats* because they reach farther down into the water-bearing layers.[17] As late as 1960, however, immediately before modern European technology was introduced on a large scale into agriculture, Iran still had some 30.000 *qanats* of which 22.000 were in good condition. Together they yielded 560.000 liters of water per second and served roughly half of the total irrigated area. Of the country's 45.000 villages, 18.000 were dependent on *qanats* and so were larger towns such as Shiraz, Kirman, Yazd, Kazwin, Tehran, etc.[18] Such data clearly demonstrate the vital importance of the *qanat* for the traditional settlement pattern. Extrapolating from these figures, we can put the total length of all working *qanats* in 1960 at 160.000 km; if we add abandoned and ruined *qanats*, the figure reaches perhaps 400.000 km.[19] Even the lower figure gives an idea of the gigantic labor effort involved in the colonization of the Plateau.

Leaving aside areas under rain-fed farming, which in long-term perspective have been of limited importance, we can roughly divide settlements on the Plateau into two analytical categories: first, the natural, river-irrigated oases, for instance Isfahan; second, the artificial, *qanat*-watered oases such as Yazd and Kirman. Each category represents a distinct phase in the history of the Plateau: while the settlements in the surface-water oases are generally old, the *qanat*-oases are much younger, most of them dating, as will be argued below, from historical times.

To sum up, in spite of evident differences in the matter of technology and water resources most of the cultivated lands on the Plateau were no less artificial than were the Mesopotomian lands. Nevertheless settlement on the Plateau proved far more resilient. It is a key argument of the present inquiry that the Plateau in general did *not* experience a decline at all comparable to what occurred in Mesopotamia. Moreover, the artificial, *qanat*-watered oases proved as viable as the natural ones. The chief exception to this overall reciliency was the Sistan Basin, which will be treated separately.

The distribution and nature of water resources largely explains the patchy settlement pattern characteristic of the Plateau. Settlements were not spread evenly, but concentrated in enclaves: i.e. dispersed oases or groups of oases separated from each other by mountains and deserts. Each enclave would have an urban center, and though larger enclaves generally contained several towns, administration, military functions, and communication out of the enclave, including caravan trade, would always be concentrated in one of the towns. There was also a concentration, though not a monopoly, of handicrafts and industry in the towns; in fact, many villages had specialized handicraft production, including production for export.[20] Transport and sale, however, was always through the towns.

Locally, the urban center of an enclave was referred to as "the city" (*shahr*). If there was a need to specify more exactly which city, one simply added the name of the enclave. Hence, the town of Katheh was commonly known as "Yazd town" or *shahr-é Yazd*. In the same way Zarandj was called (*shahr-é*) Sistan. If the functions of the center for some reason were transferred elsewhere, the name followed. Thus, in the 10th century, the name (*shahr-é*) Kirman referred to Sirdjan but later to Veh-Ardashir, at present still Kirman town. As Jean Aubin points out, this usage reflects views directly contradicting the conventional idea of a dichotomy between town and country in the Middle East.[21] The integration of town and countryside within the individual enclaves is also clear from the fact that the rural population eagerly joined in the sectarian fighting that plagued most of Iranshahr's towns from the 11th to the 13th centuries.[22]

There were of course settlements outside this simplified enclave pattern. In rugged mountainous areas there existed "free villages" where the inhabitants were presumably organized on a tribal basis. Protected by natural barriers and their own warlike traditions, they could largely ignore the town and its soldiers and tax collectors. Ibn al-Balkhi, writing in the early 12th century, describes remote villages in the Zagros and Irahistan (Fars) where the inhabitants went about armed. They were, he adds, highwaymen and footpads, exhibiting all the nasty character traits usually ascribed to mountain-dwellers.[23] Such communities, however, are of limited interest to the issues raised in the present study.

The Empire normally used the larger towns as administrative centers for extensive territories, which, however, should be kept conceptually distinct from the hinterland proper, i.e. the area which supplied the cities with basic goods and raw materials for industry as well as finished products for export. Thus around 900 Isfahan was the political capital of a region which, according to Ibn Rusteh, measured no less than 500 km in both length and breadth. However, the additional information about Isfahan provided by Ibn Rusteh and others shows that the enclave proper encompassed only the territory within a radius of two *marhaleh* (days' march), i.e. *c.* 100 km. The Nishapur enclave in the 9th and 10th centuries covered an area of similar size, while the hinterland of Shiraz did not extend beyond a radius of 50 km.[24]

Nearly all the larger towns of the Plateau consisted of two parts: (1) a walled inner city, the *sharistan* (or *madina*), and (2) surburbs, the *extra muros* quarters (mahaleh, birun, rabad).[25] The shahristan was always densely built-up, though not necessarily with domestic buildings. Here stood the citadel and the Friday Mosque, bazaars, and various public buildings and government houses. There were exceptions, of course: in Yazd the Friday Mosque stood outside the shahristan, while in Nishapur and Herat, respectively, the main bazaar and the Government House were situated in the suburbs.[26] The suburbs were usually much bigger than the shahristan, but otherwise quite varied in character. In Yazd, Nishapur, and Herat they were regular built-up areas with bazaars and mosques, while in Firuzabad they seem to have consisted largely of gardens and parks.[27] This is not unimportant, since the information provided by the sources on the size of towns often refers only to the shahristan. Hence, measurings – even if done correctly – may give little indication of the nature and actual size of a settlement. Ibn Rusteh, for instance, states that Isfahan around 900 covered 70 hectares, which means that in theory it could have had 14.000 inhabitants. This does not accord with the geographical literature which describes Isfahan as the largest and most populous city in Djibal. The explanation, of course, is that the measurement referred only to the shahristan area, without including the suburbs; of these, Yahudiyeh alone is said to have been larger than Hamadan.[28] This "Greater" Isfahan and a few other towns like Ray, Nishapur, Marv, and Herat may at one time have had populations up to and perhaps even exceeding 100.000. This estimate rests partly on the extent of the ruins of Nishapur and Marv. The rest of the towns on the Plateau were considerably smaller. While the data do not allow us to determine their size with any certainty, the descriptions in the geographical literature and the general impression of the enclaves' modest size and resources point to an estimate, perhaps rather generous, of between 10.000 and 25.000 for the ordinary town.

In any event, topography and transportation technology put limits on the size of towns. They had to live off their hinterlands because it was simply not possible to transport subsistence goods, grain above all, across the distances and natural obstacles which separated the enclaves. To be sure, at times fruit was carried from Yazd to Isfahan (c. 300 km) and grain from Quchan (Khabushan) to Nishapur (c. 100 km), but the upper limit for transporting large amounts clearly lay in the range of about 100–200 km.[29] In the 10th century al-Muqaddasi saw large caravans going with dates from Kirman to Khurasan – a journey of over 1.000 km and partly through the desert – but then the dates were precisely an exotic specialty, not a basic subsistence commodity.[30] In any case, the caravan traffic did not have the capacity to alleviate genuine shortages. That the enclaves were essentially dependent on their own subsistence production is clear from, for instance, al-'Utbi's account of the terrible famine in Nishapur in 1009/10, in which some 100.000 people were said to have perished. Sultan Mahmud, whose extortionate taxation of Khurasan had helped provoke the crisis, gave orders to open the state storehouses and distribute grain to the hungry, but this apparently had no great effect. According to al-'Utbi the situation eventually became so desperate that the flesh of humans was openly sold in the bazaars – surely a dramatic exaggeration – until the harvest the following year put an end to the misery.[31]

In short, the Plateau did not form a single unit. It was physically and economically fragmented and divided politically between the largest enclaves and the "lands" which they dominated, and from the various chronicles it appears that local feelings were strong. Ethnic differences, cultural distinctions, etc., contributed to the particular identity of individual enclaves.

Chapter 11

Early Settlement Patterns

Briefly put, the archaeological material shows that settled agriculture began to expand on the Plateau from the 6th millennium B.C., i.e. roughly at the same time as the colonization of the Mesopotamian floodplain began.[1] The earliest settlements were in the relatively well-watered intermontane valleys in the Zagros (the Kirmanshah region, Luristan, Nayriz) where rain-fed farming could be combined with other methods of subsistence. However, as early as around 5000 B.C. settlements had also been established in places where some irrigation was necessary or at least advisable (e.g. Tepe Siyalk, near present-day Kashan).[2] Whether irrigation technology was brought here by immigration or through diffusion of knowledge from earlier agricultural centers, or whether it was an indigenous invention does not matter here. Suffice it to note that by the 4th millennium B.C. agrarian settlements had spread over the entire Plateau.[3]

These early settlements were clearly confined to places with accessible surface-water. Aurel Stein had already noted this on his one-man surveys in the 1930s, and even though many new finds have been made since then, there is no reason to question Stein's conclusion.[4] Tepe Siyalk, Tepe Hissar, Khabis (Shahdab), Tepe Yahya, the Kopet Dagh settlements – some of the best known pre-historic settlements – were all located on alluvial fans near small rivers.

Outside the natural oases some agriculture was practiced with embanked fields and similar technologies which were seldom reliable enough to support permanent settlement.[5] A third form of subsistence, especially widespread in the Zagros, consisted in various forms of nomadism. In fact, specialized or "pure" nomadism seems to have evolved here during the 4th millennium B.C. in response to political pressures exerted by the large agrarian settlements in Khuzistan and the Nayriz Basin.[6]

In the largest oases irrigation and increased production provided the base for the evolution of towns and, apparently, also states; from the 3rd millennium B.C. Mesopotamian sources begin to refer regularly to political and territorial units in Iran.[7] A closer locating of these units is difficult, but on archaeological criteria the most important settlements from this early phase include the following:

The Nayriz Basin where irrigation from the Kur River created the basis for the town *Tell-é Malyan*, capital of the Elamite kingdom of *Anshan*. In the 2nd millennium B.C. it covered 150–200 hectares and was by far the largest known settlement on the western Plateau.[8] Later the Nayriz enclave became the basis for the expansionist kingdoms of the Achaemenids and the Sassanians.

Second, the Hilmand Delta in Sistan with the town *Shahr-é Sukhteh* (80 ha in the 3rd millennium B.C.). Settlement later shifted toward the north and east, but the delta remained one of the largest and most productive enclaves of the Plateau well into the Middle Ages.[9]

Third, the Marv Oasis in the Karakum Desert, colonized no later than the 3rd millennium B.C. More than 100 settlements from pre-historic times have been found, all located some 120 km north of present-day Marv. By the early 2nd millennium there was at least one urban center, the Gonur site (50 ha), with huge fortifications. From the same time date the remains of a complex irrigation system based on feeder canals 30–50 km long.[10] A gradual transfer of settlement toward the south, beginning as early as Seleucid times, may have been caused by salinity build-up and other environmental deterioration, but the oasis continued to play a key role in Iranshahr's history until the 12th or 13th centuries.

Fourth, the "Kopet Dagh corridor," i.e. the 600 km long and 80 km wide strip of land between the north slope of the Kopet Dagh and the Karakum Desert. This was watered by many streams (which were groundwater-fed and thus fairly reliable) and may have been the site of an indigenous neolithic revolution around 6000 B.C. At the beginning of the 3rd millennium there seems to have been a trend toward urbanization, although hardly so marked as in Mesopotamia. The emerging urban centers included Altyn Tepe (26 ha) and Namazga Tepe (50 ha), each with monumental buildings, fortifications, and a division of labor. Both towns were apparently abandoned during the 2nd millennium, but the area remained settled.[11]

Immediately east of Namazga, in the inland delta of the Tedzhen River, lay the Geoksyur Oasis. Here are remains, from the 4th millennium, of defensive structures and of canals several kilometers in length. In contrast to the Kopet Dagh area this oasis was abandoned in the 3rd millennium B.C. and never recolonized to any large extent.[12] In the medieval sources the delta is described as a tamarisk jungle. The reason for this may be that the Tedzhen was not a reliable source of water; later, in the Middle Ages, the town of Sarakhs, farther up the river, constantly suffered from the inadequate water supply.[13]

Finally there was the relatively well-watered southern part of the Gurgan Plain which was probably colonized roughly at the same time as the Kopet Dagh corridor. The northern part of the plain, i.e. the drier and more inhospitable area known as *Dihistan* in the Middle Ages, remained sparsely settled until the middle of the 2nd millennium B.C. Then, by an enormous labor effort, water was conducted to the area from the Atrak River. Since the Atrak apparently was already entrenched, this must have required the construction of a weir. The dammed water was then carried by a 100 km long feeder canal crossing the Sumbar, a tributary to the Atrak, westwards to at least two large secondary canals which then supplied a network   of smaller irrigation canals. The system, one of the largest and most complex in all of Southwest and Central Asia, is comparable to the Nahrawan in Mesopotamia and the Nahr al-Ta'am in Sistan and implies the existence of a centralized polity.[14]

No doubt several more enclaves should be added to this list, for instance Isfahan. But their early history today lies hidden beneath modern constructions or thick layers of sediment.

1. Technological Revolution: the Introduction of the *Qanat*

The *qanat* technology obviously revolutionized the conditions for agriculture on the Plateau by providing access to groundwater resources and thereby opening up for colonization of the arid alluvial fans along the inner slopes of the mountains. But when did this expansion occur? By themselves *qanats* and *qanat*-ruins are practically impossible to date; I am not aware of a single case where *qanats* have been dated back to pre-historical times with any reasonable degree of certainty on the sole basis of archaeological criteria. In several places which have been watered by *qanats* in historical times there remain traces of pre-historic settlement and this has led some scholars to believe that the device came into wide-spread use at a very early date.[15] In these cases, however, it seems more likely that the *qanats* were added later, either because settlement and cultivation were expanded or because the original water supply had declined as a result of the progressive forest clearing in the mountains. In Fars large mountain areas were still covered by forest in the 11th century,[16] and even as late as the early 19th century substantial forests remained. Lions were said still to live near Bushire, a sign that there must have been relatively undisturbed areas here.[17] However, precisely at this time a British traveller on his way to Shiraz saw how the locals set fire to entire mountain sides to get charcoal.[18] Over the last few centuries such destruction has greatly damaged the forest cover and reduced local water resources.

The earliest evidence of *qanat* technology seems to be the description of certain waterworks which the Assyrian king Sargon II found during his campaign against Urartu at the end of the 8th century B.C. On this basis it is generally assumed that the *qanat* had been discovered here, i.e. in the Urmiyeh region, in the beginning of the 1st millennium B.C. In the ancient cultivated area in the Kopet Dagh corridor the technology may have been discovered independently at roughly the same time.[19]

This is a fairly late dating, but the discovery – or at least the wider application – of the *qanat* technology must largely have depended on another technological advance: the use of iron. On the Plateau iron tools were not widely used until the 1st millennium B.C., earliest in the west where Urartu by the 8th century B.C. had developed into a center for the production of iron tools and weapons.[20] Even so, the mere fact that the necessary knowledge and tools were available does not prove that the pattern of *qanat*-dependent settlements was established in the 1st millennium B.C. On the contrary, most of these settlements must be considerably younger, and the *qanat*-based expansion probably did not peak until Sassanian times.

2. The Greek Description of the Plateau

The picture of the Iranian Plateau in the classical sources contains few details and is, in addition, beset with methodological difficulties to which reference has already been made. However, by following the campaigns of Alexander the Great between 331 and 323 B.C. we can obtain a rough impression of the settlement pattern, because logistics required the armies to move between the larger enclaves. When, on the way back from India, Alexander took a chance and marched into the unknown and, as it turned out, empty Gedrosia (Baluchistan-Makran), this feat of daring nearly ended in disaster, because the army could not be supplied.

Alexander's first objective after the conquest of Mesopotamia-Khuzistan was the Achaemenid homeland, i.e. the Marvdasht Plain in the Nayriz Basin with the dynastic and administrative centers of Persepolis and Pasargadae. In the classical accounts the river-watered basin is described as densely populated with numerous villages and towns;[21] but it is not clear which towns we are dealing with. The ancient capital of the Anshan kingdom, Tell-é Malyan, had been abandoned long ago,[22] and Persepolis and Pasargadae were not genuine urban settlements, though the sources refer to them as such.[23]

From pre-historic times irrigation had been practiced by simple diversions from the Kur River, and on the upper Marvdasht this technology remained the basis for agriculture. Farther downstream, however, raising of the water must have been a precondition for irrigation even in ancient times and here are in fact remains of several weirs; but whether they date from Achaemenid times is uncertain.[24] On the basis of archaeological surveys it is estimated that the population of Marvdasht in the Achaemenid era numbered no more than 30.000–40.000. If this is correct, the expansion of irrigation must largely have taken place later.[25]

The rest of Fars, beyond the Nayriz Basin, seems to have been very thinly populated. After the conquest of Persepolis, when Alexander undertook a lightning punitive expedition against the Mardi tribe in the "interior of Fars," he found only small and scattered settlements. The Mardi were apparently pastoralists whose way of life must have resembled the transhumance later practised by the nomadic and semi-nomadic groups in the area.[26]

On the coast of Fars, near present-day Bushire, stood a port, *Hieratis*, which was connected to Marvdasht through the Shapur-rud Valley. Nearby was the settlement of *Taoce*, usually identified with medieval Tawwaz.[27] *Mesembria*, i.e. the plain around Hieratis, seems to have been the only sizable enclave on the entire coastline from

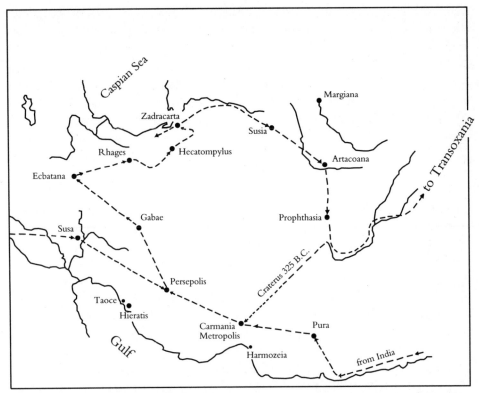

Fig. 7. Approximate Route of Alexander the Great across the Iranian Plateau (331–323 B.C.)

Hormuz to the Shatt al-Arab. Here traces of settlement go back to the 2nd millennium, and the enclave can perhaps be identified with the Elamite *Pashime* (*Mishime*). In the plain are the remains of a 40 km long canal which carried water from a small river; it is possibly Achaemenid or even older.[28] According to Alexander's admiral Nearchus the remaining settlements on the Gulf coast consisted only of small and poor fishing villages.[29]

From the Nayriz Basin Alexander marched northwards to the country of Paraeta-cena and the large *Gabae* oasis (i.e. Djay/Isfahan).[30] There is no doubt that Isfahan had long been one of the Plateau's most productive enclaves; that it was also of great military importance is suggested by the old form of the name Isfahan, *Aspadana*, meaning "the Army Camp," or "the Cavalry Camp."[31] The Achaemenids had built a palace here, a sign of the imperial interest. In 317 B.C., during the wars between the successors of Alexander, the rival generals Eumenes and Antigonus engaged in a veritable race to capture the oasis and its considerable resources. Eumenes won, and his troops were thus able to spend the winter under favorable conditions.[32]

From Paraetacena Alexander advanced into Media, i.e. Djibal, considered by the Greeks to be the largest and wealthiest province of Iran. He first occupied Hama-

dan, *Ecbatana*, the chief city of the region and a summer residence of the Achaemenids.[33] His next objective was *Rhagae* or Ray, the center of eastern Media. Because
of the growth of modern Tehran archaeological research has furnished only limited
information about this important city; nevertheless there are some indication that
settlement on this site goes back to the 4th millennium B.C.[34] According to Strabo
the Ray area was struck by an earthquake shortly after Alexander had passed
through, and "several towns and 2.000 villages" were said to have been destroyed.
This is the first mention of earthquakes as a crucial factor affecting settlement on the
Plateau. Seleucus I subsequently repaired the damages and on this occasion re-
named the city *Europos*. Later, in Parthian times, it was again re-named, as *Arsacia*,
yet it remained widely known by its original name.[35]

From Ray the Macedonians pursued the fleeing Darius eastward through the
"Caspian Gates" – the passage between the Alburz foothills and the Dasht-é Kavir –
into Choarena and Comisena, i.e. Kumis in the Simnan-Damghan region, which
was watered by streams coming down the Alburz. In Parthian times the capital of
the region was known by its Greek name *Hecatompylus*, but there are archaeological
indications that this was an important city even in pre-Achaemenid times.[36] Arrian,
however, does not mention it, while Quintus Curtius makes it a Greek foundation.
To increase the confusion, Isidore of Charax states that there was no town at all in
Comisena, thus contradicting all other classical sources as well as the Persian
historical tradition. In any case, there must have been a considerable farming
enclave, since Alexander's troops could gather the supplies necessary for further
advance.[37]

From Comisena Alexander crossed the Alburz, presumably somewhere east of
modern Shahrud, coming down into Hyrcania, i.e. the Gurgan Plain. The plain,
which lies like a wedge between the Karakum and the Iranian deserts, is watered by
the rivers Gurgan-rud and Atrak; in addition, it receives a fair amount of rainfall
(600–700 mm). Both classical and medieval sources describe it as fertile and
forested; its present-day steppe character is chiefly a result of human activity.[38]

The capital and largest city of this country was *Zadrakarta*, usually identified with
Astarabad, modern Gurgan. Yet Zadrakarta may also be identified with medieval
shahr-é Gurgan near the Gurgan-rud, 4–5 km from Gunbad-é Kabus.[39] The account
of Antiochus III's attack on Hyrcania (209 B.C.) refers to a large unfortified town,
Tambrax, and to a nearby fortress town called *Sirynx*, the real capital. As Tambrax
must have been situated immediately beyond the Alburz crossing, it might also be
identified with Astarabad. If so, Sirynx may the ancient name of Turang Tepe, the
ruins of a huge fortress in the vicinity.[40]

Strabo lists as important towns *Talabroke, Samariane,* and *Karta,* and the royal
residence *Tape.* With the possible exception of (Zadra)Karta, none of them can be
located. They should probably be sought under some of the countless Parthian
sites.[41] In any case, judging from the classical sources, we can assume that southern

Gurgan, i.e. the area around the Gurgan-rud, formed even in Achaemenid times one of the larger areas of settlement of the Plateau. In contrast, the northern areas of cultivation in Dihistan go unmentioned.

With Zadrakarta as a base Alexander conducted a short campaign against the Mardi whose country is described as mountainous and densely forested; his objective was probably the coastal plain of Mazandaran (the Amul-Babol-Sari region). However, apart from the reconnaissance expedition undertaken around 285 B.C. by a Seleucid officer, Patroclus, who sailed along the coast to the mouth of the Atrak, the Caspian coast and mountains remained largely undisturbed by the events on the Plateau during this period.[42]

It is unclear which route Alexander took after Gurgan. The assumption is that he marched up along the Atrak to the Kashaf-rud, towards Quchan where remains have been found of pre-Achaemenid settlement. He thus passed west of the country of Nisaea, i.e. the Kopet Dagh corridor, but it is possible that the Seleucids arrived there on one of the later campaigns.[43] Another ancient enclave, the *Marv Oasis*, in the Karakum Desert, was not conquered until the campaigns in Transoxania and Bactria.[44]

In any case, after Gurgan the first large settlement mentioned is *Susia*, located in the land of Aria. *If* Alexander had in fact travelled up through the Atrak Valley, Susia should be sought on the Kashaf-rud somewhere in the Mashhad region.[45] From here Alexander marched toward the capital of Aria, *Artacoana* on the River Areius.[46] This city is identified with present-day Herat or a predecessor in the immediate area.

From here Alexander then marched south over Farah toward *Drangiane*,[47] the Hilmand Delta in Sistan, and up along the Hilmand to Arachosia (al-Rukhkhadj), the ancient cultivated land along the lower Arghandab River.[48] The accounts give no details about the area, saying only that Alexander named a governor and left a garrison. Probably the garrison was stationed in the town of Arachotus mentioned by Strabo and usually identified with old Kandahar, i.e. the *Shahr-é Kuhna* ruins situated just west of present-day Kandahar. Excavations in the mid-1970s indicate that a large fortified settlement existed on this site as early as the beginning of the 1st millennium B.C.[49]

We shall disregard Alexander's campaigns outside Iranshahr, in Transoxania, Bactria, and Pandjab, and first follow him again from the autumn of 325 B.C. when he began his retreat from India. A naval force under the command of Nearchus was sent up the Gulf coast, while the rest of the army, led by Alexander himself, entered the wastelands of Gedrosia (Baluchistan-Makran), heading for Kirman and Fars. Arrian states that at no time during the campaigning in Asia did the army suffer such hardships: the guides lost their way because shifting sands constantly altered the landscape; men and draft animals died of thirst and exhaustion in the burning heat, if they did not drown when the monsoon rains suddenly poured masses of water

down the wadi where the army had made camp.[50] Other conquerors had experienced similar difficulties. Cyrus, when retreating from India, is said to have lost his
entire army here, except for seven men.[51] Many hundreds of years later, when
'Uthman was caliph in Medina, a certain Hakim b. Djabalah explored the country
and reported back that while dates were plentiful, water was scarce and the
inhabitants warlike; were the caliph to send a small army, it was certain to be
defeated, but a large one would die from hunger and thirst.[52] The Macedonians just
barely avoided this fate, and their sufferings did not end until they reached the
Gedrosian capital in the *Pura* Oasis. This must have been located somewhere on the
Bampur River, at or near the present-day town of Bampur.[53]

From Pura Alexander marched westward into Carmania (Kirman) which is
described as a fertile country with many rivers. Clearly the country in question was
the area south of the central massif of Kuh-é Lalehzar.[54] Neither Strabo nor Arrian
expressly mentions any town here. Pliny, Ptolemy, and Ammian do so, but their
information may refer to a later period.[55] However, there is reliable archaeological
evidence of at least one large urban settlement in south Kirman in Achaemenid
times: Tepe Yahya at the Kish-é Shur River in the Suwghan Valley.

The Tepe Yahya site consists partly of the remains of a fortified inner town, partly
of an area of surface debris covering several square kilometers on both sides of the
river. The original settlement is believed to go back to *c.* 4000 B.C.[56] For unknown
reasons the town was abandoned some time in the first centuries A.D., but in
Alexander's time it was probably still one of the larger settlements on the southeastern Plateau, and it is tempting to identify it with the *Carmana Metropolis* of the
classical sources. Some of the other localities named can perhaps be identified with
Bam, Rigan, and Djiruft (or their predecessors), which later traditions accord great
age. On the basis of the available information, however, such identifications must
remain tentative.[57]

On the Kirman coast Nearchus mentions two large enclaves: first, *Badis* immediately east of the entrance into the Hormuz Strait around present-day Djask, and
second, *Harmozeia*, at the mouth of the river Anamis. Both the name and the
description of the latter place point to the original site of Hormuz, i.e. Minab at the
mouth of the Duzdan.[58] Nearchus refers to Harmozeia as a district, mentioning no
town, and as late as the 10th century Hormuz in fact was just a trading post with a
mosque. Settlement consisted of small villages scattered about the coastal plain.[59]

In the vague image of Kirman drawn by classical sources, the settlement is
concentrated in the south. The land to the north is described as desert (this
information may have come from Craterus and his men, who perhaps passed
through on their return from Sistan). North Kirman was not empty, of course.
Even in pre-historical times there were settlements in the natural oases here (e.g.
Tell-é Iblis and Shahdab), but these were generally small.[60] The account given by

the Persian historical tradition, that North Kirman first became extensively colonized in Sassanian times, is certainly credible.

To sum up, the accounts of Alexander's campaigns at the close of the Achaemenid period indicate that settlements on the Plateau were still concentrated on the
old surface-water oases. Beyond these, various extensive methods of subsistence
predominated.[61] The remark that the interior of Fars was thinly populated is
supported by the surprisingly few archaeological finds of Achaemenid date, even
allowing for the fact that settlement remains may be hidden under layers from later
periods.[62]

Yet there is no doubt that by Achaemenid times the *qanat* was known and used
by the inhabitants of the Plateau. In his account of Antiochus III's march toward
Hecatompylus in 210–209 B.C. Polybius describes the territory south of the Alburz
mountains as a desert without any surface-water. Instead the inhabitants were
supplied by underground channels, and Polybius adds that the Achaemenid kings
had awarded tax exemptions for five generations to all who, with great effort and at
considerable expense, had brought land under cultivation by digging these channels.[63] Thus, when several Greek authors – among them Xenophon who himself
had been in Persian service – praised the great kings for advancing agriculture, we
need not dismiss this as edifying fiction or repetition of Achaemenid propaganda.[64]
Polybius' account shows that colonization indeed took place with state support and
involved the *qanat* technology. Considering other data on the settlement pattern,
however, the extent of this colonization seems to have been limited. It would
certainly be erroneous to assume *a priori* that all or most *qanat*-irrigated settlements
date from Achaemenid times.

3. The "Hellenized Orient" (2): the Greek Foundings

It is often said that the Greek settlement and cultural influences which followed
with Alexander's conquests had profound, long-lasting effects throughout Iranshahr
and even farther east. Thus R.N. Frye does not hesitate to speak of the Hellenization as "the most important event in the history of the Near East."[65] In Mesopotamia Greek domination was certainly a dynamic factor; yet the dynamic lay not
so much in the diffusion of Hellenic culture, which appears to have been modest,
but in the way that Greek rule promoted urbanization and the extension of the
canal system. However, events in Mesopotamia will tell us little about what
happened on the Plateau. For one thing, Mesopotamia was the core-land of the
Seleucid Empire, and the size of the Plateau simply prevented a similar degree of
control here. Yet it is often asserted that Alexander and the Seleucids consolidated
their rule by founding a network of Greek towns, *poleis*, throughout the Plateau. It
is further asserted that besides serving as political bases these towns were centers for

the diffusion of Greek culture, watchtowers of civilization in the sea of barbarism, as it were.[66]

Taken together the classical sources mention about 20 towns with Greek names on the Plateau. The names are usually dynastic, derived from the rulers' own name or that of family members: Alexandria, Seleucia, Antiochia, etc. Such names are found in all Hellenistic states.[67] Of the towns bearing Greek names on the Iranian Plateau only the following can be identified with any certainty:[68]

1. *Alexandria-in-Aria* = Herat
2. *Antiochia Margiana* = Marv
3. *Alexandria-in-Arachosia* = Kandahar
4. *Laodicia-in-Media* = Nihawand
5. *Europos* = Ray
6. *Epiphania* = Hamadan

It is obvious at once that a Greek name cannot be proof that a given town had in fact been founded by the Greeks. The towns listed above were in fact existing settlements which had been given new names. Similar cases are known from Syria where the Seleucids gave new names to ancient cities like Beirut (Laodicia) and Damascus (Demetrias).[69] Of the towns on the Plateau the classical sources explicitly refer to the following as being founded by Greeks:[70]

1. *Alexandria-in-Aria*
2. *Alexandria/Antiochia-in-Margiana*
3. *Laodicia-in-Media*. Pliny also mentions *Laodicia-in-Fars*, "west of Phrasargis, the fortress of the Magi," founded by Antiochus. This is probably the same as Laodicia-in-Media.[71]
4. *Antiochia-in-Fars*
5. *Apamia* (in the Ray or Simnan regions)
6. *Heraclia* (in the same place)
7. *Alexandropolis-in-Nisaea*
8. *Europos* (Ray)
9. *Epiphania* (Hamadan)

Ptolemy further mentions a town called Soteira, in Aria, which according to a later Byzantine source was founded by Antiochus I.[72] That the list contains both Ray and Hamadan arouses suspicion. Strabo, the source for the account of Seleucus I's founding of Europos/Ray, must have known that the town was in fact much older. So we are faced with the question: what is meant by founding?

Now Western scholarship has tended to see every founding as a replication of Alexandria in Egypt, Alexander's greatest founding scheme, or of Seleucia in

Mesopotamia; but on the Plateau we are clearly dealing with much less ambitious undertakings: here foundings consisted mainly of placing garrisons in pre-existing settlements which were then given new Greek names. The number of ethnic Greek colonists and soldiers cannot have been very large. Logistics alone set limits to the size of armies and made it extremely difficult to lead large groups of civilians across mountains and through deserts. Estimates of the size of the various foundings have been made on the basis of the size of the garrisons stationed by Alexander: 1.000 men in Susa, 3.000 in Persepolis, 13.000–14.000 in Bactria, 4.000–5.000 in Arachosia, etc.[73] But even though these figures may be reliable, they do not always refer to permanent garrisons. Many of the veterans and war invalids left behind were strongly dissatisfied with their fate and attempted to return to Europe on their own.[74]

The western territories of the Seleucid Empire did see a continual Greek immigration during the 3rd and first half of the 2nd century B.C., and the stream of immigrants certainly reached even Fars and no doubt also Media. Antiochus I, for instance, sent an unknown number of civilian colonists from Magnesia-on-the Mayandros (in Asia Minor) to the newly founded Antiochia-in-Fars.[75] Yet immigration can hardly have reached much further, as the Seleucids had poor or no control over the eastern Plateau.[76] The Hyrcani, for instance, had soon stopped paying tribute.[77] Of course, by demonstrating convincing military power, the Seleucid kings might have forced the various local rulers into submission, but this was attempted only a few times. Around 305–303 B.C. Seleucus I, during a lull in the fighting with the other Macedonian generals, conducted a campaign in the east. Then Antiochus I was in the east between 293 and 280 B.C. His base was apparently the Marv Oasis which he fortified with a wall said to be 1.500 stadia long (c. 270 km!). The city was then re-named Antiochia Margiana. No doubt this represents the high point of Seleucid influence in the east and General Demodamas' campaign or expedition in Transoxania presumably took place at this time.[78] Seleucus II, in 238–237 B.C., made an unsuccessful attack on the Parthians in Khurasan and Gurgan and, finally, Antiochus III, in 210–204 B.C., led a major campaign against local rulers in the east. Though victorious on the battlefield he was able to eliminate neither the Parthians nor the Greek-Bactrian principalities,[79] and subsequently none of the Selucid kings seem to have advanced further east than Djibal. In the early 2nd century B.C. Antiochus IV Epiphanes centered his defense against the Parthians on Isfahan.[80]

The sources, including the body of epigraphic evidence, contain a few hints of Greek presence in the east. Thus when Antiochus III attacked the Parthians in Gurgan, at the end of the 3rd century, some Greek inhabitants were found in fortified Sirynx.[81] The extent and character of their presence is unknown, however; they may have been descendants of a garrison or perhaps merchants. One of the few Greek inscriptions found on the Plateau seems also to come from Gurgan and probably dates from the reign of Antiochus I.[82] In far-off Kandahar three Greek inscriptions have been found: two of them contain a proclamation issued by the Mauryan king Asoka (c. 272–232 B.C.), indicating that, in the 3rd century at least, the population of the town included a Greek element, probably descendants of a garrison or military colony. Very likely Kandahar is identical with Alexandropolis/ Alexandria-in-Arachosia which Isidore calls *polis hellenis*, a "Greek town", a designation he applies to only few other towns. Yet excavations in Kandahar have brought forth no clues of Greek settlement in the form of remnants of buildings of unmistakable Greek origin. We must therefore assume that the original garrison or colony was placed in the existing settlement and that the founding mainly consisted in giving this settlement a new official name. Other foundings must have been made in the same way.[83] In general there are few archaeological traces of Greek presence on the plateau and most of the inscriptions, sculptures, and temple ruins which can reasonably be assumed to be of Greek origin come from the western Plateau.

However, Alexander is supposed to have been especially active founding cities east of Iranshahr – in Bactria, Transoxania, and Pandjab – and it is precisely in Bactria that French archaeologists have excavated the town of *Aï Khanum* which beyond doubt is Greek; it was probably founded while Antiochus I was in the east.[84] As might be expected, this discovery has been advanced as proof that Greek colonization and cultural diffusion indeed extended as far as the classical authors had claimed.[85] Yet before enthusiasm runs wild and we begin to take literally the tales of Plutarch that far-off barbarian tribes like the Gedrosians performed the tragedies of Sophocles and Euripides, it should be recalled that Aï Khanum together with Antiochia Margiana are virtually the only remains of large Greek settlements to be found east of the Tigris – in spite of valiant searching. A single large settlement in Bactria is not proof that the entire Iranian Plateau and Transoxania were covered by Greek towns.[86] So far, the archaeological record suggests that Aï Khanum was in fact an exceptional case.

In brief, on the Iranian Plateau the typical Greek founding must have consisted chiefly in stationing a garrison or military colony in a pre-existing settlement. No doubt these foundings were organized along the same lines as the foundings in Asia Minor and Khuzistan, where the colonists were awarded land to cultivate by local labor under their control. However, we simply do not know the details.[87] Probably the colonies were primarily placed on the western Plateau, in Media/Djibal, where Alexander was to have founded a "chain of towns as a defence against the barbarians."[88] In any case, the foundings did not alter the existing settlement pattern, because the Greeks brought with them neither additional labor nor new water technology. To credit Alexander or the Seleucids with having brought "the city" to the lands of Iranshahr east of the Tigris is simply incorrect. If we understand "cities" and "towns" to be settlements of a certain size and density, in which there is a division of labor and a concentration of administrative, commercial, and military functions, then urban settlement on the Plateau had long predated any Greek presence. Also there is no evidence that these towns grew in number or size as a result of Greek domination or that their social and economic organization were noticeably altered. In some contexts it may be correct to speak of a "Hellenized Orient;" but the Iranian Plateau was not part of it.

In addition to the Greek foundings the classical sources list several foundations and colonization schemes ascribed to the Parthians, the enemies and successors of the Seleucids. Iustin, for instance, says that Arshak (Arsaces), the first Parthian king, founded *Dara* in the country of Apavarcticena. The latter is normally identified as the southern part of the Kopet Dagh corridor, the original core-land of the Parthians.[89] In the country of Choarena (the Simnan region), immediately west of Hecatompylus, the Parthians were to have founded *Calliope* and *Issatis* as a defence against the "Medians,"[90] and at *Charax-in-Media*, near Ray, King Phraates I (*c.* 176–171 B.C.) settled Mardis, perhaps as a kind of military colonists.[91] Finally, in the *Marv* Oasis Orodes II (*c.* 57–37 B.C.) is said to have settled 10.000 Roman legionaries, prisoners from the battle of Carrhae.[92]

As might be expected, the Sassanian version of the historical tradition lists only few Parthian foundings: Narseh the Arsacide is said to have founded the city of *Dihistan*,[93] while *Istakhr* in the Nayriz Basin was founded, according to some traditions, by the Parthian king Ardavan.[94] *Darabgird* in Fars was said to have been built by "Daray, son of Daray." In the Middle Ages he was identified as an Achaemenid king (Darius I or Darius III Codomannus); but as Noeldeke suggested, on the basis of numismatic data, he was probably a local Parthian prince. On the site, located approximately 10 km from modern Darab, no remains have been found dating from the Achaemenid period.[95]

While the Parthian era is only vaguely reflected in the written sources, it is strongly represented in the archaeological record. Near Ashkhabad Soviet archaeologists have excavated a fortified temple and palace complex, apparently the remains of a closed, segregated royal residence, a "forbidden city," situated next to the ruins of an ordinary urban settlement.[96] From ostraca it appears that the official name of this residence was *Mithradadgird*.[97] According to the excavators it was built in the 1st century B.C. and abandoned in the 3rd century, i.e. when the Sassanians conquered Iranshahr. Mithradadgird is very likely the same as *Parthaunisa* or Nisaea of the classical sources, where, according to Isidore, the royal tombs were.[98] Perhaps Parthaunisa/Mithradadgird had a special political or ritual relationship to the Arsacid dynasty, similar to the relationship between by Persepolis and the Achaemenids. If so, this would explain its abandonment in the 3rd century.

If the country of Astauena, traditionally considered part of the Parthian core-area, is the upper Atrak Valley, then the town *Asaak*, where Arsaces first proclaimed himself king, might be identified with Quchan/Chabushan. The latter had reached urban size no later than Sassanian times and the surrounding area contains countless ruins of fortresses and villages which on archaeological criteria appear to be of Parthian origin.[99]

On the Gurgan Plain, where classical authors locate several towns, there is an extraordinary number of Parthian sites, some quite large, indicating a significant expansion of settlement.[100] Most of the sites are situated south of the so-called "Alexander's wall," *Sadd-é Iskander* or *Qizil Alan*, a line of walls, fortresses, and moats, extending 200 km from the Caspian Sea toward the foothills at Pish Kamar and thus screening the entire south Gurgan Plain.[101] While the Persian historical tradition credits the Sassanians with the construction of these fortifications, archaeologists believe that at least in part the line may be Parthian.[102] It is usually assumed that the walls were erected to defend Gurgan and Khurasan against "Scythians" and other nomadic raiders, and the Sassanians were in fact involved in prolonged wars with the Chul or Sul nation, presumed to have been part of the Haytal, the "White Huns." These, however, were not nomads and Dihistan, north of the wall, was certainly not nomad country. The name Chul/Sul may therefore refer to a local ruler or a state centered on the Dihistan enclave.[103]

There is archaeological evidence that the Marv Oasis also saw considerable expansion. Soviet archaeologists have estimated that the central settlement zone grew to cover 55 sq km, comprising several towns. The inner city, centered on the huge Ark-Qaleh fortress, was protected by walls 6 km long, 15 m wide, and perhaps 20 m high. Several villages beyond the urban center have also been dated to Parthian times and so have Durnali and Chihil Burdj, the remains of two large fortresses guarding the access roads to the oasis.[104] Whether the oasis served as base for the Arsacid kings (temporarily at least) or whether it formed a local principality under Parthian suzerainty cannot be determined. In any case, contemporary Chinese intelligence reports refer to *Mu-tu* (Marv) as the eastern outpost of *Ngan-si*, i.e. the Parthian Empire.[105]

In the Damghan area, just east of Hecatompylus, surface debris indicates that large-scale settlement did not occur until Parthian times.[106] Further evidence of settlement expansion in Parthian times is found in some of the larger valleys in the Zagros, e.g. Kangavar, Malayir, and Mahidasht.[107] Fars also saw several new foundings in this period. Besides Darabgird there is the Qasr-é Abu Nasr site in the arid Maharlu Basin and the ruins at Nurabad, between Shiraz and Bihbihan.[108]

To sum up, even though the archaeological data are not free of ambiguity, they indicate a general expansion during Parthian times. Whether this expansion was related to Arsacid rule is another and more difficult question. The great constructions in and around the Parthian homeland on the northeastern Plateau were perhaps the work of the Arsacid kings. In Mesopotamia they were certainly capable of executing large projects, including the founding of cities. On the Plateau, however, their power was no more effective than that of the Seleucids if we are to believe the historical tradition. Politically the two empires constituted a continuum and it is unlikely that a decentralized, "feudal" state like the Parthian would have undertaken colonization and city foundings in, for instance, Fars. Here local rulers, like the Daray who built Darabgird, must have taken the initiative. Considering that the new settlements usually required the construction of *qanats* or some other form of artificial water supply, spontaneous, unorganized expansion can hardly have been of any great importance. If the expansion was as widespread as is assumed here, the local rulers must have had a common motivation or must have been exposed to a common pressure, i.e. there must be something which caused them to respond in such uniform manner; but the period is so badly documented that any explanation will be highly tentative. Precisely this lack of documentation also makes the changes from Parthian to Sassanian times look more marked than they really were.

Chapter 12

Growth and Stabilization of the New Settlement Pattern: Djibal

With the transition from the classical sources to the Persian historical tradition and, especially, the 10th-century geographical literature, information on the Plateau increases, though it remains distributed unevenly through time and space. A complete recording of all known settlements is clearly beyond the present study; moreover, the effort is unlikely to be worth-while, since information often is too scanty and fragmentary to be of much use. Instead I have attempted to identify some general trends by focusing on a number of reasonably well-known enclaves within the various "lands" of the Plateau. However, the following is not an attempt to write the history of these oases. My purpose is simply to outline the general direction of developments and to point out the key influences.

After the Arab conquest Djibal ("the mountains") became the common name for the western Plateau, i.e. the mountainous area between Mesopotamia and the Dasht-é Kavir. Later the name *Iraq-é 'Adjami* ("Persian Iraq") came to be widely used as well. Both names roughly refer to the area which the classical authors had called *Media*.[1] Neither in Muslim times nor apparently before did Djibal form a single administrative unite, a single province. Rather, it was divided between several centers of roughly equal size. Thus Ibn Khurdadhbih limited 9th-century Djibal to the region west of Hamadan, classifying Ray and Isfahan as separate provinces. Qudama did the same, but on the other hand included Azarbaydjan.[2] Regardless of changing administrative practices there is no doubt that Djibal was a distinct territory, though its precise borders might vary (thus al-Istakhri included both Isfahan and Ray in his chapter on Djibal).[3] Ibn Khurdadhbih was well aware that this was the case, and when referring to the land of Djibal (as distinct from the administrative district Djibal) he used the designation "Pahlawi:" i.e. "the land of the Parthians."[4]

In fiscal terms Djibal was the most important region of the Plateau in Muslim times and though the tax assessment is fragmentary (see table 3), it is clear that the same was true in Sassanian times: from the very beginning the Sassanians attempted to establish direct control over enclaves such as Hamadan, Isfahan, and Qum,[5] and they further carried out several foundings and colonization projects in

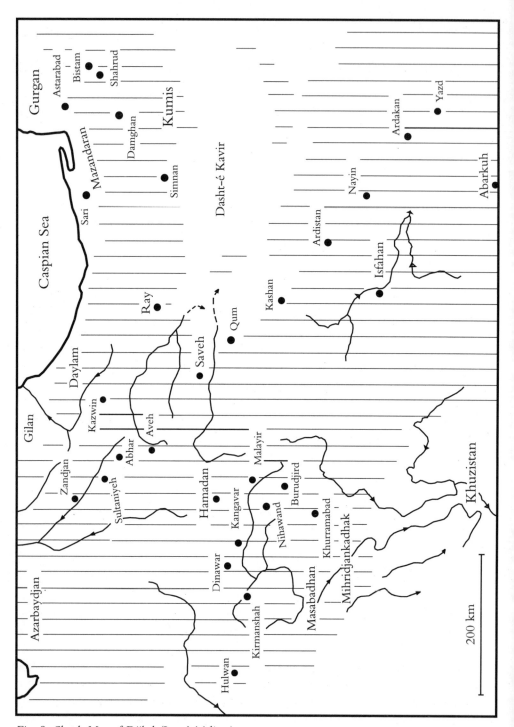

Fig. 8. Sketch-Map of Djibal (Iraq-é 'Adjam).

the country. Besides a large-scale expansion of the Isfahan enclave, the foundings are said to have included the following:

Kazwin (*Shad-Shapur*) with *Abhar* and *Zandjan*.[6]
Ram-Firuz (unidentified, but situated near Ray; perhaps part of Ray itself).[7]
Kirmanshah (which in Muslim times replaced Dinawar as center of Mah al-Kufah).[8]
Shahrazur.
Iran-Shad-Kavadh (also unidentified, situated somewhere between Shahrazur and Hulwan).[9]

These foundings had mainly military purposes: they served to enclose the wild Daylam Highlands within a line of fortified settlements, while also ensuring unhindered passage along the Khurasan road through the Zagros. Some of these foundings, for instance Kazwin and Kirmanshah, subsequently evolved into important centers in their own right. However, the existence of Nestorian sees in Isfahan, Ray, and Hamadan indicates that in Sassanian times these three ancient enclaves remained the economic and political centers of Djibal.[10]

By the 9th and 10th centuries the picture has become clearer thanks to the Muslim tax assessments and the geographical literature. However, it must be recalled that exceptional conditions may have influenced the figures of the tax assessments. For instance, it is explicitly stated for Kazwin that the assessment was low because of the costs of the continual war against the Daylamis.[11] Other enclaves were administratively expanded or contracted, something which also affected the figures.[12] It is clear, however, that the two ancient enclaves of Ray and Isfahan maintained their political and economic dominance throughout Abbasid times. Hamadan was of secondary importance, as were enclaves such as Qum, Nihawand (Mah al-Basrah), and Dinawar (Mah al-Kufah). According to Ibn Hawqal most of Djibal's cities were in fact quite small.[13]

The 1335 tax assessments (cf. table 5) and Mustawfi al-Kazwini's additional information show that Djibal as a whole remained of vital fiscal importance in Ilkhanid times. However, closer examination of the figures for the individual enclaves reveals significant changes in relative size and rank of the enclaves in relation to Abbasid times. Leaving aside Yazd, which earlier assessments had included as part of Fars, we see that by now Nihawand and Qum were only of small importance; Dinawar had disappeared, its place taken by Kirmanshah; Hamadan and Kazwin seemed stable, and a wholly new town, Sultaniyeh, had appeared. Most striking, however, is the difference which had evolved between Djibal's two traditional centers: Isfahan and Ray. While Isfahan remained highly important, accounting for no less than 1/3 of the total tax assessment, Ray had declined considerably. The city itself was more or less abandoned, having been replaced as enclave center by the nearby village of Varamin.

1. Isfahan

This ancient enclave was clearly accorded special attention by the Sassanians. Apparently it had from the very outset been subjected to direct royal administration and reports of irrigation-works, foundings of villages, deportations, and stationing of professional military further indicate that Isfahan was indeed considered a major base of the Empire on the western Plateau.

Ardashir I is said to have reorganized the distribution of water from the Zayan-deh-rud to the various rural districts; the objective may have been to prevent conflicts over water between local communities – something frequently occurring in other enclaves – and to ensure a stable water supply to Alandjan and other districts which had the special task of supporting the *dihqans*, i.e. the professional soldiers.[14] Because of its productivity Isfahan constituted one of the Plateau's large military centers, its status being reflected by the fact that Isfahani troops had the privilege of carrying into battle the royal standard of the Sassanians, the *dirafsh-é kaviyan*.[15] The traditions also state that two Sassanian kings, Bahram V Gur and Khusraw I Anushirvan, were born within the enclave, in Rusan and Ardistan respectively. In the latter place stood a Sassanian palace, and probably the enclave at times served as royal residence.[16]

In the early 5th century Yazdgird I settled Jewish colonists in a new town, Yahudiyeh, next to Djay, the original urban center of the oasis.[17] Perhaps they came from Armenia. Faustos Buzandats'i and Moses Khorenats'i, two Armenian histori-ans, relate that Shapur II carried out large-scale deportations from here: according to Faustos 91.000 Jewish and 108.000 Armenian families were deported to Meso-potamia and Khuzistan. However, Moses states that they in fact were settled precisely in Isfahan.[18] The figures stated need not be taken literally, but on the basis of what we otherwise know of Sassanian deportation practices there is no reason to doubt that they made one or perhaps several large settlements in the Isfahan enclave in the 4th and 5th centuries.[19]

In the second half of the 5th century Shah Firuz had the old urban center of Djay fortified. The work was begun by the local commandant (*pahlavan*) and was said to have cost 600.000 dirhams. On this occasion several new villages were founded, the taxes of which were to be spent on operating and maintaining the local fire temples.[20] Around the year 900 Ibn Rusteh described Djay as circular, like other Parthian-Sassanian towns such as Darabgird, Firuzabad (Gur), and Veh-Ardashir (in Mesopotamia). It covered, according to calculations made by the engineer Muham-mad al–Ludda and cited by Ibn Rusteh, an area of roughly 70 ha. This would make Djay a rather small town with a maximum of 14.000 inhabitants;[21] but then it may not have contained residential houses at all. As Isfahan's *shahristan* it may primarily have been a military and administrative center, while the majority of the civilian population probably lived in Yahudiyeh and nearby villages.

That the Isfahan enclave, regardless of the size of the urban center, must have formed one of the largest population clusters on the Plateau, is clear enough. Ibn Khurdadhbih states that it contained in Sassanian times 6.205 villages, 365 in each of the 17 subdistricts (rustaq).[22] The number of caravanserais and forts built by the Sassanians along the access roads show that the enclave was also a trade and communications center.[23]

Isfahan remained in political favor after the Muslim conquest. Successive rulers – Abbasids, Buyids, Kakuyids (a local line of princes), and Saldjuqs – enlarged and embellished the city, and the 10th-century travellers praised the flourishing agriculture, the textile industry, and the profitable long-distance trade. No other city, observed Ibn Hawqal, commanded such great numbers of camels for the caravan traffic.[24] According to Ibn Rusteh Isfahan at this time contained 20 districts with 2.300 villages. He included, however, both Qumand and Karadj (Igharayn) in his count. Other sources from the period include Yazd and Kashan.[25]

At the close of the 10th century Adud al-Dawleh constructed new city walls, 21.000 paces long (i.e. 16–20 km). Besides the inner city these walls must have surrounded also Yahudiyeh and other quarters which originally had been suburbs or villages.[26] This suggests that during Abbasid times the enclave had become increasingly urbanized, a process which occurred in many other enclaves serving as bases for the Empire (e.g. Kazwin, Ray, Nishapur). Under Saldjuq rule Isfahan achieved even greater priority, especially in the reign of Malik Shah (1072–1092) when the city became the de facto capital of Iranshahr. Malik Shah constructed several monumental buildings and laid out parks.[27] Even before this, in 1052, Nasir-é Khusraw described the city as "the most beautiful, populous, and prosperous in the land of the Persians (zamin-é pars)," adding that no ruined buildings were to be seen here.[28]

In the early 13th century, on the other hand, Yaqut saw many abandoned houses and ascribed this decline to the continual sectarian fighting.[29] The Gurwa'an and Bidabad quarters, which in 1200 had been among the most important in the city, were almost deserted by the beginning of the 14th century. Even the old shahristan, Djay, was in a state of decay. Yahudiyeh, however, had grown markedly and taken over the designation shahr-é Isfahan.[30]

Whether this shifting of settlement centers reflects decline in absolute terms is difficult to say. Mustawfi describes Isfahan of the early 14th century as a densely populated, prosperous enclave, containing 398 villages distributed over 8 districts; but the shifting administrative borders make it impossible to compare these figures with those given by Ibn Rusteh in the 10th century. Mustawfi adds that these villages were so large that in other places they would have been called towns (shahr); each village containing up to 1.000 houses in addition to bazaars, mosques, baths, etc.[31]

Of course, temporary decline may have been brought about by the various misfortunes and disasters befalling Isfahan in the time from the 10th to the 14th centuries. Severe epidemics visited the enclave in 935/36, 955/56, 1031/32 (the latter is said to have cost 40.000 lives), 1056/57 (presumably), and 1136/37.[32] Even famines were reported on several occasions, for instance in 1175.[33]

Like most other enclaves on the Plateau Isfahan was further afflicted by continual sectarian strife between Sunnis and Shi'ites and between the followers of the various Sunni law schools, primarily the Hanafi and the Shafi'i.[34] Richard Bulliet suggests that the explanation for this puzzling phenomenon must be sought in the gradual conversion to Islam in the centuries following the Arab conquest. He assumes that the first Persian converts were ostracized by their local communities. Moreover, since conversion at this time also entailed identification with the new empire, the converts gravitated to the Muslim dominated garrisons and administrative towns where they could turn their new religious status into social and material advantages. As conversion eventually became generalized, however, the descendants of the first converts attempted to maintain these advantages despite increasing pressure from the newly converted Muslims. Since the groups identified themselves with different legal schools, these conflicts took on a sectarian character.[35]

Though the details about the Mongol conquest of Isfahan are unclear, little destruction appears to have occurred on this occasions.[36] On other occasions, however, Isfahan did suffer considerable damage from warfare. When Timur-é Lenk sacked the city in 1387/88 as punishment for attacks on his tax collectors, 70.000 inhabitants are said to have been massacred.[37] Shah Rukh plundered the city at the beginning of the 15th century, and at the same time there are reports of an outbreak of *ta'un*, perhaps a reference to the plague.[38] The sack by Djahanshah Qara-qoyunlu in 1452 caused extensive damage to the irrigation systems; not surprisingly the city in 1473 made a sad impression on the Venetian Barbaro.[39]

The growth which Isfahan subsequently experienced, especially after having become the Safavid capital in 1598, need not be detailed here. European visitors in the 17th century – John Cartwright, Chardin, Olearius, Tavernier, and others – described it in flowery phrases and their estimates of the population ranged from 600.000 to 900.000. These figures must be greatly exaggerated; in 1972 Isfahan had just above 1/2 million inhabitants and it is difficulty to see how it could have supported a larger number in the past.[40]

Then, in 1722, the city was sacked by the Ghilzay Afghans after a prolonged siege which had caused famine and terrible hardship. Isfahan even lost its political status, as the capital was transferred, first to Shiraz and then to Tehran. Yet it recovered from this set-back. John Malcolm, who led a British legation to Iran in the beginning of the 19th century, believed that the city's population had in fact doubled, from 100.000 to 200.000, in the years between 1800 and 1812.[41] James Baillie Fraser, whom we already have cited as an authority on decline, was less positive. In 1834 the old capital seemed to him to be a thinly populated labyrinth of dilapidated and abandoned houses, having "about it an air of decay and fallen state which is exceedingly depressing." Unlike Isfahan, he added, Tabriz was a growing city characterized by an atmosphere of "bustle and prosperity."[42] Fraser's impression of a striking difference between these two cities reflects that in the 19th century Iran's political and economic centers were shifting to the northern provinces, largely because of the stimulus provided by the growing market in neighboring Russia for both Iranian labor and raw materials. In contrast, Isfahan's famous textile industry was nearly destroyed by the competition from the cheap European goods.[43] By the early 20th century British intelligence reports estimated Isfahan's population at 80.000, a modest figure which seems to confirm Fraser's impression of decay.[44] Besides the general economic shifting the terrible famine and the epidemics in 1870–72 may indeed have helped bring about a temporary decline.[45] However, in spite of all reverses Isfahan has survived as one of the largest settlements on the Plateau.

2. Ray

Like Isfahan, Ray was an ancient city; it probably reaches back into pre-historic times, though archaeological study of the site has been obstructed by the expansion of Tehran in recent decades.[46] But unlike Isfahan, Ray did not survive the vicissitudes of Iranian history. A combination of unfavorable environmental conditions appears to have been the underlying reason for this.

The enclave had some surface-water from streams coming down the Alburz (medieval sources list a variety of names).[47] Yet neither in size nor stability could these streams compare with the Zayandeh-rud, the river of Isfahan, and by late Achaemenid times Ray had been provided with extensive *qanat* systems which formed the basis for the dense settlement mentioned by the classical sources.[48]

About Sassanian Ray we know little, except that it must have been important. Like Isfahan it had a Nestorian bishop and a royal mint[49] and became the scene of new foundings. Thus the tradition states that Shah Firuz built the town Ram-Firuz in or close to Ray.[50] This may have been nothing more than a military base, but it is possible that the information reflects a transferring of the original settlement. A local source, cited by Yaqut, says that the city of Ray originally had been located farther east, in a place where ruins could still be seen at the time when the source was written and where the local population used to dig for buried treasure.[51] This may have been ancient Rhages. Throughout historical times the region has seen considerable seismic activity, and earthquakes may have caused the settlement to be moved in Sassanian times.

In any case, Ray was one of the settlements enlarged as an imperial base in Abbasid times: the crown prince al-Mahdi, in 774/775, founded the new quarter of *Muhammadiyeh*, outside the *shahristan* proper; he also built a palace in which his son

Harun (al-Rashid) was born.[52] Later, in the 10th century, Ray served as capital for the Buyids. At this time the geographical literature describes Ray as the largest and most prosperous city in the entire east after Baghdad. Besides being politically important, Ray was a center of caravan traffic along the Khurasan road and had a famed textile industry. To be sure, Nishapur was more extensive, Ibn Hawqal says, but not so densely populated.[53] Ray was said to cover 1 or 1 1/2 sq *farsakh*. Although this figure hardly can be taken as a literal expression of the extent of the built-up area, all available evidence is that 10th-century Ray was one of the major settlements on the Plateau.[54]

By the 14th century it was virtually abandoned. Usually the Mongols get the blame for this. Ibn al-Athir, for instance, says that they first sacked the city in 1220/1221, then returned in 1224 to destroy it completely. A later compiler, Ahmad al-Razi (16th century), cites information that 700.000 people were massacred on this occasion.[55] This seem to reflect myth rather than reality. One of Djalal al-Din Mankubirti's officials, Muhammad al-Nasawi, was in Ray in 1228/29 but says nothing about the destruction of the city.[56] Another Persian official, Djuwayni, writing in the 1270s, says that Ray capitulated peacefully; at no point does he refer to massacres or large-scale destruction.[57]

Yaqut, who visited Ray shortly before the arrival of the Mongols, says that 2/3 of all the houses were already in ruins at this time. He was told that the destruction was caused by violent sectarian fighting, first between Sunnis and Shi'ites, and then, after the Shi'ites had been eliminated, between Hanafis and Shafi'is. The entire enclave had been involved; even the rural population from the surrounding villages had armed themselves with their agricultural implements and then flocked to the city to join in the fighting.[58] Sectarian conflicts afflicted most of the towns on the Plateau, but seems to have been especially destructive in Ray and Nishapur, perhaps because the various hegemonic states intervened in the tensions here.

Yet other conditions must certainly have contributed to the decline of the ancient city. As early as 300 B.C. the enclave had been seriously damaged by an earthquake; other major shocks were recorded in 864/65 and 957/58. No doubt several smaller shocks occurred as well without being registered in the sources.[59] Both the larger and the smaller earthquakes must have damaged the *qanats* which formed a vital part of the water supply. Second, Ray was notorious for its frequent epidemics. The enclave was not only visited by the larger, transregional epidemics, but was apparently also the focus of some dangerous and highly contagious diseases of endemic character.[60] In both respects Ray clearly differed from Isfahan which enjoyed a "healthy climate" and was spared serious earthquakes.[61]

In the early 14th century one of the "good kings," Ghazan Khan, gave orders for Ray to be rebuilt, but without lasting results. The city was deserted for good and would not even be replaced by a new urban center nearby.[62] That Ray was abandoned does not mean that the entire enclave went out of cultivation as well. It

Table 9. The Abbasid assessment of Djibal (8th–10th Centuries) in dirhams; 'Ali b. 'Isa's figures in dinars, however.

	788	819/20	c. 840	840–73	918/19
Mihridjankadhak and Masabadhan[a]	4.000.000	2.200.000	2.500.000	2.700.000	74.496
Shahrazur[b]	1.000.000	2.750.000	3.500.000		
Mah al-Kufah (Dinawar)	7.000.000	5.000.000	5.700.000	3.000.000	195.198
Mah al-Basrah (Nihawand)	5.500.000	4.800.000	1.000.000		453.156
Karadj (Igharayn)		3.100.000[c]	3.400.000	"as Dinawar"	
Ray	12.000.000	20.200.000[d]	10.000.000	10.000.000	587.722
Kazwin		1.628.000[e]	1.500.000	1.200.000	174.000
Isfahan	11.600.000	10.500.000	10.000.000	7.000.000[f]	599.512
Qum		3.000.000	4.500.000	2.000.000	277.458
Hamadan	11.500.000	1.700.000	6.000.000		206.269

Sources:
Ibn al-Mutarrif (788).
Qudama (819/20).
Ya'qubi (c. 840).
Ibn Khurdadhbih (840–873).
'Ali b. 'Isa (918/19).
Note that *Hulwan* is not included. According to Ya'qubi (tr.: 68) this district belonged geographically to Djibal, but fiscally to Mesopotamia. Qudama (tr.: 185), however, maintains that it is included in the assessment of Djibal.

[a] These districts, with the towns Saymareh and Sirawan, were situated in the Zagros foothills south of Kirmanshah.
[b] Shahrazur stood in the foothills northwest of Kirmanshah.
[c] Variant: 3.800.0007.
[d] "Including Demawand."
[e] Variant: 1.828.000; Zandjan and Abhar were often included in the Kazwin assessment.
[f] Isfahan with Qum farmed for 16.000.000.

still contained several villages and by the 14th century one of these, Varamin, had taken over the function of enclave capital. However, it never approached ancient Ray in size or importance.[63] Later, Varamin was replaced by another small town, Tehran, situated just beside the ruins of Ray. The Spanish emissary Clavijo, in the early 15th century, described this town as large but unfortified, surrounded by a densely populated (and extremely hot) countryside.[64]

Shortly before 1800 Tehran became the capital of all Iran, but in size and economic activity it could not compare with large ancient cities like Isfahan. For some time it seems to have functioned like the *ordu-bazars* of earlier times, i.e. as service center for a travelling court. Hence, its population increased when the Shah was in residence and declined when he was not. British emissaries in the early 19th century estimated the resident population of the town to be no more than 10.000.[65] Not until the end of the century did Tehran's population exceed 100.000, a figure which ancient Ray may have equalled in its heyday.[66] Later Tehran grew quickly, especially after the Second World War; yet this growth took place under conditions quite different from those under which the towns and enclaves of the Plateau had existed in former times. We need only mention the introduction of modern means of communcation and transportation, modern water supply technology, and the development of the oil industry which for the first time provided the Iranian state with a substantial source of income independent of agriculture. The sprawling metropolis of modern Iran thus arose in a new historical context which also stimulated growth in most other towns, albeit to a less dramatic degree. Clearly present-day Tehran does not constitute a genuine continuation of the ancient city of Ray. On the contrary, seen within the framework of pre-industrial Iran, Ray must be counted as an indisputable case of decline.

3. The *Qanat*-Oases of Djibal

In the case of Ray the combination of unfavorable influences must have been unique, for its fate was certainly *not* representative of the *qanat*-based settlements in Djibal as a whole. Three such settlements will be briefly discussed here: Kazwin, Kashan and Yazd, each the center of a medium-sized enclave.

C. 150 km northwest of Ray, on an important road to the Daylami Highlands, Shapur I founded the fortified town Kazwin, officially called *Shad-Shapur*.[67] It was primarily a military base with a garrison of professional cavalry soldiers whose task was to fight the intractable Daylamis. The soldiers' maintenance was secured by the local agriculture through a system resembling the Muslim *qati'a* allotments.[68] This arrangement presupposed a sizable agricultural surplus. Kazwin was located in a thinly populated arid area, however, and thus the founding of the town had to be accompanied by the creation of an oasis which could supply the garrison.[69]

After the Arab conquest Kazwin remained an important military and adminis-trative center, the Empire's bastion against Daylam. The caliph al-Hadi (785–786) had it enlarged with new quarters;[70] Harun al-Rashid built a new Friday mosque and began construction of walls which would enclose both the original *shahristan* and the new quarters outside. These walls were not finished until 868/69 by Musa b. Buqa, a general under the caliph al-Mu'tazz. Musa also carried out an adminis-trative reorganization, transferring several districts to Kazwin. The town later profited from similar administrative rearrangements.[71]

Although Kazwin had originally been far away from the main lines of communi-cation and caravan routes, its military and administrative functions eventually attracted traffic. This served as an incentive to the rise of a textile industry and extensive camel-raising, and by the 10th century the geographical literature ranked Kazwin among the large and important towns in Djibal.[72]

This position was achieved in spite of the inadequate water supply of the site. With only a few seasonal streams, the town and enclave was highly dependent on *qanats*;[73] but as travellers noted, these were few and of quite moderate capacity.[74] Though governors and the local nobility often invested in extensions, there was apparently little overall improvement in the situation.[75] Earthquakes may have been partly responsible for this. A major shock occurred in 864/65 and was no doubt followed by others.[76] The town also saw a good deal of sectarian strife and wartime destruction. No less than 40.000 inhabitants are said to have lost their lives fighting Djebe and Sübedei's Mongols in 1220/21.[77] However, the information that Kazwin was razed on this occasion is just another exaggerated account of Mongol devastations in Iran. At least, Zakariyeh al-Kazwini and Mustawfi al-Kazwini both describe their native town as large and prosperous; European travellers from the 15th century give similar impressions.[78] In the period from 1555 to 1598 Kazwin was the capital of all of Iran and, as a result, expanded considerably. Decline inevitably followed when the Safavids transferred the capital to Isfahan.[79] Despite this and despite the wars of the 18th century Kazwin remained an important center for caravan traffic and textile production. Only at the beginning of this century, with the emergence of modern transportation technology and Tehran's increasing monopolization of economic activities, did Kazwin lose much of its traditional importance.

Kashan, on the edge of the Dasht-é Kavir between Isfahan and Ray, was founded by Harun al-Rashid's wife Zubaydah according to one tradition. Other traditions, such as the Arab accounts of conquest, suggest that it must in fact be older.[80]

Situated on a small seasonal river, Kashan in historical times has relied on *qanats* as well as on cisterns storing winter rain.[81] In the 10th century it is described as a small town, center of a fertile enclave, famous for its production of *kashi* porcelain and notorious for its poisonous scorpions and the "Shi'ite" beliefs of the inhabitants.[82] It is reported to have been ravaged by the Mongols in 1224,[83] but if this is correct, the consequences cannot have been lasting, for precisely in Ilkhanid times Kashan seems to have seen considerable growth thanks to its silk production and its location on the important north-south caravan route. Mustawfi states that the enclave contained 18 large villages, and around 1500 al-Ghiyati considered Kashan the most important town of Djibal after Isfahan.[84] European travellers of the 15th and 16th centuries described the town in positive terms as well. The English merchant Lionel Plumtree, in 1572, especially praised the puritan work ethic and discipline of the inhabitants:

"An idle person is not suffered to live amongst them. The child that is but five yeeres old is set to some labour. No ill rule, disorder or riote by gaming or otherwise is there permitted."

Playing cards or dice, he noted approvingly, was punishable by death.[85] Kashan survived all the disastrous reverses of the 18th century: the Afghan invasion, Nadir

Shah's campaigns, and the Zand-Qadjar wars. In the early 19th century it was described as "one of the most prosperous towns in Persia."[86]

Standing on the edge of the great desert, constantly threatened by the shifting sands, Yazd has survived through the constructing and maintaining of some of the largest *qanat* systems on the Plateau.[87] According to the *Tarikh-é Yazd*, a local chronicle from the 15th century, the town of Yazd (*shahr-é Yazd*), also called Katheh (Kete), was founded by Yazdgird b. Bahram, i.e. either Yazdgird I or Yazdgird II. Perhaps the story is just an etymological construction, yet it states in some detail who financed the various *qanats* and constructed the villages.[88] While neither Hamza Isfahani nor Tabari count any of the Yazdgirds among the great Sassanian colonizers, Yazdgird I does occupy a prominent place in the *Shahristan* list's shorter version of the foundation traditions (though without any specific reference to Yazd). In any case, the Arab accounts of conquest make it clear that Yazd must have existed before the middle of the 7th century. So the dating of Yazd to Sassanian times seems plausible.

Tenth-century Yazd is described as an attractive medium-sized town, noted for its textile production and export of dried fruit.[89] Unlike Kazwin and Ray, Yazd did not constitute an important base for the Abbasid empire and was therefore not enlarged at imperial command. From the 11th century Yazd formed the core of an independent principality ruled by successive dynasties: Kakuyids, Atabegs, Muzaffarids. All of these local rulers saw to it that new *qanats* were built, villages and fortifications constructed, and tamarisks planted to check the sand drifts.[90] Moreover, they did not challenge superior opponents and by voluntarily paying tribute they generally managed to save Yazd from large-scale wartime destruction. Marco Polo, who visited the town in 1271, described it as

"... a very fine and splendid city and a centre of commerce. A silken fabric called *yazdi* is manufactured here in quantity and exported profitably to many markets."[91]

Mustawfi al-Kazwini also speaks approvingly of the textile industry and the commercial activities, and in the tax assessments of the 14th century Yazd appears as Djibal's most important enclave after Isfahan.[92]

Later in the 14th century the Yazd enclave did suffer reverses. In 1391/92 it was sacked by Shah Mansur, one of the many warlords who fought for power on the Plateau after the collapse of the Ilkhanid Empire. In 1396, after a revolt, it was subjected to prolonged siege by Timur-é Lenk, and though Timur in this case departed from his usual procedure by refraining from massacre or destruction of the rebellious town, the famine accompanying the siege is said to have claimed the lives of 30.000 people. During the Timurid wars of succession new destructions followed, and in 1457 Pir Budaq, one of the Qara-qoyunlu leaders, extorted a huge

Table 10. The Assessment of Djibal, 1335–1341 (according to Mustawfi al-Kazwini).

	Dinar-é rayidj
Isfahan (incl. Firuzan)	984.500
Yazd	251.000
Hamadan	241.000
Kirmanshah/Kurdistan	201.500
Sultaniyeh	200.000
Ray	151.000
Kashan	117.000
Kazwin	110.000
Tarum[a]	64.000
Gulpaygan (Djurbazqan)	42.000
Aveh and Saveh	42.000
Qum	40.000
Nihawand	37.000
Farahan	37.000

Some smaller enclaves are not included in the list. When Mustawfi's figures are added together, the total assessment of Djibal reaches 2.849.400 dinar-é rayidj. Mustawfi (Nuzhat, tr.: 54) also lists a total sum, but only of 350.000 dinar-é rayidj. However, this is clearly a transcription error (the same figure is given for the city of Isfahan alone).

[a] The area between Zandjan and the Alburz mountains.

ransom from the enclave.[93] Apparently none of this had lasting consequences. Barbaro, in 1473, described Yazd as "v miles in circuite, with very great subvrbes, and yet in maner they all arr wevers and makers of divers kindes of sylkes." These textiles, he added, were exported far and wide, to India, Turkey, Chagatay, and China. Other European travellers in the 16th and 17th centuries have left similar descriptions.[94] During the Afghan wars in the beginning of the 18th century Yazd bought off the invaders, and in the early 19th century it was described by British officers as large and populous, an important trade center containing 24.000 houses.[95]

4. River-Irrigated Oases of Djibal

Hamadan, at an altitude of 1800 meters and notorious for its icy winter cold, was adequately supplied with surface-water by streams coming down from Mount Alvand.[96] In Achaemenid times it had been one of the imperial capitals and presumably Djibal's largest city. Not much is known of Hamadan in Sassanian times, except that it continued to be of considerable importance. Thus it was placed directly under royal administration and also housed a Nestorian see. The obviously incorrect statement in the Shahristan list that the city originally was founded by Yazdgird I perhaps reflects that some Sassanian constructions were carried out here.[97]

However, by early Muslim times, if not before, Hamadan had fallen behind Ray and Isfahan. The 10th-century geographers still describe it as an important town, covering 1 sq *farsakh* and surrounded by a fertile agricultural enclave; it also remained a center of communication between Mesopotamia and the Plateau.[98] But in most of the tax assessments it is ranked far below Ray and Isfahan. Probably this was not because Hamadan had suffered a decline; rather, the difference seems to reflect the growth of Ray and Isfahan.

During the Middle Ages Hamadan was afflicted by largely the same misfortunes as Ray: earthquakes, epidemics, sectarian fighting, and wartime destruction.[99] As usual the latter is said to have culminated with the Mongol invasion when, according to Ibn al-Athir, the inhabitants were massacred in 1220/21 and again in 1224.[100] Again it is doubtful whether this information is accurate. Nasawi confirms that Djebe and Sübedei plundered the enclave during their lightning campaign, but says nothing of an outright destruction. Djuwayni states that the city surrendered voluntarily, and nowhere says that it was destroyed.[101] That Hulagu later could use Hamadan as a base for his attack on Mesopotamia, strongly suggests that it had not in fact been razed.[102] Admittedly Ibn al-Faqih, in the 10th century, classified 765 villages as belonging to Hamadan, while Mustawfi, four hundred years later, listed only 212. But as Hamadan's administrative role had been reduced in the meantime, these figures cannot be taken as documentation for the decline caused by the ravages of the Mongols.[103] On the contrary Hamadan figures in the Ilkhanid tax assessments as one of the important enclaves of Djibal, though far below Isfahan.[104] Later Hamadan appears as an important stronghold, the site of frequent fighting against the Ottomans in the 16th and 18th centuries.[105] According to Kinneir, in the early 19th century it contained but 10.000 "meanly-built houses," yet remained a center of communication and caravan traffic. The hinterland is described as covered by villages and gardens.[106]

Two other oases need only be touched upon briefly. Qum must have been an enclave of some importance as early as in Parthian times, since the first Sassanians placed it directly under royal administration.[107] The center of the enclave in Sassanian times was located in Manidjan, a settlement where the existence of a pre-Muslim citadel is recorded in the 9th century. According to one tradition the center only took on urban character at the beginning of the 8th century, when Arab immigrants built walls around Manidjan and 6 other villages. The enclave was said to have contained a total of 40 villages at this time.[108]

The immigrants also carried out regulation of the water supplies by enforcing an agreement on water distribution upon the upriver settlements.[109] Qum certainly had hydrological problems. Though the local river was perennial, in summer the water turned quite salty and could be used for irrigation only, not for drinking.

Since the groundwater in the wells also turned salty, the inhabitants had to rely on rain-water stored in cisterns.[110]

In the 10th century the town is described as fairly large and surrounded by a fertile hinterland which produced, among other things, saffron. However, Qum was not noted for any industrial production.[111] The town was afflicted by both natural disasters, including a flood in 904/5, and war. As usual we have accounts of an especially destructive Mongol attack (1224), and by the early 14th century the town was in a state of advanced decay, if we can believe Mustawfi al-Kazwini.[112]

Yet Qum enjoyed some special advantages which helped it survive. Very early it had become a recognized center of Shi'ite learning and thus attracted students from throughout Iranshahr. To further enhance the town's status it was asserted that the Shi'ite saint Fatimah, sister to the eighth imam 'Ali al-Riza, had been buried here in 816/17. This important discovery seems first to have been made after the 14th century.[113] In any case, Fatimah's grave became a popular shrine to the town's great advantage, especially in Safavid times when the lords of Iran themselves were Shi'ites. Qum's religious status, on the other hand, caused the Sunni Afghans to pounce savagely on it in 1722. After the wars of the 18th century it made a sad impression on Kinneir and other British emissaries who described it as "a vast ruin."[114] Thanks to its religious status, however, Qum survived this setback as well.

Kirmanshah, according to most versions of the historical tradition, was founded by Kavadh I (i.e. at the beginning of the 6th century).[115] It stands in a valley on the outer edge of the Zagros watershed and is watered by the Qareh Su River. Ibn al-Faqih described the town as the "most pleasant between al-Mada'in (Ctesiphon) and the Oxus," and it served both in Sassanian times and after as a royal summer residence. Kirmanshah's location directly on the Khurasan road indicates that strategic considerations also played a role in its founding.

Kirmanshah belonged to Mah al-Kufah, i.e. the part of Mah (Media) which in early Muslim times was administered from Kufah. The center of this province was originally the town of Dinawar, situated in a valley between Kangavar and Kirmanshah. Dinawar, which in the 10th century was described as a considerable town of a size "2/3 of Hamadan's," no longer exists as an urban settlement. Its demise is generally attributed to Timur-é Lenk,[116] but decline had in fact begun long before and seems to have been closely related to the rise of Kirmanshah. By the 12th century Kirmanshah had surpassed Dinawar in size, taking over and subsequently retaining the function as the center of the region.[117] In the early 14th century Mustawfi al-Kazwini describes Dinawar as a small town with a prosperous hinterland. He adds that Kirmanshah too had declined considerably, perhaps because with Mesopotamia's collapse the Khurasan road lost some of its traditional importance.

After the Ottoman conquest of Mesopotamia, Kirmanshah frequently became a battleground. It is also mentioned as a center for semi-autonomous Kurdish princi-palities.[118] From the end of the 18th century Kirmanshah entered a phase of prolonged growth, partly as a result of Iran's gradual integration into the world market.

Summary

The history of Djibal shows no general trend towards decline. The cases cited present a confusing picture of fluctuations, involving growth as well as decline and, in a few cases, even settlement cessation. We see that in this respect the *qanat*-based enclaves did not differ from other oases in any marked way. Obviously the nature of the water resources was not decisive for the survival of the enclaves. The size of the water resouces was important, of course, but this problem was common to both *qanat*-irrigated and river-irrigated enclaves. Yet we note that both Kazwin and Qum survived in spite of inadequate water supplies. As to Ray, one of the most noticeable cases of decline on the Plateau, it is in fact difficult to point to any particularly decisive factor or set of factors. The Mongols can be excluded simply because the city was already in decline long before they appeared on the scene. Earthquakes probably were far more important, just as they were in the case of Nishapur in Khurasan. Yet other enclaves even more *qanat*-dependent than Ray, for instance Kazwin, survived frequent earthquakes. Ray even enjoyed the addi-tional advantage of being situated on the Khurasan road, Iranshahr's most important line of trade and communciation.

Location on the caravan routes is often cited as a factor which would ensure a settlement's survival in spite of natural disasters and wars, because trade brought with it income from service functions and customs duties and further stimulated the manufacturing of specialties and luxury goods for export. In the cases of Yazd and Kashan there is no doubt that precisely their location on the important caravan road along the edge of the Dasht-é Kavir contributed to their resiliency and prosperity. Yet Ray is not the only case in which strategic location failed to ensure survival.

Around 1200 the Ilkhans Arghun and Uldjaytu built a new imperial capital, Sultaniyeh, directly on the route between Tabriz and Kazwin. Even though Sultaniyeh was the official capital, it did not function as a residential city in the traditional sense, because the Ilkhans did not live permanently in one place; rather, they travelled continually with their camp, the *ordu*, between summer and winter pastures. As the plains east of Zandjan were favored as a summer camp, the new town was situated here to serve as an *ordu-bazar*, i.e. service and trading center for the rulers and their entourage.[119] Owing to this function Sultaniyeh attracted people from all parts of the Empire. By the mid-14th century it had reached 12.000 paces in circumference. It was said to contain more monumental buildings than any other town apart from Tabriz, and a large number of *qanats* and wells had been built provide water.[120]

The collapse of the Ilkhanid Empire did not have immediate consequences for the town, which retained its functions into Timurid times. Thus Clavijo described it in the beginning of the 15th century as populous, though smaller than Tabriz. Its commercial activity, on the other hand, was more extensive. The summer months in particular would see the arrival of large caravans with spice from India, silks from Gilan, cotton and silks from Shiraz, Yazd, and Khurasan, and pearls from Hormuz. These goods were then resold in Sultaniyeh to Turkish and Syrian merchants.[121]

Shortly afterwards, however, the town was sacked by Qara Yusuf Qara-qoyunlu who deported part of the population to Tabriz, Maragheh, and Ardabil.[122] Moreover, the post-Timurid rulers, the Qara-qoyunlus, the Aq-qoyunlus, and the Safavids, ceased using it as *ordu-bazar*, preferring instead Tabriz and Kazwin. Thus Barbaro, in the early 1470s, remarked that Sultaniyeh was now "but evill enhabited, having between vij and viij^{ml} people in it, peradventure more." When John Cartwright passed through in 1603, the town had been completely deserted.[123]

An example of a smaller *ordu-bazar* is Abarkuh, situated between Yazd and Shiraz and, strictly speaking, a part of Fars rather than Djibal. Abarkuh is described in the 11th century as a smallish, *qanat*-based oasis, productive but of no great importance.[124] It stood, however, on the nomads' route between summer and winter pastures, and since the nomads' political and military role grew in Ilkhanid times, the town evolved into a local *ordu-bazar* and even succeeded in attracting much of the caravan traffic going from Shiraz to Isfahan. This traffic had until then followed routes further to the west, passing through Yazd-é Khwast.[125]

As a result of the political changes in Safavid times, Abarkuh lost its commercial functions and quickly returned to its former state as a small, insignificant agricultural enclave. As a reminder of its brief period of flowering in the 14th and 15th centuries, there remain a few monumental buildings, among them a huge Friday Mosque. Their dilapidated state endows the small town with a gloomy air of decay.

Obviously caravan routes were not unchangeable. They shifted with the rise and fall of new markets, the degree of security on the roads, and the like, and these changes could deprive a city of important economic assets. This was the case with Abarkuh, but not with Sultaniyeh: the route between Tabriz and Kazwin remained an important line of trade and communication. Sultaniyeh declined because it was no longer used by the rulers and their court. In brief, the degree of political favor was a factor at least as important as strategic location and water resources.

Note: Kumis and Gurgan

Since these two peripheral regions are mentioned only briefly in the medieval sources, it is difficult to discern any processes of change. The land of *Kumis* consisted of the narrow strip between the Alburz and the Dasht-é Kavir, east of Ray. One of Iranshahr's smallest territories, it was important to the Empire primarily because the Khurasan road ran through it. Fiscally it was certainly of little importance. But in our context the land is interesting because here we find some key environmental influences similar to those in Ray and Kazwin.

In Parthian times Kumis had possessed a political center of some importance in Hecatompylus, although this town had been abandoned as early as the time of the birth of Christ. The reason may have been that the Arsacids ceased residing in it after their conquest of Mesopotamia when the imperial center was transferred to the west. In Sassanian times we hear of Kumis mainly in connection with military affairs. Thus, in the 5th century, Yazdgird II used *shahristan-é Kumis* as base for his war against the Chul/Sul, an ethnic or political group in the Gurgan region.[126] *Shahristan-é Kumis*, or *shahristan-é Yazdgird* as it is called in Syriac and Armenian sources, must have been identical with present-day *Damghan* which was the regional capital when the Arabs arrived in the 7th century.[127] Local traditions, collected in the 10th century, tell of Sassanian irrigation-works, including a dam with branching canals at Chesmeh-é 'Ali, a spring situated above Damghan town.[128]

Surface finds in the Damghan area, however, indicate that settlement expansion during Parthian and Sassanian times was limited. If the dating is correct, the majority of the *qanats* adding to the modest supplies of surface-water were probably not built until early Muslim times, perhaps as part of an urbanization process.[129] In spite of these *qanats*, water supplies remained inadequate. Besides, Damghan was struck by frequent earthquakes. The worst shock appears to have occurred in 856/857.

Though the number of victims is obviously inflated in the sources, the figures leave the impression of an extraordinary disaster. Finally, Damghan is said to have been taken by the Mongols in 1220/1221.[130] To this we can add further disasters and wartime destruction in later times. The point is that Damghan, like Kazwin, survived environmental handicaps such as inadequate water supply and earthquakes. The two other ancient towns in Kumis, Simnan and Bastam, both suffering similar problems, also survived. The fourth town of the region, Shahrud, situated near Bastam, is believed to be of more recent date.[131]

The *Gurgan* Plain, thanks to its rivers and rainfall, enjoyed hydrological advantages over the rest of the Plateau. As we have seen, it was densely settled as early as in Achaemenid and Parthian times, and there are archaeological indications that the noticeable expansion in the Parthian era continued into the Sassanian. The historical tradition adds that Shah Firuz built a town here, *Rawshan-Firuz*, perhaps identical with the 200 hectare archaeological site known as Bibishirvan, about 100 km west of Gunbad-é Kabus.[132]

Otherwise Gurgan appears in the historical tradition primarily as the scene of endless wars against the Chul and the Haytal. The disastrous battle in 484, which cost Firuz his life and destroyed the entire Sassanian eastern army, was probably fought here.[133] The tradition ascribes the construction of the *Sadd-é Iskandar* (*Qizil Alan*), i.e. the long line of fortifications stretching across the Gurgan plain, to Firuz and his successors, Kavadh I and Khusraw I. However, as already noted there are signs that construction had in fact begun as early as Parthian times. A similar defensive line was built by the Sassanians farther towards the west at Tamis (Tamiseh), near Bandar-é Gaz in Mazandaran.[134] Against whom these massive fortifications were erected remains unclear, but they do show that Gurgan in the 5th and 6th centuries was the scene of violent events. The reference to a Nestorian bishop and a *marzban* would suggest that the Sassanians maintained a foothold in the region. In connection with the early raids before 650 the Arab accounts of conquest mention a "king of Gurgan" called Raznan (or Rawzan) Sul. This may be an indication that during the Sassanian civil wars the Chul had conquered part of Gurgan; on the other hand it may simply mean that parts of Gurgan formed a Sassanian vassal state.[135]

In the 10th and 11th centuries, Gurgan had two large urban centers: Gurgan town, the *shahr-é Gurgan*, situated a few kilometers from present-day Gunbad-é Kabus, and *Astarabad*, today known as Gurgan. The capital, the *shahr-é Gurgan*, which according to some traditions had been founded by the Arab general Yazid b. Muhallab in 716/717, stood on the Gurgan river. In the geographical literature it is famed for its fertile hinterland, its abundance of cheap foodstuffs, and its textile industry. It is further said that the town was nearly as large as Ray.[136] This is no doubt much exaggerated. The remains of the town today cover about 150 ha, but Old Nishapur, which was always referred to as one of the few cities comparable to Ray, covered during the same period more than 1500 ha. Mustawfi al-Kazwini also more modestly estimates the circumference of *shahr-é Gurgan* as 7.000 paces. According to his settlement statistics this would make the *shahr-é Gurgan* a "medium-sized town."[137]

Gurgan town and the region as a whole were notorious for something else: a lethal rate of infection. It was even known as "the graveyard of the people of Khurasan," and legend had it that when the angels divided the world amongst them, the Angel of Death received Gurgan as part of his share. The sources ascribe the frequency of pestilences to the changeable and damp weather.[138]

In Saldjuq times Turkoman nomads immigrated into the region. However, this does not seem to have affected agriculture adversely. The nomads were presumably assigned pastures in the Atrak region, north of the arable lands proper, and were closely supervised by the Saldjuk state.[139] The Saldjuqs, and especially Malik Shah, according to Mustawfi al-Kazwini favored Gurgan town; the remains of various buildings from Saldjuq times support this information.[140] Later the town is said to have been stormed by the Mongols and – if we are to believe Mustawfi – it never recovered from this. Since the site has yielded no sherds nor remains of buildings from the time after the 13th century, he may be right, even though it must be clear by now that we cannot accept the accounts of Mongol excesses without reservation.[141] In any case, a new urban settlement, Gunbad-é Kabus, arose immediately next to Gurgan town.

In Ilkhanid times, Astarabad, situated in the western part of the region, became the regional capital, the new *shahr-é Gurgan*. This town was apparently visited by the plague in the middle of the 14th century; in 1384 it was taken by Timur, who massacred the inhabitants. Astarabad survived these disasters and in Safavid times achieved some importance as base for a Turkish noble family, the Qadjars, who shortly before 1800 conquered the Plateau.[142]

Owing to the fragmentary nature of the data, it is difficult to catch the nuances. Perhaps the Gurgan region did suffer some settlement decline by the standards of Parthian-Sassanian times, but the extent and causes are unknown. In any case, settlements were not widely discontinued, nor was agriculture generally replaced by extensive methods forms of subsistence. In spite of the wars of the 18th century and the constant danger of Turkoman raids, Astarabad in the mid-19th century had about 18.000 inhabitants.[143] Neither the new nor the old *shahr-é Gurgan* can have had substantially larger populations in earlier times.

However, cessation of settlement did occur in Dihistan, the old agricultural enclave north of the Atrak. Soviet archaeologists have ascribed this to destructions by the Mongols and later by Timur-é Lenk.[144] Yet there are chronological objections to this explanation. Al-Muqaddasi, in the 10th century, certainly states that the capital of Dihistan, Akhur (not localized), was the center of an agricultural enclave, which he described as the most populous in Gurgan. This would indicate continuity of the ancient Dihistan enclave, yet both al-Istakhri and Ibn Hawqal describe Dihistan as thinly populated, containing only a few forts and villages which largely relied on fishing in the Caspian Sea.[145] If the latter authors are right, intensive cultivation and settlement in the area must already have been strongly reduced by the 10th century. The causes, then, should not be sought in the Mongol wars, but rather in the break-down of the old canal systems which had carried water from the Atrak. However, the available data do not allow us to establish a precise chronology nor the exact causes for this decline.

Chapter 13

Fars

According to the Abbasid assessments Fars was the most important region on the Plateau after Djibal. That it had occupied a similar position in earlier times is clear from the fragmentary Sassanian assessment and from the large-scale colonization activities which the Sassanian kings carried out here. The historical tradition records in considerable detail four major city-foundings:

Gur (*Firuzabad*), founded by Ardashir I in the Shur Valley. The port of Siraf was possibly part of this project.[1]

Rev-Ardashir (*Rishahr*), also founded by Ardashir I and subsequently peopled with prisoners of war by Shapur I. The precise location is unknown, but in late Sassanian times the town was important enough to be the seat of the Nestorian metropolitan bishop of all Fars.[2]

Veh-Shapur (*Bishapur*), founded by Shapur I near present-day Kazirun. Ibn al-Balkhi says that Shapur was not content with building the town itself, but also carried out construction projects in the surrounding areas.[3]

Arradjan, founded by Kavadh I on the border between Khuzistan and Fars. The official name of the town was *Veh-az-Amid-Kavadh*, "Kavadh's-(town)-better-than-Amida," presumably because some of the captives from Amida (Diyarbakir) were settled here. The names "Ram-Kavadh" and "Bar-Kavadh" are also mentioned.[4] Ibn al-Faqih further says that Kavadh founded a town named *Kavadh-Khurreh*. According to Ibn al-Balkhi this name referred to the Arradjan region, but the earlier geographers, though not making it quite clear whether it was a town or a district, locate it southeast of Firuzabad, near present-day Qir.[5]

From the archaeological material and diverse information in the written sources it appears that construction activity and colonization in Sassanian times went considerably beyond these four towns. First, settlement and irrigation was extended on the Marvdasht Plain in the Nayriz Basin, the original homeland of the Sassanian dynasty, and in the adjacent Maharlu Basin.[6] Second, Fasa – in Achaemenid times little more than a fort on the road between Marvdasht and southern Kirman – was enlarged. In the 10th century it is described as one of the major settlements in Fars, highly dependent on *qanats*.[7]

Finally, there is evidence of a considerable colonization effort in the desolate, inhospitable lands south and east of Firuzabad and Fasa: Mandistan, Irahistan, and Laristan. Apart from the coastal stretches, which receive some monsoon rains, this region is extremely arid. The discharge of the rivers is negligible, and the ground-

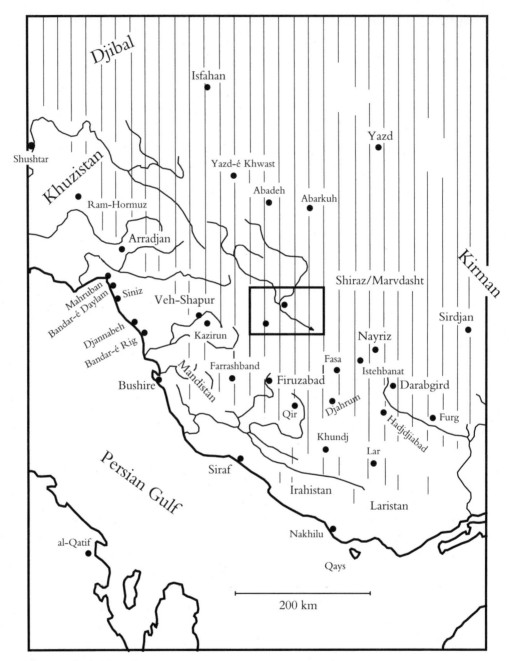

Fig. 9. Sketch-Map of Fars.

Table 11. The assessment of Fars.

	Dirhams
6th Century (Sassanians)	c. 57.000.000[a]
788.	27.000.000[b]
819.	24.000.000[c]
840–70	33.000.000[d]
911/12	18.000.000[e]
918/19	c. 38.000.000[f]
c. 960	c. 40.000.000[g]
c. 980	c. 49.000.000[h]
1335.	c. 13.700.000[i]

In the 1335 assessment Shabankareh is included as part of Fars, but Yazd is not. On the other hand, Yazd is included in the earlier assessments. According to Ibn Hawqal (tr., II: 298), 'Ali b. 'Isa extended taxation to include vineyards and fruit trees which until then had been exempt.

[a] Ibn Khurdadbih (tr.: 34) gives the figure as 40 million *mithqals* of silver. Ibn al-Balkhi (tr.: 83) has a more modest figure, 36 million dirhams in the time of Khusraw I. Ibn al-Faqih (tr.: 249) has 40 million dirhams.
[b] According to al-Mutarrif (el-'Ali: 1971).
[c] Qudama (de Goeje tr.: 184).
[d] Ibn Khurdadbih (tr.: 34); Ibn al-Faqih (tr.: 247) has 33–35 million.
[e] Ibn al-Furat cited by Miskawayh (tr., IV: 268).
[f] 'Ali b. 'Isa cited in von Kremer (1888: 313f); the figure given is 1.892.560 dinars (converted at the rate of 1:20).
[g] Ibn Hawqal (tr., II: 299). He says that Fars paid more than 1.500.000 dinars (convertion rate 1:20), to which should be added half a million from Arradjan.
[h] Ibn al-Balkhi (tr.: 83ff): 2.466.000 dinars in the reign of Adud al-Dawleh. Here converted at the rate of 1: 20. Ibn al-Balkhi himself used a rate of 1: 12, which yields 29.6 million dirhams.
[i] Mustawfi (*Nuzhat*, tr.: 112, 137): 3.137.300 *dinar-é rayidj*, here converted according to silver weight.

water in most places is too deep to be reached by *qanats*.[8] Agriculture was widely practiced by various dry farming methods. For instance, Ibn al-Balkhi in the 11th century describes how the inhabitants of Irahistan planted date palms at the bottom of deep pits which collected the winter rain and prevented wasteful run-off.[9]

In this region there are few archaeological traces of pre-historic settlement, no doubt because the extensive agriculture could support only a dispersed and mobile population.[10] Permanent settlement had to await the construction of water works for collecting and storing the winter rain, and this did not happen until Sassanian times. This assumption is based on the many remains of cisterns, storage dams, fire temples, and settlements which from technical and stylistic features can be dated to this period. Among these remains are a large dam at Qutabad (some 20 km north of Djahrum), a considerable site at Khundj, and the ruins at Hadjdjiabad between Lar and Darabgird. The latter can be precisely dated to the reign of Shapur II (4th century).[11]

The medieval sources list the names of several settlements in the arid southeastern parts of Fars, but with the exception of Ibn al-Balkhi's *Fars-nameh* they provide little additional information. It is clear, however, that the large *qanat*-watered settlement of Djahrum had existed already in Sassanian times;[12] no doubt the same is true of most of the other small towns mentioned. Lar, later the most important town in the area, first appears in the sources in the 13th century, at the time when the caravan routes from Shiraz to Hormuz began to attract growing traffic. Yet this says little about the age of the settlement.[13]

The expansion of settlement in Irahistan and Laristan appears to have been an extension of the colonization of southern Fars. No doubt it was the Sassanian crown which began this expansion in the same way as it did in the arid north Kirman. The motive must be sought primarily in military considerations. Commercial interests can only have been of secondary importance, as the caravan routes from the Gulf to the interior of Fars in this period ran from Siraf. However, a military consolidation in southeastern Fars – as well as in any other arid and peripheral region – must have required some agricultural expansion to provide income for the soldiers.

In the assessment from 1335 Fars still appears as one of the Plateau's most important regions, although the prosperous Yazd enclave had been administratively transferred to Djibal. The figures reproduced by Mustawfi al-Kazwini further show that Shiraz, with 450.000 *dinar-é rayidj* out of a total assessment of three million, was by far the most important enclave. However, since the earlier Abbasid assessments do not provide figures for individual enclaves, but only a total for the whole country, a comparison will not reveal whether significant shifts had occurred in the intervening period.

That changes must have occurred at some later date is clear from the sad picture of Fars drawn by European travellers in the 19th century. Their descriptions are often so precise that the impression of decline cannot be ascribed solely to the different perspective of the Europeans. But lack of sources makes it difficult to determine when (and why) this decline had taken place. Thanks to Ibn al-Balkhi's *Fars-nameh* we have a reasonably clear picture of Fars around 1100, but after this date there is an almost complete gap until Safavid times. The information provided by Mustawfi al-Kazwini, apart from the figures of the 1335 assessment, is largely a paraphrase of the *Fars-nameh*. Ibn Battuta travelled twice in Fars, shortly before 1330 and again in 1347, but he provides little more than descriptions of Shiraz and Lar. Hence, the changes which took place in Fars during the Middle Ages can only be roughly identified.

1. Shiraz and Marvdasht

The archaeological surveys in the Nayriz Basin, the ancient center of Fars along the Kur River, have focused particularly on the pre-historic settlement and little effort has been made to distinguish later historical periods. So much is clear, however, that Sassanian and early Muslim times together saw a marked expansion of settlement.[14]

This expansion was based on the construction of several weirs across the Kur and

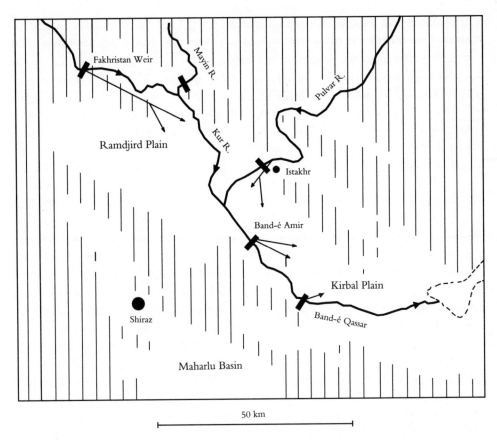

Fig. 10. Sketch-Map of Shiraz and the Marvdasht Plain (11th Century). Cf. Kortum (1976).

its tributaries. Sources from the 10th and 11th centuries mention several such weirs. Ibn al-Balkhi thus lists four, one in Ramdjird (the northern part of Marvdasht) and three in Kirbal farther down the Kur River. At least two of these were pre-Muslim.[15]

One was the Ramdjird weir. Ibn al-Balkhi says that it had been damaged during the Arab conquest and later repaired by the Saldjuq Atabeg Djauli around 1100. As the Atabeg bore the official honorary name Fakhr al-Dawleh, the restored weir was renamed *Fakhristan*. Presumably it is identical with the ruins of the Band-é Dukhtar in the Durudzan Canyon above Ramdjird.[16] The second pre-Muslim weir was the *Band-é Qassar*, also called *Band-é Fayzabad*, which raised water for the lower Kirbal Plain. This, too, was repaired by Djauli.[17]

Ibn al-Balkhi does not say in so many words who built these two weirs, and the ruins themselves fail to provide any clear indications of age. As stated, they may go back to Achaemenid times. On the other hand Marvdasht was less densely settled in

Achaemenid times than later and would not yet have needed extensive irrigation works. Most likely, therefore, the two weirs were of Sassanian origin, though they may have been extensions of smaller, earlier constructions. The remains of a large diversion from the Pulvar, a tributary to the Kur, means that near Istakhr there must have existed yet another weir, though this is not mentioned by Ibn al-Balkhi.[18]

A further expansion of the irrigation systems and the cultivated area occurred in the 10th century, under Buyid rule, when Adud al-Dawleh built the famous *Band-é Amir* weir. It raised water for the upper Kirbal Plain, an area which until that time had remained uncultivated. Another large weir across the Mayin, a small tributary to the Kur on the northern plain, should perhaps be dated to this period as well.[19]

During this expansion the political and urban center of the Nayriz region was transferred from Istakhr to Shiraz. Istakhr, located immediately north of the Marv-dasht Plain proper, had in Sassanian times enjoyed considerable favor. It had been the center of the Anahita cult and the native town of the dynasty, and seems to have retained a particular relation with the royal family, similar to Persepolis' relations with the Achaemenids. This did not prevent Istakhr from also becoming the seat of a Nestorian bishop.[20] Yet it did not take any administrative or political precedence over Fars' other towns: Veh-Shapur, Firuzabad, Darabgird, Rev-Ardashir and Arradjan. The size of the site shows that Istakhr was in fact a rather small town.[21]

The Arab conquest of Fars was hard-fought; according to Ibn al-Balkhi Istakhr rebelled several times and was subjected to retaliatory massacres.[22] At the end of the 7th century, however, the Arabs built a new *shahristan* next to the Sassanian town, and this means that Istakhr in spite of everything continued to serve as the local center.[23] At the end of the 10th century the town was severely damaged in the fighting which followed the collapse of Buyid rule, and Ibn al-Balkhi says that in his time (*c.* 1100), it was largely abandoned.[24] The reason for this can hardly have been wartime destructions alone. First Istakhr had lost its religious status with the conversions, and then it had to compete with the neighboring urban center of Shiraz.

Situated in the arid Maharlu Basin 50 km south of Istakhr, Shiraz had been founded as a *misr*, a garrison town, by the Arabs in the late 7th century. Nearby was an existing Parthian-Sassanian settlement, which perhaps already bore the name Shiraz (today the remains of this settlement is known as Qasr-é Abu Nasr).[25]

By Abbasid times Shiraz had achieved pre-eminence above the other towns in Fars. Ibn Khurdadhbih refers to it as capital not only of the old Firuzabad region, but of the whole country, and his route descriptions show that it had become the center of all trade and communication in Fars.[26]

During the 10th and 11th centuries Shiraz was further favored by the Buyids. They improved the water supply and built palaces, a hospital, and walls 12.000 *zira'* (*c.* 7 km) long. Adud al-Dawleh even built a new quarter, *Fana-Khusraw-gird*, with bazaars and houses for the garrison. The rents of the shops alone brought the state

16.000 dinars a year, a sign of the town's prosperity in this period.[27] The construction of the Band-é Amir and the expansion of cultivation on the Marvdasht Plain was closely linked to this enlargement of Shiraz. The town could not be supplied from its own immediate hinterland in the dry Maharlu Basin, but got both food and raw materials for the textile industry from within a radius of 50 km. Most came from Marvdasht, the largest agricultural enclave in Fars.[28]

In the second part of the 11th century Shiraz, together with most of Fars, suffered much destruction during the Shabankareh wars. Around 1100 the town was practically in ruins, and Adud al-Dawleh's newly constructed quarter had been razed and literally plowed over.[29] Later, Saldjuq governors succeeded in pacifying most of the country and began rebuilding. The Atabeg Djauli in particular is praised for his efforts in this respect.[30]

In the 12th, 13th, and 14th centuries Shiraz and Marvdasht formed the basis for successive semi-independent rulers such as the Salghurids, the Indju'ids, and the Muzaffarids. Owing to their protection the town regained its trade and reputation for prosperity. The Salghurids thus entered into a voluntary tributary agreement with the Mongols, thereby sparing the region new wars.[31]

Around 1300 Shiraz appears virtually as a republic ruled by the leading merchant families (formally under Ilkhanid sovereignty of course). Ibn Battuta visited the town in the mid-14th century and describes it in effusive tones.[32] Later it was apparently ravaged twice by Timur, in 1387 and 1393, and subjected to extortionate taxation by the Qara-qoyunlus around 1460.[33] Nevertheless ten years later Barbaro describes it as

"very great, of 20 miles compass, reckoning the suburbs withall. It contains innumerable people and is full of merchants (...) and may contain 200 thousand houses, or peradventure more."[34]

Another Italian who visited Shiraz at the same time estimated the population at a more modest 200.000, but added that it was Persia's most important city.[35] While these figures are improbable, they show that Shiraz impressed even those travellers who had visited other large cities.

Shiraz' subsequent fate was characterized by fluctuations, which may be very briefly summarized here. Largely on the basis of European travel descriptions the Safavid period (the 16th and 17th centuries) is thought to have been one of stability and prosperity. During the Afghan wars, in the beginning of the chaotic 18th century, Shiraz was plundered, but as capital of Karim Khan Zand (1750–1779), whose rule extended over most of southern and central Iran, the city again enjoyed political favor. A large new bazaar was built and the water supply improved.[36] Thanks to the political astuteness of the patricians Shiraz was spared during the wars between the Zand and the Qadjars,[37] and by the 19th century it had again attained

status as one of Iran's largest and most important cities, even though it made
different impressions on the British diplomats and agents in John Malcolm's suite.
To Ouseley Shiraz appeared to be "rapidly hastening to decay," while Kinneir
described it favorably as a center of trade and industry with 40.000 inhabitants.[38]
Later in the 19th century the increasing flood of European manufactured goods and
the general northward shift of economic activity disrupted local economies in
Shiraz and the rest of southern and central Iran, but this development lies outside
the scope of the present inquiry.

From travel descriptions and from the existence of many deserted villages, it
appears that settlement and cultivation on the Marvdasht Plain saw continuous
fluctations as well. These were caused by wartime destructions, especially in the
18th century, and by changes in fiscal practices, but clearly by hydrological changes
and salination as well.[39] Today it is estimated that up to 1/5 of the agricultural land
on the plain is salinated to varying degrees, the situation being worst in the
low-lying areas close to the Nayriz salt lake. Ouseley, at the beginning of the 19th
century, observed that it was precisely the Kirbal district farthest down the Kur
River which contained most deserted settlements. On the other hand "Bandamir,"
i.e. the Band-é Amir district, was densely populated. Kinneir also thought that
Marvdasht was "rich and populous."[40]

In the long term, then, Shiraz and Marvdasht constituted a resilient enclave in
spite of continuous fluctuations. This resiliency is thrown in relief by the fact that
nearly all other towns in Fars declined and in some cases even ceased to exist
between the 11th and 19th centuries.

2. Firuzabad

Firuzabad, situated on the Shur River in a valley 125 km south of Istakhr, was
founded by Ardashir I, no doubt to commemorate the victories which had made
him master of central Fars. According to the historical tradition it was precisely this
founding which provoked the Parthian high king's anger and precipitated the
Sassanian revolt.[41] The official name of the town was *Ardashir-Khurreh*, but it was
commonly known as *Gur* (Djur in Arabic), until Adud al-Dawleh in the 10th
century renamed it Firuzabad. Apparently "Gur" (which can also mean "tomb")
sounded a little too ominous.[42]

The historical accounts and the site itself show that the founding was planned on
a large scale. First Ardashir built a great fortress, the Qaleh-é Dukhtar, and then he
drained the swampy valley and regulated the river. The tradition has it that the latter
projects were carried out by a famous master-engineer, Burazeh, who was killed
during the final tunnel work. The town itself was circular, like Veh-Ardashir in
Mesopotamia, and covered an area of about 300 hectares.[43] It too became the seat of
a Nestorian bishop.[44]

In itself the founding of Firuzabad marked an advance into the hitherto thinly populated areas of southern Fars, but the new town apparently also served as base for further expansion. Mihr Narseh, one of Bahram V's generals, who owned or controlled large areas in the Ardashir-Khurreh district, is said to have colonized Farrashband, 50 km west of Firuzabad. He founded four villages with fire temples and laid out three plantations with 12.000 olive trees, 12.000 date palms, and 12.000 cypress trees respectively. Remains of the fire temples can still be seen.[45]

Also Siraf (now Bandar-é Tahiri), the largest and most important port of Fars in the 9th-11th centuries, was a Sassanian foundation. The remains of numerous Sassanian cisterns and caravanserais lining the routes leading from Siraf to the towns in the interior, i.e. Firuzabad, Fasa, Darabgird, indicate that Siraf had been the major port even in pre-Muslim times.[46] According to the historical tradition Ardashir I further founded a port, *Batn-Ardashir*, on the east coast of Arabia near al-Qatif. This is perhaps a sign that the Sassanians systmatically attempted to gain control over the trade and maritime traffic in the Gulf. If so, Siraf must have held a key position.[47]

In the 10th century Firuzabad was described as a prosperous medium-sized town, surrounded by gardens and parks and a fertile hinterland that extended for one *marhaleh*. The enclave was especially noted for its roses and the production of *djuri* rosewater, a specialty which was exported as far as "Maghrib and China." Firuzabad also enjoyed the favor of the Buyids, as Adud al-Dawleh occasionally used it as residence.[48]

Ibn al-Balkhi says nothing of destructions during the Shabankareh wars, but the anonymous copyist who brought Ibn Hawqal up to date remarks that by the middle of the 12th century Firuzabad was in decline.[49] At some later date it was deserted for unknown reasons and replaced by a new settlement a few kilometers away. But this settlement never achieved the reputation or size of Old Firuzabad. Waring, who passed through in the summer of 1802, thought that it was about the size of Shiraz, but added: "the houses are falling into decay." Shortly afterwards Kinneir called it "an inconsiderable place." However, both observed that the valley remained under fairly intensive cultivation.[50] Yet in 1857 consul Abbott was told that the entire Firuzabad district contained but 700 families.[51] Much of the decline and de-urbanization so obvious in the Firuzabad enclave by the 19th century thus seems to have occurred rather recently.

3. Darabgird and Fasa: De-urbanization and Decline in Eastern Fars

Darabgird, the model of Firuzabad, dated from Parthian times. In Sassanian times it too became the seat of a Nestorian bishop and is described, in the 10th century, in the same terms as Firuzabad: prosperous, medium-sized, and surrounded by a productive hinterland. The water, however, was said to be of poor quality. The specialty of Darabgird was *mumiya*, a kind of bitumen, which was widely exported as a remedy against fractures and disease.[52]

Around 1100, Ibn al-Balkhi tells us, Darabgird was largely in ruins. No explanation is offered, however. The Shabankareh princes subsequently transferred the political center of eastern Fars to the fortress of Shahr-é Idj, located in a small valley north of Darabgird. Diversion of water here may have adversely affected the water supplies of Darabgird and contributed to the town's decline. In the mid-14th century the Muzaffarids destroyed Shahr-é Idj and though the valley remained under cultivation the fortress was never reconstructed. Darabgird, however, was rebuilt just north of its old location, on a site where the conditions for diverting water from the River Rudbal were more favorable.[53]

In the British reports from the early 19th century Darabgird itself is described as dilapidated but its hinterland as well-cultivated. Kinneir estimated that the town had 15.000–20.000 inhabitants, yet this seems overly optimistic; even in its heyday the original Darabgird cannot have had more.[54] Fifty years later, Abbott thought Darabgird "a mere casabeh or large village." The entire enclave contained 64 villages with a settled population of no more than 2.300 families. The Darab Plain now served as winter pasture for the Baharlu tribe, part of the Khamseh federation (the summer pastures were located on the Marvdasht Plain).[55]

Abbott was further told that the number of date palms in the preceeding fifty years (i.e. since Kinneir's time) had fallen from 100.000 to 30.000. No explanation is given. At the time of Abbott's visit Darabgird had been attacked by locusts for seven years in succession, which, not surprisingly, had caused the peasants "the utmost distress."[56] As with Firuzabad, it is not clear why and when the decline occurred, but again there are indications that at least some of the decline noted in the European accounts must have been fairly recent.

In the Middle Ages the Darabgird district contained another fairly important town, *qanat*-watered Fasa. It had textile industries and a considerable caravan trade and was said to be as large as Shiraz or even Isfahan, a considerable exaggeration in view of the actual extent of the site.[57] By 1100 it was declining like most other towns in Fars. After the Shabankareh wars a new town was founded a few kilometers farther north, but this failed to regain the prosperity and size of its predecessor. Ouseley, in the early 19th century, found Fasa decayed and impoverished, no doubt because the *qanats* of the enclave had been systematically destroyed during the Qadjar war of succession a few years before. In the middle of the century Abbott described Fasa as "merely a large village of some 900 families," surrounded by an enclave with 33 small villages. Like Darabgird, Fasa had been ravaged by locusts Abbott's visit, and this may explain why the consul formed such an extremely sorry impression of the place.[58]

A third town in eastern Fars, Nayriz, had also been deserted by the early 19th century. Apart from agriculture there remained little economic activity in this area, except in the small town of Istahbanat where Ouseley noted some textile production and a ceramic industry that turned out imitations of Chinese porcelain.[59]

4. Veh-Shapur and Arradjan: De-urbanization and Decline in Western Fars

Veh-Shapur (Bishapur), founded by Shapur I in a narrow river-watered valley 130 km west of Shiraz, was another large-scale project that included th: construction of both irrigation works and huge palaces. The site still covers about 800 hectares.[60] The palaces, together with the reliefs which the Sassanian kings carved on the cliffs to commemorate victories and coronations, suggest that the town had a special relationship, perhaps of a ritual nature, with the dynasty. This, however, did not prevent the town from being the seat of a Nestorian bishop.[61]

By the early 9th century the town of Naubandegan (Nawbandjan) farther north had taken over Veh-Shapur's position as regional center, and towards the end of the 10th century Veh-Shapur, according to al-Muqaddasi, was rapidly declining.[62] The fall of the Sassanians had deprived the town of imperial favor and that may have been the major factor in the decline, but an exceptional level of infection seems to have contributed as well. The sources describe the surroundings of the town as "unhealthy" and the inhabitants as "yellow and sickly," an indication of endemic malaria. The reservoirs and the extensive rice fields must have provided perfect conditions for this disease and for other water-borne infections as well.[63] In addition both Veh-Shapur and Naubandegan suffered severely during the Shabankareh wars; the latter town was apparently stormed and burnt. Though the Atabeg Djauli is praised for his repair works in both towns, they never really recovered.[64]

Instead, during the 10th and 11th centuries, Kazirun, a small enclave irrigated by both *qanats* and wells, emerged as the new regional center. The town itself is said to have been built by Shapur I in connection with the founding of Veh-Shapur. Other traditions add that Shah Firuz and Kavadh also built on the site.[65] In contrast to Veh-Shapur Kazirun enjoyed a healthy climate, but the water supplies were considered inadequate. It developed a considerable linen production; the Buyids favored it as a commercial center and, in the 11th century, it became the center of a Sufi order founded by Shaykh Abu Ishaq Ibrahim b. Shahriyar. According to Ibn Battuta, Shaykh Abu Ishaq was regarded as a kind of saint of the sailors on the Indian Ocean, and the hospice that he had founded in Kazirun received considerable gifts of money from far away.[66] Because of these advantages Kazirun survived both the Shabankareh wars and a Mongol attack in 1284.[67]

In southwestern Fars, on the borders of Khuzistan, Kavadh I founded or enlarged the town of *Veh-az-Amid-Kavadh*, usually called Arradjan. Tradition has it that Shapur I originally built a bridge and a weir across the Tab River (today: the

Marun). He also dug canals, perhaps to provide water for Rev-Ardashir, another Sassanian founding in the vicinity (its precise location is unknown). Kavadh then built the town of Arradjan and populated it with prisoners of war from Amida (i.e. Diyarbakir, conquered in 502).[68]

In the 10th century Arradjan was the fourth largest town in Fars, the center for the traffic between Khuzistan and Shiraz and Isfahan, and famous for its textile production and export of the medicinal bitumen, *mumiya*. For a time the town even became *de facto* capital of one of the Buyid kings, Rukn al-Dawleh. His son and heir, Adud al-Dawleh, used to praise the enclave for its fiscal contributions, which is understandable, since it, according to Ibn Hawqal, paid no less than 1/4 of the total tax from Fars during this period.[69]

Nasir-é Khusraw visited the town in 1052 and was told that the adult male population numbered 20.000. He admired the irrigation systems and the intensively cultivated, fertile hinterland.[70] Fifty years later, however, the town was largely abandoned. Ibn al-Balkhi blames the Isma'ili wars, but a major earthquake in 1085/86, reported by Ibn al-Athir, may have caused worse damage.[71] In any case, no later than the mid-14th century Arradjan had been replaced by a new town, Bihbihan, a few kilometers to the south.[72] Though much of the land remained intensive cultivation, Bihbihan never equalled Old Arradjan, probably because the decline of Khuzistan had robbed the area of trade and communication. Nevertheless Bihbihan survived the wars and disturbances of the 15th–18th centuries and, around 1800, it still held an estimated population of 10.000.[73]

5. Siraf and the Gulf Ports

At the end of the 4th century B.C. Alexander's admiral, Nearchus, reported only one large settlement on the entire coast between the Shatt al-Arab and Hormuz. This was Hieratis-Mesembria, presumably identical with the site of Rishahr just south of present-day Bushire. Settlement here goes back to the Elamite times (2nd millennium).[74]

However, by the 10th century we find several fairly important settlements on the coast: Mahruban, Siniz, Djannabeh and, of course, Siraf. On the basis of the Arab accounts of conquest and archaeological indicators they can be dated back to Sassanian times at least, when settlement was also extended into the interior of Fars.

All of these towns were located in places where the conditions for agriculture were bad, either because the soil was too poor, or because water supplies were inadequate or of bad quality. They existed on a combination of pearl fishing, trade and shipping, as well as textile production, including *tiraz*: i.e. luxury fabrics for official use produced in state factories.

The largest and wealthiest of these seaports was *Siraf* (today Bandar-é Tahiri), center of navigation from Fars to Africa, India, and China. The trade in exotic luxury goods such as ivory, precious stones, spice, sandalwood, and other aromatic products created fabulous fortunes for the town's merchants and captains, which they spent on building houses of rare African woods. The wealth also brought corruption; at least that is what the rather puritan al-Muqaddasi thought, as he indignantly observed that adultery, usury, and extravagance were prevalent. When Siraf was heavily damaged by an earthquake, in 977, he deemed it a fitting punishment from God.[75]

Al-Muqaddasi admits, however, that the decline of the town had begun before this, because many residents had emigrated to 'Uman after the Buyids had gained control over Fars; but why the Sirafis should have been opposed to the Buyids is not explained. Ibn al-Balkhi makes no mention of this and dates the decline of the town to the period after the collapse of Buyid rule, when pirate princes from the small island of Qays would attack Sirafi ships with impunity.[76] Siraf apparently remained a local market until the 15th or 16th centuries, but its role as center for the long-distance trade was over by the 11th century. Siraf was not an isolated case, however, as decline struck nearly all the ports on the Farsi coast about this time:

Djannabeh (now Ganaveh, just north of Bandar-é Rig), originally the port of Veh-Shapur and Kazirun, and famous for both pearl fishing and *tiraz* production, seems to have been in decline as early as the 10th century. The reason may have been the Qarmatian wars or extremely poor water supplies.[77]

Tawwaz (Tawwadj), founded in the 7th century as an Arab *misr* (garrison town), probably on the Shirin-Hilleh River near present-day Borazdjan, was also known for *tiraz* production. Described in the 10th century as nearly as large as Arradjan, Tawwaz was practically deserted by the 12th century.[78]

Siniz, presumably identical with the large site at Hisar (south of Bandar-é Daylam), also had *tiraz* production and maritime trade. It was stormed and sacked by the Qarmatians in 933/34. Yaqut cites a local source, Abu Bakhr Ahmad b. Mahmud al-Ahwazi, who says that 1.280 inhabitants were massacred on this occasion. Even though Ibn al-Balkhi states that Siniz still existed in the early 12th century, its prosperity and importance was greatly reduced.[79]

Mahruban, located just 25 km north of Bandar-é Daylam, had originally served as port for Rev-Ardashir and Arradjan. With the decline of Djannabeh and Siniz, however, it became the chief port of all of western Fars in the 11th and 12th centuries. Nevertheless no later than the 14th or 15th centuries, it too had been abandoned.[80]

Local factors, ranging from earthquakes to wartime destruction, must certainly have played a role in each single case. Yet the chronology, and the fact that no new ports arose to replace the old, indicate that the decline of the coastal settlements was related to the general decline of southern Fars from the 11th century onward. The small coastal settlements described by the European travellers in the 16th and 17th centuries, i.e. ports such as Bandar-é Daylam, Bandar-é Rig, Nakhilu, etc., were certainly less impressive than their medieval predecessors, having neither textile industry nor long-distance trade. According to Pedro Teixeira the trade of Bandar-é Rig was indeed modest: it consisted chiefly of export of onions to Basrah. These small towns survived on a little agriculture, a bit of local trade, and, given the opportunity, piracy.[81]

In the 18th century Bushire temporarily became the chief port in the Gulf owing to the favors of Nadir Shah and the Zand rulers, and this caused the British and Dutch to move their factories here from Bandar-é Abbas.[82] But during the Zand-Qadjar wars navigation in the Gulf practically stopped, and Kinneir, around 1800, found Bushire to be "a mean place" of 400 houses.[83] It since grew into a considerable port thanks to British activity in the Gulf, but this development lies outside the scope of our inquiry.

Summary

The history of Fars from the 3rd to the 16th centuries is roughly marked by three phases. The first of these phases, i.e. the Sassanian period (3rd to 7th centuries), saw an extensive and largely state-directed colonization. Settlement and cultivation was intensified in existing enclaves such as Marvdasht and new settlements were established in the peripheral areas in southern Fars, including the coastal region. As in Mesopotamia and Khuzistan, this expansion involved the typical Sassanian combination of city-founding, construction of irrigation works, deportations and forcible resettlements.

The second phase, the age of the Abbasids and the Buyids (8th-10th centuries), was characterized by a concentration of both political, administrative, and commercial functions in a single city: Shiraz. Consequently Shiraz grew in size and importance, eventually overshadowing the other towns. The only exception was Siraf which occupied a special position as center of the martitime trade on the Indian Ocean.

The third phase, from the 11th century onwards, was marked by a marked de-urbanization all over southern Fars. Practically all the towns founded or enlarged by the Sassanians were deserted, and though some of them, e.g. Arradjan and Veh-Shapur, were replaced by other smaller urban settlements in the vicinity, the final result was a considerable shrinkage of settlement and cultivation.

Ibn al-Balkhi points to the Shabankareh wars, around 1100, as the immediate cause. The fighting caused extensive material destructions, and the general lawlessness made the caravans seek new routes in Kirman. Consequently the old towns of Fars lost much of their economic base.[84] Djahrum and Lar, however, as well as a few small towns like Khundj and Fal, also situated in southeastern Fars, profited from this, because they were situated on the new caravan routes connecting Hormuz and Qays to Shiraz.[85]

Why were the deserted towns and reduced enclaves in southern Fars not reestablished when political stability returned in the 12th and 13th centuries? We have seen how towns in Djibal recovered from disasters much worse than the Shabankareh wars. Part of the explanation must be that Shiraz' growth and dominant position prevented this. Shiraz had certainly also been seriously affected by the Shabankareh wars, but apparently it had no difficulty recovering. In sharp contrast to the decline in the south, the Shiraz enclave, including Marvdasht, was basically stable and, in spite of the shifting of caravan routes, the city continued to attract long-distance trade.

An additional explanation for the lack of re-colonization may lie in the diffusion of nomadic methods of subsistence. Not that Fars was a case of "bedouinization:" i.e. forcible diffusion of nomadism at the cost of settled agriculture. A large part of Fars' population had always been tribally organized and combined extensive agriculture with nomadism. The Shabankareh war was a struggle for political domination in Fars, not a conflict between the nomads and the sedentary population. However, a temporary collapse of political power, the destruction of irrigation works, and similar occurrences may have encouraged nomadic or seminomadic subsistence.[86] Later, during the 15th and 16th centuries, Turkish nomads belonging to clans such as Afshar, Purnak, Baharlu, Aynalu, Qashqa'i, etc. immigrated or, rather, were transferred from Syria, Anatolia, and Azarbaydjan. Though, in the 18th century, some of them were sent onward to Khurasan, nomadism became more widespread in Fars, but this happened long after the contraction of settlement had begun. If Fars was "bedouinized," it seems to have been a consequence rather than a cause of the decline in settled agriculture. Nomadism and other extensive methods of subsistence were a means of filling up the vacuum, as it were. However, once established such ways of life together with their particular political structures were not easily disrupted.

A third, and perhaps decisive, cause of the de-urbanization and contraction of settled life was the lack of political favor. The towns which survived in the south did so largely because of their religious status. Kazirun was the center of a Sufi order and had a shrine which, though not approaching the prestige of Qum, nevertheless attracted pilgrims and thereby sustained economic activity. Something similar held good of Lar and Khundj.[87] The other towns were allowed to decline. In Djibal the towns and enclaves were restablished following earthquakes and wartime destructions, but in southern Fars there was no political power capable of reconstruction. Without political, or religious, favor the old towns could no longer attract long-distance trade or other economic activities, and Fars, Shiraz excepted, sank back into provincial obscurity.

Chapter 14

Kirman

As indicated by the tax assessments, Kirman occupied a somewhat peripheral position within Iranshahr. It was an arid land of dispersed settlements, far from the imperial centers, a refuge for rebels and dissidents. Its resources were modest, and for long periods the local rulers were left reasonably undisturbed.[1]

In physical terms the land consisted, roughly speaking, of two parts. "Warm Kirman," *Garmkirman*, i.e. the region south of the central Kuh-é Lalehzar massif, was watered by several streams, but as these were mostly seasonal, many settlements were supplied with extra water from *qanats* or cisterns. "Cold Kirman" (the *sardsir*), north of the central massif, was a region of desolate basins and valleys facing the great desert Dasht-é Lut. Settlement in pre-historical and early historical times was here limited to a few small, natural oases.

In Sassanian and early Muslim times both parts of Kirman saw considerable settlement expansion. Later, however, there was a divergence: the south, which apparently offered the best conditions for settlement, declined, while settlement in the north, inspite of the inhospitable environment, the frequent natural disasters and wars, proved resilient.

1. The Colonization of North Kirman

The north of Kirman was one of those arid areas on the edge of the great Iranian deserts which the *qanat*-technology opened up for colonization. Expansion of settlement began in earnest in the 3rd century when Ardashir I, immediately after his conquest of Kirman, founded a new town, *Veh-Ardashir*, on the edge of the Dasht-é Lut. The name was eventually transformed into *Bardasir* or *Guwashir*.[2] Ardashir's intention was no doubt to establish a military base, but in this barren, isolated country even a small garrison could subsist only in an oasis, so this had literally to be constructed together with the town. In the 10th century Veh-Ardashir, which had then just become the capital of all Kirman, is described a small heavily fortified town surrounded by gardens and watered by many *qanats*, wells, and cisterns. We have no earlier descriptions, but the Sassanian town must have looked much the same.[3]

Local traditions has it that a Sassanian governor founded the town of Mahan at the foot of Mount Djupar, southeast of Veh-Ardashir.[4] Further colonization of "Cold Kirman" took place in the 4th century when Shapur II settled prisoners of war from his Arabian campaign in "Aban." Le Strange identifies this place with

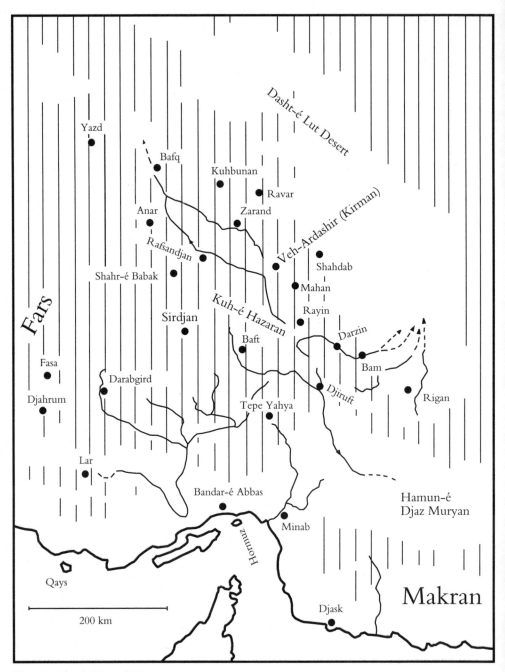

Fig. 11. Sketch-Map of Kirman.

Table 12. The assessment of Kirman.

	Dirhams
788	4.500.000[a]
819/20	6.000.000[b]
826/27	5.000.000[c]
911/12	5.000.000[d]
918/19	c. 7000.000[e]
c. 960	c. 10.000.000[f]
11th–12th centuries	c. 3.900.000[g]
1335	c. 3.000.000[h]

[a] al-Mutarrif (el-'Ali: 1971).
[b] Qudama (de Goeje tr.: 184).
[c] Ibn Khurdadhbih (tr.: 25); here it is also said that Kirman in "the time of Kisra" paid 60 million. This figure, also found in Ibn al-Faqih (tr.: 249), is highly improbable and must be due to an error in a common source.
[d] Ibn al-Furat, cited by Miskawayh (tr., IV: 268).
[e] 'Ali b. 'Isa cited by von Kremer (1888: 314); the figure is in fact 364.380 dinars, here converted at the rate of 1:20 (with a slightly different conversion rate this would accord with the figure given by Ibn al-Furat).
[f] Ibn Hawqal (tr., II: 309): actually 500.000 dinars. Presumably the figure refers to tax farming rather than the tax assessment proper. See also Schwarz (286f) and Spuler (1952: 471f).
[g] Mustawfi (Nuzhat, tr.: 138); the figure is actually 880.000 dinar-é rayidj in "Saldjuq times."
[h] Mustawfi (Nuzhat, tr.: 138); the figure is really 676.500 dinar-é rayidj, here converted according to silverweight. Hormuz alone paid 1/10 (60.000 dinars).

present-day Anar, a small qanat-watered oasis on the edge of the desert between Yazd and Rafsandjan.[5]

To sum up, during Sassanian times the northern desert fringe of both Fars and Kirman was being systematically colonized, and the process may well have included the founding, or at least the enlargement, of the whole string of small qanat-oases in northern Kirman: Zarand, Rafsandjan, Bafq, etc.[6] As an echo of this activity Ibn al-Faqih, in his description of Kirman, remarks that in "Kisra's time" the entire country had been brought under cultivation through the construction of gigantic qanats, some of which were said to be five marches long. He also refers to a strange legend about the expansion being accompanied by a widespread planting of trees.[7]

As in the case of Veh-Ardashir the chief motives behind the colonization must have been military: important lines of communication and trade routes had to be protected and recalcitrant mountain peoples kept in check. Khusraw I made a great massacre of the Pariz tribe, living in present-day Djibal Bariz, and deported the survivors. Yet even such harsh measures did not permanently solve the problem of independent (and, no doubt, predatory) groups, as the Muslim period saw further bloody retaliations against the Pariz and Qufs tribes.[8] The colonization schemes and the campaigns against the tribes may further have been prompted by a wish to secure control of Kirman's deposits of metal ore (the sources mention iron, copper, gold, silver, lead, and zinc).[9]

Within the Sassanian Empire Kirman apparently ranked as a kind of vassal kingdom. Shapur I, who gives Kirman a rather humble place on his list of possessions, mentions a certain Ardashir as king of that country. Tabari says that this individual was a Sassanian prince, a son of Ardashir I.[10] In any event, it later became customary to confer the rule of Kirman region on princes from the royal family, who were then given the title of "Kirmanshah."[11] One of them, the later Bahram IV, is said to have built a town in Kirman, an indication that the Kirmanshahs may have been as energetic colonizers as the great kings.[12]

2. Contraction in South Kirman

In spite of the expansion in the north the political and economic center of Kirman remained in the old cultivated zone south of the Kuh-é Lalehzar. In the Rud-é Gushk Valley there are signs of a marked expansion in Parthian-Sassanian times. The remains of settlement lie in lineal extension of each other, indicating that the expansion was linked to the introduction or enlargement of *qanats*.[13]

The historical tradition explicitly credits the Sassanians with several colonization schemes in the south, especially in the Bam region. Thus Ardashir I is said to have founded the fortified caravan town of Narmashir on a little river east of Bam. This story may simply be based on an etymological construction, but in view of the founding of Veh-Ardashir it is likely that the Sassanians did in fact establish a base here as well. Other stories credit Ardashir's wife with financing some new irrigation works at Nisa, a locality in the Narmashir district where the remains of a dam are still to be seen.[14]

For unknown reasons the old Tepe Yahya settlement, in the Suwghan valley, was abandoned in Parthian or early Sassanian times. It was replaced, however, by Sirdjan and Djiruft which, together with Bam, constituted the principal enclaves in the south.

Sirdjan, situated in western Kirman, remained the political center of the country until the 10th century.[15] The villages in the enclave had water only from wells, and Sirdjan had to put up with inadequate water supplies even though the Saffarids, in the 9th century, built new *qanats*. Even so, Sirdjan was a considerable town and, according to some sources, larger than Djiruft.[16]

The latter town, located on Kirman's largest river, the Halil-rud, was center of the most productive enclave, however. Ample water supplies provided for the cultivation of water-demanding crops such as sugar cane and indigo, and Djiruft's commercial quarter, *Kamadin*, famous as Marco Polo's "Camadi," was an entrepot for long-distance trade with Sistan, Khurasan, and – via the port of Hormuz (today Minab) - India.[17]

The center of eastern Kirman was heavily fortified Bam on the Tah River. Though the river was perennial, it tended to turn salty during the summer, and therefore huge *qanats* had been built to augment the water supply of the oasis. The town itself was noted for its textile industry and caravan trade, and was described in the 10th century as larger than Djiruft.[18] In the hinterland stood several smaller towns, among them Narmashir, an important stopping point for caravans and pilgrims from Sistan, Khurasan, and the Indus River Valley. The town of Rayin was also noted for an important textile industry.[19]

By the 12th century the picture had changed, and Yaqut found that Kirman in his time (the early 13th century) had been depopulated and destroyed because of wars and the tyranny of the sultans.[20] Sirdjan had apparently been the first to suffer a decline. In the middle of the 10th century a local ruler, Abu 'Ali b. Ilyas, officially governor for the Buyids, had chosen to transfer the administrative center to impregnable Bardasir. In consequence, the little town now became *shahr-é Kirman*, "City of Kirman."[21] Deprived of its political status and without any large agricultural production in the surrounding enclave (because of the inadequate water supplies), Sirdjan was quickly reduced to secondary importance. In the 14th century it repeatedly suffered wartime devastations, and in 1411 it was destroyed by the Timurid Iskandar b. 'Umar Shaykh, who then deported the survivors to nearby Bimand. At the end of the 18th century a new town, Sa'idabad, was founded 10 km from Old Sirdjan, and eventually this settlement took over the name Sirdjan as well. However, the enclave never regained the position it had once held in the early Middle Ages.[22]

Djiruft and its suburb Kamadin suffered severely in the Saldjuq wars of succession and in the Ghuzz invasion at the end of the 12th century and, according to Vaziri's *Tarikh-é Kirman* (19th century), the city was abandoned at this time because a dam or weir was breached.[23] This can hardly be true, for Marco Polo visited the town in 1271 on his way to Hormuz. The Venetian did conclude, however, that it was in a state of decline, for which he, incorrectly, blamed the Mongols. The hinterland remained under cultivation, though constantly harassed by bands of robbers known as the Karaunas.[24] Subsequently, Djiruft was in fact abandoned and *not* replaced by any other new town in the region. Intensive agriculture also contracted. Precisely when this happened cannot be determined, but no later than the 19th century the enclave had become grazing land for nomads.[25]

Bam also declined, though to a less drastic degree. During the Saldjuq wars of succession and the Ghuzz invasion in the 12th century the irrigation works were damaged and the caravan trade compelled to seek new and less dangerous routes. The waterworks were eventually repaired, but the trade could not be recaptured because of the general lawlessness in the region, and this harmed Bam's textile industry. By the 15th century this industry had ceased altogether, and the economic activities in the oasis were largely reduced to subsistence agriculture. Jean Aubin estimates that Bam at that time had only 5.000 inhabitants, but we have no information about how many more it might have had earlier.[26]

The decline affected the entire Bam region. Though the small towns farther up the Tah-rud Valley survived, their economic base was reduced. For example, the textile industry disappeared completely from Rayin.[27] Narmashir, which in the 12th century was still described as prosperous and surrounded by gardens and palm groves, was completely abandoned; again we do not know precisely when.[28] Even around 1800 a British traveller, Lieutenant Pottinger, observed that the Narmashir district was well-irrigated and densely populated, though subject to frequent Baluchi raids. Koruk now figured as the largest settlement in the district.[29]

It seems that some of the decline in southeastern Kirman has in fact occurred quite recently. The town of Rigan, located in the district of Narmashir and also known to us from 10th century sources, still appeared to Pottinger as "a neat little town." A hundred years later it had been reduced to a small settlement of some 200 people around a fort.[30]

Bam, because of its strategic position, retained some importance, and the oasis survived as the largest settlement on the southeastern Plateau. In the 19th century it even experienced a new period of growth. First, the Qadjars made it their local military and administrative center; second, the caravan trade with India via Baluchistan stimulated the production of, for instance, henna.[31] Then, around 1840, Bam was physically moved a little distance to the southwest, and today the old town constitutes the Plateau's most well-preserved urban site. It is also a reminder that the presence of ruins may have nothing to do with settlement cessation.[32]

3. The Resiliency of North Kirman

As the new political and administrative center Bardasir – or just *(shahr-é)* Kirman, a name it has since retained – attracted prestige investments as well as trade and manufacturing, especially textiles. Ibn Khurdadhbih, al-Istakhri, and Ibn Hawqal make it clear that traffic from the western Plateau in the 9th and 10th centuries generally preferred the route over Sirdjan and Djiruft, and from there onward to Hormuz or Bam.[33] However, the local Saldjuq dynasty in Kirman exploited the political turmoil in Fars in the 11th century to attract the traffic to Bardasir/Kirman. Turanshah (1085–1097) even constructed an entirely new quarter with caravanserais to accommodate the merchants. Eventually the road from Djiruft over Bardasir/Kirman to Yazd developed into an important caravan route. Among the many who travelled this way was Marco Polo.[34]

So, by the middle of the 12th century Bardasir had become the chief town of Kirman: prosperous and densely populated, surrounded by intensively cultivated land.[35] Town and enclave was repeatedly afflicted by drought, famine, and no doubt also by earthquakes, while sand-storms constantly threatened to overwhelm the fields.[36] Neither did the town escape wartime devastations during the Saldjuq wars of succession and the Ghuzz invasion. The bazaar quarter was plundered in 1166/67 and the entire city was sacked in 1195/96.[37] However, together with the rest of the region, the enclave escaped the Mongols, because a new dynasty of local rulers, the Qutlugh-khanids, voluntarily submitted to Mongol suzerainty, and during their rule the region is said to have experienced renewed expansion and construction.[38]

Except for Sirdjan, attacked in 1396, Kirman suffered little damage in Timur's campaigns. However, the subsequent Timurid wars of succession caused widespread destruction. In 1411 Iskandar b. 'Umar Shaykh conducted a campaign which is described by Hafiz-é Abru and al-Samarkandi as an attempt to destroy the land systemtically. Buildings were razed, canals destroyed, orchards felled, and the surviving inhabitants deported. Not even the most remote corner of Kirman escaped this disaster, it is said. Shah Rukh, Iskandar's rival and Hafiz-é Abru's employer, is praised for having repaired the damage and for restoring cultivation by reducing taxes and giving seed to the peasants. One suspects that the Timurid court historians used the description of the fighting to de-legitimate Iskandar as a destroyer, a "bad king," in contrast to the "good king" Shah Rukh.[39] The list of wartime devastations and accompanying disasters can be extended. Qara-Qoyunlu warlords levied extortionate taxes in the first half of the 15th century and the Uzbeks plundered in the beginning of the 16th century. In the early part of the 18th century the Afghan wars and Nadir Shah's campaigns were said to have caused seven years of famine.

The worst disaster in the history of Bardasir/Kirman happened in 1794, when Aqa Muhammad Qadjar sacked and partly destroyed the town. All male inhabitants were allegedly killed or blinded, and the women and children enslaved.[40] Aqa Muhammad's barbarous behavior made a deep impression on his contemporaries – which was precisely his intention – and left the town devastated.[41] Yet it remained the capital of the region and in the 19th century it experienced considerable growth. Qadjar governors repaired the war damage and built new qanats and villages. At the same time some of Kirman's traditional products, carpets and shawls, began to find new and greater markets.[42]

This resiliency characterized not only the Bardasir/Kirman enclave, but all of "Cold Kirman." Of course, settlement must have fluctuated in response to the shifting of caravan routes, change in local environments, etc. However, if we take the 10th century description as a point of departure, only a few settlements seem to have actually been abandoned. Djanzarud, a small river oasis between Bardasir/Kirman and Zarand, has disappeared,[43] or rather the name has disappeared, for the settlement can perhaps be identified with one of those still existing in the area. A parallel can be made with the small town of Unas. The name has also disappeared, but the actual settlement must be either identical with or succeeded by Bahramabad/Rafsandjan.[44] Also abandoned were two smaller towns in the mountains south of the Kirman Basin, Ghubayra and Kughun, the former presumably in Ilkhanid times.[45]

Yet none of these cases can compare with the abandonment of important centers like Djiruft and Sirdjan or of secondary towns like Narmashir. In the north the settlement pattern remained basically intact. Why this contrast? In the case of Sirdjan we can point to the shifting of caravan routes, inadequate water supplies, and the loss of political favor. In the case of Djiruft, however, other factors must have been decisive. On first sight, the conventional view of a progressive "bed-ouinization" of Iran seems to provide an explanation. *If* a substantial immigration of nomads had in fact occurred, the south would certainly have appeared far more attractive as grazing lands than the barren north. Marco Polo, travelling in the beginning of the 1270s from Bardasir/Kirman to "Camadi" (Djiruft), observed that even though the Kirman Basin was densely populated and covered by villages, the slopes on the south side of the central massif were inhabited only by nomads. Here had once been villages, he added, but they were deserted.[46]

Planhol has used this information to argue that southern Kirman had been "bedouinized" as a result of the Ghuzz invasion in the 12th century.[47] However, nomadic existence was established in Kirman long before the invasion. Transhu-mant nomads such as the Qufs used the area south of the central massif as their winter residence. Together with the other pastoralists, they always had resisted state attempts to levy taxes and regulate their way of life.[48] It is possible that Marco Polo simply mistook the empty seasonal dwellings of the transhumant herders for abandoned villages. Moreover, the size of the Ghuzz groups was modest; perhaps they were simply absorbed, as A.K.S. Lambton assumes, into the existing patterns of settlement and subsistence through stock-raising and caravan traffic.[49] On one occasion the Ghuzz themselves stated their number at 10.000 to appear as menacing as possible, but this figure seems to have been a considerable exaggeration.[50] Also, Marco Polo describes the Rudbar area (i.e. the country around Djiruft) as densely populated and under cultivation, all of which argues against the Ghuzz having converted cultivated land into pasture. Planhol does not cite this part of the description.[51] Neither the Mongol invasion, which largely by-passed Kirman, nor the campaigns of Timur seem to have brought with them any significant immigra-tion of nomads. The Afshars, the largest nomadic group in the 19th century, were first brought to the country by Nadir Shah in the early 18th century. Other tribes (e.g. the Lak Lurs) arrived at the same time, i.e long after the beginning of the decline.[52]

There is no doubt that nomadic existence extended over large areas of south Kirman in the 18th and 19th centuries, perhaps becoming even more widespread than before, although this is difficult to determine. However, it is unlikely that the expansion of nomadism directly caused the de-urbanization and the shrinkage of settled agriculture. Rather, southern Kirman was a parallel to Fars where lack of political favor and recolonization schemes created a vacuum which was then filled by nomads and extensive agriculturalists.

Chapter 15

Khurasan

Developments in far-off Khurasan, the land between the great *kavirs* to the west and the Amu Darya (Oxus) to the east, remain extremely vague in the classical sources. With the Persian historical tradition and the Muslim accounts of conquest the picture becomes a little clearer; but not until the 9th and 10th centuries do we get an overall impression of the wide expanse of desert and steppe lands.

By the 5th century Nestorian sees were established in Marv, Nishapur and Herat, the most important and probably also the largest enclaves in Sassanian times.[1] From the second half of the 6th century synodal records mention additional sees in Abivard, Marv al-Rud (Bala Murghab) and Pushang.[2] Now tradition has it that the latter two towns were Sassanian foundings. As the Nestorian church usually cooperated closely with the Sassanian state, the establishing of sees precisely in these towns may reflect Sassanian efforts to extend control beyond the Murghab River, the traditional eastern frontier of the Empire.[3]

Tax assessments for 827/28, reproduced by Ibn Khurdadhbih, show that Marv, Nishapur, and Herat remained the largest enclaves in Khurasan proper, an impression generally confirmed by Ibn Hawqal and other 10th-century travellers.[4] We shall, therefore, take these three enclaves as starting-points for an outline of the historical trends in Khurasan.

1. Marv

Ibn Khurdadhbih's figures are somewhat misleading, as they refer to a period when Nishapur had temporarily become the capital of Khurasan. This position was usually held by Marv which thus was known as *al-shahidjan*, "Royal Marv." In Sassanian times the oasis had been residence of the Nestorian metropolitan of all Khurasan.[5] As it was Nestorian practice to let the size and status of the residence towns determine the ranking of the dioceses, we may assume that the Marv bishop's position within the Nestorian hierarchy reflected the importance of Marv to the Empire.

In particular, the Sassanians used the oasis as their main military stronghold on the eastern frontier and they therefore made special efforts to maintain control across the wide distances separating Marv from the core-lands to the west. They deposed the Parthian prince of the oasis and replaced him with a regular governor,[6] and they stationed an army of professional soldiers. These, like their colleagues in garrison

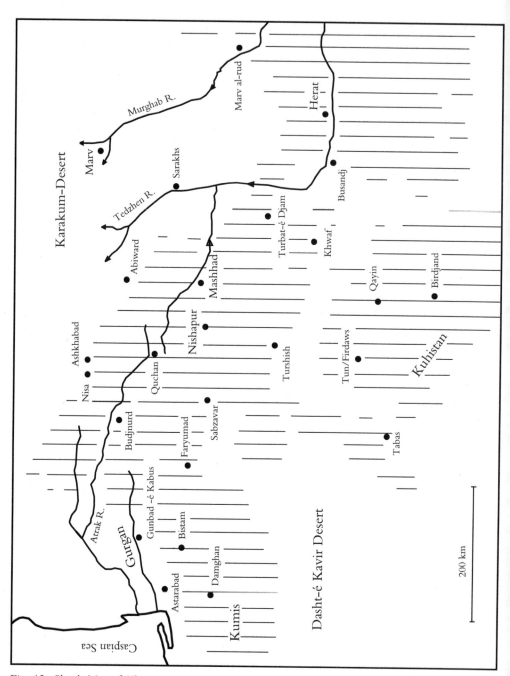

Fig. 12. Sketch-Map of Khurasan.

Table 13. The assessment of Khurasan, 828 (according to Ibn Khurdadhbih).

	Dirhams
Tabasayn	113.800
Kuhistan	787.880
Nishapur	4.108.900
Tus	740.860
Nasa	893.400
Abivard	700.000
Sarakhs	307.440
Marv	1.147.000
Marv al-Rud	420.400
Badghis	440.000
Herat	1.159.000
Bushandj	559.350
Guzganan (Djuzdjan)	154.000
Balkh "with Khuttalan"	193.300
Taliqan	21.400
Khulm (Tash-Qurghan)	12.300
Faryab	55.000
Zamm	106.000
Amul (Amuyah)	293.400

Note: This list includes only the regions of Khurasan proper. Transoxania, Sistan, Ghur, Ghardjistan and additional areas in the Afghan highlands are not included.

towns like Isfahan and Kazwin, were paid through *qati'a*-like allotments.[7] That the oasis was able to support an army strongly indicates a sizable population and a considerable agricultural production. When the Arabs penetrated Khurasan, Marv paid the largest tribute: between one and two million dirhams besides large deliveries of wheat and barley.[8]

After the Arab conquest Marv remained the military center in the east, serving as a forward base for raids into Transoxania. Initially the garrisons rotated until Ziyad b. Abihi, in 672/73, sent 50.000 men and their families from Mesopotamia. They were settled in the villages outside Marv city, registered in a *diwan*, and paid with the surplus of the oasis through the *al-'ata* system.[9]

The Arab soldiers soon tired of their hazardous military duties and began looking for other occupations. Many of them moved into Marv city, perhaps attracted by the opportunity to engage in the lucrative trade with the Transoxanian towns.[10] In order to restore the military balance the caliph Hisham, in 734, dispatched another 20.000 soldiers from Mesopotamia.[11] We need not dwell on the motives behind the Empire's actions, i.e. to rid Mesopotamia of discontented and unruly Arab warriors; nor need we detail the continuous struggles between the veterans and new arrivals or between *dihqans* and *mawalis*, all of which made Marv a hotbed of discontent culminating in the Abbasid rebellion in 749. Suffice it to say that the Arab settlement in Marv, as in other places on the plateau, led to increased urbanization. One indication of this are new bazaars and government houses built by Abu

Muslim.[12] In the early 9th century when Harun al-Rashid attempted to divide peacefully the Empire between his sons al-Amin and al-Ma'mun, Marv was the obvious choice as the latter's capital.

Shortly after, the Tahirids made Nishapur the capital of Khurasan and this may explain the decline which al-Muqaddasi and others believed had occurred in the quarters along the al-Raziq Canal in Marv; but more likely the abandoned houses simply reflected minor hydrological changes, because the Tahirids in fact enlarged Marv city along the westerly Hormuzfarrah Canal.[13] In any case, Marv remained one of Khurasan's largest cities, notable for both its agriculture and its textile industry and in the 11th-12th centuries, under Saldjuq rule, it regained its position as capital. Political favor brought with it new investments in fortifications and irrigation works.[14] From the 10th century we have brief and rather vague descriptions of the irrigation system on which rested the fame and productivity of Marv:[15]

First there was an embankment at the village of al-Raziq (also written "Zarq"), one day's march (*marhaleh, c.* 40 km) up the Murghab. The purpose of this must have been to prevent the river from changing its course during the spring floods. Probably there was also a weir at al-Raziq, since Ibn Hawqal refers to canals branching out here and conducting water to the agricultural districts.

The second element was a weir 1 *farsakh* above Marv, where the water was raised up into four canals: the Nahr As'adi, the Nahr Raziq, the Nahr Madjan and the Nahr Hormuzfarrah (counted from east to west). These canals delivered water to Marv's urban quarters as well as to the rural districts north of the city.

Around Marv the cultivated area extended for a distance of one or two marches. Repairs, maintenance, and distribution of water were entrusted to a special department led by a "water director," the *muqassim al-ma'* or *amir-é ab*. According to Ibn Hawqal this official commanded a labor force of no less than 10.000 men.[16] While the figure may be inflated, it nevertheless gives an idea of the toil required to keep the oasis in operation under environmental circumstances that were rather less favorable than the flowery descriptions of medieval Marv might suggest.

First, the Murghab was an unpredictable river; because of the limited catchment area drought (and eventual famine) were constant threats. Flash floods occurred as well. In 1162/63, for instance, a flood washed away the main weir and, despite several attempts at repair, operations were resumed only after the Khwarizmshah had sent expert engineers.[17] Second, salinity hazards appears to have been greater in Marv than elsewhere on the Plateau. Though al-Ma'mun praised Marv's sweet water, it was widely known that the water was in fact brackish and bitter. Ibn Hawqal further noted that the soil was covered by salt.[18] A third danger was the shifting sands which choked the canals and threatened to overwhelm the fields.[19] Finally, the man-made environment proved a fertile breeding-ground for a number of pathogenic parasites. *Filaria medinensis* was thus considered virtually unavoidable, and in spite of Yaqut's assurances to the contrary, Marv was notorious for its "unhealthy air."[20] The great epidemic which in 855/56 spread from Sarakhs to most of Iran[21] must also have visited Marv (if it did not originate there). The same must be true of the other great epidemics ravaging Khurasan in the Middle Ages. To sum up, compared to the Iranian Plateau in general the Marv oasis suffered extraordinary environmental problems.

In explaining why medieval Marv was transformed into a deserted ruin, both the medieval sources and modern scholarship primarily blame the wars and barbarian invasions which swept Khurasan in the 12th and 13th centuries. The city was first ravaged by the Khwarizmshah in 1141/42; then, in 1153, came the Ghuzz Turks from their unexpected victory over Sultan Sandjar and sacked it for three days.[22] The damage was apparently not irreparable, for Yaqut who spent three years in Marv in the early 13th century described it in flowery terms.[23]

According to most sources the turning point in Marv's history came with the Mongols. In 1220 two of Djenghiz Khan's generals, Djebe and Sübedei, advanced across the northern Plateau toward Hamadan in an attempt to capture the Khwarizmshah Muhammad and thus weaken organized resistance. On their way they encouraged the towns to surrender peacefully, enter into tributary agreements, and accept a governor appointed by them. Like Nishapur, Sarakhs, and Tus, Marv at first accepted such an agreement, apparently because the city's Shaykh al-Islam had advocated this.[24] Shortly after, however, the Shaykh was murdered by a political rival who took power with support from "the rabble" (aubash) and renounced the agreement.[25] These events obviously were related to the intense factional struggles and sectarian conflicts known to us from Nishapur and most other towns on the Plateau. In these struggles the rival factions did not hesitate to involve the Ghaznavids, the Saldjuks, and even the heathen and barbarian Mongols.

In the spring of 1221 when the Mongols, led by Tolui, began the systematic subjugation of Khurasan, they consistently punished the towns which had not respected the treaties with Djebe and Sübedei. Though Marv withstood the first Mongol assault, it was decided to surrender the city. This did not save it from the wrath of the Mongols, however. Djuwayni describes the bloodbath carried out in Marv, adding that he had heard from a reliable source – a sayyid said to have spent 13 ghastly days counting corpses – that the number of killed exceeded 1.3 million; and this figure did not even include the victims in the rural districts. Only 400 craftsmen and some children were spared and enslaved. The neighboring town of Sarakhs had remained faithful to the original agreeement and accordingly rendered military assistance to Tolui. The troops from Sarakhs enthusiastically took part in the massacre, which goes to show that the enclaves of Khurasan did not uniformly see the Mongol invasion as an ominous threat to Muslim civilization, but just as much as an opportunity for political maneuvering and for striking back at local opponents. In any case, Djuwayni's vivid description of the butchery is greatly exaggerated. The fortifications were quickly repaired and, at the end of the year, one of the Khwarizmshah Djalal al-Din's generals could occupy the city with support from the anti-Mongol faction. In 1222 the Mongols recaptured Marv and on this occasion, according to Djuwayni, slaughtered 100.000 people. After yet another rebellion, in 1223, the city was razed for a third time, and now only 100 survivors remained in the entire oasis, if we are to believe Djuwayni. Finally, in 1268, it was raided by the Chagatay.[26]

Ibn Battuta, who travelled through Khurasan in the 1330s, did not himself visit Marv but was told that it was still in ruins.[27] Mustawfi says the same, placing the blame on internal struggles, however.[28] Two Timurid court historians, Hafiz-é Abru and 'Abd al-Razzak al-Samarkandi, vividly describe how Tolui's attack had reduced Marv to a heap of rubble, inhabited only by wild animals. They add that for the next two hundred years the ancient capital had remained deserted. This is somewhat exaggerated, for in Timur's time the oasis in fact served as cantonment and as a base for campaigns, a clear indication that agricultural production had not completely ceased.[29]

Then, in 1409/10, Shah Rukh ordered the city rebuilt and it is, of course, this initiative which Hafiz-é Abru and al-Samarkandi wished to emphasize. Laborers were conscripted from all of Khurasan, the weir was repaired, the silted canals cleaned out, and a new feeder canal, 12 *farsakh* long, was constructed. Five hundred families were settled to reclaim the abandoned land, and in Marv city new mosques were built, as were baths, caravanserais, etc. The city became once more a regional capital, and at the end of the 15th century the Herati historian Isfizari asserted that no other province grew so much grain and cotton as did Marv.[30]

From Hafiz-é Abru's description it appears, however, that Shah Rukh in fact did not restore Old Marv. The new weir was situated 12 *farsakh* from the rebuilt town, i.e. much farther up the Murghab than the old weir mentioned in the 10th- and 11th-century sources. The canals now branched off at a locality called Bakhsh-ab. Finally Hafiz explicitly states that the old cultivated area farthest down the Murghab had been overwhelmed by the shifting sands – Mustawfi also mentions this – and was not reclaimed.[31] Settlement and cultivation had clearly shifted towards the south. Something similar had happened earlier in Marv's history and left the ruins of successive settlements in the desert. Part of the explanation for this shift must be that salination and formation of dunes, the results of intensive cultivation, had made environmental conditions worse.

The new Marv remained a modest enclave lacking the military importance of its predecessor. The empire built by Shah Rukh out of Timur's conquest was largely a Khurasani state in which Marv had no great strategic value until, in 1500, Khurasan was again divided along the Murghab owing to the rise of two new states, the Safavids in the west and the Shaybanids in the east. The former chose to expand Mashhad as their principal base, abandoning Marv to recurrent raids. The worst of these occurred in 1788 when the khan of Bukhara, Shah Murad, also known as

Begi Djan, systematically destroyed the waterworks of the oasis, slaughtered the inhabitants, and deported the survivors to the Transoxanian slave markets. According to local traditions 700.000 people perished on this occasion, a figure as unrealistic as that given for Tolui's massacre. Other sources state that 27.000 families were deported. Whatever the reliability of the figures the massacre seems to have marked the nadir of Marv's stormy history. In the early 19th century British intelligence reports estimated that only 3.000 inhabitants remained.[32]

During the 19th century the oasis was partly recolonized by Turkoman immigrants. An Irish journalist, E. O'Donovan, spent a few months there in 1880, estimating the total population at 500.000. This seems rather optimistic considering the additional information he provides on settlement structures and methods of subsistence:[33] Marv no long possessed a regular urban center; the population lived in small villages, each containing between 50 and 200 houses. No taxes were levied, apart from some small duties on local caravan traffic, because there no longer was any central political authority in Marv. This did not prevent the population from raising labor to build fortifications, to maintain a simple but serviceable weir of earth and fascines across the Murghab, and to clean the two canals conducting water from the weir into a network of small irrigation canals.[34]

From O'Donovan's description it also appears that since Timurid times settlement and cultivation had again shifted, this time toward the west. Higher up the river, O'Donovan saw the remains of an old weir, which had once raised water for the settlements now standing in the desert, east of the existing oasis.[35] The economic activities had also changed. The peasants still grew grain, some rice, and a good deal of fruit, including the famous melons which since ancient times had been dried and exported;[36] but cotton and silk had disappeared together with the textile industry. The only remaining craft of any commercial importance was carpet weaving which used local wool and some silk thread purchased in Bukhara.[37] Also gone was *filaria medinesis*, the traditional scourge of Marv, no doubt because irrigation had been reduced. The few cases which O'Donovan heard about were all the result of visits to Bukhara.[38]

To sum up, though settlement in the Marv oasis survived both wars and environmental deterioration, it did so by shifting location and changing character. "Royal Marv," the old capital of Khurasan, was abandoned and buried by the sand drifts and in its stead emerged a decentralized, subsistence-oriented community.

2. Nishapur

Nishapur – or Abrashahr as it was also called – was not an ancient city like Marv. It was an artificial oasis founded in the middle of the 3rd century by Shapur I on the western slope of the Binalud Mountains where *qanats* could tap the groundwater resources and supplement the few streams coming down from the mountains.[39] The reasons for the founding seem largely to have been military: in the 450s Yazdgird II used Nishapur as a base in the Haytal wars, as did Khusraw II Parviz's Armenian general, Smbat Bagratuni, in the early 7th century.[40]

On the basis of aerial photos of the site and the placenames in the Muslim sources R.W. Bulliet concludes that Sassanian Nishapur was a small town; although heavily fortified, it probably had just a few thousand inhabitants.[41] Yet the importance of the enclave should not be judged from the size of its urban center alone. Nishapur became the seat of a Nestorian bishop,[42] a sign of political status, and from later accounts it appears that even in Sassanian times the hinterland contained many villages. The tributary agreement, which paid the Arabs one million dirhams, further indicates a considerable population and agricultural production.[43]

The growth of Nishapur city began in earnest when 'Abdullah b. Tahir, in 830, made it the capital of Khurasan at the expense of Marv. At the same time he invested one million dirhams in new qanats and built a new suburb, Shadyakh.[44] The Tahirids' successors as lords of Khurasan – the Saffarids, the Samanids, and the Ghaznavids – added new structures, even though they did not use the city as their capital. 'Amr b. Layth, for instance, built a new dar al-imara (government house), and Mahmud of Ghazna paid 100.000 dinars to have the bazaar covered, perhaps to compensate for the extortionate taxation which had made him so unpopular.[45] Local patricians like the Mikali family, who through several generations held the office of ra'is al-balad or "leader," i.e. middleman between the Empire and the local community, also invested in villages and qanats.[46]

During the 9th and 10th centuries the urbanization of Nishapur proceeded so vigorously that both the suburb Shadyakh and 65 villages were eventually incorporated into the city and, according to Bulliet, the population may have reached and even exceeded 100.000.[47] The entire enclave was said to contain 2.000 villages, most of them qanat-watered, and Ibn Hawqal states, that Nishapur's agriculture was the most productive in all of Khurasan. Even so, the city had to import foodstuffs from the neighboring enclaves of Sarakhs and Quchan.[48] Because of its political status Nishapur attracted trade and developed large textile and ceramic industries. It also won a reputation as a center of learning because jurists, theologians, and other scholars flocked to the city to benefit from the generosity of the rulers.[49] A proper political center must of course have not only magnificent buildings, but also the trappings of elite culture.

However, by the 12th century the great city of Nishapur was heading for ruin as a result of intense sectarian fighting, earthquakes, and war. Like most other Iranian towns, Nishapur became the scene of bitter struggles between Hanafis and Shafi'is. A third part in the conflict was the fundamentalist Karramiyeh movement which, unlike the two law schools, derived support from the lower classes, i.e. the weavers and the peasants, and only to a lesser extent from craftsmen and merchants. The same was true of Marv and Herat, where the movement was also strong. In a social context it thus seems to have represented the underprivileged Muslims. In Nishapur the movement may have been furthered by the economic decline which the city must have suffered when it lost its status as capital. The Samanids and Ghaznavids resided, respectively, in Bukhara and Ghazna, and in the 11th century, under Saldjuq rule, Marv was the nearest thing Khurasan had to a capital.[50] The sectarian struggles paralyzed the local political cooperation needed, for instance, to repair the damages done to the city by wars and natural disasters. Bulliet therefore sees factional strife as the single most important cause of the ruin of Nishapur.[51]

The Nishapur region also saw considerable seismic activity between the 9th and 17th centuries. Earthquakes struck the city as early as 818/19 and 856, and after a new major shock, in 1145/46, some of the inhabitants emigrated, among other places to Kazwin.[52] Then, in 1153/54, Nishapur was thoroughly ravaged by the Ghuzz Turks who killed several thousand people. The historian al-Rawandi, after describing the massacre, adds that no sooner had the Ghuzz left than the sectarian fighting in the city broke out with unabated fury, completing the destruction where the Ghuzz had left off.[53]

During the next decade what remained of the city was further plundered by roving bands of Ghuzz, by a troop of *ayyaran*, and by the Ghurids.[54] In 1161 one of Sandjar's generals made himself master of the enclave and began to repair the damage; an anonymous source reports that in 1184 the new Nishapur, now centered upon the Shadyakh quarter, was even more prosperous than the old.[55] Then another earthquake occurred in 1208/9, and this time the Khwarizmshah ordered a reconstruction. A few years later, in 1216, Nishapur was visited by Yaqut who describes it as flourishing, beyond comparison with other towns. However, this account seems to be stereotyped, for after comparing the site with the place-names found in the written sources Bulliet concludes that with hardly more than 30.000 inhabitants the new Nishapur was a mere shadow of the old.[56]

It was thus a considerably reduced Nishapur which entered into an agreement with Djebe and Sübedei in 1220. Subsequently rumors of Djalal al-Din's victories caused the city to renounce the agreement, exposing it to retalitation from the Mongols. A first Mongol attack was turned back in November 1220, but the following spring Tolui and his main force razed Nishapur and massacred its inhabitants. Djuwayni's description closely resembles his description of what had occurred shortly before in Marv; even the selection of the 400 craftsmen is included. This may be a stereotype, but on the other hand it may reflect that Mongol retribution in fact followed a standard procedure.[57] Djuwayni says nothing of the number killed, but a later historian, Sayf al-Harawi, in the beginning of the 14th century cites the figure of 1.7 million which is improbable, to say the least: not only was Nishapur's economic and demographic apogee long past by the time the

Mongols arrived, but the entire enclave, considering technology and water resources, cannot in pre-industrial times have supported much more than 500.000
people, the same as it did around 1950.

Both Mustawfi and Hafiz-é Abru pass lightly over the massacre, instead attribut-
ing the destructions to earthquakes. New shocks in fact occurred in 1251 and 1270
(both dates are uncertain) and the latter destroyed Shadyakh.[58] Again the city was
rebuilt, this time on the initiative of Vadjih al-Din Faryumadi, the vizier of
Khurasan. Ibn Battuta visited Nishapur in the beginning of the 1330s and thought it
both large and well-irrigated, with a considerable textile industry and extensive
bazaars. It had even preserved its reputation as a center of learning.[59] Mustawfi states
that the new Nishapur measured 15.000 paces (gam) in circuit, i.e. about 12 km,
and had thus reached the same size as the famed Nishapur of old. If he is referring to
the urban district proper, excluding suburbs, gardens, etc., the information cannot
possibly be correct. Aerial photos show that the remains of the 14th century walls
circumscribe an area of 105 hectares, less than 1/10 of the urban area in the 10th
and 11th centuries.[60]

During the Sarbadar wars, in the second half of the 14th century, the king of
Herat, Ghiyaz al-Din Pir 'Ali, ravaged the enclave, cut down all the trees and
destroyed the canals. In 1389 a new earthquake struck.[61] Nevertheless Clavijo, who
visited the city on his way to Timur in Samarkand, thought it "very large and well
supplied with all things, surrounded by gardens, and very handsome houses."[62] But
immediately afterwards, in November 1405, Nishapur was again struck by a violent
earthquake which lasted several days and is said to have cost 30.000 lives. Shah
Rukh gave orders for yet another reconstruction and Hafiz-é Abru dutifully assures
us that the city once again was heading for prosperity: as we already have seen in the
cases of Kirman and Marv, Shah Rukh was cast in the role of the "good king," the
rebuilder whose efforts to advance civilization could not fail.[63] In fact, Nishapur
never regained its former size or status. After new devastations during the prolonged
Uzbek wars and the establishing of the Qadjar state, which need not be discussed
here, British intelligence reports from the early 19th century estimated that the city
had at most 15.000 inhabitants. Moreover it was "now destitute of water" because
most of the qanats were in disrepair. The hinterland, containing around 90 villages,
was still cultivated to some extent.[64]

Precisely this lack of water, noticed by the British agents, points to a key
influence in the history of Nishapur. There is no denying that wartime destructions
played an important part, but it may have been the extraordinary high frequency of
earthquakes which in the end prevented reconstruction. Major shocks, such as
those occurring in 1145, 1270, and 1405, must inevitably have damaged most, if
not all, of the qanats, the core-element in the water supply of the enclave. With the
repeated destructions, motivation for investing in repairs must have declined,
especially as another town, Mashhad, arose nearby. Located just on the other side of

the Kuh-é Binalud and surrounded by an aura of sanctity, Mashhad attracted increasing political interest and economic activity at the expense of Nishapur.

Originally Mashhad had just been a village called Sanabad, in the Tus-district. 'Ali al-Riza, later recognized as the eighth Shi'ite Imam, died here in 818, and his grave eventually became a popular shrine known as "the place of martyrdom," i.e. Mashhad.[65] With the pilgrim traffic followed trade, industry, donations, and investments in public buildings, pious foundations, and extension of the water supplies. Clavijo calls it a "large town" and notes the throng of pilgrims.[66] Not later than Timurid times Mashhad had become the largest and most important city in western Khurasan.[67] Contributing to this growth was tax exemptions granted by successive rulers out of respect for the shrine.[68]

Later developments need only be described briefly. The Safavids further enlarged Mashhad, both as a shrine and as a military stronghold against the Uzbeks. It was plundered repeatedly but remained in Persian hands. In the 18th century, under Nadir Shah, it briefly became the capital of the entire Empire. Mashhad was not spared in the wars following Nadir's death, but neither its existence nor its position was endangered. On the basis of information from Persian sources Kinneir estimated that immediately after the final Qadjar conquest (1803) Mashhad still had 50.000 inhabitants, even though several of the quarters were in ruins. The textile industry had also survived and the city continued to be the center for caravan trade between Iran, Transoxania, and Afghanistan. The hinterland was described as "rich and well-watered."[69]

3. Herat

This great city and oasis on the Hari-rud was actually beyond the reach of the Mesopotamia-based empires, regardless of how often they claimed sovereignty, for instance in their official historiography.[70] Thus the Persian tradition claims that Shapur I founded the fortified town of Pushang (Bushandj, present-day Ghuryan on the road from Nishapur to Herat. If true, this would indicate some degree of Sassanian control of the Hari-rud Valley; yet local traditions assert that the town was in fact much older, going back to the mythical hero Afrasiab. Under Bahram V Gur (421–439) Sassanian armies were said to have advanced all the way to Balkh. In the process they may also have occupied Herat, as the Nestorian synodal records refer to a bishop here at this time.[71] In any case, Sassanian control of Herat must have ceased, at the latest, in the disastrous year 484 when Shah Firuz and most of the Sassanian eastern army fell in battle with the Haytal princes. In order to obtain peace the Empire had to surrender all its bases east of Marv and even pay tribute.[72]

When Khusraw I, around 560, finally subjugated the Haytal princes and pushed the border of the Empire forward to Taliqan (between Marv al-Rud/Bala Murghab and Maymaneh), Herat again came under some kind of Sassanian control. At the same time we have reports of a Nestorian bishop in Pushang,[73] and even as late as the end of the 6th century the famous general Bahram Chubin could use Herat as base for fighting the Turks. But during the civil wars in the west, which began immediately afterwards, the oasis slipped out of Sassanian hands. By the early 7th century it was considered enemy territory. When the Arabs arrived they found in Herat no *marzban*, contrary to what they had done in safely held Sassanian bases such as Marv and Nishapur.[74]

The stereotyped Arab accounts of conquest of course mention the conquerors Herat (there are several candidates for this honor) as well as the size of the tribute (1.000.000 dirhams). In reality the enclave was more an allied principality than a subjugated province;[75] only under the Abbasids and later the Tahirids, Saffarids, Samanids, Ghaznavids, and Saldjuqs was Herat incorporated into larger regional political structures without, however, serving as a capital. Therefore it did not yet enjoy the extraordinary favor alternately bestowed upon Nishapur and Marv.[76]

Nevertheless, owing to favorable environmental conditions, the Herat oasis was one of the largest and most important enclaves of Khurasan. Though famines occurred, for instance in 794/95 and again in 833/34, Ya'qubi in the 9th century characterized Herat as the most prosperous city in the country; Ibn Rusteh counted 400 villages in the enclave which in all the 10th-century sources is famed for its fertility and its textile and metal industries.[77]

Herat was not spared disasters. An earthquake struck in 1101/2, and sectarian fighting broke out between Shi'ites and Sunnis;[78] but neither in frequency nor in intensity were these disasters comparable to what occurred in Nishapur. At the end of the 12th century, under the short-lived Ghurid rule, Herat is said to have contained no fewer than 6.000 baths, 12.000 shops, and 444.000 dwellings. Needless to say, these figures must be greatly exaggerated.[79]

Then, in 1221, came the Mongols. The city offered resistance and succeeded in repulsing the initial attack. Nevertheless the inhabitants chose to surrender voluntarily, and Tolui was therefore content to slaughter the Khwarizmi garrison and install a pro-Mongol governor. Later in the year Herat rebelled, this time suffering heavy retaliation. After a prolonged siege it was stormed in June 1222, and as punishment the Mongols carried out a massacre which, according to Saif al-Harawi, cost the lives of 1.6 million people. The hinterland, including Badghis, was also thoroughly ravaged. Al-Harawi, who recorded the local traditions a hundred years after the attack, explains that the enclave was completely razed; the few remaining inhabitants survived by robbing caravans. Another historian, Djuzdjani, closer to the events, reports that no fewer than 2.4 million people perished.[80] Both figures are entirely arbitrary, of course, and cannot be used to reconstruct the size of Herat in pre-Mongol times.[81]

In the case of Herat, then, the sources also represent the Mongol invasion as a major disaster, but considering the city's later history this seems to be exaggerated and stereotyped. As early as 1236 Herat was officially pardoned and repair work permitted. The kings of the Kart dynasty, who ruled the enclave from 1245 to 1373, initially as Ilkhanid governors, were energetic builders and colonizers; Ibn Battuta describes Herat under their rule as the greatest city of Khurasan.[82] Mu'izz al-Din Kart (1333–1370) built huge walls around the entire city, including the suburban districts. They were said to enclose an area of 1 sq *farsakh* (36 sq km). In practice they proved impossible to defend and Timur subsequently had them demolished.[83]

Herat had surrendered to Timur without a struggle in 1381. Disturbances the following year led to reprisals in the form of extra taxes and some arbitrary killings, but because Herat had obviously been dragged involuntarily into the rebellion, Timur did not carry out any serious punishments or massacres.[84] His son and successor, Shah Rukh, made Herat the capital of a large Khurasani state and the object of considerable political favor.[85] The local historian Isfizari says that at the end of the 15th century the *shahristan* of Herat, i.e. the fortified inner town, formed a square with a circuit of 7.300 paces (1.900 on each side). This would give an intramural area of approximately 200 ha with a hypothetical maximum population of 40.000. However, the city was far larger than that. Outside the walls were suburbs 1 *farsakh* in length, with mosques, bazaars, palaces, and gardens (thus they did not form entirely built-up areas); beyond the suburbs a dense settlement of villages extended for several *farsakhs* farther.[86] In Timurid times agricultural production of the enclave was also expanded through the construction of new irrigation systems. Cultivation had previously been concentrated south of the city, while the area to the north was described as desert. This area was now brought under plow when several new canals were constructed, first by Timur himself who had the army dig canals in the Murghab district northeast of the city, then by by Abu Sa'id (1459–1469), Husayn Bayqara (1469–1506), and others.[87] Thus Herat acquired the reputation for being a most beautiful and pleasant place. Mirza Muhammad Haydar, author of the *Tarikh-é rashidi*, recalled the city of his childhood, around 1500, as "a paradise."[88]

Disasters continued to afflict the enclave, however. In 1435 an outbreak of plague killed 600.000 people in the city and an additional 400.000 in the rural districts. Shah Rukh, away on campaign in Djibal, is said to have forbidden the army to receive letters from Khurasan for fear that the reports of the ravages of the plague would undermine the morale of his troops. Another serious plague epidemic broke out in 1463/64.[89] Djahanshah Qara-qoyunlu briefly occupied Herat in 1458, and when his soldiers retreated they plundered so thoroughly that famine ensued. During the Uzbek wars the enclave was ravaged several times (1507, 1529, 1554, 1585, and 1604).[90]

None of these events caused lasting damage. While Herat never regained the position it had held as the Timurid capital, it remained one of Khurasan's major enclaves. A British officer, Captain Christie, who visited Herat at the beginning of the 19th century, remarked that "no city, perhaps, in the East, has so little ground unoccupied. It is computed to contain one hundred thousand inhabitants (...) it is the emporium of the commerce carried on between Cabul, Kashmere, Bockhara, Hindostan and Persia." The hinterland Christie described as intensively cultivated, covered by villages and gardens.[91] The development of Herat was thus the opposite of that of Marv: an example of resiliency and continuity in Khurasan.

4. Summary

Conventional explanations of the alleged decline of Khurasan focus on the fact that the country had to bear the brunt of the barbarian invasions of the 12th and 13th centuries. This is little more than a paraphrase of the horror stories told by the medieval sources. Even though Khurasan was perhaps more exposed to wars and invasions than Iranshahr's other lands, these reports in fact wildly exaggerate the extent and consequences of wartime destruction. Rashid al-Din, for instance, includes as a matter of fact Sarakhs (on the Tadjand/Tedzhen River between Nishapur and Marv) in his list of towns razed by the Mongols. Djuwayni, who was closer to the events, explicitly states, however, that Sarakhs capitulated voluntarily and even placed troops at the disposal of Tolui for his attack on Marv. Apparently some disturbances occurred later in the town, yet they did not provoke any destructive reprisals. When Ibn Battuta visited Sarakhs in the 1330s, he found nothing unusual to report. He knew that Marv, in contrast, was in ruins. Mustawfi al-Kazwini lists Sarakhs as a thriving medium-sized town, 5.000 paces in circuit.[92]

The consequences of Timur's campaigns have been exaggerated as well. In fact, they did not cause great destruction to Khurasan. The exception is Tus where, in 1388, Miran Shah, one of Timur's sons, carried out a retaliatory massacre.[93] In contrast, during the prolonged wars between the Safavids and the Uzbeks in the 16th century most of the towns in western Khurasan were repeatedly plundered. Still, the history of the large enclaves does not confirm the idea of an absolute and general decline. The overall impression is, rather, one of constant fluctuations and shifts in which the destructions produced by the Mongols and others are but one among several factors. In Nishapur, for instance, earthquakes seem to have been the key influence in the decline and the transferring of the center of western Khurasan to Mashhad.

The many smaller enclaves of Khurasan present a similar picture of fluctuations rather than general decline. Of course, cases of de-urbanization and even abandonment of settlement can be found. If we briefly examine Ibn Khurdadhbih's assessment lists from the 9th century and the geographical descriptions from the 10th century, we see two such cases: Nisa (Nasa) and Abivard (Baward). These towns, located one day's journey from each other in the old cultivated area on the northern slopes of the Kopet Dagh, were described in the 10th century as medium-sized, but unhealthy. Nisa in particular was said to be strongly infected with *filaria medinensis*.[94] Apparently no further information is available about the time and causes of the abandonment of these two settlements. Nisa, originally the secular part of old Parthaunisa, was struck by an earthquake in 943, and 5.000 people were said to have perished. Later the town was stormed by the Mongols, who allegedly massacred 70.000, including a large number of refugees from Khwarizm.[95] Yet this cannot have been the only cause of the abandonment of Nisa, as Soviet archaeologists date the last traces of settlement much later. Perhaps the town was simply stifled by the Uzbek wars and the disturbances of the 18th century.[96] By the beginning of this century Nisa had been replaced by Ashkhabad, some twenty kilometers to the east.

Abivard, identified with the site of Kuhna-Abivard near the village of Kahka, presumably suffered a similar fate.[97] By the 14th century the district was referred to as a winter pasture of nomads, but this in itself explains little, since both the Abivard and Nisa districts also retained some cultivation.[98]

Most of the remaining enclaves on Ibn Khurdadhbih's list survived, although they too underwent fluctuations and settlement shifts; in some cases they also changed their names. One example of the resiliency of the secondary enclaves is Quchan (Khabushan) in the upper Atrak Valley, an area which in medieval times was called Ustuwa. Archaeological evidence suggests that during Sassanian times the town grew to about 30 ha; perhaps it should be identified with Shahr-Kavadh, a town which Ibn al-Faqih lists as having been founded by Kavadh I between Nishapur and Gurgan.[99] As center of the Ustuwa district Quchan grew considerably in Muslim times; today the site covers about 180 ha. Yaqut calls it a "small town," but adds that the surrounding district contained 93 villages.[100] Later it suffered damage, either during the Mongol wars or by earthquakes. However, Hulagu Khan, who is otherwise notorious as the destroyer of Baghdad, brought *muqannis* from Kuhistan to repair the water supply; his successors are said to have favored the town further. We should also note that many of the ruined dams still existing in Khurasan can be dated by their technical features to Ilkhanid and Timurid times, an indication of continued political will to keep the enclaves under cultivation.[101] After new earthquakes Old Quchan was abandoned in the 19th century and a new town built a bit further to the east. A British officer, C.M. MacGregor, estimated that this town in the 1870s had 2.000 houses. He also observed that the area was still under intensive cultivation.[102]

Sabzavar, center of the Bayhaq district and therefore often called *(shahr-é)* Bayhaq, suffered similar changes in fortunes. Yaqut states that the center of the district had originally been the town of Khusrawdjird. However, in his time (early 13th century) Khusrawdjird had been replaced by Sabzavar, perhaps as a result of the earthquake which had occurred in 1052.[103] Sabzavar is said to have been sacked by the Mongols, but if Mustawfi al-Kazwini's information is up to date, it had recovered from this by the beginning of the 14th century. In Ilkhanid times the town temporarily lost its traditional function as an entrepot for the caravan trade between Nishpaur and the western Plateau. Political favoring of the small town of Faryumad attracted the traffic to an alternative route through the Isfarayin Valley. No doubt this change of fortune contributed to make Sabzavar the center for the *Sarbadars*, a quasi-religious movement which sought to gain autonomy from the successive hegemonic states in Khurasan. The movement was finally suppressed by Timur-é Lenk in 1381.[104] Sabzavar later became an important Safavid base and was repeatedly conquered and plundered by the Uzbeks. Like countless other Khurasani settlements Sabzavar suffered from the chaos of the 18th century and the constant Turkoman raids from the steppes east of the Caspian Sea. Only the Russian expansion in Central Asia in the second half of the 19th century finally put a stop to these incursions. However, Sabzavar survived all this.[105]

Note: Kuhistan

Another example of resiliency is the enclaves in Kuhistan, the arid and earthquake-plagued mountain area immediately east of the large *kavirs*. The geographical literature from the 10th century and onwards lists several *qanat*-watered towns, among them Qayin, Tun, Djunabad, Turshish, Buzdjan (today Turbat-é Djam), Zaveh (today Turbat-é Haydariyeh), Khwaf, and the two Tabas (Tabasayn), i.e. Tabas Gilaki on the edge of Dasht-é Lut and Tabas Masina east of Birdjand, on the present border of Afghanistan. All these towns are described as small and with inadequate supplies of water. Qayin, usually considered the capital of the region, was the largest, nearly the size of Sarakhs. Besides agriculture the economic activity of the Kuhistani settlements included textile manufacture and caravan trade. In the steppe and desert areas between the enclaves nomadic existence was widespread, which incidentally argues against the idea that the region was later exposed to progressive "bedouinization."[106]

   Kuhistan was a seismically active area and the *qanat*-watered enclaves must have been repeatedly damaged by earthquakes. For the period before 1500 we can document at least two major destructive shocks: in 1336 (the Khwaf area) and in 1493 (east of Birdjand). The loss of human life was considerable in both cases. Further serious shocks are registered in the 16th and 17th centuries. Local legends, vaguely hinting at previous earthquakes, may therefore have historical foundation.[107]

   Kuhistan was also exposed to repeated wartime destructions. As base for the Isma'ilis the area was attacked several times by the hegemonic states from the 11th century and onwards. However, it was first with Hulagu Khan's campaign in 1256, in which Tun was razed and its inhabitants massacred, that an end was put to the autonomy of Kuhistan.[108] In 1381 Turshish was destroyed by Timur-é Lenk and the successor settlement, Sultanabad (now Kashmar), may not have been established until Nadir Shah's time (18th century). The Uzbek wars and continuous Turkoman raiding can be added to the list of misfortunes.[109] As a result considerable change and fluctuation occurred within the individual enclaves. Tun (presently Firdaws) was, according to Nasir-é Khusraw, already in marked decline long before the Mongol attack, while in contrast the village of Birdjand, first mentioned by Yaqut, grew to urban size in Ilkhanid times.[110]

In general, the small enclaves of Kuhistan, despite the severe environment and the hydrological problems, survived both natural disasters and wars. Some of them, e.g. Buzdjan and Zaveh, were favored by having shrines (the tombs of Sufi saints) of some supraregional reputation. Around 1900 Sykes estimated that Zaveh/Turban-é Haydariyeh had a population of 15.000. It hardly can have had substantially more at any earlier date.[111] European descriptions from the latter half of the 19th century certainly present a rather sad picture of decline and poverty in the remote territory. Especially Qayin, the old capital, which at the beginning of the 19th century still had been a prosperous and important town with 20.000 families, had declined markedly. MacGregor did not think that it had more than 800 inhabited houses, and Sykes called it "the most desolate-looking town I have ever seen." Its place as the capital of Kuhistan had been taken over by Birdjand.[112] However, these accounts were written shortly after the terrible famine and epidemics in the early 1870s, disasters which had hit the eastern Plateau most severely. Added to this came the competition from European goods which deprived Kuhistan's towns of an important part of their traditional economic activity. If Kuhistan did decline, the causes must largely lie with particular conditions in the 19th century.

Admittedly Quchan, Sabzavar, and Kuhistan are only examples. They are fairly representative examples, however, of the small enclaves of eastern Iran. Considered all together, then, there is little in the available evidence to support the idea of a dramatic demographic decline or massive expansion of extensive methods of subsistence in Khurasan during the Middle Ages.[113]

Chapter 16

Azarbaydjan

Azarbaydjan comprises the northwestern corner of the Iranian Plateau, from the Qizil Uzan and the Tarum Highlands in the south to the Aras (Araxes) in the north. Arran , i.e. the territory further to the north, between the Aras and the Kur River and largely identical with the former Soviet Republic of Azarbaydjan, was usually considered a separate region, even though it was sometimes administered together with Azarbaydjan proper.[1]

On the Plateau each country, indeed each oasis, had a certain individuality of its own which was the outcome of its history and particular environmental conditions. What made Azarbaydjan distinct was, in the first place, hydrological conditions: several fairly large perennial rivers, including the Aras, the Qizil Uzan, the Qareh Su, and the Zarineh Rud flowed through the country. Second, topographical barriers kept it rather isolated, with the Zandjan Valley as the most important line of communication to the outside. Medieval sources further remarked the distinctive ethnic character of the country even before immigration, beginning in the 13th century, transformed it into the major Turkish-speaking region in Iranshahr.[2] All of this explains, in part at least, why Azarbaydjan also had a tradition of autonomy not found in other places on the western Plateau. Its marginal position in relation to the Empire in Abbasid times is reflected by the tax assessments (cf. Table 4). By Ilkhanid times (13th and 14th centuries), this situation had changed completely. Azarbayjdan now occupied a key fiscal position and had even become the seat of the hegemonic power.

Settlement and intensive agriculture in Azarbaydjan was traditionally concentrated in the basins between the mountains. The largest of these is the Urmiyeh Basin with the lake bearing the same name. Like the large and small *kavirs* farther to the east, the Urmiyeh Basin is a closed drainage basin. The soil along the banks of the lake is saline and unsuitable for agriculture. On the slopes farther away, however, conditions are more favorable, owing to the natural drainage and the water supplied by streams and rivers falling into the lake. Since pre-historic times this fertile belt has been the primary settlement zone of Azarbaydjan. Extensive methods of subsistence otherwise seem to have been widespread, especially in the eastern part of the country.[3]

In the early 1st millennium B.C. the Urmiyeh Basin was part of Urartu, a state centered on the Van region in eastern Anatolia. According to the German archaeo-

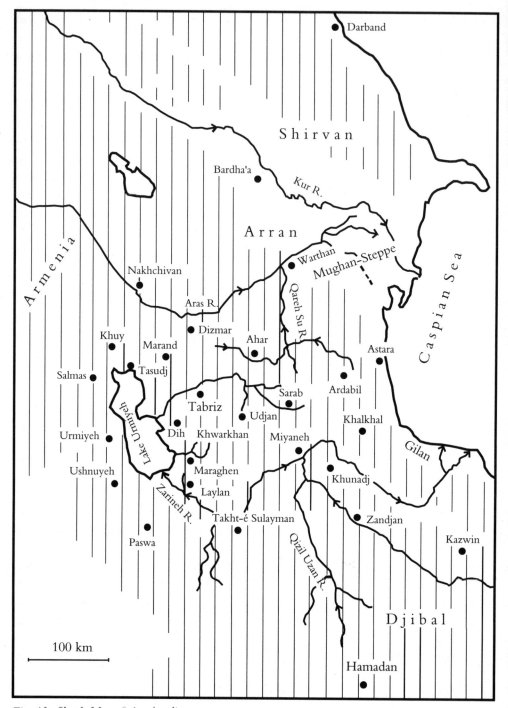

Fig. 13. Sketch-Map of Azarbaydjan.

logists, who carried out several surveys and excavations in the Basin the 1960s and 1970s, this period saw a marked expansion of settlement.[4] In their inscriptions the Urartu kings boast of having built both fortifications and irrigation works, and like their Assyrian enemies they seem to have carried out deportations and forcible resettlements.[5] The inscriptions also mention several placenames, but few of these seem to refer to Azarbaydjan. In any case, identification with known localities is subject to considerable uncertainty.[6] This is true also of the place names found in the accounts of the Assyrian campaigns. Yet Ulhu, a fort stormed by Sargon II, in 714 A.D., would seem to be identical with the ruins at Livar in the Marand region.[7]

The Urmiyeh Basin must have formed the core of the satrapy mentioned by Herodotus as *Matiene*, but the sources offer little additional information about the region in the Achaemenid era. As neither Alexander nor his successors came here, no information was gathered which could be integrated into the classical image of Persia. Later Strabo sought to make up for this gap by collecting information from participants in Marcus Antonius' Azarbaydjan campaign in 36 B.C.[8] Apparently Alexander was content with appointing (or simply acknowledging) a Persian, Atropates, as vassal prince of the country.[9] During Seleucid and Parthian times the successors of Atropates ruled Azarbaydjan (now known by the dynastically derived name *(Media) Atropatene* as an autonomous principality. Its capital was in Ganzak, a town located on a tributary to the Zarineh Rud in the southeastern corner of the Urmiyeh Basin.[10]

1. On the Fringes of the Empire: Azarbaydjan in Sassanian and Abbasid times

Little more is known about Azarbaydjan in Sassanian times. It was certainly considered part of Iranshahr proper – as, for instance, adjacent Armenia was not – but may have retained some measure of autonomy. At least, Ibn Khurdadhbih mentions "Azarbaydjan-shah" and "Barashkan-shah" as titles of local rulers.[11] On the other hand the shrine in Shiz (Takht-é Sulayman) seems to have had special functions in relation to the Sassanian crown.[12] Apart from this, the sources primarily focus on Azarbaydjan's strategic importance. Through the lowland passages at Darband and Batumi nomad raiders from the Black Sea steppes would make forays against the enclaves in northern Djibal and Djazirah, while the Sassanians, with Azarbaydjan as a base, would attack Armenia and thereby outflank the Roman and Byzantine *limes* in northern Syria.[13]

The foundings traditionally ascribed to the Sassanians in the region were certainly of a military character: thus *Shahram-Firuz* (also known as *Firuz-gird*, *Budan-Firuz* and presumably identical with Ardabil), founded in the 5th century by Firuz, was a counterpart to the fortress town of Kazwin, in Djibal.[14] Outside Iranshahr proper, in Caucasian Albania, Firuz also founded the base *Firuz-Kavadh* (Parthaw). In

Table 14. The assessment of Azarbaydjan.

	Dirhams
788	4.700.000[a]
819	4.500.000[b]
c. 840	4.000.000[c]
840–70	2.000.000[d]
918/19	c. 4.500.000[e]
c. 960	10.000.000[f]
1335–1341	11.000.000[g]

[a] al-'Mutarrif (el-'Ali: 1971).
[b] Qudama (de Goeje tr.: 190).
[c] Ya'qubi (tr.: 72).
[d] Ibn Khurdadhbih (tr.: 93).
[e] 'Ali b. 'Isa (von Kremer, 1888: 315); Miskawayh (tr. !V, p. 54) informs us that the amount (converted from 220.000 dinars) represented the surplus from *iqta's* and that it was not paid.
[f] Ibn Hawqal (tr., II: 327f). The figure presumably represents money paid for tax-farming.
[g] Mustawfi(*Nuzhat*: ch. 8); the actual figure is 2.5 million *dinar-é rayidj*, here converted according to silver-weight.

Arran, on the border with Armenia, Kavadh is said to have founded another base, *Bardha'a*, which is later mentioned as a large and important town.[15] Above all, the Sassanians enlarged the fortification of the lowland passages already begun by local rulers in Parthian times: at Darband, Kavadh and Khusraw I built a line of walls and forts 20 *farsakh* long, guarded partly by garrisons of professional soldiers, partly by prisoners of war settled in military colonies. They also constantly put pressure on the Byzantines to contribute money to this defensive line which they saw as mutually advantageous.[16]

Ordinary settlements are given only vague mentions in the sources: Ganzak in the 5th century was the seat of Azarbaydjan's Nestorian bishop, an indication that this town for some time remained the capital, as it had been in Parthian times. But when the Arabs arrived in the 7th century, Ardabil appears as the political center, seat of the *marzban*, the Sassanian governor or, perhaps, vassal prince.[17] The Urmiyeh Basin remained the principal settlement zone, however, with the two largest towns besides Ardabil: Maragheh and Urmiyeh.[18]

Apparently this pattern did not change in the centuries following the Muslim conquest. Azarbaydjan was an unruly land, the scene of continuous warfare against the Byzantines and the Khazars, and a refuge of Arab tribesmen from the Djazirah fleeing imperial control. Outside the larger enclaves the Sassanian successor states did not succeed in making their rule effective.[19] Moreover, in 816 the peasants of Azarbaydjan rose up in a widespread messianic, anti-Muslim revolt, the Khurrami-yeh. It cost the Empire large resources and 20 years of savage fighting to suppress it. In the end the effort was to no avail: by the late 9th century the Abbasid caliphate, weakened by internal political crisis, had lost control of the land to local warlords.[20] This explains why Azarbaydjan appears only marginally in the Abbasid tax assessments. The figures cannot be taken as proof that the region was unproductive and thinly populated, as the following anecdote will show.

In 965 Rukn al-Dawleh, the Buyid lord of Djibal, assisted a vassal prince, Ibrahim al-Salar, in conquering Azarbaydjan. Rukn al-Dawleh's vizier, who had participated in the campaign and studied the country, subsequently reported that Ibrahim was quite unsuitable as a ruler: because of his compliance toward Kurdish and Daylami *iqta'*-holders, his drinking and general incompetence, Ibrahim did not collect more than two million dirhams in taxes from this potentially rich land. The vizier therefore suggested that Ibrahim be pensioned off together with his beloved singers and jesters and that he (the vizier) assume administation of the country; in return, he promised to levy no less than 50 million dirhams. Rukn al-Dawleh rejected the offer saying that it was inconsistent with his prestige to take the country from an old friend and ally.[21] The vizier's offer was no doubt improbably high, but the story reminds us that the Abbasid tax figures reflect political rather than purely economic conditions.

The 10th-century geographical accounts describe Azarbaydjan as covered by small enclaves, each containing a number of fortified minor towns.[22] The principal zones of settlement were:

The *Urmiyeh Basin*, with two large towns, Maragheh and Urmiyeh, and several smaller ones: Tabriz, Dih Khwarkhan, Laylan, Paswa, Ushnuyeh, Salmas (now Shahpur), and Tasudj.

The *Ardabil enclave*, watered by many streams from the Sabalan massif.

Among the secondary enclaves were:

The *Khuy Basin*, with the towns Khuy and Marand.

Sarab (Sarav).

Miyaneh, located on a tributary to the Qizil Uzan.

Khalkhal, south of Ardabil.

Ardabil and Maragheh were the dominant towns, each extending 2/3 *farsakh* in length and width, and alternating as political center of the country. The remaining towns, with the exception of Urmiyeh, were described as small.[23]

From Yaqut's eye-witness account of Azarbaydjan certain changes can be seen to have occurred between the 10th and the 13th centuries: towns such as Salmas, Ushnuyeh, Udjan, Marand, and Khunandj, the latter an important place of call for caravans going through the Zandjan Valley, had declined; in contrast, Tabriz had grown into a large city.[24] In some cases the decline was only temporary, however, and the overall settlement structure had remained largely unchanged. Nor had there been any decisive changes when Mustawfi al-Kazwini wrote in the 14th century, after the large nomad invasions had begun.

The Ghuzz Turks arrived in the 11th and 12th centuries. They were assigned grazing lands in northern Azarbaydjan, including the Mughan steppe where they could serve as fighters for the Faith, *ghaziyan*, against Armenians and Georgians.

Table 15. Azarbaydjan: larger enclaves in the 14th century. (According to the 1335–1341 tax assessment, as cited in Mustawfi al-Kazwini: *Nuzhat al-qulub*: ch. 8).

	Dinar-é rayidj
1. Urmiyeh region	
Tabriz	1.150.000
Maragheh	255.500
Urmiyeh	74.000
Salmas	39.000
Paswa	25.000
Dih Khwarkhan	23.600
Ushnuyeh	19.300
Laylan	10.000
Tasudj	5.000
2. Ardabil region	
Ardabil	85.000
Khalkhal	30.000
Shahrud district	10.000
3. Sarab (with 100 villages)	81.000
4. Khuy region	
Khuy (with 80 villages)	53.000
Marand	24.000
5. Dizmar (north of Tabriz)	40.800
6. Darmuzin (with 100 villages)	29.000
7. Miyaneh	25.800
8. Azad (on the Aras River)	18.300
9. Ahar region	
Ahar (with 30 villages)	15.000
Pishkin	5.200
10. Naw-Diz (between Tabriz and Ardabil)	11.000
11. Arran with Mughan	303.000
12. Nakhchivan	113.000

Note: a number of smaller settlements with low assessments are not included.

The Ghuzz presumably numbered some tens of thousands and can hardly have disturbed subsistence patterns to any great extent; in fact, the mountains of Azarbaydjan already contained a more or less nomadic population of Kurds.[25] The Mongol invasion, on the other hand, brought considerable immigration. No less than a half million nomads, with their herds, were brought west and settled in Azarbaydjan, Arran, and Anatolia. Later, successive Turkish rulers on the northern Plateau – the Qara-qoyunlu, the Aq-qoyunlu and especially the Safavids – transferred many of these nomads from Anatolia to Azarbaydjan and other places in Iran.[26]

Though some eventually were sedentarized, the total number of nomads in Azarbaydjan grew considerably because of these immigrations. No doubt this led to increased political turmoil. Yet there is no evidence that nomadic immigration by itself led to a lasting shrinkage of settled agriculture. The nomads, it should be recalled, were not distributed evenly over the country, but were concentrated in areas with good grazing such as the Mughan steppe and the districts of Khalkhal and

Daravard. The nearby plains around Zandjan in northern Djibal were also popular grazing lands. Yet to cite the Mughan steppe as an example of the "bedouinisation directe," as Xavier de Planhol does, would carry more weight, had the steppe ever been an agricultural enclave of any significance.[27] Rather than causing decline, the nomad immigration seems in fact to have contributed to the growth in Azarbaydjan from Ilkhanid times onward.

2. Tabriz: The Emergence of a New Political Center

On the heels of the nomads followed the hegemonic power, and so increased political favor was bestowed on Azarbaydjan. The explanation for this is simple enough: from Ilkhanid times the rulers of Iranshahr based their military power on the mobilization of nomads rather than on professional armies. This was a momentous change which will be taken up later. To maintain contact with (and control over) its military basis, the Empire therefore moved its center to the grazing lands of Azarbaydjan. Thus Hulagu Khan, founder of the Ilkhanid state, made the ancient town of Maragheh his capital. Subsequently, Ghazan Khan moved the imperial center, first to Udjan and then to Tabriz, and the latter's spectacular growth reflected the position of Azarbaydjan as the new heartland of the Empire.

Tabriz, founded or fortified by invading Arab warlords in the 9th century, was originally a small town overshadowed by the old towns of Maragheh, Ardabil, and Urmiyeh. Then, in the middle of the 10th century, it was chosen as base by the Musafirids, one of the local lines of rulers struggling to control larger or smaller parts of Azarbaydjan. Because of this, the town seems to have grown considerably.[28]

In 1042/43 Tabriz was heavily damaged by an earthquake said to have cost 40.000 lives. Yet when Nasir-é Khusraw visited the town a few years later, it was again flourishing and populous. He measured it as 1400 paces in length and breadth and called it the administrative center of the country (*qasabeh-é Azarbaydjan*).[29] We have similar descriptions from the 12th and 13th centuries, for instance by Yaqut, who himself had resided in Tabriz in 1213/14. He adds, however, that Maragheh remained Azarbaydjan's largest town.[30]

Tabriz' success in attracting long-distance trade was noted by Marco Polo. Visiting the town in 1271, shortly before it was made the capital, he saw merchants from Baghdad, Mosul, Hormuz, India, and even Europe, who had all come to Tabriz to trade in precious stones and luxury textiles, especially the brocades manufactured in the town itself.[31] At this time the circuit of the walls, according to Mustawfi, measured 6.000 paces. By comparison, he mentions that Urmiyeh had a circumference of 10.000 paces, Salmas of 8.000, Khuy of 6.500, and Udjan of 3.000. Like Khuy, Tabriz was still just a "medium-sized town," *shahr-é wast*.[32]

But when Ghazan Khan made it his capital around 1300, he and magnates like the vizier Rashid al-Din began building on a large scale. Among the projects was the construction of 900 new *qanats* intended to supplement the water provided by the streams from the Sahand massif. Suburbs (*shahrche*) were built and surrounded by new walls 25.000 paces long. In a short time Tabriz thus grew to become one of Iranshahr's largest cities, and the many new *qanats* provided for expanded and intensified agricultural production in the hinterland.[33]

The concentration of political and commercial activity in Tabriz presumably caused some of Azarbaydjan's other towns to stagnate or even decline.[34] Ardabil escaped that fate because, in Ilkhanid times, it had become seat of a highly respected Sufi order led by the Safavid family. The tomb of Shaykh Safi al-Din, the founder of the order, eventually became a venerated shrine.

As Azarbaydjan became the Empire's new core-land, its fiscal importance increased. Although the assessments include duties on long-distance trade, the figures must nonetheless reflect a genuine growth in settlement and cultivation. In support of this we can point to Mustawfi's information about the expansion of agriculture in the Tabriz enclave and to the archaeological surveys which indicate a continuous settlement growth from Ilkhanid times.[35]

Tabriz remained one of Iranshahr's largest and most important cities, even though it lost its status as capital in the 16th century and was visited by wars and natural disasters. The plague struck in 1347 and 1487; more outbreaks are registered in the 18th and 19th centuries.[36] Serious earthquakes occurred on several occasions: thus in 858/59 the town was apparently destroyed and had to be rebuilt. In 1042/43 it was partly destroyed and 40.000 inhabitants perished. Mustawfi refers to later shocks (probably those occurring in 1274 and 1304), adding that they did not cause serious damage. However, in 1550 and in 1721 Tabriz was again struck by major earthquakes.[37] Moreover, owing to its location Tabriz became the scene of prolonged fighting between the Ottomans and the Safavids in the 16th and 18th centuries. During these wars the city changed hands several times and was plundered and otherwise damaged.[38]

No doubt it was the wars and recurrent outbreaks of plague that had reduced Tabriz to its depressing state around 1800. Kinneir called it "one of the most wretched cities I have seen in Persia," estimating its population at below 30.000. Yet several of the other towns in Azarbaydjan were described in much more positive terms in the British reports[39] and the decline was temporary in any case. As early as 1834 James Baillie Fraser thought Tabriz was "a city which is every day improving, and its population increasing," and this despite the fact that the cholera had ravaged the city and the rest of Azarbaydjan just a few years before.[40] In the 1860s British diplomats estimated that the city was now Iran's largest, with over 100.000 inhabitants. Fiscally Tabriz together with the rest of Azarbaydjan also occupied a clear first place.[41]

The rapid economic growth in Azarbaydjan in the 19th century was largely caused by the world market, more particularly the increasing trade with Russia.

These developments are outside the scope of this study;[42] but it must be stressed that the shifting of both political power and economic activity toward the north and northwest of Iranshahr had been under way already in Ilkhanid times. Changes in the Empire's resource base had given the nomads increasing military importance. Consequently, the Empire's interest was directed toward Azarbaydjan with its strategic resources in the form of pastures. Expansion of trade, urbanization, and agriculture resulted from this.

Chapter 17

Recapitulation and Comparison:
Contrasting Highlands with Floodplain

Like Mesopotamia, the Plateau clearly saw a considerable expansion of settlement and irrigation in Parthian and Sassanian times. Moreover, again like Mesopotamia, state-directed colonization appears to have been a key part in the process, at least in the Sassanian period. Unlike Mesopotamia, however, the Plateau did not later experience continuous and general decline. The Iranian author Muhammad Dja-malzadeh relates from his youth that one night on the banks of the Zayandeh-rud the wind whispered to him about Isfahan that the city's history had been written with

"(...) the pen of tyranny, with killing, plunder, famine, and turmoil. Yet it still lives, breathes, and struggles (...) Different tribes and peoples burned the rich works of art which toil, suffering, cleverness, and intelligence had created during the centuries. But these peoples soon disappeared and Isfahan still stands."[1]

The wind could have whispered the same of countless other large and small enclaves. Of course, some settlements did decline or were even abandoned: Ray, Marv, the southern parts of both Fars and Kirman are obvious examples. In contrast, however, we can cite the economic and demographic growth in Tabriz, Herat, and other places.

Except for the gradual shift of political power and economic activity toward the north no general trend can be readily discerned. Each enclave had its own history, where changing phases of growth and decline seem largely to have been the result of local hydrological conditions, the severity and frequency of natural disasters, the degree of political favoritism, etc. While the individual enclaves thus constantly were caught up in change, the overall effect does not seem to have been drastic qualitative changes for the Plateau as a whole. Of course, the lack of quantitative data means that we cannot categorically rule out that some long-term decline did in fact occur. If it is correct that pre-industrial settlement reached its high point in Sassanian and early Muslim times, then the expansion of extensive methods of subsistence during the Middle Ages must reflect a decline in the total area of settled cultivation. However, it was largely a retreat from marginal areas. The idea that

settlement on the Plateau generally became the victim of a forcible "bedouinization" should be dismissed.

In any case, the Plateau did not experience anything comparable to the depopulation and de-urbanization of Mesopotamia. As we have already seen from the
tax assessments, the long-term development of the two principal environmental
regions of Iranshahr was strikingly different. Yet they were exposed to roughly the
same influences in the form of natural disasters, famine, wartime destructions and
plunderings (carried out, incidentally, by Iranshahr's own rulers as well as by
invaders). On one point, however, there was perhaps a significant difference in the
frequency and severity of these disasters: it would seem that epidemic diseases,
including plague, played a less prominent part on the Plateau than in Mesopotamia.

As stated, infectious diseases are not simply a matter between the host organism
and the disease-producing microparasite. There are also affected by environmental
factors, the methods of subsistence, etc. This means that we cannot infer from
Mesopotamia what was the nature of epidemics on the Plateau and their consequences. Thus the influence of local environments seems to be reflected in the
geographical literature's classification of "healthy" and "unhealthy" places. While
Isfahan was famed for its invigorating climate, Ray and Gurgan were notorious for
frequent, lethal epidemics. No doubt this classification contains some stereotypes,
but it may well be based on real local differences, e.g. in the quality of the water
resources. We can be reasonably certain that several chronic infections such as
trachoma, leprosy, and tuberculosis in different forms had spread over most of the
Plateau at an early stage. Malaria presumably followed in the wake of the *qanat* and
irrigated agriculture. But the acute person-to-person infections would have had
more difficulty in gaining an endemic foothold, given the great distances, the
dispersed settlement, and the small size of the individual enclaves. Even though
oases like Ray, Nishapur, Marv, and Isfahan in some periods reached a couple of
hundred thousand inhabitants, they must still have been too small to constitute
permanent reservoirs for infections like measles.

Of course, the Plateau was not spared epidemic disease, because infections could
quite easily be transmitted from the two adjacent disease pools, Mesopotamia-
Khuzistan and the Indus River Valley. The summary below, however, indicates
that many of the infections which came to the Plateau from these areas, remained
geographically limited. In many places epidemics must have occurred after an
interval of several generations. When they finally did strike, the risk of contagion
was high because few if any inhabitants had immunity from the diseases. However,
precisely because the diseases after all did arrive with some regularity from the
permanent reservoirs, the population of the Plateau cannot be considered a "virgin"
population like the pre-Columbian Americans. In the very long term the total
infection pressure was probably lower on the Plateau than in Mesopotamia; hence,
the conditions for a demographic recovery after a period of heavy mortality would

be more favorable. This is hypothetical, of course. There are no data to verify it statistically. By now we have seen, however, that settlement on the Plateau was basically resilient, a sign that the demographic balance here was in fact much less fragile than in Mesopotamia. It seems plausible (if unprovable) that a lower level of infection was a contributory factor.

A preliminary summary shows the following major outbreaks of epidemic diseases on the Plateau during the Muslim era:

c. 800	*Shar'uta* (plague?) in Mughan (Azarbaydjan).[2]
819/20	*Waba'* in Khurasan and surrounding countries.[3]
841/42	*Waba'* in Sistan.[4]
855/56	Great epidemic spreading from Sarakhs in east Iran to Mesopotamia.[5]
877/78	Epidemic in Kumis.[6]
900/901	Epidemic in Azarbaydjan.[7]
935/36	Epidemic in Isfahan.[8]
937/38	Smallpox in Azarbaydjan.[9]
955/56	Great epidemic over several years affecting both Khurasan and Djibal. Women and children are said to have died disproportionately.[10]
989/90	*Waba'* in Gurgan.[11]
1010/11	*Waba'* in Sistan.[12]
1031/21	Widespread epidemic striking Fars, Djibal, and Mesopotamia. In Isfahan alone 40.000 are said to have died.[13]
c. 1040	Epidemic in Herat.[14]
1056/57	Great epidemic spreading over the entire Middle East.[15]
1094	Smallpox in Isfahan. The extent of this epidemic remains unclear.[16]
1136/37	Epidemic in Djibal (Hamadan, Isfahan) spreading to Mesopotamia.[17]

A closer examination of the Iranian local histories in particular may reveal several more outbreaks and perhaps correct the impression of the frequency of infection: i.e. high in the 9th to 11th centuries, lower in the 12th and 13th centuries.

The list shows that besides local cases, there were several epidemics which affected all or at least large parts of the Plateau and the areas around it. The precise nature of these infections is impossible to determine. Plague can be excluded, however, as it was nowhere in evidence during the period covered by the list. Even when plague did occur, i.e. in the 6th to 8th centuries and again from the 14th century onwards, it apparently failed to spread to the Plateau. On first sight this seems well-nigh impossible considering that plague, especially the pneumonic strain, is extremely contagious. As regards the first pandemic, this absence may of course be a simple optical illusion caused by the scarcity of sources. Thus Thomas of Marga's remark about an outbreak of *shar'uta* (the Syriac term for *ta'un*) in the Mughan area at the end of the 8th century may refer to plague. But besides this there is little to either confirm or disprove the spread of plague on the Plateau at that time. The same uncertainty applies to Europe outside the Mediterranean region. It is tempting to make up for the lack of sources by infering from later and better known pandemics; yet this is not as simple as it may seem. The progress of later pandemics show considerable variations: the risk of infection and the virulence depend greatly, for instance, on whether or not the pneumonic strain is present. Without a shred of supporting evidence we cannot be certain that plague in the first pandemic spread widely across the Plateau.

The progress of the second pandemic is nearly as obscure, though the 14th century is considerably better documented than the 6th and 7th centuries. While we can reconstruct the course of the first epidemic, i.e. the Black Death, in Egypt and Syria and draw a rough outline of the frequency and extent of subsequent outbreaks, the situation in Iranshahr remains unclear. All we know is that on its first appearance, in the middle of the 14th century, the plague struck Tabriz and presumably Gurgan, besides Mesopotamia.[18] A few later outbreaks are also recorded:

1408:   Isfahan. Though this epidemic is classified as *ta"un*, the description does not indicate a high death rate.[19]

1435:   Herat. Al-Isfizari states that at its peak the plague killed 4.700 people a day. He estimates the total number of dead for the entire enclave at no less than one million.[20]

c. 1460:   Herat.[21]

1487/88: *Ta'un* in Tabriz.[22]

So what we have are five or six outbreaks distributed over nearly a century and a half and occurring mainly on the northern fringe of the Iranian highlands. This does not suggest that the plague had gained a firm foothold on the Plateau.[23] Given the ease with which the disease ordinarily spread this seems incredible, but even in Europe some areas suffered comparatively low mortality from the Black Death (e.g. Milan and Bohemia).[24] Thus it is possible, at least in theory, that the plague did in fact enter the plateau, but that the sources failed to record it because the disease did not cause severe loss of life. Yet this is very unlikely. Everywhere else the Black Death manifested itself so dramatically as to exclude any doubt that this indeed was a new and extraordinary disease; if we take al-Isfizari's description of the plague in Herat in 1435, we get precisely this impression of a unique disaster. Unless Iranian local chronicles or similar sources on closer inspection will provide further evidence, it would seem that particular circumstances on the Plateau prevented or at least limited the spread of the plague.

It is difficult, however, to imagine what these circumstances might have been. It is not enough to point out that the Plateau was thinly populated and that the enclaves lay far from each other, separated by mountains and deserts. Population density would have little effect on the spread of the bubonic strain. Scotland and Scandinavia, including such remote places as Iceland, were also sparsely settled, yet suffered heavy mortality from the plague. We may further note that other contagious infections both before and afterwards spread over large parts of the Plateau. Thus in 1822/23 an epidemic, cholera most likely, had no difficulty spreading from India over Shiraz to Hamadan and Sultaniyeh.[25]

In his study of the Black Death in Egypt and Syria M.W. Dols has suggested that the political turmoil following the collapse of the Ilkhanid Empire in the middle of the 14th century might be the reason: as long-distance trade across the Iranian Plateau stopped, dissemination of the infection was prevented.[26] Now the Plateau may have lost some of its traditional importance as a transit area during post-Ilkhanid times; yet Clavijo's description of Tabriz and Sultaniyeh in the early 15th century, to take but one example, makes it clear that caravan trade continued on a considerable scale. Moreover caravans were not the only conceivable carriers of infection. The armies which in this period constantly marched across the Plateau could have spread the disease as well.

A later hypothesis by M.W.Dols suggests that the dissemination of plague was hindered because rats are rare on the Plateau: both *rattus rattus* and *rattus norvegicus* thrive in the Caspian coastland and along the Gulf, but the Plateau proper is too dry for them.[27] This explanation must be viewed with some skepticism as well. Other rodents, such as the house mouse, found throughout the Plateau, can carry plague (though the mouse flea may be less willing to turn to human hosts than the rat flea);[28] in fact, about 200 species of mammals, including most domestic animals, may serve as secondary carriers. In view of this, the importance of rats and other rodents in the dissemination of plague would seem to be somewhat overestimated, especially in British and American research. Moreover when plague has first been transmitted to people, the human flea will probably serve quite effectively as vector. In the case of pneumonic plague the infection is easily spread in densely settled areas by airborne droplets, quite independently of animal carriers.

There is little doubt that the pneumonic strain did in fact occur in some of the outbreaks of plague on the Plateau. Among the victims of the epidemic in Herat in 1435 was the esteemed *'alim* (legal scholar) Shaykh Zayn al-Din Khwafi, who died just two days after having led the Friday prayer. The short duration of the disease as well as al-Isfizari''s general description of heavy mortality would indicate that pneumonic plague was present.[29] One could imagine that in an isolated enclave like Herat the highly contagious, virulent pneumonic plague would have burned itself out before further dissemination could have occurred. On the other hand, the spread of the less virulent (but still lethal) bubonic strain would still have been possible, especially as Herat in Timurid times was the center for widespread commercial and military activity. However, we have simply no documentation or indications that this in fact happened.

During the second pandemic the plague gained a foothold among wild rodent populations in the Kurdistan mountains. From this new focus several epidemics were disseminated, ravaging Mesopotamia, the Caucasus, and northwestern Iran in the 17th to 19th centuries. But these later epidemics also failed to spread across the Plateau. Like the Black Death, they were restricted largely to Azarbaydjan, the Caspian coast, Gurgan-Mazandaran, and Kurdistan. The cases of plague reported from Khurasan (Mashhad) in the 19th century were probably offshoots of the outbreaks in Gurgan. It is not clear to what extent pneumonic plague appeared during this later phase.[30]

Even if the Black Death and subsequent plague epidemics did not bypass the Plateau, their influence would have been small when compared to Mesopotamia. Where plague did strike, i.e. in Herat, Tabriz, and (perhaps) Isfahan, no long-lasting damage is discernible. This cannot be because the disease assumed a less virulent form in these enclaves. The key factor must have been infrequency: on the Plateau plague came in isolated epidemics; i.e. it did not recur at short intervals and thus the pattern of cumulative high mortality was avoided. John Fryer, a British traveller who visited Isfahan at the end of the 17th century, was told that "the plague" had not come to Iran since 1600.[31] Here the word "plague" must certainly be understood simply as referring to lethal epidemic disease in general and, taken literally, the information is hardly correct. However, it lends some support to the impression that the total pressure of infection was relatively lower on the Plateau proper.

In itself plague cannot explain the historical differences between the regions of Iranshahr. Though it was certainly decisive in Mesopotamia during the crisis of the 7th century, agricultural contraction and settlement abandonment continued here in the following plague-free periods. So the course of the plague pandemics would indicate that the historical difference between the two main regions was basically related to their respective environmental characteristics.

Part 4
Sistan

Chapter 18

Environment and Early Settlement

On the eastern fringe of the Iranian Plateau, far from the imperial centers in Mesopotamia, lies the land of Sistan. In terms of geomorphology it consists of an inland drainage basin, closely resembling the arid *kavirs* farther west. Yet in other respects Sistan differs from the rest of the Plateau: its environment, characterized by the existence of sizable freshwater lakes, as well as its remarkable history mark it as a distinct unit within Iranshahr. This individuality has been accentuated by the east Iranian Highlands, i.e. the Qayin-Birdjand mountains and the Kuh-é Taftan, which physically separate the country from the rest of the Plateau.

Rainfall in Sistan occurs largely as torrential downpours during the winter. The annual average is between 50 and 100 mm, while potential evaporation reaches almost 3.000 mm. Under such extreme climatic conditions intensive agriculture and large-scale settlement is wholly dependent on irrigation. Water for this is brought to Sistan by the 1.000 km long Hilmand River that rises in the western Hindu Kush. On its way across the Dasht-é Margo and Rigistan, the desolate steppes of Sistan, the river has downcut its channel some 15–20 meters; here irrigation is impossible, at least with pre-industrial technology. In the lowest part of the basin, however, where it flows into a string of shallow freshwater lakes (the *Hamun-é Hilmand*), the river forms a dendritic delta suited for irrigation. Of course, the delta environment alternatively provides conditions favorable for extensive methods of subsistence, including hunting and fishing.

Maximum flows of the Hilmand occur in spring, from March until May, when the snow of the Hindu Kush is melting. The various channels of the delta then become unstable and floods occur frequently. At this time the lakes also reach their maximum extent, around 4.000 sq. km, contracting to half this size in summer and autumn. As the precipitation over the Hindu Kush fluctuates, the discharge of the Hilmand fluctuates as well: flooding in one season may be followed by droughts, sometimes so severe that the Hamun-é Hilmand dries out completely (this has happened several times in the last hundred years). Furthermore, owing to high rates of sediment deposition and the effect of the earth's rotation, the Hilmand tends to alter its course through the delta. We can complete the hydrological outline by mentioning two smaller rivers flowing into the Hamun, the Khash-rud and the Farah-rud. They are seasonal, i.e. in summer they usually run dry in the lower parts of their channels.

The instability of the Hilmand was not the only problem that agrarian society in

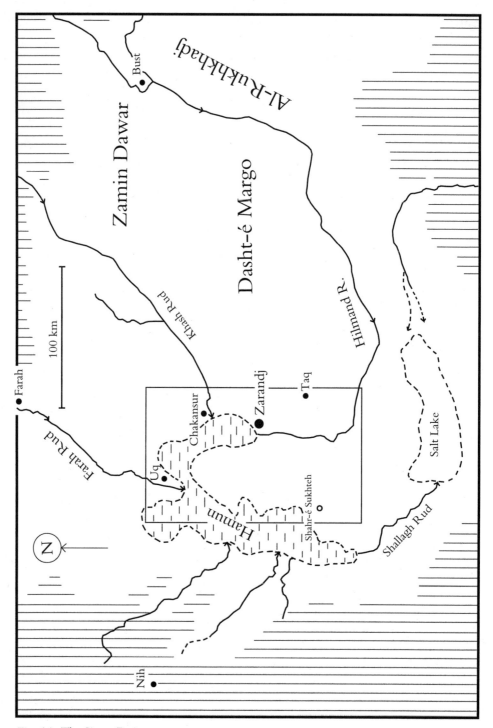

Fig. 14. The Sistan Basin.

Sistan had to face. At least since the Middle Ages sand drifts and dunes have posed a constant threat. Today the sands cover several thousand square kilometers and is kept in perpetual motion by the "120-days wind," a strong northwesterly wind that blows almost without interruption between May and October. The sands have partly been formed naturally, by wind erosion of clay surfaces, but erosion of dikes and levees must have contributed to the process. The conditions for settlement and agriculture are thus rather different from those in most other enclaves on the Plateau. The nearest parallels would be the large river oases such as Isfahan and Marv, although the hydrological system of Sistan involved much larger amounts of water.[1]

A distinctive feature of present-day Sistan is its countless ruins. The contrast between past and present is even more striking here than in Mesopotamia: in the 9th and 10th centuries Sistan was described as flourishing and prosperous, with numerous towns and villages; the only negative aspects mentioned were the shifting sands and the vipers.[2] By the 19th century European travellers found a wind-swept, desolate wasteland.[3] None of the medieval towns existed any longer and settlement had been reduced to a few impoverished enclaves in the delta. The total population at the beginning of this century was estimated at 161.000 and this was after the Iranian state, from the 1860s onwards, had made considerable effort to attract colonists to the country.[4] Even if many of the ruins must represent successive settlements, there can be no doubt that Sistan has seen a decline of vast proportions.

This shrinkage of settlement has made the country well-suited for archaeological research.[5] During the re-drawing of borders in the 19th century the ancient cultivated lands in the Hilmand Delta were divided between Iran and Afghanistan, however, and as far as the historical epochs are concerned, it is chiefly the Afghan part that has been surveyed. Yet even here most of the sites remain unindentified and only roughly dated on the basis of surface finds.

The first agriculturalists seem to have settled in Sistan around 3000 B.C. at the Rud-é Biyaban, a dried-up bed which was once one of the main channels of the Hilmand. According to available archaeological information the settlement grew steadily during the 3rd millennium B.C.: remains have been found of some 30 small villages and one major settlement, *Shahr-é Sukhteh*, the "Burnt Town." The latter appears to have been a genuine town, covering *c.* 80 ha and having a developed division of labor. The inner city – presumably the seat of institutionalized political power – was fortified and around it were several industrial quarters containing pottery workshops, weaving rooms, and workshops for the processing of lapis lazuli and turquoise. An estimated 50.000 ha of the town's hinterland was under irriga- tion, making the settlement in the Hilmand Delta one of the largest and oldest irrigated enclaves on the Plateau.[6] Thus the early *Sistani* society has a superficial resemblance to the early Mesopotamian city states; but the background for the urbanization process must have been different, because *Shahr-é Sukhteh* was apparently the only major settlement in the region. There were no other centers nearby to compete for the available resources.

It is generally thought that the settlements in the enclave were abandoned around 2000 B.C.[7] The causes behind this apparent collapse are not known. *Shahr-é Sukhteh* may have been deserted because the Hilmand altered its course, yet this fails to explain why the rest of the delta was also depopulated. The abandonment in Sistan has been linked with the settlement decline that allegedly occurred all over southwest Asia at this time. However, this general decline may be nothing but an illusion caused by the lack of representative data; so the question must remain open.

1. From Zranka to Sakastan: Sistan in Achaemenid and Parthian Times

At any rate, from the 1st millennium B.C. settlements again appear in the archaeological record. Two are dated to Achaemenid times: Dahan-é Ghulaman, a small settlement in the western delta, and Tepe Surkh Dagh at Nad-é 'Ali (the site of medieval Zarandj).[8] If these are representative, settlement seems by now to have shifted from the Rud-é Biyaban farther down into the delta, no doubt because of hydrological changes.

Under the name Zranka (Greek: Drangiane) Sistan appears in several of Darius' inscriptions, while Herodotus lists it as part of the "14th satrapy."[9] The accounts of the campaigns of Alexander and the Seleucid kings mention three towns here: Prophthasia, Propasta and Karkoe. Polybius adds that Antiochus III, during his great eastern campaign (210–203 B.C.), had his army winter a year in Sistan.[10] Because of the evident similarity Karkoe, which Isidore calls Korok, must be Karkuyeh (Karkuy) which in Sassanian and early Muslim times was famous for its fire-temple. Later local traditions ascribe great age to this town.[11] Propasta, identified on etymological grounds as Farah, and mentioned by Isidore in the more recognizable form of Phra, was outside the Hilmand Delta proper. Tomaschek views Prophthasia as a parallel form to Propasta, while others would identify Propasta with the later Zarandj, the capital of Sistan in the Middle Ages.[12] Though the latter identifications are uncertain, Sistan in the 4rth and 3rd centuries B.C. must have been a productive enclave (how else could Antiochus' army have wintered here?) with at least a few urban settlements. Whether Zarandj was among them is not clear.

The four centuries of the Parthian era lie almost completely in the dark. Yet it was precisely in this period that the country changed its name from Zranka to Sakastan from which were later derived names such as Segistan, Sidjistan, and Sistan. Literally Sakastan means "the land of the Saka," and these Saka, it is assumed, must be the Iranian nomads originally living on the steppes around the Oxus and the Djaxartes. On the basis of a few bits of epigraphic and numismatic material and hints in classical and Chinese sources, scholarship has constructed a scenario of vast migrations avalanching through Central Asia and the Hindu Kush, causing the rise and fall of ephemeral "nomad empires" in Pandjab-Afghanistan. Allegedly, all this had been set in motion by the pressure of the Hsiung-nu "empire" on its neighbors along the eastern frontier of Chi'in-China. In this connection the Saka, or a part of them, are said to have migrated to Sistan and to have given the country its new name. This dramatic scenario seems altogether speculative.[13]

It is remarkable that Isidore of Charakene, writing in the 1st century, still distinguishes between Zarangiane – i.e. the Hilmand Delta proper – and, 63 *schoinoi* (over 300 km) away, *Sakastane*. Here Sakastan must refer to what later came to be known as Zamin Dawar.[14] Of course, his information may be out of date and may in fact refer to the situation a hundred or two hundred years before. In any case, from Sassanian times there is no longer any doubt that the name Sakastan refers primarily to the delta region.[15] But why Achaemenid Zranka changed its name to Sakastan, we simply do not know (on the whole it does not seem to be a very important question either).

In Parthian Zarangiane Isidore locates two towns: *Korok* (Karkuyeh) and *Parin*, perhaps a misspelling of Zarin, i.e. Zarandj.[16] In Sakastane he locates the towns of Barda, Min, Palacenti, Sigal, and Alexandria, the latter presumably identical with the Alexandria listed in Arachosia (i.e. Kandahar).[17] In the country of "Anauon," 21 *schoinoi* (over 100 km) north of Zarangiane, Isidore lists four towns: Phra (Farah), Nie, identical with the medieval caravan-town Nih, as well as Gari and Bis.[18] We are given no information whether the three regions listed by Isidore formed a political unit in Parthian times as they did later.

Available archaeological information suggests that a marked expansion of settlement began in Parthian times and continued into Sassanian times: some of the large settlements, e.g. the Pust-é Gav site (north of Chakansur), Sar-u-Tar, and the gigantic fortress SirChehel Burdj, apparently originated in Parthian times; many other Parthian structures are no doubt masked by later Sassanian constructions.[19] As will be discussed below, the location of Pust-é Gav and other sites suggest that the expansion was accompanied by an enlargement of canals as well as by advances in irrigation technology: the forerunners of the large-scale and complex canal systems known from Muslim times must already have been constructed during this period. The political context in which this happened remains unknown, however.[20]

Chapter 19

The Zenith of Sistan

1. The Political Context

Although remote from the imperial centers, Sistan was certainly a part of Iranshahr: not only did the great kings claim suzerainty over the country, they also made it the scene of some typical feats of advancement of civilization; at least, that is what the Persian historical tradition would have us believe. Ardashir I is thus credited with founding Zarandj when the original capital, Ram-Shahristan, was destroyed in a dam breach.[1]

In practice it must have been difficult for the Sassanians to control a country so far away from the imperial center in Mesopotamia. During the reign of Ardashir I, Sistan was in fact ruled by a local Parthian prince, Ardashir, "King of the Saka," and his recognition of Sassanian suzerainty may have been largely a matter of form.[2] But Shapur I mentions one of his sons, Narseh, as *Sakanshah*, no doubt installed at the expense of the local ruler.[3] We should be careful, however, of taking this as proof of a genuine centralization. In a political structure like the Sassanian Empire, with no fixed rules for succession within the royal family, a productive enclave like Sistan must in fact have been an excellent base for unruly and ambitious princes. That the Empire in the 4th century employed *Sistani* soldiers against the Romans on the Euphrates front is not proof of centralization either. Most likely, these soldiers were mercenaries of which Sistan later became a great supplier.[4]

Besides Narseh, three other princes are known to have held the title of Sakanshah: Bahram (late 3rd century), Shapur, a brother of Shapur II (4th century) and Hormizd (mid-5th century). Of the four, only Shapur failed to mount the imperial throne.[5] Apparently Hormizd was the last of the royal Sakanshahs. His brother and successor as great king, Firuz (459–484), installed a nobleman of the Karen family as governor, a move presumably dictated by the need to prevent further dynastic conflicts and to mobilize the resources of Sistan for the Haytal wars.[6]

As long as the Sassanian kings themselves resided on the eastern borders of Iranshahr, they no doubt made their rule effective in Sistan. Later, however, the position of governor became de facto hereditary, always a sign that central government had limited control. In the time of Khusraw II Parwiz (591–628) Sistan was ruled by an *aspahbad* (governor), Bakhtiyar b. Shah Firuz, who claimed descent directly from Rustam himself. Incidentally this Bakhtiyar must have been a remark-

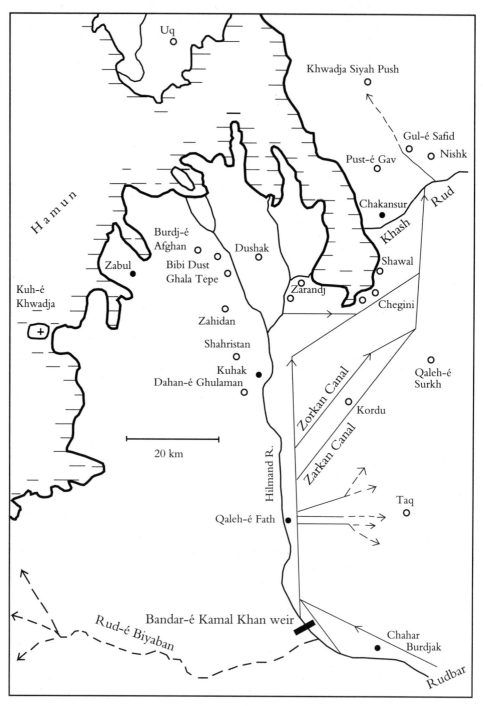

Fig. 15. Sketch-Map of the Hilmand Delta and the Nahr al-Ta'am (10th century).

able person, for his exploits subsequently formed the basis for one of the Sassanian historical romances, the *Bakhtiyar-nameh*. His grandson, Rustam b. Azadkhu, was also *aspahbad* of Sistan, while the latter's son, Iran b. Rustam, ruled as "Shah of Sistan" when the Arabs appeared in the mid-7th century.[7] As late as the 10th century the *Tarikh-é Sistan* includes a descendant of Bakhtiyar, Muhammad b. Hamdun, among the nobility of Sistan.[8]

In Sistan, as in most of eastern Iranshahr, it is somewhat exaggerated to speak of a regular Arab conquest. When the first Arab bands reached the country in 650/651, they met dogged resistance until the local *marzban* (who must have been Iran b. Rustam mentioned above) entered into a peace treaty: he formally acknowledged Muslim suzerainty and agreed to pay an annual tribute of 1.000.000 dirhams, but he was otherwise left to rule Sistan as before, together with the dihqans.[9] Arab governors periodically came out from Basrah to collect the tribute, usually supported by armed forces; but according to Ya'qubi the country was in a state of virtually constant rebellion until the time of Ziyad b. Abihi.[10]

Arab armies were also sent out to use Sistan as a base for raids into the territories east of the Hilmand Delta: Zamin Dawar, al-Rukhkhadj, and Zabulistan, where a king with the title of *Zunbil* ruled from the town of Ghazna. Around 670 Ziyad b. Abihi sent a Persian official, Hasan al-Basri, with the task of systematizing the collection of the *kharadj* in Sistan. This was done not to undermine the power of the local dihqans, but to create the financial basis for an *al-'ata* system and thereby for a garrison of Arab warriors, exactly as had been done in Marv.[11] In Sistan, however, the plans of Ziyad and al-Hadjdjadj were frustrated. The warriors from Basrah and Kufah were not attracted by the prospect of bitter fighting in the wild mountains of Zabulistan and therefore refused to remain in Sistan.[12] Meanwhile, the Umayyad governors posted here had little effective control. Between the local opposition on the one hand and the *Zunbil* on the other, they had to choose: either they could use their military resources to collect the tribute with armed force, and thus lose local support in fighting the *Zunbil* (who had proved a redoubtable opponent), or they might cooperate with the local noblemen – but then they had to avoid offending these by intruding upon traditional autonomy.

Also the Abbasids failed to control Sistan, even in the short period when al-Ma'mun ruled the eastern half of the Empire from Marv (809–817). In fact, attempts to make the tax collection more efficient and to bring a part of the surplus out of the country only sharpened local resistance.[13] The Tahirids who ruled Khurasan and the rest of the east from 821 to 873, formally as Abbasid governors, had no better luck.[14]

The hegemonic states encountered other problems besides those obviously springing from logistics, and thanks to the *Tarikh-é Sistan* we can see why it was so difficult to control Sistan from without. The governors sent out from Mesopotamia invariably sought to cooperate with the *mashayikh va buzurgan*, i.e. the patrician families of Zarandj. In return for offices in the juridical and fiscal administration, they could be brought to recognize the suzerainty of the Empire, and their local prestige would then endow the governors with some authority.[15] Outside Zarandj, in the small towns and the rural districts, the situation was quite different. Here the sworn enemies of the Muslim Empire, the Kharidjites, had won a solid foothold by the middle of the 8th century, and they stubbornly opposed every attempt to tax and otherwise establish outside control.[16] The Kharidjites of Sistan were largely of aristocratic origin and did not represent a popular resistance movement; but their struggle against taxation seems, not surprisingly, to have won more or less passive support from the peasantry.

Eventually the discontent and the conflicts culminated in a great Kharidjite revolt which not only put a definitive end to the Empire's influence in Sistan, but also spread across large parts of eastern Iranshahr. The leader of the revolt, the famous Hamza b. 'Abdallah, descended from a dihqan family in Ravin-va-Djul, a village in Sistan, and agitated eagerly against unjust taxes. The *Tarikh-é Sistan* says that his career as a rebel in fact began when he killed a tax collector in his native village. In his continuous campaigns, Hamza subsequently executed any tax collector who fell into his hands.[17] The patricians of Zarandj, nurturing no sympathy for the Kharidjites, certainly continued to recognize the suzerainty of the Empire, but Hamza resolutely prevented the transfer of any tribute from Sistan. The Kharidjites themselves took nothing, says the *Tarikh-é Sistan*, but got what they needed by raiding the heathen lands of Ghur and Sind.[18] Nor after Hamza's death, in 829, did the representatives of the Empire and their allies in Zarandj succeed in breaking Kharidjite control of the rural districts. To obtain money for the continued warfare a Tahirid governor even resorted, in 837, to confiscations in Zarandj and that cannot have made him or his masters more popular.[19]

At this time a new factor arose, or at least now it appears in the sources: i.e. the *ayyaran*. The literal meaning of the word is "scoundrels" or "vagabonds," though it seems to have been used as a nickname. Groups or movements having this name appeared throughout Iranshahr and the Middle East between the 9th and 12th centuries; but who they were and how they were recruited and organized is not altogether clear. Sometimes they appear as mercenaries or common highwaymen or as self-appointed guardians of law and order and public morality; on still other occasions as mafia-like organizations. In his study of social movements in the towns of the medieval Middle East Claude Cahen states that the *ayyaran* – in spite of superficial local differences – shared certain characteristics: they were organizations of men from the lowest social strata in the towns who had come together to improve their social standing.[20] In Sistan, however, where the *ayyaran* appeared earliest and had their greatest political strength, Cahen's definition does not fit. First, the *ayyaran* of Sistan were not part of the urban population. Some of them may have been recruited from among the lower classes in the towns, but the

Tarikh-é Sistan distinguishes them expressly from the ordinary rabble, citing several examples of open conflicts between the two groups.[21] Second, the *ayyaran* always came to Zarandj from outside. Their haunt was the notoriously unruly border town of Bust, the outpost against the kingdom of the *Zunbil* and base for raids into the heathen lands.[22] Barthold at one time suggested that the Transoxanian *ayyaran* were a mixed group of destitute townsmen, fugitive peasants, criminals, and other marginal elements, who had joined the ranks of the volunteers fighting for the Faith, the *ghaziyan va muttawi'ah*, hoping to make a living and achieve status by raiding the infidels. In Sistan, a similar explanation seems more plausible than that of Cahen.[23] Yet from the *Tarikh-é Sistan* it appears that the *ayyaran* of Sistan were not just fighters for the Faith or mercenaries. In spite of the resemblance in name and appearance to other armed and rebel groups, they were a local phenomenon.

The *ayyaran* played a key role in Sistan for over 200 years, not least because they were the original supporters of the sons of Layth, Ya'qub and 'Amr. We need not detail the amazing career of the two brothers in the second half of the 9th century: in spite of their humble birth they became masters of Sistan and, for a brief period, of large parts of the rest of Iranshahr as well. This attempt to create a hegemonic state with Sistan as its center eventually failed when, in 900, 'Amr was defeated and imprisoned by the Samanids at Balkh. After that, Sistan had to yield first to Samanid and later Ghaznavid suzerainty. Yet owing not least to the *ayyaran*, it remained as before very much a semi-independent principality, now ruled by the descendants of Ya'qub and 'Amr, the Saffarids, so-called because Ya'qub was said to have been a coppersmith (*saffar*) by trade.[24] This goes to prove that in Iranshahr considerable political continuity could exist at the local level, regardless of how often the hegemonic states changed hands.

2. The Development of Large-Scale Irrigation: the Construction of the Nahr al-Ta'am

The short-lived rise of Sistan under the redoubtable Layth brothers occurred in a particular historical context: it was precisely at this time that settlement and irrigation reached its high point. The dating of the expansion rests primarily on archaeological indicators, i.e. the surface debris and the architectonic and stylistic features of the sites. The *Tarikh-é Sistan*, however, by mentioning abandonments and reclamation schemes also points to the period before the year 1000 as the period of maximum settlement and cultivation.

In the western delta the historical settlement maximum is marked by a string of sites extending from Burdj-é Afghan over Bibi Dust and Ghala Tepe, down to Zahidan and onward to Shahristan. Most of them can be dated to Sassanian times, even though there is evidence that the expansion had begun earlier.[25] In the Rud-é

Biyaban delta farther south lie remains of a large cluster of settlements which also date from Sassanian–Parthian times.[26]

East of the Hilmand, Zarandj presumably goes back to pre-Achaemenid times, although it did not develop into a large city until later. The mounds rise in some places to more than 35 meters, a sign of prolonged occupation.[27] As already said, Taq (Sar-u-Tar, Shahr-é Ghulghula) dates from Parthian times. North of Taq the ruined forts and the area of surface debris between Kordu and Qaleh-é Surkh are believed to be Sassanian.[28] The immense sites in the Chakansur region, including genuine urban settlements like Nishk, Chigini, Shawal, Gul-é Safidka, are of Sassanian and early Muslim origin, i.e. built before the 11th century; but again there are traces of settlement dating back to Parthian times. The same is true of non-fortified settlements like Gul-é Safid, Pust-é Gav, Khwadja Siyah Push, and Di-wal-é Khudaydad, and many villa-like complexes dispersed across the landscape.[29]

Few of the sites can be identified with historically known settlements. The sources, primarily the geographical literature of the 10th century, describe Sistan in general terms as a prosperous, densely populated country, but provide few topographic details.[30] Zarandj, or just *shahr-é Sistan*, is described as one of the great cities of Iran; the Arab accounts of conquest indicate that it had been a large settlement even in Sassanian times. In the 9th century, Ya'qubi says, Zarandj had a circumference of four *farsakh* (24 km): around the heavily fortified inner town (*shahristan*) extended the suburbs for a distance of 1/2 *farsakh*, and these were in turn surrounded by walls. The city had much trade and a large textile industry and was famed as a center of learning.[31]

Among the small towns are mentioned Karkuyeh (northeast of Zarandj), Qarnin (in the Khash-rud area and famous as the birthplace of the Layth brothers), Taq, Uq (by the Farah-rud), and others. The towns of Nih, Farah, and Bust were also politically part of Sistan in this period, but stood far from the delta (and were thus subjected to different environmental conditions).

The expansion beginning in Parthian/Sassanian times had pushed settlement into areas with few or no water resources, for instance around Chakansur where the small Khash-rud was quite inadequate for supplying the new settlements with water. These had to be supplied from the Hilmand by a system of feeder canals similar to those constructed in Mesopotamia. From al-Istakhri's account, reproduced by later geographers and compilers, it appears that the core-area of 10th-century Sistan was irrigated by six large canals (here listed from south to north): the Nahr al-Ta'am, the Nash-rud, the Sana-rud, the Nahr Sha'beh, the Nahr Mili and, finally, the Nahr Zaliq.[32] The context indicates that the Sana-rud was simply the main channel of the Hilmand in the branching delta; otherwise the information is too vague for a detailed reconstruction of the system. Nor can the cited canals be identified positively with the old river and canal beds still visible in the landscape.

The only exception is the Nahr al-Ta'am, the main feeder canal of the entire area east of the Hilmand. Al-Istakhri expressly states that it had its intake 1 day's march (*marhaleh*) south of Zarandj and that it carried water all the way up to Nishk (Nishak) by the Khash-rud. On this basis it seems reasonable to identify the Nahr al-Ta'am with the remains of a large canal which left the Hilmand at Chahar Burdjak. At Bandar-é Kamal Khan are the remains of what must have been one of the weirs that raised water for the canal. This may even have been the main weir, later known as the *Band-é Rustam*. From aerial photographs it is possible to follow the course from here: some 30 km north of the weir the Nahr al-Ta'am branched out into several channels, including the old beds today known as Zorkan and Zarkan; these must have supplied the Kordu-Qaleh-é Surkh region. Ten km south of Chakansur the channels again flowed together, crossed the Khash-rud and delivered water to Gul-é Safid, Khwadja Siyah Push, and further north. With a total length of at least 150 km the system bears comparison with the great Mesopotamian canals.[33]

The *Tarikh-é Sistan* states that the canal was constructed on the initiative of an Umayyad governor, Qa'qa b. Suwayd, in 723/24.[34] This can only be true, how-ever, of the northern sections (where the majority of sites are also of Muslim origin).[35] The main part of the system must be older, since the extensive Parthian-Sassanian settlement areas from Taq and up to the Khash-rud must have been served by large feeder canals. Al-Baladhuri, in his account of the Muslim conquest of Sistan, in fact mentions "the old canal," *Dju-yé kuneh*, which flowed all the way down to Rudbar. Most likely this was the Sassanian precursor of the Nahr al-Ta'am.[36]

As in Mesopotamia responsibility for building and maintaining the essential parts of the irrigation system fell to the state. According to a budget reproduced by the *Tarikh-é Sistan*, and probably dating from the early 11th century, the state annually set aside the following amounts of money for the maintenance of the waterworks:

1. Repair of flood damage . . . .   4.000 dirhams
2. Weirs (*band-é bastanha*) . . . .   25.000   –
3. Sand fighting (*rig-é bastanha*) . . . .   30.000   –
4. Embankments (*paranha*) . . . .   50.000   –
5. Bridge and canal construction . . . .   30.000   –

Additional sums were held in reserve in the event of extraordinary floods or other natural disasters.

At first sight this does not amount to much compared to the other items in the budget: thus 300.000 dirhams went to the upkeep of military structures, mosques, and hospitals, and to wages to police and officials, while no less than 2.000.000 dirhams were allocated to something called *timuq* (the meaning of this word is not clear).[37] However, the expenditures listed for the maintenance of production probably included only salaries to specialists. Among these were the expert sand dammers who by clever use of hedges and fences constructed of brushwood and rushes made the constant wind turn the sand drifts away from the fields. Ibn Hawqal provides a description of their work.[38] The basic routine work such as repairing dikes and embankments, cleaning existing canals, and digging new ones was done largely by corvée labor (hashar).[39] This did not necessarily involve compulsory measures; on the contrary, there are several examples of the Sistanis voluntarily carrying out repairs and construction works: in the late 13th century, for instance, the inhabitants of the Dar al-Ta'am quarter in Zarandj dug a new canal to Taq and rebuilt the old fortress. It was not that the state had begun to neglect such tasks, because at the time it was in fact engaged with large-scale schemes in the northern end of the Nahr al-Ta'am system. The Sistanis were apparently so used to disciplined, collective labor that local organizations at community level could tackle quite extensive projects.[40]

Distribution of the water also rested with the state. An amir-é ab ("water director") ensured that this was done properly. His office was considered one of the most important and prestigious in the country, and Ya'qub b. Layth used to say that the welfare and prosperity of all of Sistan depended entirely on how the amir performed his duties.[41] Strict and fair supervision of the water resources was necessary because the need for irrigation was greatest immediately before the autumn sowing, i.e. when the flow of the Hilmand was at its lowest (the harvest then took place in June–July).[42]

Both the hydrology and the agricultural cycle resembled what we have seen in Mesopotamia, and indeed Sistan had a similar reputation for extraordinary productivity. The British consul Abbott, in the mid–19th century, reported that seed-yield ratios of 1:25–100 were normal in the Hilmand Delta.[43] By then, however, intensive cultivation was confined to the most favorable areas and average yields in the Middle Ages, when marginal areas were also sown, must have been considerably lower. Besides the basic winter crops of wheat, barley, and millet, the Sistanis also grew summer crops in intensive horticulture, including fruit (melons, grapes, pomegranates) and raw materials for the textile industry (silk). The gardens were surrounded by high walls for protection against the continuous wind. The same wind drove the characteristic windmills which lifted the water up to the gardens.[44] The date palm was widespread over the entire country. By the 19th century it had practically disappeared and the Sistanis imported dates from Baluchistan.[45]

Tenth-century sources also refer to a large textile industry both in the towns and the villages. Incidentally the weavers seem to have formed a militant element in the country's internal conflicts. Around 920, when rival ayyaran and patrician groups fought each other and the caliphal representatives and the Saffarid princes, a weaver from Uq temporarily made himself amir of Sistan with support from "the rabble" (ghawgha).[46]

Chapter 20

The Decline of Sistan

As in Mesoptamia the first signs of trouble in Sistan follow immediately upon the high-water mark of expansion. The *Tarikh-é Sistan* states that already under 'Amr b. Layth's successor, Tahir b. Muhammad, revenues began falling off and a general decline in the prosperity of the country became discernible.[1] Perhaps the anonymous author exaggerated to highlight the good times under the brothers Ya'qub and 'Amr. The available tax figures certainly reveal a downward trend, but by themselves they are too dispersed and too heterogeneous to allow conclusions about the general economic situation. Other sources, however, confirm that the *Sistani* state in fact was having financial difficulties. While Ya'qub b. Layth is said to have refrained from taxing people who owned less than 500 dirhams,[2] later rulers certainly could not afford such consideration. At the end of the 10th century Khalaf b. Ahmad stated that no one, not even merchants, needed to own more than 10 dirhams. His systematic confiscations paved the way for the Ghaznavid occupation of the country in 1002.[3]

That it was more than a case of financial difficulties for the state, is indicated by Ibn Hawqal. When he visited Sistan around 970 it was still prosperous, but he remarked that the soil was covered by salt, and that productivity, and hence the ability to pay taxes, had declined in certain areas. Shortly after, the sands temporarily broke into Zarandj itself, a further sign that agriculture was beginning to suffer from environmental problems.[4]

During the 11th century the decline in cultivation and settlement became evident when the Bar Zareh district along the Barg Canal was abandoned. The precise location is unkown, but from the context it appears that the *Tarikh-é Sistan* refers to areas in the northern end of the Nahr al-Ta'am system.[5] Archaeological evidence indicates that a considerable number of settlements in the north were in fact abandoned at this time.[6] The 11th–13th centuries seem altogether to have been a difficult time for the country: the *Tarikh-é Sistan* lists several disasters such as epidemics, floods, and famine.[7] Of course, natural disasters had occurred also during the expansion phase,[8] but they may well have become more frequent as a result of increasing evironmental instability. Wartime destruction certainly became more widespread. To the continuous internal conflicts were added attacks by Turkomans, Ghaznavids, Isma'ilis, and Mongols. Zarandj was sacked no less than four times, and Nih and several small towns were destroyed.[9] Incidentally the Mongols, having razed Nih, do not otherwise seem to have caused great damage. Djuzdjani's

Table 16. The assessment of Sistan.

	Dirhams
788	5.000.000[a]
819	1.000.000[b]
826	6.776.000[c]
c. 840	10.000.000[d]
c. 960	4–5.000.000[e]
Beginning of 11th Century	3.957.000[f]

[a] al-Mutarrif (el-'Ali 1971: 307).
[b] Qudama (de Goeje tr.: 184, 190).
[c] Ibn Khurdadhbih (tr.: 28f). The figure includes Zamin Dawar and Zabulistan. Bust, however, was assessed separately at 90.000 dirhams.
[d] Ya'qubi (tr.: 97).
[e] Ibn Hawqal (tr., II: 411f). The exact information is that Sistan (including al-Rukhkhadj and Bust) pays "the Lord of Khurasan" 200.000 dinars and 1.100.000 dirhams.
[f] TS: 30ff. This figure includes Bust, Zamin Dawar, al-Rukhkhadj and Zabulistan. It is not dated but no doubt refers to the beginning of the 11th century, when the major part of the chronicle was composed.

information that they destroyed Zarandj is certainly incorrect.[10] On three occasions in the 11th century, the small town of Darag, in the Farah-rud area, had to pay great sums of money to escape sack: 300.000 dirhams, 100.000 dirhams and, finally, 15.000 dinars. This goes to prove that despite everything there was still something left to rob.[11]

During this period the *ayyaran* also disappeared as suddenly as they had emerged a few centuries before. They are mentioned for the last time in *Tarikh-é Sistan* as defending the Taq-fortress in 1051.[12] They had long been staunch defenders of the autonomy of Sistan, but apparently many of them eventually threw their support to Mahmud of Ghazna, the great *ghazi*. Perhaps the last of the *ayyaran*, together with other volunteers, followed him on the campaigns to India. Raiding the rich lands here must have been more attractive than staying in impoverished Sistan or making a precarious living as marauders in the mountains of Afghanistan.

Towards the end of the 13th century the picture again changed: the princes of Sistan now repaired the Barg Canal and reclaimed the Bar Zareh district; repair work in Uq and at the Khash-rud is also mentioned, and two new canals were constructed from the Hilmand (or rather, from the Nahr al-Ta'am) to the areas north and east of Zarandj. Nih was rebuilt and new lands brought under cultivation. The small town of Divarak (location unknown), sacked by the Mongols, was rebuilt as well and provided with new canals. Finally, as we have seen, a group of townsfolk in Zarandj dug a new canal to Taq, which attracted numerous new colonists.[13] At that time the rulers of Sistan were involved in continuous wars with the Kart kings of Herat and the Nigudari Mongols. Yet apparently they were able to protect the country.

Wartime destruction, however, this time on a dramatic scale, struck Sistan at the end of the 14th century. In 1383 Timur-é Lenk took Zarandj and made a systematic retaliatory massacre of the inhabitants. Having destroyed Taq as well, Timur then marched toward Bust which was also razed. On the way, according to 'Ali Yazdi, Timur destroyed the main weir, the *Band-é-Rustam*.[14] As this must have been located somewhere south of Taq, it is probably identical with the Bandar-é Kamal Khan weir, where, as stated, one of the main channels of the Nahr al-Ta'am had its intake.

The *Ihya al-Muluk*, a local chronicle from the early 17th century, however, does not blame Timur, but his son Shah Rukh. On his Sistan campaign, in 1407, Shah Rukh is said to have destroyed a masonry weir (*band-é havang*) dating from "the time of Garshasp." From the descriptions it is clear that this was a major weir, as it raised water for the canals east of the Hilmand, "from Taq and up to Uq," as well as for the canals running westward to Havzdar and Kundar.[15] Thus it seems that the *Band-é Rustam* and the *band-é havang* must be the same. The nearly contemporary account of 'Ali Yazdi's *Zafar-nameh* would appear more reliable than the later *Ihya al-Muluk*; on the other hand, the latter is supported by the Timurid historian al-Samarkandi's account of Shah Rukh's campaign in Sistan: according to al-Samarkandi there was in fact three weirs across the Hilmand; "they had been built in the time of Rustam," he states, adding that "the first bore the name *Shalak*, the second *Band-é shahr*, while the third, and largest, was called *Bal'aghani*. They were all destroyed (...) and both towns and fields were destroyed in every conceivable way."[16] No doubt there existed several weirs, but what little information we have indicates that only one of them was considered the main one and that this was located somewhere south of Taq. Thus *Bal'aghani* must simply be another name for *Band-é Rustam* and the "masonry dam" of the *Ihya al-Muluk*. That it was destroyed or damaged in Timurid times is fairly certain. Whether Timur or Shah Rukh was the culprit remains an open question, yet it need not concern us here. The important question is whether the destruction really was the turning point in the history of Sistan as the chroniclers would have us believe.

They all state that Sistan now entered into continuous decline. The *Herati* historian Isfizari, for instance, noted, in the late 15th century, that the country had been completely laid waste by the Timurid wars of succession.[17] This is somewhat exaggerated: as early as 1386 Timur had ordered the reconstruction of Zarandj, and even though it did not come to much, several new settlements were in fact founded during the 15th and 16th centuries, among them a new capital (identified by Tate with Qaleh-é Fath).[18] In the area around the old fortress of Taq some cultivation and settlement continued up to the 16th century.[19] A Mughal force, which in 1639 had occupied Kandahar and advanced into Sistan, even managed to find a weir to destroy.[20] In connection with Nadir Shah's campaign in the first half of the 18th century Uq and Qaleh-é Kah (both located in the Farah-rud area) are mentioned as being inhabited; part of the ruins in Uq-Djuwayn Lash are in fact so well-preserved that they cannot be very old.[21]

At this time, however, the Nahr al-Ta'am had long ceased conducting water northwards. The archaeologists date the massive abandonment of settlements in the areas along the great canal to Timurid times, another indication that precisely this period was especially critical.[22] The surviving settlements in the north thus only had water from the Farah-rud and the Khash-rud, and the area under intensive cultivation must therefore have been limited.

Tate cites a local chronicle, the *Shadjarat al-Muluk*, for information that the local rulers even around 1800 constructed or repaired several large canals in the northern delta. They also had water delivered to Havzdar through the old bed of the Rud-é Biyaban.[23] This latter project implies the existence of a weir quite far up the Hilmand. The British officer Christie, one of the first Europeans to visit Sistan in modern times, described, in 1810, the country's capital, "Dushak," as small, but quite populous and surrounded by well-cultivated land.[24] Presumably it is identical with a settlement later known as Djallalabad.

Together with the last remaining large settlements in Sistan, i.e. Havzdar and Kundar (both in the Rud-é Biyaban region), Dushak was deserted during the 19th century, a period of extreme political instability and Baluchi immigration. It is unknown to what extent these factors actually caused the abandonment, however. In the 1860s the *amir* of Qayin, acting on behalf of the Qadjars, began to assert political control over the Hilmand Delta and start reclamation schemes. The Afghans had occupied Farah in 1856 and to forestall them in Sistan proper the *amir* gradually forced the local nobles to accept Qadjar suzerainty. He also founded a new capital, Nasirabad (now Zabul), and brought in 20.000 colonists from Qayin and Khurasan. The weirs and canals were improved to divert as much water as possible into Qadjar territory.[25] British intervention, however, prevented further expansion and in the end the ancient land was arbitrarily divided between Qadjar Iran and the new Afghan state.

From the European descriptions of the 19th century it appears that since Timurid times a further decline had occurred. Permanent settlement and intensive cultivation had now largely contracted to an area in the northwestern delta, called the *Shahristan*, between the Hilmand and the village of Sekuheh (*c.* 30 km south of Zabul). In some places along the Khash-rud and the Hilmand, where simple inundation irrigation was possible, patches of intensive cultivation were also found. However, all the towns had disappeared. There remained only some villages, inhabited by peasants and weavers. The largest had perhaps a population of a few thousand.[26] The basis of intensive cultivation in the *Shahristan* enclave was a weir at Kuhak, the *Band-é Sistan*, which raised the water of the Hilmand into a large westward-running canal. This canal fed numerous small distributaries that supplied the individual villages: the principle of irrigation was the same as before, but the scale was much smaller. Around Chakansur a little grain was raised by rain-fed farming and in the rush beds and tamarisk jungles of the delta there was shifting agriculture and cattle raising. By now cattle were practically the only commodity Sistan had to offer.[27]

Summary

In broad outline the decline of Sistan occurred in three distinct phases: the first began immediately after the maximum expansion of the 9th-10th centuries and lasted until the end of the 13th century. Renewed expansion was short-lived, and was followed by another phase of marked decline from the end of the 14th century. It was then that the huge Nahr al-Ta'am system finally stopped working. Finally the first half of the 19th century saw a further shrinkage of settlement. In our context this phase is less interesting because Sistan by now was long sunk into poverty and obscurity.

The second phase was accompanied by a series of dramatic events which at first sight appear to have been the chief causes of the decline of flourishing Sistan. The Persian historians, as stated, blamed the destructive campaigns of Timur and Shah Rukh, and this explanation has been widely accepted ever since.[28] One could object that other enclaves such as Isfahan were also subjected to systematic massacres at Timur's command. In Sistan, however, the fatal blow is said to have been the deliberate destruction of the Hilmand weir, the cornerstone of the irrigation system.

Two objections can be invoked against the idea that Timur's (or Shah Rukh's) destruction of the weir by itself decisively turned the history of Sistan. The first is of course that decline had been noticeable long before. For this reason alone the destructions in Timurid times cannot constitute an adequate explanation. Second, it is not obvious why the destruction of the weir should have had such disastrous and irreversible results: in the 19th century the *Sistanis*, despite demographic decline and political decentralization, were still able to construct quite serviceable weirs across the Hilmand. The British border commission, in 1870, saw how this was done:

"The dimensions of the "Band" are as follows: entire length, 720 feet; length across original bed of river, 520 feet; breadth at broadest part, 110 feet; depth 18 feet on the river side. It is formed of fascines of tamarisk branches closely interwoven together with stakes driven into them at intervals: the branches used for this purposes are green and fresh, but of no great size, while the interlacing of them is very close (...) The present "Band" was constructed by 2000 men in three months, all classes in Sistan giving their aid to a work on which their own prosperity was so much dependent. The great part of the labour was in bringing from a distance the enormous quantity of tamarisk required; but it is said that once the branches were collected, the actual construction was performed in a short time by one man, a native of Banjár, the sole possessor of this art, and who refuses to impart his knowledge to any one but his own son. The "Band" still requires a small yearly repair when the spring floods are over, and its face towards the river is annually increased by a yard or more, but these repairs are now easily accomplished by fifty or sixty men."[29]

Tate, who witnessed the rebuilding of the weir in 1904, says that the work began in the middle of August (i.e. between harvest and sowing), lasted a good month, and involved 40.000 people in all. For the construction itself no less than 450.000 fascines of tamarisk branches were used.[30] No doubt a weir of tamarisk fascines is less imposing than a masonry structure, but the fact remains that Sistan had both the expertise and the labor force to raise the waters of the Hilmand for irrigational purposes. In view of this it is difficult to accept the destruction of the *Band-é Rustam* as the sole cause of the massive settlement decline and the abandonment of the Nahr al-Ta'am system. New weirs were in fact constructed, though farther down the river, so that the total area which could be brought under irrigation was smaller than before.

The chronology of the decline suggests another disaster as decisive: the plague pandemic of the 14th and 15th centuries. Prolonged excess mortality must have had roughly the same consequences for Sistan as for Mesopotamia. However, we do not know whether the plague actually reached Sistan. Mustawfi assures us that like Isfahan Sistan was only rarely afflicted by disease, but this seems to be just another of the many stereotypes he weaved into his text.[31] In epidemiological terms the country must in fact have resembled Mesopotamia. The *Tarikh-é Sistan* reports major epidemics (*waba'*) in 841/842 and 1010/1011,[32] and it is difficult to see how Sistan could have escaped other outbreaks which spread across most of eastern Iranshahr (e.g. in 955/956 and 1056/1057). But documentation is lacking. Around 1300 *Sistani* troops were infected by epidemic disease (*bimari*) in Kirman, but whether they brought it home with them is not known.[33]

Yet the movements of armies and long-distance trade must have exposed Sistan to infections. Plague struck Herat at least twice during the 15th century, and considering Herat's location and the regular contacts it is tempting to assume that the disease also spread to Sistan. In 1905, during the third plague pandemic, Sistan was in fact easily infected from the Indian ports.[34] Yet there is no documentation that this actually happened during the second pandemic. In view of the unpredictable way in which the plague ran its course in other places, it must remain an unprovable (if plausible) assumption that plague was a key influence in the decline of Sistan. Yet even if the plague did strike Sistan with full strength, this still fails to explain why the decline had in fact begun long before.

Clearly, the decline of Sistan cannot be attributed to a single disaster (or even series of disasters). Wars certainly played an important role by killing off labor and damaging the irrigation works. Very likely plague had much the same effect. However, these factors must be seen in a broader context, as other changes reduced the ability of the country to recover from disasters. Because of the environmental conditions of the Hilmand Delta and the extent of irrigation in the Middle Ages, considerable salination and build-up of sand drifts must have occurred. As stated, such processes were rarely observed by the medieval authors. Ibn Hawqal, however, noted that Sistan's soil was covered by salt. Together with his description of the *Sistanis'* constant struggle against the shifting sand this would indicate that ecological difficulties had arisen as early as the 10th century.[35] Today concentrations of salt can be seen all along the old Nahr al-Ta'am system, from Taq up to the Khash-rud, another sign that salinity had built up while the region was under irrigated cultivation.[36]

The dramatic history of medieval Sistan thus took place in the context of an environment becoming more and more precarious. The radical manipulation of the water resources, for instance through the construction of the Nahr al-Ta'am system, together with the removal of natural vegetation and other modifications of the environment, created an unstable agriculture, vulnerable to disturbances from outside. In this sense it resembled the type of farming which had developed in Mesopotamia.

Conclusion

Chapter 21

Decline and Resilience:
Patterns in the History of Iranshahr

Taking the long view of Iranshahr's history, we can now discern certain broad patterns in the continuous changes and fluctuations. These patterns, however, are not altogether consistent with the notion of a general decline in the Middle East. What stands out in the overall picture of Iranshahr is, first of all, the considerable expansion of settlement and irrigation occurring in Parthian and Sassanian times, i.e. from the 2nd century B.C. until the 6th century. Under the Sassanians this expansion was largely the result of a royal policy of colonization. This would seem to have been the case under Arsacid rule as well, at least in the imperial core-areas, but that period is so badly documented that conclusions can only be tentative.

The general expansion ended towards the close of the Sassanian era, quite abruptly in some places. From then on patterns became more diverse, marked by regional differences. Severe demographic and economic decline occurred in Mesopotamia and Sistan, the two great river-watered enclaves of Iranshahr. In Mesopotamia the end of expansion was marked by a series of linked disasters: the floods, plagues, and wars of the 6th and 7th centuries. Though the Sassanian successor states sought to repair the damage done to the irrigation- works by these disasters, in the long run their efforts were in vain. The crisis turned into a continuous decline, and no later than the 16th century once productive Mesopotamia had been reduced to a virtual wasteland. In Sistan the turning point seems to have been less dramatic, but from the 10th century there are clear indices of decline. The final result was no less depressing than in Mespotamia.

In both countries decline was a cumulative process that cannot be explained by a single factor or a single set of circumstances. Wars, natural disasters, administrative misrule and, in Mesopotamia at least, a high level of infection were all key influences. However, they must be set in the proper historical context. What made Mesopotamia and Sistan particularly vulnerable to disasters was their increasingly fragile environments: the strong manipulation and coercion of the environment which came with the settlement expansion caused hydrological changes, accumulation of windblown sands, and salination. Whether environmental deterioration alone would have eventually destroyed large-scale irrigation agriculture in Mesopotamia and Sistan must remain an object of speculation. It is certain, however, that environmental difficulties made the systems creak in the joints before they were struck by other blows.

On the Iranian Plateau the period after the general expansion phase presents a quite different picture. Fluctuations and shifts took place constantly, but on the whole the settlement pattern proved remarkably resilient. Of course, in purely quantitative terms some decline may have occurred during the Middle Ages, but the overall pattern is certainly qualitatively different from that in Mesopotamia and Sistan. Yet the cultivated lands on the Plateau were certainly no less artificial than those of Mesopotamia and Sistan: the network of ruined as well as still operating *qanats* testify to the huge labor effort required to maintain the oases. Nor did the Plateau escape problems with salination and accumulation of windblown sand. In Marv, for instance, it seems that precisely these factors led to a drastic reduction of settlement and cultivation. In general, however, the harmful effects of irrigation and intensive cultivation were less severe than in the river-irrigated lowlands owing to special physcial circumstances (limited water resources, a higher degree of natural drainage etc.). Apparently the Plateau also suffered a lower level of infection. If so, this should be attributed to environmental conditions as well. Settlement on the Plateau did not constitute a connected system, i.e. disasters in one enclave did not necessarily have noticeable consequences for other enclaves. In Mesopotamia and Sistan, on the other hand, breaches of a major dike or weir in one place would inevitably affect the entire system.

The progressing environmental collapse in Mesopotamia drained away the strength of the Persian Empires. The rest of Iranshahr had neither the economic potential nor the population to compensate for the decline of the imperial heartland. It should be noted that Iranshahr, compared to other pre-industrial great powers, was a demographic lightweight. Obviously we have no way of arriving at exact figures for pre-industrial populations: the available quantitative data are too dispersed, too uncertain, and virtually never representative; but research in historical demography can at least provide a general impression of the relative size of populations. Thus the Roman Empire in the 1st century probably had around 50 million.[1] T'ang China, about A.D. 600, had 60 million taxpayers (which must refer to the adult, male population); this figure doubled during the following centuries.[2] The Ottoman Empire, in the 16th century, contained between 30 and 35 million, of which 8 million lived outside the Middle East, in southeast and central Europe. This estimate is based on tax registers and includes both Egypt and Iraq.[3] Pre-conquest Peru probably had a total population of 9 million.[4] By the late 16th century the most populous of the western European states, France, had close to 20 million inhabitants.[5] At no time could Iranshahr have had more than 10–15 million and throughout most of its history the actual figure must have been lower.[6] The largest single population cluster was in Mesopotamia and the tax assessments clearly show that in fiscal terms it was primarily Mesopotamia that sustained the Empire.

Iranshahr's other lands, taken together, had as many or perhaps even more tax-payers, but topographical barriers and the dispersed character of the settlement precluded any effective centralized control over the surplus of the entire Plateau under the given technological conditions. Moreover the oases of the Plateau failed to increase production, though they were pressed by the extortionate methods of tax-collecting that at times resembled regular warfare against the taxpayers. During its long history the Plateau saw many fluctuations and more or less permanent shifts, yet as far as the ability to produce a surplus was concerned, no marked qualitative change occurred after the introduction of the qanat.

Compared with the history of western Europe this of course looks like stagnation, backwardness, and lack of development; but such concepts give a distorted image of Iranshahr's history. One can no doubt find obstacles which on purely theoretical grounds hindered development (understood as sustained economic growth), for instance the heavy-handed political control of economic life or the high frequency of natural disasters, especially earthquakes which destroyed qanats and other capital equipment.[7] But such speculations are of interest only if a genuine potential for growth can be shown to have existed. If we consider agrarian society on the Iranian Plateau in environmental as well as long-term perspective, it is difficult to see where such a potential could have existed. Admittedly the use of iron tools and the qanat was a major technological revolution that made new resources available; but subsequently there occurred no innovations of importance. The resource base remained largely static. This does not imply that the stagnation of Iranshahr was simply caused by lack of innovation. We must ask what kind of technological innovations or political changes could have expanded the resource base and thereby created the preconditions for a substantial increase in production.[8]

Extortionate taxation no doubt deprived the peasants of a margin of safety and made them vulnerable to climatic variations, wars, etc. Had the Plateau enjoyed more of Adam Smith's "peace, easy taxes and a tolerable administration of Justice," the peasants could perhaps have achieved a higher living standard, but productivity and patterns of subsistence would not have been markedly different. It is telling that Iranian agriculture during this century, in spite of considerable investments and the transfer of modern, western agrarian technology, has not increased productivity – rather the opposite, if we look at production per area unit. The point is that resource scarcity, primarily lack of water, has imposed fundamental limits on production, limits which until now neither more capital nor improved technology nor alternative forms of social organization have been able to transcend. In this sense Iranshahr differs from both pre-industrial Europe and the wet-rice societies of Asia.[9]

In the Persian Empire the decline of the main resource base led to a fateful military transformation which eventually made nomad leaders the masters of Iran-shahr. Unlike several other pre-industrial empires, e.g. Rome, Byzantium, China under the Chin, Han, Sui, and T'ang dynasties, the Persian Empires never made use of citizen armies and certainly not of the *levée en masse* of "Oriental hordes."[10] Until the 13th century they based their military power on professional armies, recruited and paid in different ways; both mercenaries and aristocratic warrior castes were used. In almost all pre-industrial societies the need to maintain permanent military forces eventually led to the professionalization of the armies as illustrated by the development of the Roman Army and peasantry during the Republic. The process invariably created serious financial problems, because standing armies were expensive. In Byzantium a military force of 120.000 men, on paper at least, absorbed more than half of the state's cash budget in the 9th century, to which should be added further costs in the form of deliveries of raw materials, corvée on fortifications, etc.; moreover this was the situation *after* military reforms designed to reduce costs.[11] When the citizen army in T'ang China, in the 8th century, was replaced by professional armies, military expenses rose immediately: they doubled between 715 and 755 and by the early 9th century had developed into a crushing economic burden; eventually the increasing tax load led to peasant rebellions and widespread "banditry."[12]

In Iranshahr the quantitative data are too few and dispersed to allow us to calculate the military expenses in exact terms.[13] Yet the sources do reveal that the army represented by far the largest item in the Empires' budget and securing its maintenance became increasingly hard as the fiscal erosion worsened. Bitter conflicts between various groups over the distribution of the dwindling surplus caused political instability and meanwhile the military forces of the central government disintegrated. The core of the Abbasid army consisted of Turkish cavalry, said to have numbered 70.000 men in al-Mu'tasim's time (833–842); but now there were no longer funds for salaries, horses, armor, or purchase of new slaves. (Since al-Mu'tasim's reorganization the élite regiments of the army had consisted of *mamluks*, usually of Turkish origin, who technically speaking were slaves).[14]

On the Plateau local rulers maintained their own small armies like the 5.000 men whom Tahir b. al-Husayn brought with him when he joined al-Ma'mun in Marv.[15] The larger regional states raised armies of considerable size. At the height of its power, under Mahmud b. Sebüktegin, the Ghaznavid Army perhaps numbered 50.000, both cavalry and heavy infantry, strengthened by many costly war-elephants. It was paid in cash, partly with money extorted from Khurasan and Transoxania, partly with the booty and tribute gathered during the campaigns in India.[16] As we have seen, the heavy taxes made the Ghaznavids hated in Khurasan, and the loyalty of the country to the dynasty was undermined. Herat went so far as to ally herself with Turkoman nomads in an attempt to break free of Ghaznavid rule.[17] Something similar had happened to the Ghaznavids' immediate predecessors as rulers over the eastern plateau, the Samanids. They had originally been praised for their mild taxation, but eventually military expenses, said to have reached 20 million dirhams a year, led to tax increases which weakened the loyalty of the *dihqans*.[18]

In the late 11th century the Saldjuk ruler Malik Shah still had 46.000 men registered on his official payroll (that the troops were now increasingly paid through the *iqta'* institution is of minor importance in this context).[19] But this was the last great standing army in Iranshahr. After the collapse of Saldjuk rule in the middle of the 12th century and the Mongol conquest in the 13th century, armies were raised largely from among the nomads who, until then, had not played any prominent military role. The Saldjuks, themselves of nomad origin, had in fact attempted to send their unruly tribesmen further west, preferring to build up a regular army on the Ghaznavid model.

According to the prevailing view nomads possess a military superiority somehow rooted in the discipline, endurance, and equestrian skills, which their way of life breeds in them. This potential was simply waiting, so it is said, for a talented leader to channel it into plunder and conquest. At first sight, the swift and extensive Mongol conquests in the 13th century would seem to confirm such assumptions, but they are in fact little more than stereotypes, often repeated but seldom scrutinized more closely.[20]

That the nomads' mobility gave them certain tactical and logistical advantages is no doubt correct, but the armies of agrarian societies were for long periods nevertheless able to suppress and even terrorize nomad societies. Nomad armies were certainly not invincible: the battle of Leignitz (1241), where the Mongols decimated a hastily summoned, numerically inferior German-Polish army, can be contrasted with the battles of Ayn Djalut (1260), Albistan (1277), and Homs (1281), where the heavy Egyptian *mamluk* cavalry defeated Mongol armies. In the 14th century the Lithuanians and Russians gained similar victories over the Golden Horde (e.g. at Voya in 1378 and Kulikovo in 1380).

The rulers of the Middle East, in contrast to later western historians, were not impressed overmuch by the nomads' effectiveness or by their rapidly shifting political loyalties. They preferred, as far as it was within their means, to rely on regular armies. With such a regular army, consisting of disciplined infantry armed with guns and small arms, the Ottomans inflicted on nomad armies the historic defeats at Bashkent (1473) and Chaldiran (1514). If firearms were decisive here, we should not forget that another professional army, the Egyptian *mamluks*, had defeated nomad invasions without making use of them. The development of weapons technology is not the only reason that the nomads were contained and eventually defeated.

Several agrarian societies have sometimes suffered nomad conquest or have been obliged to pay some form of tribute to nomad leaders. However, *prolonged* nomad rule seems to have been a particularly Iranian and Transoxanian phenomenon.[21] The reason that nomads had the military and political capacity to dominate an old agrarian society like Iranshahr for centuries should therefore be sought in the specific conditions within Iranshahr, not in the alleged invincibility of the nomads. In the long term the Persian Empires with their declining economic and demographic resources were unable to maintain the costly regular armies. In this situation, the nomads offered a kind of ad hoc solution, i.e. they were a cheap alternative. They supplied their own weapons and horses, were paid with plunder and, what is economically important, could be sent home again when the campaign had ended. However, such cheap alternatives have their disadvantages. The need of finding pasture for the horses, for instance, imposed seasonal restrictions on the use of nomad armies which never evolved complicated logistical systems. Of course, such systems would have robbed them of their chief tactical advantage: mobility. Moreover the nomads were difficult to keep under political control once the conquests were over. Ambitious princes and other pretenders were always ready to enlist the support of those warriors and *khans* who felt they had received inadequate reward or status for their efforts. One way of preventing this was to wage war continuously and thus keep up the flow of booty. This was, roughly speaking, the strategy of Timur-é Lenk. The alternative was to allow the nomad leaders a share of the agrarian surplus by appointing them to high offices such as governorships. Yet such a combination of military power and fiscal resources gave the *khans* a high degree of genuine autonomy.[22] The Safavids, who conquered Iranshahr with a nomad army in the early 16th century, learned from both the battle of Chaldiran and the recalcitrance of the *khans*. Consequently they attempted to build up a regular army, organized on Ottoman lines; but in the end they did not have the necessary resources.[23]

Thus large-scale mobilization of the nomads led to several centuries of extraordinary political instability, characterized by the weakening of the hegemonic state, perpetual wars of succession, and conflicts among nomad groups over the agrarian surplus. The point is that this was part of a larger historical confluence beginning with the changes Iranshahr had undergone during the Middle Ages. The process which eventually led to nomad domination shows that the history of Iranshahr cannot be explained in terms of a few external influences, be they Hellenism, the Arab conquest, the spread of Islam, the Mongols, or the fluctuations of long-distance trade. Such influences should rightly be seen as variables in the specific historical context, alongside other influences such as environmental conditions and epidemic diseases. That nomads, as well as merchants, legal scholars, and townsmen in general, figure much more prominently in the sources than do the peasants, must not lead us to ignore that agriculture formed the material base of Iranshahr. Seen in the long-term perspective, the societies of Iranshahr reveal particular internal dynamics which sprang precisely from the conditions in agriculture, i.e. the clash between the environmental and technological limitations of agricultural production and the political demands for surplus.

Nature, whether pristine or coerced and modified by human agency, will in all societies set specific limiting conditions. In Iranshahr the limits were narrower than in most other places. From this it does not follow, however, that decline was an unavoidable result of the severe environmental conditions. Though the fate of Iranshahr certainly emphasizes that society and nature constitute a single system, this must not lead us into the trap of ecological reductionism. We must not forget that the environment itself is shaped by complex historical processes. Neither the construction of the huge canal systems in the lowlands nor the building of artificial oases on the Plateau was absolutely necessary for human survival. They were built largely because the rulers of Iranshahr chose to do so, primarily with the aim of expanding the state's resource base. The environmental costs, ranging from desertification to diseases, were at the expense of later generations, reminding us that some of the problems of the Third World countries today listed by the Brundtland Commission are deeply rooted in the past.

Bibliography

Sources

The texts are listed according to the generally accepted forms of the authors' names. As regards oriental names, smaller elements such as "ibn" and "al-" are ignored. Anonymous sources are listed according to title, collections of sources according to editor's name.

Abbé Carré: *The Travels of Abbé Carré in India and the Near East, 1672–1674*, trans. C. Fawcett, 3 vols. (London: Hakluyt Society, 1947–48).

Abu Yusuf Ya'qub ibn Ibrahim al-Ansari (dead 798): *Kitab al-kharadj*, trans. A. Ben Shemesh, *Taxation in Islam* vol. 3 (Leyden 1969).

Abbott, K.E.: "Notes Taken on a Journey Eastwards from Shiráz to Fessá and Darab," *JRGS* 27, 1857: 149–184.

Cities and Trade: Consul Abbott on the Economy and Society of Iran, 1847–1866, ed. A. Amanat (London 1983).

al-Ahri, Abu Bakr al-Qutbi (*c.* 1360): *Tarikh-é Shaykh Uways*, ed. and trans. J.B. Van Loon (s'Gravenhage 1954).

Ammianus Marcellinus (*c.* 390): *Rerum Gestarum Libri qui Supersunt*, trans. J.C. Rolfe (London: Loeb Classical Library, 1935).

ibn 'Arabshah, Abu Muhammad Ahmad (dead 1450): *Tamerlane or Timur, the Great Amir*, trans. J.H. Sanders (London 1936).

Arrian, Flavius (2nd Century): *The History of Alexander and Indica*, trans. E.I. Robson (London: Loeb Classical Library, 1929–1933).

al-Baladhuri, Ahmad ibn Yahya (dead *c.* 892): *Kitab futuh al-buldan*, trans. P.K. Hitti (vol. 1) and F.C. Murgotten (vol. 2), *The Origins of the Islamic State* (New York 1916–1924).

Bal'ami, Abu 'Ali Muhammad (*c.* 970): *Chronique de Tabari sur la version persane de Bel'ami*, trans. M.H. Zotenberg, 4 vols. (Paris 1867–1874).

ibn al-Balkhi (*c.* 1100): *Fars-nameh*, ed. G. Le Strange and R.A. Nicholson (London: *GMS* N.S. 1, 1921). Part. trans. G. Le Strange, "Description of the Province of Fars in Persia," *Asiatic Society Monographs* XIV (London 1912).

Barbaro, Josafa: *Travels to Tana and Persia by Josafa Barbaro and Ambrogio Contarini*, trans. Lord Stanley of Alderley (London: Hakluyt Society, 1873).

Bar-Hebraeus (dead 1286): *The Chronography of Gregory Abu'l-Faraj (...) commonly known as Bar Hebraeus*, ed. and trans. E.A.W. Budge (London 1932).

Bar-Penkaye, John (late 7th Century): *Rish Mellé*, ed. and part. trans. A. Mingana, *Sources Syriaques* 1/2 (Mosul 1908). Part. trans. S.P. Brock, "North Mesopotamia in the Late Seventh Century: Book XV of John Bar Penkaye's Rish Melle," *Jerusalem Studies in Arabic and Islam* 9, 1987: 51–75.

ibn Battuta, Abu 'Abdallah Muhammad: *al-Rihla*, trans. H.A.R. Gibb, *The Travels of Ibn Battuta, 1325–1354*, 3 vols. (Cambridge: Hakluyt Society, 1958–1971).

Bayhaqi, Abu al-Fazl Muhammad ibn al-Husayn (dead 1077/78): *Tarikh-é mas'udi*, ed. Q. Ghani and 'A. Fayyad (Tehran 1945).

Benjamin of Tudela: *Contemporaries of Marco Polo*, ed. M. Komroff, pp. 253–322 (London 1927).

Cassius Dio (early 3rd century): *Roman History*, trans. E. Cary (London: Loeb Classical Library, 1914).

Chou Shu: *Accounts of Western Nations in the History of the Northern Chou Dynasty*, ed. and trans. R.A. Miller (Berkeley 1959).

Clavijo, Ruy Gonzalez de (*c.* 1405): *Narrative of the Embassy of Ruy Gonzalez de Clavijo to the Court of Timour*, trans. C.R. Markham (London: Hakluyt Society, 1859).

Constantine VII Porphyrogenitus (10th century): *Excerpta de Legationibus*, part. trans. E. Doblhofer, *Byzantinische Diplomaten und Östliche Barbaren* (Graz 1955).

Contarini, Ambrogio (15th century): *Travels to Tana and Persia by Josafa Barbaro and Ambrogio Contarini*, trans. Lord Stanley of Alderley (London: Hakluyt Society, 1873).

Ctesias of Cnidos (*c.* 400 B.C.): Die Persika des Ktesias von Knidos, ed. and trans. F.W. König. *Archiv für Orientforschung*, Beiheft 18 (Graz 1972)

Cyprian, Thascus Caecilius (dead 258): *De Mortalitate*, ed. and trans. M.L. Hannan (Washington: Patristic Studies 36, 1933).

Dijk, J. Van et al.: *Early Mesopotamian Incantations and Rituals*, Yale Oriental Series, Babylonian Texts 11 (New Haven 1985).

Diodorus Siculus (dead *c.* 20 B.C.): Ed. and trans. C.H. Oldfather (London: Loeb Classical Library, 1932); ed. and trans. P. Goukowsky (Paris 1978).

Dionysius of Tell-Mahré (*c.* 840): *Chronique de Denys de Tell-Mahré. Quatriéme partie*, ed. and trans. J.B. Chabot (Paris 1895).

Dionysius of Halicarnassus (1st century B.C.): *Roman Antiquities*, trans. E. Cary (London: Loeb Classical Library, 1937).

al-Djahiz, Abu 'Uthman 'Amr ibn Bakr (dead 868): *Kitab al-buhala*, trans. Ch. Pellat, *Le livre des avares* (Paris 1951 and in *Arabica* 2, 1955: pp. 322–352).

al-Djahshiyari, Abu 'Abdallah Muhammad ibn 'Abdus (dead 942): *Kitab al-wuzara' wa'l-kuttab*, part trans. J. Latz, *Das Buch der Wezire und Staatssekretäre von Ibn 'Abdus al-Gahsiyari*, Walldorf-Hessen 1958).

ibn Djubayr, Abu al-Husayn Muhammad ibn Ahmad (dead 1217): *al-Rihla*, trans. R. Broadhurst, *The Travels of Ibn Jubayr* (London 1952).

Djuwayni, 'Ala al-Din 'Ata-Malik ibn Muhammad (dead 1283): *Tarikh-é djahan-gushay*, ed. Mirza Muhammad Kazvini (London: *GMS* 16, 1912–1937); trans. J.A. Boyle, *The History of the World-Conqueror by Juvayni*, 2 vols. (Manchester 1958).

Djuzdjani, Abu 'Umar 'Uthman (*c.* 1260): *Tabaqat-é nasiri*, trans. H.G. Raverty, 3 vols. (London 1881).

Elias Bar-Shinaya of Nisibis (*c.* 1020): "Fragmente Syrischer und Arabischer Historiker," part. ed. and trans. F. Baethgen, *Abhandlungen für die Kunde des Morgenlandes* VIII/3 (Leipzig 1884).

Eusebius of Caesarea (dead 340): *The Ecclesiastical History*, trans. Kirsopp Lake and J.E.L. Oulton (London: Loeb Classical Library, 1926–1932).

ibn al-Faqih al-Hamadani (*c.* 900): *Mukhtasar kitab al-buldan*, ed. M.J. de Goeje (Leyden: *BGA* 5, 1885); trans. H. Massé, *Abrégé du livre des pays* (Damascus 1973).

Fasa'i, Hasan-é (late 19th century): *Farsnameh-yé nasiri*, trans. H. Busse, *History of Persia under Qajar rule* (New York-London 1972).

Fraser, J.B.: *Travels in Koordistan, Mesopotamia &c.* 2 vols. (London 1840).

Geller, M.J.: *Forerunners to UDUG-HUL: Sumerian Exorcistic Incantations*. Freiburger Altorientalische Studien 12 (Stuttgart 1985).

al-Ghiyati (or al-Baghdadi), 'Abdallah ibn Fath'allah (*c.* 1500): *Turkmenische Herrscher des 15. Jahrhunderts in Persien und Mesopotamien nach dem Tarih al-Giyati*, trans. M. SchmidtDumont (Freiburg-in-Breisgau 1970).

Grayson, A.K. trans.: *Assyrian Royal Inscriptions*, 2 vols. (Wiesbaden 1972).

Assyrian and Babylonian Chronicles (Locust valley: Texts from Cuneiform Sources 5, 1975).

Babylonian Historical-Literary Texts (Toronto: Toronto Semitic Texts and Studies 3, 1975).

Grignaschi, M. ed. and trans.: "Quelques spécimens de la litterature sassanide conservés dans les bibliothéques d'Istanbul," *Journal Asiatique* 254, 1966: 1–142.

Hafiz-é Abru, Shihab al-Din (dead 1429/30): *Djughrafiya*, part. ed. and trans. D. Krawulsky, *Horasan zur Timuridenzeit*, 2 vols. (Wiesbaden: TAVO Beiheft B 46/1–2, 1982–1984).

Zayl-é Djami' al-tavarikh, trans. K. Bayani, *Chronique des rois mongols en Iran* (Paris 1936).

Hakluyt, R.: *The Principal Navigations, Voyages, Traffiques & Discoveries of the English Nation*, 2 vols. (London, 2nd. ed. 1598–1600).

Hamza al-Isfahani (*c.* 960): *Ta'rikh sini muluk al-ard wa'l-anbiya'*, ed. and latin trans. J.M.E. Gottwaldt (Leipzig 1848).

Han Shu (mid-5th century): "Les pays d'Occident d'après le Heou Han Chou," trans. E. Chavannes, *T'oung Pao*, 2nd ser., vol. 8, 1907: 149–234.

ibn Hawqal, Abu al-Kasim Muhammad (*c.* 980): *Kitab surat al-ard*, ed. J.H. Kramers (Leyden 1938–1939); trans. J.H. Kramers and G. Wiet, *Configuration de la terre*, 2 vols. (Paris 1964).

Herodian (*c.* 250): trans. C.R. Whittaker (London: Loeb Classical Library, 1970).

Herodotus (late 5th century B.C.): *The Histories*, trans. A. de Selincourt (Harmondsworth 1954).

Hilal al-Sabi' (dead 1056): *Ta'rikh*, ed. and trans. H.F. Amedroz and D.S. Margoliouth, *The Eclipse of the Abbasid Caliphate*, vols. 3 and 6 (Oxford 1920–1921).

Hoffmann, G. trans.: "Auszüge aus Syrischen Akten Persischer Märtyrer," *Abhandlungen für die Kunde des Morgenlandes* 7, 1880.

Hudud al-'Alam (*c.* 982/83): Trans. V. Minorsky, *Hudud al-'Alam, "the Regions of the World." A Persian Geography 372 AH/982 AD* (London: GMS, N.S. 11, 1937).

ibn Isfandiyar, Muhammad ibn al-Hasan (1216): *Tarikh-é tabaristan*, part. trans. E.G. Browne, *An Abridged Translation of the History of Tabaristan* (Leyden: GMS 2, 1905).

al-Isfizari, Mu'in al-Din Muhammad (1491/92): *Rauzat al-djannat fi ausaf madinat harat*, part. trans. M. Barbier de Meynard, "Extraits de la chronique persane d'Herat," *Journal Asiatique,* 5th ser. 1861 (Extrait no. 11) and 1862: 268–319.

Isidore of Charax (1st century): *The Parthian Stations*, ed. and trans. W.H. Schoff (London 1914).

al-Istakhri (or al-Farisi), Abu Ishaq Ibrahim ibn Muhammad (*c.* 950): *Kitab al-masalik wa'l-mamalik*, ed. M.J. de Goeje (Leyden: BGA 1, 1870); trans. A.D. Mordtmann, *Das Buch der Länder* (Hamburg 1845).

Iustin (*c.* 200): *Epitoma historiarum philippicarum Pompei Trogi*, ed. F. Ruehl (Leipzig 1886); trans. O. Seel, *Pompeius Trogus: Weltgeschichte von den Anfängen bis Augustus* (Zürich-München 1972).

John of Ephesus (dead 586): *The Third Part of the Ecclesiastical History of John, Bishop of Ephesus*, trans. R. Payne Smith (Oxford 1860).

"Lives of the Eastern Saints," ed. and trans. E.W. Brooks, *Patrologia Orientalis* 17, 1923: 1–307; 18, 1924: 513–698; 19, 1925: 153–185.

Ps. Joshua the Stylite (507): *The Chronicle of Joshua the Stylite*, trans. W. Wright (Cambridge 1882).

Karnameh Artakhsir i Papakan: Ed. and trans. D.D.P. Sanjana (Bombay 1896).

al-Kazwini, Zakariya ibn Muhammad (*c.* 1280): *Zakarija ben Muhammed ben Mahmud al-Kazwini's Kosmographie*, trans. H. Ethé (Leipzig 1868).

ibn Khallikan, Ahmad ibn Muhammad (dead 1282): *Ibn Khallikan's Biographical Dictionary*, trans. M.G. de Slane, 4 vols. (Paris-London 1842–1871).

al-Khatib al-Baghdadi, Ahmad ibn Thabit (11th century): *Ta'rikh Baghdad*, part. ed. and trans. G. Salmon, *L'Introduction topographique à l'histoire de Bagdadh de (...) al-Khatib al-Bagdadhi* (Paris 1904); part. trans. J. Lassner, *The Topography of Baghdad in the Early Middle Ages* (Detroit 1970, pp. 45–118).

Khundji, Fazlallah ibn Ruzbihan (*c.* 1500): *Tarikh-é 'alam-ara-yé amini*, part. trans. V. Minorsky, *Persia in AD 1478–1490. Royal Asiatic Monographs* 26 (London 1957).

Mihman-nameh-yé bukhara, trans. U. Ott, *Transoxanien und Turkestan zu Beginn des 16. Jahrhunderts* (Freiburg-in-Breisgau 1974).

ibn Khurdadhbih, 'Ubaydallah ibn 'Abdallah (late 9th century): *Kitab al-masalik wa'l-mamalik*, ed. and trans. M.J. de Goeje (Leyden: *BGA* VI, 1889).

The "Khuzistan Chronicle" (late 7th century): Trans. T. Noeldeke, "Die von Guidi herausgegebene Syrische Chronik," *Sitzungsberichte der Philologisch-Historischen Klasse der Kaiserlichen Akademie der Wissenschaften* 128 (Wien 1893).

Kinneir, J. McDonald: *A Geographical Memoir of the Persian Empire* (London 1813).

Kitab al-tadj (9th century): Trans. Ch. Pellat, *Le livre de la Couronne* (Paris 1954).

Koçi Bey, Mustafa (1631): Trans. W. F. Behrnauer, "Kogabegs Abhandlung über den Verfall des Osmanischen Staatsgebaüdes seit Sultan Soleiman dem Grossen." *ZDMG* 15 (1861).

Labat, R. ed. and trans.: *Traité akkadien de diagnostics et pronostics médicaux* (ParisLeyden: Collection de travaux de l'académie internationale d'histoire des sciences 7, 1951).

Langlois, V. ed. and trans.: *Collection des historiens anciens et modernes de l'Arménie*, 2 vols. (Paris 1867–1869).

Luckenbill, D.D. trans.: *Ancient Records of Assyria and Babylonia*, 2 vols. (Chicago 1926–1927).

Marco Polo (13th century): *Il Milione*, ed. R. Alluli (Rome 1954).

ibn Masawayh, Yuhanna (early 9th century): *Kitab al-azmina*, trans. G. Tropeau, "Le livre de temps de Jean ibn Masawayh," *Arabica* 15, 1968: 113–142.

al-Mas'udi, Abu'l-Hasan 'Ali ibn Husayn (dead 956): *Kitab al-murudj al-dhahab*, ed. and trans. C. Barbier de Meynard and P. de Courteille, *Les prairies d'or*, 9 vols. (Paris 1861–1877).
    Kitab al-tanbih, trans. B. Carra de Vaux, *Le livre de l'avertissement* (Paris 1896).

Michael the Syrian (dead 1199): Ed. and Trans. J.B. Chabot, *Chronique de Michel le syrien*, 4 vols (Paris 1899–1910).

ibn Miskawayh, Abu 'Abdallah Ahmad ibn Muhammad (dead 1030): *Tadjarib al-umam*, ed. and trans. H.F. Amedroz and D.S. Margoliouth, *The Eclipse of the Abbasid Caliphate*, vols. I-II and IV-V (Oxford 1920–1921).

Moses Khorenats'i (8th century): Trans. R.W. Thomson, *History of the Armenians* (Cambridge, Mass. 1978).

al-Muqaddasi (or al-Maqdisi), Abu 'Abdallah Muhammad ibn Ahmad (*c*. 990): *Ahsan al-taqasim*, ed. M.J. de Goeje (Leyden: *BGA* III, 1906); part. trans. G.S.A. Ranking and R.F. Azoo (Calcutta: Bibliotheca Indica 137, 1897).

ibn al-Muqaffa' (dead 759/60): *Risala fi al-sahaba*, ed. and trans. Ch. Pellat (Paris 1976).

al-Mustawfi al-Kazwini, Hamd'allah (*c*. 1340): *Nuzhat al-qulub*, ed. and trans. G. Le Strange, *The Geographical Part of the Nuzhat al-Qulub* (London: *GMS* 23, 1919).
    Tarikh-é guzideh, ed. and part. trans. E.G. Browne, 2 vols. (London: *GMS* 14, 1910–1913). The section concerning the history of Kazwin has been translated by M.C. Barbier de Meynard in *Journal Asiatique*, 5th ser., vol. 10, 1857: 257308.

ibn al-Nadim, Abu'l-Faradj Muhammad (dead 995): *Kitab al-fihrist*, ed. and trans. B. Dodge, 2 vols. (New York 1970).

Narshaki, Abu Bakr Muhamad ibn Dja'far (dead 959): *Tarikh-é bukhara*, trans. R.N. Frye, *The History of Bukhara* (Cambridge, Mass. 1954).

Nasawi, Muhammad ibn Ahmad (13th century): *Sirat al-sultan Djalal al-din mankubirti*, ed. and trans. O. Houdas, *Vie de Djelaleddin Mankobirti*, 2 vols. (Paris 18911895).

Nasir al-Din Tusi (dead 1274): *Zidj-é ilkhani*, ed. and trans. M. Minovi and V. Minorsky, "Nasir al-Din Tusi on Finance," *BSOAS* 10, 1941: 755–789.

Nasir-é Khusraw (11th century): *Safar-nameh*, ed. and trans. C. Schefer, *Relation du voyage de Nassiri Khosrau* (Paris 1881).

Nizam al-Mulk, Abu 'Ali Hasan ibn 'Ali (dead 1071): *Siyasat-nameh*, ed. C. Schefer (Paris 1891); trans. H. Darke, *The Book of Government, or Rules for Kings* (London 1960).

Oppenheim, A.L. trans.: *Letters from Mesopotamia* (Chicago 1967).

Ouseley, W.: *Travels in Various Countries of the East; more particularly Persia*, 3 vols. (London 1819–1823).

Pliny (dead 79): *Natural History*, trans. H. Rackham (London: Loeb Classical Library, 1938).

Plutarch (dead 120): *Lives*, trans. B. Perrin (London: Loeb Classical Library, 1914–1926).

Polybius (*c.* 120 B.C.): *The Histories*, trans. W.R. Paton (London: Loeb Classical Library, 1922).

Pritchard, J.B. ed.: *Ancient Near Eastern Texts Relating to the Old Testament* (Princeton: 3rd ed., 1969).

Procopius of Caesarea (*c.* 560): *History of the Wars*, trans. H.B. Dewing (London: Loeb Classical Library, 1914).

Ptolemaeus, Claudius (*c.* 150): *Geography of Claudius Ptolemy*, ed. and trans. E.L. Stevenson (New York 1932).

Purchas, Samuel: *Hakluytus Posthumus or Purchas his Pilgrimes*, 20 vols. (reprint. New York 1965)

Qudama ibn Dja'far al-Katib (dead *c.* 930): *Kitab al-kharadj*, ed. and part. trans. M.J. de Goeje (Leyden: BGA VI, 1889); part. trans. A. ben Shemesh, *Taxation in Islam*, vol. 2 (Leyden 1968).

Quintus Curtius Rufus (1st century): *History of Alexander*, trans. J.C. Rolfe (London: Loeb Classical Library, 1946).

ibn Qutayba, Abu Muhammad 'Abdallah ibn Muslim (dead 889): *'Uyun al-akhbar*, part. trans. J. Horowitz, *Islamic Culture* vol. 4 (1930): 171–198, 331–362, 487–529; vol 5 (1931): 1–27, 194–224.

Rashid al-Din, Fazlallah (dead 1318): *Djami' al-tavarikh*, part. ed and trans. E. Quatremére, *Histoire des mongols de la Perse* (Paris 1836); part. trans. J.A. Boyle, *The Successors of Genghis Khan* (London 1971).

al-Rawandi, Muhammad ibn 'Ali (*c.* 1200): *Rahat al-sudur wa ayat al-surur*, ed. Muhammad Iqbal (London: GMS N.S. 2, 1921).

ibn Ridwan, 'Ali (11th century): *Kitab daf' madarr al-abdan*, ed. A.S. Gamal and trans. M.W. Dols, *Medieval Islamic Medicine* (Berkeley 1984).

al-Rudhrawari, Abu Shudja' (dead 1095): *Dhayl tadjarib al-umam*, ed. and trans. H.F. Amedroz and D.S. Margoliouth, *The Eclipse of the Abbasid Caliphate*, vols. III and VI (Oxford 1920–1921).

ibn Rusteh, Abu 'Ali Ahmad ibn 'Umar (*c.* 910): *Kitab al a'laq al-nafisa*, ed. M.J. de Goeje (Leyden: BGA VII, 1891); trans. G. Wiet, *Les atours précieux* (Cairo 1955).

al-Salmani, Tadj (15th century): *Shams al-husn*, ed. and trans H.R. Roemer (Wiesbaden: Akademie der Wissenschaften und der Litteratur. Veröffentlichungen der Orientalischen Kommission 8, 1956).

al-Samarkandi, Kamal al-Din 'Abd al-Razzak (dead 1482): *Matla'-é sa'dayn wa madjma'-é bahrayn*, part. trans. M. Quatremére (Paris: Notices et extraits des manuscrits de la bibliothéque du Roi et autres bibliothéques 14, pp. 1–514).

ibn Sarabiyun, Suhrab (*c.* 900): *Kitab 'adja'ib al-aqalim al-sab'ah*, ed. and trans. G. Le Strange, "Description of Mesopotamia and Baghdad (...) by Ibn Serapion," *JRAS* 1895: 1–76, 255–315.

Ps. Sebeos (*c.* 700): *Histoire d'Héraclius par l'évéque Sebeos*, trans. F. Macler (Paris 1904).

The "Se'ert Chronicle" (11th century): Ed. and trans. Mgr. Addai Scher, "Histoire nestorienne inédite," *Patrologia Orientalis* vol. 4 (1908): 215–313; vol. 5 (1910): 219–344; vol. 7 (1911): 97–203; vol. 13 (1919): 437–639.

Scriptores Historia Augusta (*c.* 400): Trans. D. Magie (London: Loeb Classical Library, 1922–1932).

Shahristanha-yé Iran (8th century): Ed. and trans. J. Markwart, "A Catalogue of the Provincial Capitals of Eranshahr," *Analecta Orientalia* 3, 1931.

Shapur, Kaba of Zoroaster (SKZ): Trans. A. Maricq, "Res Gesta Divi Saporis," *Syria* 35, 1958: 295–360.

Smith, S. trans.: *Babylonian Historical Texts* (London 1924).

Strabo (early 1st century): *Geography*, trans. H.L. Jones (London: Loeb Classical Library, 1917).

Strategicon (*c.* 600): *Das Strategikon des Maurikios*, ed. G.T. Dennis, tr. E. Gamillscheg. Corpus Fontium Historiae Byzantinae XVII (Wien 1981).

al-Suli, Muhammad ibn Yahya (dead 946/47): *Kitab al-awraq*, trans. M. Canard, "Akhbar al-radi-billah wa'l-muttaqi-billah," *Publications de l'institut d'études orientales de la faculté des lettres d'Alger* 10 (1946) and 12 (1950).

Synodicon Orientale: Ed. and trans. J.B. Chabot (Paris 1902).

The Syriac Book of Medicine: Ed. and trans. E.A.W. Budge, 2 vols. (London 1913).

al-Tabari, Abu Dja'far Muhammad ibn Djarir (dead 923): *Ta'rikh al-rusul wa'l-muluk*, part. trans. T.

Noeldeke, *Geschichte der Perser und Araber zur Zeit der Sasaniden* (Leyden 1879); E. Marin, *The reign of al-Mu'tasim* (American Oriental Series 35, 1951); J.A. Williams, *The Abbasid Revolution* (Albany: the History of al-Tabari 27, 1985); G. Saliba, *The Crisis of the Abbasid Caliphate* (Albany; the History of al-Tabari 35, 1985); M.G. Morony, *Between Civil Wars. The Caliphate of Mu'awiyah* (Albany: the History of al-Tabari 18, 1987).

al-Tabari, Abu al-Hasan Ahmad ibn Muhammad (late 10th century): Part. trans. M. Rihab, "Der Arabische Artz at-Tabari. Übersetzung einzelner Abschnitte aus seinen "Hippokratischen Be-handlungen," *Archiv für Geschichte der Medizin* 19, 1927: 123–168.

Tacitus (dead *c.* 117): *The Annals*, trans. J. Jackson (London: Loeb Classical Library, 1931).

Tansar-nameh: trans. H. Kirketerp-Møller, *Tansar's Brev til Gushnasp, Konge af Tabaristan* (Copenha-gen: Selskabet til Historiske Kildeskrifters Oversættelse XIII/16, 1965).

al-Tanukhi, al-Muhassin ibn 'Ali ibn Muhammad ibn Dawud (dead 994): *Nishwar al-muhadara*, trans. D.S. Margoliouth, *The Table Talk of a Mesopotamian Judge* (London 1922); continued in *Islamic Culture* vol 3 (1929): 490–522; vol 4 (1930): 1–28, 223–228, 363–388, 531–557; vol. 5 (1931): 169–193, 352–371, 559–581; vol. 6 (1932): 47–66, 184–205, 370–396.

Tarikh-é Sistan (late 11th century with short continuation up to 1325): ed. Muhammad Taqi Bahar (Tehran 1935); trans. M. Gould (Rome 1976).

ibn Tayfur, Ahmad (dead 893): Ed. and trans. H. Keller, *Sechster Band des Kitab Baghdad von Ahmad ibn abi Taifur* (Leipzig 1908).

Teixeira, Pedro: *The Travels of Pedro Teixeira*, trans. W.F. Sinclair (London: Hakluyt Society, 1902).

al-Tha'alibi, Abu Mansur al-Husayn ibn Muhammad (dead 1038): *Ta'rikh ghurar al-siyar*, part. ed. and trans. H. Zotenberg, *Histoire des rois des perses par al-Tha'alibi* (Paris 1900).
  Lata'if al-ma'arif, trans. C.E. Bosworth, *The Book of Curious and Entertaining Information: the Lata'if al-Ma'arif of Tha'alibi* (Edenburgh 1968).

Theophanes (dead 818): Part. trans. L. Breyer, *Bilderstreit und Arabersturm in Byzanz* (Graz 1957).

Thomas of Marga (*c.* 840): *The Book of Governors. The Historia Monastica of Thomas Bishop of Marga*, ed. and trans. E.A.W. Budge, 2 vols. (London 1893).

Thucydides (dead *c.* 400 B.C.): trans. C.F. Smith (London: Loeb Classical Library, 1920).

al-'Utbi, Abu Nasr Muhammad ibn 'Abd al-Djabbar (*c.* 1030): *Kitab al-yamini*, trans. J. Reynolds, *Historical Memoirs of the Amir Sabaktagin and the Sultan Mahmud of Ghazna. Translated from the Persian Version of the Contemporary Chronicle of al-Utbi* (London 1858).

ibn al-Wardi, Abu Hafs 'Umar (dead 1349): *Risala al-naba' an al-waba'*, trans. M.W. Dols in *Near Eastern Numismatics, Iconography, Epigraphy and History. Studies in Honor of George C. Miles*, ed. D.K. Kouymjian, pp. 443–455 (Beirut 1974).

Waring, E.S.: *A Tour of Sheeraz* (London 1807).

Wassaf al-Hazrat, 'Abdallah ibn Fazlallah (14th century): *Tarikh-é Wassaf*, part. ed. and trans. J. von Hammer-Purgstall, *Geschichte Wassaf's* (Wien 1856).

Wiseman, D.J. trans.: *Chronicles of Chaldaean Kings (626–556 B.C.)* (London 1956).

Xenophon (early 4th century B.C.): *Anabasis*, trans. C.L. Brownson (London: Loeb Classical Library, 1922).
  Cyropaedia, trans. W. Miller (London: Loeb Classical Library, 1914).

Yahya ibn Adam (dead 818): *Kitab al-kharadj*, trans. A. ben Shemesh, *Taxation in Islam*, vol. I (Leyden 1967).

al-Ya'qubi, Abu al-Abbas Ahmad ibn abi Ya'qub (*c.* 900): *Kitab al-buldan*, ed. M.J. de Goeje (Leyden: BGA VII, 1891); trans. G. Wiet, *Les pays* (Cairo: Publications de l'institut francais d'archéologie orientale du Caire 1, 1937).

Yaqut al-Rumi, Abu 'Abdallah al-Hamawi (dead 1229): *Mu'djam al-buldan*, part. trans. C. Barbier de Meynard, *Dictionnaire de la Perse. Extraits de mo'djem al-bouldan de Yaqout* (Paris 1861); W. Jwaideh, *The Introductory Chapters of Ya'qut's Mu'jam al-Buldan* (Leyden 1959).

Zosimus (*c.* 500): *Nouvelle Histoire*, ed. and trans. F. Paschoud (Paris 1971).

Modern works

Abrams, Ph.:
1978: "Towns and Economic Growth: some Theories and Problems," in *Towns and Societies*, ed. Ph. Abrams and E.A. Wrigley, pp. 9–33 (Cambridge).

Adamec, L.W., ed.:
1976: *Historical Gazetteer of Iran*, I-III (Graz).

Adams, R. McC.
1958: "Survey of Ancient Watercourses and Settlement in Central Iraq," *Sumer* 14: 101–103.
1962: "Agriculture and Urban Life in Early Southwestern Iran," *Science* 136: 109–122.
1965: *Land behind Baghdad. A history of Settlement on the Diyala Plains* (Chicago).
1970: "Tell Abu Sarifa," *Ars Orientalis* 8: 87–119.
1972: "Patterns of Urbanization in Early Southern Mesopotamia," in *Man, Settlement, and Urbanism*, ed. P.J. Ucko et al., pp. 735–749 (Cambridge, Mass.).
1974: "Historic Patterns of Mesopotamian Irrigation Agriculture," in *Irrigation's Impact on Society*, ed. T. Downing and McGuire Gibson, pp. 1–6 (Tucson: Anthropological Papers of the University of Arizona 28).
1978: "Strategies of Maximation, Stability, and Resilience in Mesopotamian Society, Settlement, and Agriculture," *Proceedings of the American Philosophical Society* 122: 329–335.
1981: *Heartland of Cities. Surveys of Ancient Settlement and Land Use on the Central Floodplain of the Euphrates* (Chicago).

Adle, C.:
1971: "Contribution á la géographie historique du Damghan," *Le Monde Iranien et l'Islam*, pp. 69–90 (Geneve: Hautes Etudes Islamiques et Orientales d'Histoire Comparée 4).

Albaum, L.I. and B. Brentjes:
1972: *Wächter des Goldes. Zur Geschichte und Kultur Mittelasiatischer Völker vor dem Islam* (Berlin).

al-'Ali, S.:
1968: "Al-Mada'in and its Surrounding Area in Arabic Literary Sources," *Mesopotamia* 3–4: 417–439.
1971: "A New Version of Ibn al-Mutarrif's List of Revenues in the Early Times of Harun al-Rashid," *JESHO* 14: 303310.

Alizadeh, A.:
1985: "Elymaean Occupation of Lower Khuzistan during the Seleucid and Parthian Periods: a Proposal," *Iranica Antiqua* 20: 175–195.

Allan, J.W.:
1979: *Persian Metal Technology, 700–1300 A.D.* (London)

Altheim, F. and R. Stiehl:
1954: *Ein Asiatischer Staat: Feudalismus unter den Sassaniden und ihren Nachbarn* (Wiesbaden).

Ambraseys, N.N.:
1979: "A Test Case of Historical Seismicity: Isfahan and Chahar Mahal," *Geographical Journal* 145: 56–71.

Ambraseys, N.N. and C.P. Melville:
1977: "The Seismicity of Kuhistan, Iran," *Geographical Journal* 143: 179–199.

Appleby, A.B.:
1975: "Nutrition and Disease: the Case of London, 1550–1750," *Journal of Interdisciplinary History* 6: 1–22.
1980: "The Disappearance of the Plague: a Continuing Puzzle," *The Economic History Review* (2nd ser.) 33: 161–173.

Ashtor, E.:
1968: "An Essay on the Diet of the Various Classes in the Medieval Levant," in *Biology of Man in*

History. Selections from the Annales, ed. R. Foster and O. Ranum, pp. 125–162 (Baltimore 1975).

1969: *Prix et salaires dans l'Orient médiéval* (Paris).

1976: *A Social and Economic History of the Near East in the Middle Ages* (London)

Aubin, J.:

1955: "Références pour Lar médiévale," *Journal Asiatique* 243: 491–501.

1956: "Deux sayyids de Bam au XVe siècle," *Akademie der Wissenschaften und der Litteratur* 7 (Wiesbaden).

1959: "La ruine de Siraf et les routes du Golfe persique aux XIe et XIIe siècle," *Cahiers de Civilisation Médiévale* 2: 295–301.

1965 : "Un soyurghal Qara-qoyunlu concernant le buluk de Bawanat-Harat-Marwast," in *Documents from Islamic Chanceries*, ed. S.M. Stern and R. Walzer, pp. 159–170 (Oxford).

1967: "Un santon Quhistani de l'époque timouride," *REI* 35: 183–216.

1968: "Comment Tamerlane prenait les villes," *Studia Islamica* 19: 83–122.

1969: "La survie de Shilau et la route du Khundj-o-Fal," *Iran* 7: 21–37.

1970: "Éléments pour l'étude des agglomerations urbains dans l'Iran médiévale," in *The Islamic City*, ed. A.H. Hourani and S.M. Stern, pp. 65–75 (Oxford: Papers on Islamic History I).

1971: "Réseau pastoral et réseau caravanier: les grand'routes du Khurassan à l'époque mongole," *Le Monde Iranien et l'Islam* I: 105–130 (Hautes Études Islamiques et Orientales d'Histoire Comparée 4).

1976a: "Le khanat de Cagatai et le Khorassan, 1334–1380," *Turcica* 8: 16–60.

1976b: "Aux origines d'un movement populaire médiéval: le cheykhisme du Bayhaq et du Nishapour," *Studia Iranica* 5: 213–224.

1986: "Chiffres de population urbaine en Iran occidental autour de 1500," *Moyen Orient et Océan Indien* 3: 3754.

Azarnoush, M.:

1983: "Excavations at Hajjiabad, 1977," *Iranica Antiqua* 18: 159–176.

Ayalon, D.:

1946: "The Plague and its Effect upon the Mamluk Army," *JRAS*: 67ff.

1956: *Gunpowder and Firearms in the Mamluk Kingdom* (London).

1975: "Preliminary Remarks on the Mamluk Military Institution in Islam," in *War, Technology, and Society in the Middle East*, ed. V.J. Parry and M.E. Yapp, pp. 44–58 (London).

1985: "Regarding Population Estimates in the Countries of Medieval Islam," *JESHO* 28: 1–19.

Aymard, M.:

1975: "Pour l'histoire d'alimentation: quelques remarques de méthode," *Annales* 30: 431–444.

Ball, W. and J.C. Gardin:

1982: *Archaeological Gazetteer of Afghanistan* I-II (Paris).

Barkan, Ö.L.:

1957: "Essai sur les donées statistiques des registres de recensement dans l'empire Ottoman aux XVe et XVIe siécles," *JESHO* 1: 9–36.

1970: "Research on the Ottoman Fiscal Surveys," in *Studies in the Economic History of the Middle East*, ed. M.A. Cook, pp. 163–171 (London).

Barnett, R.D.:

1963: "Xenophon and the Wall of Media," *Journal of Hellenic Studies* 83: 1–26.

Barthold, V.V.:

1910: *Nachrichten über der Aral-See und dem unteren Lauf des Amu-darja von der ältetsten Zeiten bis zum 17. Jahrhundert* (Leipzig: Quellen und Forschungen zur Erd- und Kulturkunde 2).

1928: *Turkestan down to the Mongol Invasion*, 2nd ed. (London: GMS n.s. 5).

1956: *Four Studies on the History of Central Asia* I-III (Leyden).

Bean, J.M.W.:

1962: "Plague, Population, and Economic Decline in England," *Economic History Review* 15: 423–437.

Beaumont, P., G.H. Blake and J.M. Wagstaff:
  1976: *The Middle East. A Geographical Study* (London).
Bémont, F.:
  1973: *Les Villes de l'Iran* (Paris).
Bernard, P.:
  1967: "Aï Khanum on the Oxus: a Hellenistic City in Central Asia," *Proceedings of the British Academy* 53: 71–95.
  1974: "Un problème de toponymie antique dans l'Asie centrale: les noms anciens de Qandahar," *Studia Iranica* 3: 171185.
Bernstein, L.:
  1962: "Salt-affected Soils and Plants," *Arid Zone Research* 18: 139–174 (Paris: UNESCO: The Problems of the Arid Zone).
Biberstein-Kazimirski, A. de:
  1886: *Menoutchehri. Poète persan du 11ème siècle* (Paris).
Bickerman, E.:
  1966: "The Seleucids and the Achaemenids," *La Persia e il Mondo Greco-Romano* pp. 87–117 (Rom: Accademia Nazionale dei Lincei).
Biraben, J.N.:
  1975: *Les hommes et la peste en France et dans les pays européens et mediterranéans* I-II (Paris).
Biraben, J.N. and J. LeGoff:
  1969: "The Plague in the Early Middle Ages," in *Biology of Man in History: Selections from the Annales*, ed. R. Foster and O. Ranum, pp. 48–80 (Baltimore 1975).
Biscione, R.:
  1977: "The Crisis of Central Asian Urbanism in II Millennium B.C.," *Le Plateau Iranien et l'Asie Centrale des Origines à la Conquête Islamique*, pp. 113–127 (Paris: Colloques Internationaux du C.N.R.S. 567).
Biscione, R. et al.:
  1974: "Archeological Discoveries and Methodological Problems in the Excavation of Shahr-i-Sokhta, Sistan," in *South Asian Archeology*, ed. J.E. van Lohuizen-de Leuw and J.M.M. Ubaghs, pp. 12–52 (Leyden).
Bivar, A.D.H.
  1970: "Hariti and the Chronology of the Kusanas," *BSOAS* 33: 10–21.
  1981: "The Second Parthian Ostracon from Qumis," *Iran* 19: 81–84.
  1982: "Seal Impressions of Parthian Qumis," *Iran* 20: 161–170.
Bivar, A.D.H. and G. Fehervari:
  1966: "The Walls of Tammisha," *Iran* 4: 35–50.
Blaikie, P. and H. Brookfield:
  1987: *Land Degradation and Society* (London).
Blair, S.S.:
  1986: "The Mongol Capital of Sultaniyya," *Iran* 24: 139–152.
Boak, A.E.R.:
  1955: *Manpower Shortage and the Fall of the Roman Empire in the West* (Ann Arbor).
Bobek, H.:
  1954: "Klima und Landschaft Irans in Vor- und Frühgeschichtlicher Zeit," *Geographischer Jahresbericht aus Österreich* 25: 1–42.
Bonine, M.E.:
  1979: "The Morphogenesis of Iranian Cities," *Annals of the Association of American Geographers* 69: 208–224.
  1980: *Yazd and its Hinterland* (Marburg/Lahn: Marburger Geographische Schriften 83).

1982: "From Qanat to Kort: Traditional Irrigation Terminology and Practices in Central Iran," *Iran* 20: 145–159.

Bosworth, A.B.:

1976: "Errors in Arrian," *Classical Quarterly* 26: 117–139.

Bosworth, C.E.:

1960: "The Rise of the Karamiyah in Khurasan," *The Muslim World* 50: 5–14.

1963: *The Ghaznavids* (Edinburgh). Ref. to 2nd ed. Beirut 1973.

1968a: *Sistan under the Arabs. From the Islamic Conquest to the Rise of the Saffarids* (Rom: Istituto Italiano per il Medio ed Estremo Oriente XI).

1968b: "The Armies of the Saffarids," *BSOAS* 31: 534–554.

1970: "Dailamis in Central Iran: the Kakuyids of Jibal and Yazd," *Iran* 7: 73–95.

1971: "The Banu Ilyas of Kirman," in *Iran and Islam*, ed. C.E. Bosworth, pp. 107–124 (Edinburgh).

1975: "Recruitment, Muster, and Review in Medieval Islamic Armies," in *War, Technology and Society in the Middle East*, ed. V.J. Parry and M.E. Yapp, pp. 59–77 (London).

1979: "The Heritage of Rulership in Early Islamic Iran and the Search for Dynastic Connections with the Past," *Iranian Studies* 11: 7–34.

Boucharlat, R.:

1985: "Suse, marché agricole ou relais du grand commerce. Suse et la Susiane à l'époque des grands empires," *Paléorient* 11/2: 71–81.

1987: "Suse à l'époque sasanide," *Mesopotamia* 22: 357–366.

Boucharlat, R. and J.-F. Salles:

1987: "L'Arabie Orientale: d'un bilan à un autre," *Mesopotamia* 22: 277–309.

Bowden, M.J. et al.:

1981: "The Effect of Climatic Fluctuations on Human Populations: Two Hypotheses," in *Climate and History*, ed. T.M.L. Wrigley et al., pp. 479–513 (Cambridge).

Boyd, R.:

1972: "Urbanization, Morbidity, and Mortality," in *Man, Settlement, and Urbanism*, ed. P.J. Ucko et al., pp. 345–352 (Cambridge, Mass.)

Boyle, J.A.:

1971: "The Capture of Isfahan by the Mongols," in *La Persia nel Medioevo*, pp. 331–336 (Rome: Accademia Nazionale dei Lincei).

Braudel, F.:

1967: *Capitalism and Material Life, 1400–1800* (London 1973).

Bray, F.:

1983: "Patterns of Evolution in Rice-Growing Societies," *Journal of Peasant Studies* 11: 3–33.

Briant, P.:

1975: "Villages et communautés villageoises d'Asie achéménide et hellénistique," *JESHO* 18: 165–188.

1978: "Colonisation hellénistique et populations indigénes," *Klio* 60: 57–92.

1979: "L'élevage ovin dans l'empire achéménide," *JESHO* 22: 136–161.

1980: "Communautés rurales, forces productives et mode de production tributaire en Asie achéménide," *Zaman* 2: 75–100.

1981: "Appareils d'état et développement des forces productives au Moyen-Orient ancien: le cas de l'empire achéménide," *La Pensée* 217/218: 9–23.

1982a: "Colonisation hellénistique et populations indigénes II," *Klio* 64: 83–98.

1982b: *État et pasteurs au Moyen-Orient ancien* (Cambridge).

1983: "Communautés de base et "économie royale" en Asie achéménide et hellénistique," in *RSJB* 41 (Communautés Rurales 2): 315–344.

1984: "La Perse avant l'empire," *Iranica Antiqua* 29: 71–118.

Brinkman, J.A.:

1968: "A Political History of Post-Kassite Babylonia, 1158722 B.C.," *Analecta Orientalia* 43.

1979: "Babylonia under the Assyrian Empire, 745–627 B.C.," *Mesopotamia* 7: 223–250.

Browne, E.G.:

1900: "Some Account of the Arabic Work Entitled Niháyatu'lIrab...," *JRAS*: 195–259.

1901: "Account of a Rare Manuscript History of Isfahan," *JRAS*: 411–446, 661–704.

1902: "Account of a Rare, if not Unique Manuscript History of the Seljuqs," *JRAS*: 567–610, 849–887.

Brunschvig, R.:

1957: "Probléme de la décadence," in *Classicisme et déclin culturel dans l'histoire de l'Islam*, ed. R. Brunschvig and G. von Grunebaum, pp. 29–46 (Paris).

Bulliet, R.W.:

1972: *The Patricians of Nishapur. A Study in Medieval Islamic Social History* (Cambridge, Mass.: Harvard Middle Eastern Studies 16).

1973: "The Political-Religious History of Nishapur in the Eleventh Century," in *Islamic Civilization, 950–1150*, ed. D.S. Richards, pp. 71–91 (Oxford).

1975: *The Camel and the Wheel* (Cambridge, Mass.).

1976: "Medieval Nishapur: a Topographic and Demographic Reconstruction," *Studia Iranica* 5: 67–89.

1978: "Local Politics in Eastern Iran under the Ghaznavids and the Seljuks," *Iranian Studies* 11: 35–56.

1979: *Conversion to Islam in the Medieval Period. An Essay in Quantitative History* (Cambridge, Mass.).

Buringh, P.:

1957: "Living Conditions in the Lower Mesopotamian Plain in Ancient Times," *Sumer* 15: 30–46.

Burnet, McF. and D.O. White:

1972: *Natural History of Infectious Disease*, 4th ed. (Cambridge).

Busse, H.:

1972: "Kerman im 19. Jahrhundert nach der Geographie des Waziri," *Der Islam* 49: 284–312.

Butz, K. and P. Schröder:

1985: "Zu Getreideerträgen in Mesopotamien und dem Mittelmeergebiet," *Baghdader Mitteilungen* 16: 165–209.

Butzer, K.W.:

1961: "Climatic Change in Arid Regions since the Pliocene," in *A History of Land Use in Arid Regions*, ed. L. Dudley Stamp, pp. 31–56 (Paris, UNESCO: Arid Zone Research 17).

1978: "The Late Prehistoric Environmental History of the Near East," in *The Environmental History of the Near and Middle East Since the Last Ice Age*, ed. W.C. Brice, pp. 5–12.

Cahen, C.:

1951: "Le service de l'irrigation en Iraq au début du XIe siècle," *Bulletin des études orientales* 13–14: 117–143.

1953: "L'Évolution de l'iqta du IXe au XIIIe siècle," *Annales* 8: 25–52.

1954: "Fiscalité, propriété, antagonismes sociaux en Haute Mésopotamie au temps des premiers 'Abbasides," *Arabica* 1: 136–152.

1955: "L'Histoire économique et sociale de l'Orient musulman médiéval," *Studia Islamica* 3: 93–115.

1957: "Les facteurs économiques et sociaux dans l'ancylose culturelle de l'Islam," in *Classicisme et déclin culturel dans l'histoire de l'Islam*, ed. R. Brunschvig and G. von Grunebaum, pp. 195–207 (Paris).

1958: "Mouvements populaires et autonomisme urbain dans l'Asie musulman au moyen age," *Arabica* 5–6: 225–250, 25–56, 233–265.

1960: "Réflexions sur l'usage du mot "féodalité," *JESHO* 3: 2–20.

1968: *Der Islam* I (Frankfurt a.M.: Fischer Weltgeschichte 14).

1973: "Nomades et sédentaires dans le monde musulman au milieu du moyen age," in *Islamic

Civilization, 950–1150, ed. D.S. Richards, pp. 93–104.

1975: "Les changements techniques militaires dans le Proche Orient et leur importance historique," in *War, Technology, and Society in the Middle East*, ed. V.J. Parry and M.E. Yapp, pp. 113–124 (London).

1982: "La Communauté rurale dans le monde musulman médiéval," *RSJB* 42 (Les Communautés Rurales 3): 9–27.

Calmeyer, P.:

1983: "Die Yauna," *AMI* Ergänzungsband 10: 153–167.

Cameron, A.:

1969: "Agathias on the Sassanians," *Dumbarton Oaks Papers* 23–24: 67–183.

Cameron, G.G.:

1973: "The Persian Satrapies and related Matters," *JNES* 32: 47–56.

Canard, M.:

1959: "Le riz dans le Proche Orient aux premiers siècles de l'Islam," *Arabica* 6: 113–131.

Carmichael, A.G.:

1983: "Infection, Hidden Hunger, and History," *Journal of Interdisciplinary History* 14: 249–264.

Carter, E. and M.W. Stolper:

1984: *Elam. Surveys of Political History and Archaeology* (Berkeley/Los Angeles).

Cavallero, M. Carnevale:

1967: "The Excavations at Choche, Area 2," *Mesopotamia* 2: 48–56.

Charles, M.P.:

1988: "Irrigation in Lowland Mesopotamia," *Bulletin on Sumerian Agriculture* IV: 1–39 (Cambridge).

Chaumont, M.-L.:

1958: "Le culte d'Anahita à Staxr et les premiers Sassanides," *Revue de l'Histoire des Religions* 154: 154–175.

1968: "Les ostraca de Nisa," *Journal Asiatique* 256: 11–35.

1971: "Documents royaux à Nisa," *Syria* 48: 143–164.

1975: "États vassaux dans l'empire des premiers Sassanides," *Acta Iranica* 4: 89–156.

Christensen, A.:

1925: "Le règne du roi Kawadh 1. et le communisme mazdakite," *Det Kongelige Danske Videnskabernes Selskab, Historisk-Filologiske Meddelelser* IX.6 (Copenhagen).

1936: *L'Iran sous les Sassanides* (Copenhagen). Ref. to 2nd ed. 1944.

Christensen, P.:

1987: "The Qajar State," in *Contributions to Islamic Studies: Iran, Afghanistan and Pakistan*, ed. C. Braae and K. Ferdinand, pp. 4–58 (Aarhus).

Christiansen-Weninger, F.:

1961: "Alte Methoden der Wassergewinnung für Bewässerungszwecke im Nahen und Mittleren Osten unter besonderer Berücksichtigung der Kanate," *Wasser und Nahrung* 1: 28–31, 73–84.

Claxton, R.H.:

1985: "Climate and History: the State of the Field," in *Environmental History: Critical Issues in Comparative Perspective*, ed. K.E. Bailes, pp.104–134 (Lanham).

Clevenger, W.M.:

1969: "Dams in Horasan. Some Preliminary Observations," *East and West* 19: 387–394.

Cockburn, A.:

1963: *The Evolution and Eradication of Infectious Diseases* (Baltimore).

1971: "Infectious Diseases in Ancient Populations," *Current Anthropology* 12: 45–62.

Cockburn, A. and E. Cockburn eds.:

1980: *Mummies, Disease, and Ancient Cultures* (Cambridge).

Cohen, G.M.:

1978: "The Seleucid Colonies," *Historia*, Einzelschriften 30 (Wiesbaden).

Conrad, L.I.:

1981: "Arabic Plague Chronologies and Treatises," *Studia Islamica* 54: 51–93.

1982: "Tā'ūn and Wabā', Conceptions of Plague and Pestilence in Early Islam," *JESHO* 25: 268–307.

Cook, J.M.:

1983: *The Persian Empire* (London).

Cook, M.A.:

1974: "Economic Developments," in *The Legacy of Islam*, ed. J. Schacht and C.E. Bosworth, pp. 210–243 (2nd ed. Oxford).

Crosby, A.W.:

1972: *The Columbian Exchange: Biological and Cultural Consequences of 1492* (Westport).

1976: "Virgin Soil Epidemics as a Factor in the Aboriginal Depopulation in America," *William and Mary Quarterly* 33: 289–299.

Daniel, N.:

1960: *Islam and the West: the Making of an Image* (Edinburgh).

1966: *Islam, Europe, and Empire* (Edinburgh).

Davary, D.:

1975: "Die Ruinenstadt Bost am Helmand," *Acta Iranica*, 2nd ser., 1: 201–208.

Debevoise, N.C.:

1938: *A Political History of Parthia* (Chicago).

Defrémery, M.:

1846: "Recherches sur trois princes de Nichabour, 548–595 de l'hégire," *Journal Asiatique*, 4th ser. vol. 8: 446–482.

Dijk, J. van:

1965: "Une insurrection générale au pays de Larsa avant l'avènement de Nuradad," *Journal of Cuneiform Studies* 19: 1–25.

Dilleman, L.:

1962: *Haute Mesopotamie et pays adjacents*, Institut Francais d'Archéologie de Beyrouth: Bibliothèque Archéologique et Historique 72 (Paris).

Dollfus, G.:

1985: "Le peuplement de la Susiane au cours du Ve millénaire," *Paléorient* 11/2: 7–20.

Dols, M.W.:

1974: "Plague in Early Islamic History," *JAOS* 94: 371–383.

1977: *The Black Death in the Middle East* (Princeton).

1979: "The Second Plague Pandemic and its Recurrences in the Middle East, 1347–1894," *JESHO* 22: 162–189.

1981: "The General Mortality of the Black Death in the Mamluk Empire," in *The Middle East, 700–1900*, ed. A.L. Udovitch, pp. 397–428 (Princeton).

1983: "The Leper in Medieval Islamic Society," *Speculum* 58: 891–916.

1984: *Medieval Islamic Medicine: Ibn Ridwan's Treatise "On the Prevention of Bodily Ills in Egypt."* (Berkeley/Los Angeles).

Driel, G. van:

1987: "Continuity or Decay in the Late Achaemenid Period: Evidence from Southern Mesopotamia," in *Achaemenid History I: Sources, Structures, and Synthesis*, ed. H. Sancisi-Weerdenburg, pp. 159–182 (Leyden).

1988: "Neo-Babylonian Agriculture," *Bulletin on Sumerian Agriculture* IV: 121–159 (Cambridge).

Ebeling, E.:

1955: "Ein Neuassyrisches Beschwörungsritual gegen Bann und Tod," *ZA* 17: 167–179.

Eckholm, E.:

1976: *Losing Ground: Environmental Stress and World Food Prospects* (New York).

Eddy, S.K.:

1961: *The King is Dead. Studies in the Near Eastern Resistance to Hellenism, 334–31 B.C.* (Lincoln).

Ehlers, E.:

1975: *Traditionelle und Moderne Formen der Landwirtschaft in Iran. Siedlung, Landwirtschaft und Agrarso-zialstruktur im nördlichen Khuzistan seit dem Ende des 19. Jhr.s.* (Marburg/Lahn: Marburger Geographische Schriften 64).

Ehrenkreutz, A.S.:

1964: "The Tasrif and Tas'ir Calculations in Medieval Mesopotamian Fiscal Operations," *JESHO* 7: 46–56.

Ehrlich, P.R. and J. Roughgarden:

1987: *The Science of Ecology* (New York).

Ellis, M.:

1976: *Agriculture and the State in Ancient Mesopotamia* (Philadelphia).

Ellison, R.:

1981: "Diet in Mesopotamia: the Evidence of the Barley Ration Texts," *Iraq* 43: 35–45.

English, P.W.:

1966: *City and Village in Iran. Settlement and Economy in the Kirman Basin* (Madison).

1968: "The Origin and Spread of Qanats in the Old World," *Proceedings of the American Philosophical Society* 112: 170–181.

Fahd, T.:

1970: "Conduite d'une exploitation agricole d'après "l'agriculture nabatéenne," *Studia Islamica* 23: 109–128.

1971: "Un traité des eaux dans al-filaha an-nabatiyya," in *La Persia nel Medioevo*, pp. 277–325 (Rome: Accademia Nazionale dei Lincei).

1977: "Materiaux pour l'histoire de l'agriculture en Irak: al-filaha an-nabatiyya," in *Handbuch der Orientalistik, Abt, 1, vol. 6/6: Wirtschaftsgeschichte des Vorderen Orients in Islamischer Zeit 1*, ed. B. Spuler, pp. 276–377 (Leyden).

1983: "La communauté rurale selon l'agriculture nabatéenne," *RSJB* 41 (communautés rurales 2), pp. 475–504.

Fairservis, W.A.:

1961: "Archeological Studies in the Seistan Basin," *Anthropological Papers of the American Museum of Natural History* 48: 1–128.

Fiey, J.M.:

1964: "Vers la réhabilitation de l'histoire de Karka d'Bét Sloh," *Annalecta Bollandiana* 82: 189–222.

1967a: "The Topography of al-Mada'in," *Sumer* 23: 3–28.

1967b: "Auteur et date de la chronique d'Arbeles," *L'Orient Syrien* 12: 265–302.

Finster, B.:

1976: "Sistan zur Zeit Timuridischer Herrschaft," *AMI* 9: 207–215.

Finster, B. and J. Schmidt:

1976: "Sassanidische und Frühislamische Ruinen im Iraq," *Baghdader Mitteilungen* 8.

Fischer, K.:

1967: "Zur Lage von Kandahar an Landverbindungen zwischen Iran und Indien," *Bonner Jahrbücher* 167: 129–232.

1973: "Archaeological Field Surveys in Afghan Sistan," in *South Asian Archaeology*, ed. N. Hammond, pp. 132–155 (London).

1976: "Geländebegehungen in Sistan 1955–1973 und die Aufnahme von Dewal-i Khodaydad 1970," *Veröff. d.Forschungsstelle f. Orient. Kunstgeschichte an der Univ. Bonn, Reihe A. Bd. 1.* (Bonn).

Flannery, K.V.:

1965: "The Ecology of Early Food Production in Mesopotamia," *Science* 147: 1247–1256.

1969: "Origins and Ecological Effects of Early Domistication in Iran and the Near East," in *The Domistication and Exploitation of Plants and Animals*, ed. P.J. Ucko et. al., pp. 73–100 (Chicago).

Flohn, H.:

1973: "Klimaschwankungen und Klimamodifikation," *Universitas* 28: 1293–1300.

Forand, P.G.:
   1971: "The Status of the Land and Inhabitants of the Sawad during the Two First Centuries of Islam," *JESHO* 14: 25–37.
Fraser, P.M.:
   1979: "The Son of Aristonax at Kandahar," *Afghan Studies* 2: 9–19.
Frier, B.:
   1982: "Roman Life Expectancy: Ulpian's Evidence," *Harvard Studies in Classical Philology* 86: 213–251.
Frumkin, G.:
   1970: "Archaeology in Soviet Central Asia," *Handbuch der Orientalistik*, Abt. 7, Bd. 3/1 (leyden).
Frye, R.N.:
   1959: "Biyabanak: the Oases of Central Iran," *Central Asiatic Journal* 5: 182–197.
   1962: *The Heritage of Persia* (London).
   1971: "History and Sassanian Inscriptions," in *La Persia nel Medioevo*, pp. 215–223 (Rome: Accademia Nazionale dei Lincei).
   1975: *The Golden Age of Persia* (London).
Frye, R.N. ed.:
   1973: *Sassanian Remains from Qasr-é Abu Nasr* (Cambridge, Mass.).
Funck, B.:
   1976: "Zur Innenpolitik des Seleukos Nikator," in *Wirtschaft und Gesellschaft im Alten Vorderasien*, ed. J. Harmatta and G. Komoróczy, pp. 505–520 (Budapest).
Fussman, G.:
   1966: "Notes sur la topographie de l'ancienne Kandahar," *Ars Asiatiques* 13: 33–45.
Gagé, J.:
   1964: *La Montée des Sassanides* (Paris).
Ganssen, R.:
   1968: *Trockengebiete: Böden, Bodennutzung, Bodenkultivierung, Bodengefährdung* (Mannheim).
Gardin, J.C.:
   1963: *Lashkari Bazar*. Mémoires de la délégation archéologique francaise en Afghanistan 18 (Paris).
Gaube, H.:
   1973: *Die Südpersische Provinz Arragan/Kuh-Giluyeh von der Arabischen Eroberung bis zur Safawidenzeit*. Österreichische Akademie der Wissenschaften, Phil.Hist. Klasse 107 (Wien).
   1977: "Innenstadt – Aussenstadt. Kontinuität und Wandel im Grundriss von Herat," in *Beiträge zur Geographie Orientalischer Städte und Märkte*, ed. G. Schweizer, pp. 213–240 (Wiesbaden: TAVO B24).
   1978: *Iranian Cities* (New York).
Gelb, I.J.:
   1973: "Prisoners of War in Early Mesopotamia," *JNES* 22: 70–98.
Gentelle, P.:
   1977: "Quelques observations sur l'extension de deux techniques d'irrigation sur le plateau iranien et en Asie centrale," in *Le plateau iranien et l'Asie centrale des origines à la conquête islamique*, pp. 249–269. Colloques internationaux du C.N.R.S. 567 (Paris).
   1978: *Étude géographique d'Aï Khanum et de son irrigation depuis les temps antiques* (Paris: C.N.R.S. Centre des recherches archéologiques).
Gerasimov, I.P.:
   1978: "Ancient Rivers in the Deserts of Soviet Central Asia," in *The Environmental History of the Near and Middle East Since the Last Ice Age*, ed. W.C. Brice, pp. 319–334 (London).
Gibson, McGuire:
   1972: *The City and Area of Kish* (Miami).
   1973: "Population Shift and the Rise of Mesopotamian Civilization," in *The Explanation of Cultural Change*, ed. C. Renfrew, pp. 447–463 (London).

1974: "Violation of Fallow and Engineered Disasters in Mesopotamian Civilization," in *Irrigation's Impact on Society*, ed. T. Downing and McGuire Gibson, pp. 7–19. Anthropological Papers of the University of Arizona 28 (Tucson).

Gilliam, J.F.:

1961: "The Plague under Marcus Aurelius," *American Journal of Philology* 82: 225–251.

Goblot, H.:

1979: *Les Qanats. Une technique d'acquisition de l'eau*. Industrie et artisanat 9 (Paris).

Göbl, R.:

1971: *Sassanian Numismatics*. Manual of Middle Asian Numismatics 1 (Braunschweig).

Goetze, A.:

1955: "An Incantation Against Disease," *Journal of Cuneiform Studies* 9: 8–18.

Goldsmid, F.J.:

1876: *Eastern Persia. An Account of the Journeys of the Persian Boundary Commission, 1870–1872*, I (London).

Golombek, L.:

1974: "Urban Patterns in Pre-Safavid Isfahan," *Iranian Studies* 7: 18–44.

Goodblatt, D.M.:

1979: "The Poll Tax in Sasanian Babylonia: the Talmudic Evidence," *JESHO* 22: 233–295.

Grayson, A.K.:

1964: "Akkadian Prophecies," *Journal of Cuneiform Studies* 18.

Grigg, D.:

1974: *The Agricultural Systems of the World. An Evolutionary Approach* (Cambridge).

1980: *Population Growth and Agrarian Change. A Historical Perspective* (Cambridge).

Grignaschi, M.:

1971: "La riforma tributaria di Hosro I e il feudalesimo Sassanide," in *La Persia nel Medioevo*, pp. 87–147 (Rome: Accademia Nazionale dei Lincei),

Grmek, M.D.:

1983: *Les maladies à l'aube de la civilisation occidentale* (Paris).

Gropp, G.:

1970: "Bericht über eine Reise in West- und Südiran," *AMI* 3: 149–160.

Gullini, G.:

1964: "First Report of the Results of the First Excavation Campaign at Seleucia and Ctesiphon," *Sumer* 20: 63ff.

Haas, J.D. and G.G. Harrison:

1977: "Nutritional Anthropology and Biological Adaption," *Annual Review of Anthropology* 6: 69–101.

Haerinck, E.:

1987: "La neuviéme satrapie: archéologie confronte histoire?" in *Achaemenid History I: Sources, Structures and Synthesis*, ed. H. Sancisi-Weerdenburg, pp. 139–146 (Leyden).

Haeser, H.:

1882: *Lehrbuch der Geschichte der Medicin und der Epidemischen Krankheiten* I-III (Jena 1875–1882).

Hahn, I.:

1959: "Sassanidische und Spätrömische Besteuerung," *Acta Antiqua* 7: 149–160.

Hallier, U.W.:

1974: "Neh – eine Partische Stadt in Ostpersien," *AMI* 7: 173–190.

Halm, H.:

1967: *Die Traditionen über den Aufstand Ali ibn Muhammads, des "Herrn der Zang"* (Bonn).

1971: "Der Wesir al-Kunduri und die Fitna von Nisapur," *Die Welt des Orients* 6: 205–233.

Hamilton, J.R.:

1973: *Alexander the Great* (London).

Hammond, N.G.L.:

1981: *Alexander the Great. King, Commander, and Statesman* (London).

1983: *Three Historians of Alexander the Great* (Cambridge).

Hansman, J.:

1967: "Charax and the Karkheh," *Iranica Antiqua* 7: 21–58.

1968: "The Problem of Qumis," *JRAS*: 111–139.

1972: "Elamites, Achaemenians, and Anshan," *Iran* 10: 101125.

1975: "An Achaemenian Stronghold," *Acta Iranica* 2nd ser. III, pp. 289–312.

1978: "Seleucia and the Three Dauraks," *Iran* 16: 154–161.

1984: "The Land of Meshan," *Iran* 22: 161–166.

Hansman, J. and D. Stronach:

1970: "Excavations at Shahr-i Qumis, 1967," *JRAS*: 29–62.

Helbaek, H.:

1960: "Ecological Effects of Irrigation in Ancient Mesopotamia," *Iraq* 22: 186–196.

Helms, S.W.:

1979: "Old Kandahar Excavations 1976: a Preliminary Report," *Afghan Studies* 2: 1–8.

Henning, W.B.:

1939: "The Great Inscription of Sápúr I," *BSOS* 9: 823–849.

Henrickson, E.F.:

1985: "The Early Development of Pastoralism in the Central Zagros Highlands (Luristan)," *Iranica Antiqua* 20: 142.

Herrenschmidt, C.:

1976: "Désignation de l'empire et concepts politiques de Darius Ier d'après ses inscriptions en vieux-perse," *Studia Iranica* 5: 33–65.

Herzfeld, E.:

1932: "Sakastan," *AMI* 4: 1–116.

Hinz, W.:

1949a: "Das Rechnungswesen Orientalischer Reichsfinanzämter im Mittelalter," *Der Islam* 29: 1–29, 113–141.

1949b: "Ein Orientalisches Handelsunternehmen im 15. Jahrhundert," *Die Welt des Orients*: 313–340.

1950: "Das Steuerwesen Ostanatoliens im 15. und 16. Jahrhundert," *ZDMG* 100: 177–201.

1955: Islamische Masse und Gewichte, *Handbuch der Orientalistik*, Ergänzungsband 1, Heft 1 (Leyden).

Hirsch, A.:

1881: *Handbuch der Historisch-Geographischen Pathologie* (Stuttgart: 2nd ed.).

Hole, F.:

1966: "Investigating the Origins of Mesopotamian Civilization," *Science* 153: 605–611.

Hopkins, K.:

1978: "Economic Growth and Towns in Classical Antiquity," in *Towns in Society*, ed. Ph. Abrams and E.A. Wrigley, pp. 35–77 (Cambridge).

Houtsma, M.T.:

1885: "Zur Geschichte der Selgugen von Kerman," *ZDMG* 39: 362–402.

Hunt, R.C.:

1988: "Hydraulic Management in Southern Mesopotamia in Sumerian Times," *Bulletin On Sumerian Agriculture* 4: 189–206 (Cambridge).

Ingram, M.J. et al.:

1981: "Past Climates and their Impact on Man: a Review," in *Climate and History*, ed. T.M.L. Wigley et al., pp. 3–50 (Cambridge).

Invernizzi, A.:

1976: "Ten Years' Research in the al-Mada'in Area," *Sumer* 32: 167–175.

Issawi, C.:

1966: *The Economic History of the Middle East 1800–1914. A Book of Readings* (Chicago).

1970: "The Decline of Middle Eastern Trade, 1100–1850," in *Islam and the Trade of Asia*, ed. D.S. Richards, pp. 245–266 (Oxford).

1971: *The Economic History of Iran 1800–1914* (Chicago).

1977: "Population and Resources in the Ottoman Empire and Iran," in *Studies in Eighteenth Century Islamic History*, ed. T. Naff and R. Owen, pp. 152–164 (Carbondale).

1980: "Europe, the Middle East, and the Shift in Power: Reflections on a Theme by Marshall Hodgson," *CSSH* 22: 487–504.

Jacobsen, T.:

1958: "Summary of a Report by the Diyala Basin Archaeological Project," *Sumer* 14: 79–89.

1960: "The Waters of Ur," *Iraq* 22: 174–185.

1969: "A Survey of the Girsu (Telloh) Region," *Sumer* 25: 103–109.

1982: "Salinity and Irrigation Agriculture in Antiquity. Diyala Basin Archaeological Projects: Reports on Essential Results, 1957–1958," *Bibliotheca Mesopotamica* 14 (Malibu).

Jacobsen, T. and R. McC. Adams:

1958: "Salt and Silt in Ancient Mesopotamian Agriculture," *Science* 128: 1251–1258.

Jones, E.L.:

1981: *The European Miracle. Environments, Economies, and Geopolitics in the History of Europe and Asia* (Cambridge).

Jutikkala, E. and M. Kauppinen:

1971: "The Structure of Mortality during Catastrophic Years in a Pre-Industrial Society," *Population Studies* 25: 283–285.

Kass, E.H.:

1971: "Infectious Diseases and Social Change," *Journal of Infectious Diseases* 123: 110–114.

Keal, E.J.:

1975: "Parthian Nippur and Vologases' Southern Strategy," *JAOS* 95: 620–632.

1977: "Political, Economic, and Social Factors on the Parthian Landscape of Mesopotamia and Western Iran," *Bibliotheca Mesopotamica* 7: 81–89.

1981: "The Qal'eh-i Yazdigird Pottery; a Statistical Approach," *Iran* 19: 33–80.

1982: "Qal'eh-i Yazdigird: an Overview of the Monumental Architecture," *Iran* 20: 51–72.

Kimball Armager, O.:

1978: "Herodotus' Catalogues of the Persian Empire," *Transactions of the American Philological Association* 108: 1–11.

Kinneir Wilson, J.V.:

1967: "Organic Diseases of Ancient Mesopotamia," in *Diseases in Antiquity*, ed. D. Brothwell and A.T. Sandison, pp. 191–208 (Springfield, Ill.)

Kippenberg, H.G.:

1984: "Mahdist Movements in Abbasid Iran," in *Religion and Rural Revolt*, ed. J.M. Bak and G. Benecke, pp. 243–255 (Manchester).

Kirkby, M.J.:

1976: "Land and Water Resources of the Deh Luran and Khuzistan Plains," in *Studies in the Archaeological History of the Deh Luran Plain*, ed. F. Hole, pp. 251–288 (Ann Arbor: Memoir of the Museum of Anthropology, University of Michigan 9).

Kister, M.J.:

—1968: "Al-Hira: Some Notes on its Relations with Arabia," *Arabica* 15: 143–169.

Kiyani, Y.:

1982a: "Excavations on the Defensive Wall of the Gurgan Plain," *Iran* 20: 73–79.

1982b: "Parthian Sites in Hyrcania," *AMI* Ergänzungsband 9.

Kleiss, W.:

1972: "Bericht über Erkundungsfahrten in Iran im Jahre 1971," *AMI* 5: 135–242.

Klima, J.:

1983: "La communauté rurale dans la Babylonie ancienne," *RSJB* 41 (Les Communautés Rurales 2): 107–132.

Kohl, Ph. L.:

1984: *Central Asia: Paleolithic Beginnings to the Iron Age* (Paris).

Korbel, G.:

1983: "Archäologische Ergebnisse einer Geländebegehung im Gebiet von Torbat-é Djam," *AMI* 16: 18–55.

Kortum, G.:

1973: "Ländliche Siedlungen im Umland von Shiraz," in *Kulturgeographische Untersuchungen im Islamischen Orient*, ed. R. Stewig and H.G. Wagner, pp. 177–212 (Kiel: Schriften des Geographischen Instituts d. Universität Kiel 38).

1975: "Siedlungsgenetische Untersuchungen in Fars," *Erdkunde* 29: 10–20.

1976: *Die Marvdasht-Ebene in Fars* (Kiel: Kieler Geographische Schriften 44).

Kramer, S.N.:

1963: *The Sumerians* (Chicago).

Krawulsky, D.:

1978: *Das Reich der Ilhane* (Wiesbaden: TAVO B 17).

Kreeb, K.:

1964: *Ökologische Grundlagen der Bewässerungskulturen in den Subtropen* (Stuttgart).

Kreissig, H.:

1973: "Die Polis in Griechenland und im Orient in der Hellenistischen Epoche," in *Hellenistische Poleis* III, ed. E. Welskopf, pp. 1074–1084 (Berlin).

1977: "Landed Property in the "Hellenistic" Orient," *Eirene* 15: 5–26.

1983: "Die Dorfgemeinde im Orient in der Hellenistischen Epoche," *RSJB* 41 (Les Communautés Rurales 2): 301–314.

Kremer, A. von:

1875: *Kulturgeschichte des Orients unter den Chalifen*, I-II (Wien).

1880: "Ueber die Grossen Seuchen des Orients nach Arabischen Quellen," *Sitzungsberichte der Kaiserlichen Akademie der Wissenschaften*, Philologisch-Historische Klasse 96/1, pp. 69–156 (Wien).

1888: "Ueber das Einnahmebudget des Abbasidenreiches vom Jahre 306 H. (918–919)," *Denkschriften der Kaiserlichen Akademie d. Wissenschaften*, Philologisch-Historische Klasse 36, pp. 283–362.

1889: "Ueber das Budget der Einnahmen unter der Regierung des Harun al-Rashid," *Berichte des VI. Internationalen Orientalistencongresses (1886)*, 1–19.

Krenkow, F.:

1951: "The Construction of Subterranean Water Supplies during the Abbaside Caliphate," *Transactions of the Glasgow University's Oriental Society* 13: 23–32.

Kroll, S.:

1984: "Archäologische Fundplätze in Iranisch OstAzarbaidjan," *AMI* 17: 13–134.

Kuhrt, A.:

1987: "Survey of Written Sources Available for the History of Babylonia under the Later Achaemenids," in *Achaemenid History I: Sources, Structures and Synthesis*, ed. H. Sancisi-Weerdenburg, pp. 147–158 (Leyden).

Laere, R. van:

1980: "Techniques hydrauliques en Mésopotamie ancienne," *Orientalia Lovaniensia Periodica* 11: 11–53.

Lamberg-Karlovsky, C.C.:

1971: "An Early City in Iran," *Scientific American* 224: 208–217.

1972: "Tepe Yahya 1971: Mesopotamia and the Indo-Iranian Borderlands," *Iran* 10: 89–101.

1975: "Third Millennium Modes of Exchange and Modes of Production," in *Ancient Civilization and Trade*, ed. J.A. Sabloff and C.C. Lamberg-Karlovsky, pp. 341–368 (Albuquerque).

Lamberg-Karlovsky, C.C. and M. Tosi:

1973: "Shahr-i Sokhta and Tepe Yahya: Tracks of the Earliest History of the Iranian Plateau," *East and West* 23: 21–58.

Lambton, A.K.S.:

1937: "The Regulation of the Waters of the Zayande Rud," *BSOS* 9: 663–673.

1947: "An Account of the Tarikhi Qumm," *BSOAS* 12: 586–596.

1953: *Landlord and Peasant in Persia* (London). Ref. to 2nd ed. 1969.

1957: "The Administration of Sanjar's Empire as Illustrated in the "Atabat al-Kataba," *BSOAS* 20: 367-388.

1965: "Reflections on the Iqta"," in *Arabic and Islamic Studies in Honor of H.A.R. Gibb*, ed. G. Makdisi, pp. 358–376 (Leyden).

1966: "Justice in the Medieval Persian Theory of Kingship," *Studia Islamica* 16: 91–119.

1973: "Aspects of Saljuq-Ghuzz Settlement in Persia," in *Islamic Civilization, 950–1150*, ed. D.S. Richards, pp. 105–125 (Oxford).

1977: "Aspects of Agricultural Organisation and Agrarian History in Persia," in *Handbuch der Orientalistik, 1. Abteilung, Band 6/6 (Wirtschaftsgeschichte des Vorderen Orients in Islamischer Zeit 1)*, ed. B. Spuler, pp. 160–187 (Leyden).

1981: "Reflections on the Role of Agriculture in Medieval Persia," in *The Islamic Middle East, 700–1900*, ed. A.L. Udovitch, pp. 283–312 (Princeton).

1984: "The Dilemma of Government in Islamic Persia: the Siyasat-nama of Nizam al-Mulk," *Iran* 22: 55–66.

Lapidus, I.M.:

1969: "Muslim Cities and Islamic Socities," in *Middle Eastern Cities*, ed. I.M. Lapidus, pp. 47–79 (Berkeley/Los Angeles).

1973: "The Evolution of Muslim Urban Society," *CSSH* 15: 21–50.

1981: "Arab Settlement and Economic Development of Iraq and Iran in the Age of the Umayyad and Early Abbasid Caliphs," in *The Islamic Middle East, 700–1900*, ed. A.L. Udovitch, pp. 177–208 (Princeton).

Lassner, J.:

1970: *The Topography of Baghdad in the Early Middle Ages* (Detroit).

1980: *The Shaping of Abbasid Rule* (Princeton).

Lattimore, O.:

1951: *Inner Asian Frontiers of China* (New York).

Layard, A.H.:

1856: "A Description of the Province of Khuzistan," *JRGS* 16: 1–105.

Leemans, W.F.:

1983: "Trouve-t-on des "communautés rurales" dans l'ancienne Mésopotamie?" *RSJB* 41 (Communautés Rurales): 43–106.

Leriche, R.:

1974: "Aï Khanum, un rempart hellénistique en Asie Centrale," *Revue Archéologique*: 231–270.

1977: "Problèmes de la guerre en Iran et en Asie Centrale dans l'empire perse et à l'époque hellénistique," *Le Plateau Iranien et l'Asie Centrale des Origines à la Conquête Islamique*, pp. 297–312. Colloques Internationaux du C.N.R.S. (Paris).

Le Rider, G.:

1965: *Suse sous les Séleucides et les Parthes*. Mémoires de la mission archéologique en Iran 38 (Paris).

Le Strange, G.:

1905: *The Lands of the Eastern Caliphate* (Cambridge).

Levine, L.D.:

1973: "Geographical Studies in the Neo-Assyrian Zagros," *Iran* 11: 1–12 and *Iran* 12 (1974): 99–124.

Lisitsina, G.N.:

1969: "The Earliest Irrigation in Turkmenia," *Antiquity* 43: 279–288.

Lombard, M.:
  1980: *L'Islam dans sa premiére grandeur* (Paris).
Lozinski, B.Ph.:
  1984: "The Parthian Dynasty," *Iranica Antiqua* 19: 119–139.
Læssøe, J.:
  1951: "The Irrigation System at Ulhu, 8th Century B.C.," *Journal of Cuneiform Studies* 5: 21–32.
  1953: "Reflections on Modern and Ancient Oriental Water Works," *Journal of Cuneiform Studies* 7: 5–26.
McDowell, R.G.:
  1972: "The History of Seleucia from Classical Sources," in *Topography and Architecture of Seleucia on the Tigris*, ed. C. Hopkins, pp. 149–163 (Ann Arbor).
MacGregor, C.M.:
  1879: *Narrative of a Journey through the Province of Khurasan*, I-II (London).
McKeown, T.:
  1977: *The Modern Rise of Population* (London).
  1988: *The Origins of Human Disease* (Oxford).
McNeill, W.H.:
  1976: *Plagues and Peoples* (London). Ref. to Penguin ed. 1979.
  1979: *The Human Condition. An Ecological and Historical View* (Princeton).
  1982a: "A Defence of World History," *Transactions of the Royal Historical Society*, 5th ser., 32: 75–89.
  1982b: *The Pursuit of Power. Technology, Armed Force, and Society since A.D. 1000* (Chicago).
McNicoll, A.:
  1976: "Excavations at Kandahar, 1975," *Afghan Studies* 1: 41–53.
Maekawa, K.:
  1984: "Cereal Cultivation in the Ur III Period," *Bulletin on Sumerian Agriculture* 1: 73–96 (Cambridge).
Makdisi, G.:
  1959: "The Topography of Eleventh Century Baghdad," *Arabica* 6: 281–309.
Malek, E.A.:
  1961: "The Ecology of Schistosomiasis," in *Studies in Disease Ecology*, ed. J.M. May, pp. 261–327 (New York).
Malcolm, J.:
  1829: *A History of Persia*, I-II (London).
Maricq, A.:
  1959: "Vologésias, l'emporium de Ctésiphon," *Syria* 36: 264276.
Markwart (also Marquart), J.:
  1885: "Beiträge zur Geschichte und Sage von Eran," *ZDMG* 49: 628–672.
  1896: *Untersuchungen zur Geschichte von Eran* (Göttingen 1896–1905).
  1901: *Eranshahr nach der Geographie des Ps.Moses Xorenac'i*. Abhandlungen der Königlichen Gesellschaft der Wissenschaften zu Göttingen. Philologisch-Historische Klasse, N.F., Band III/2.
Mason, H.:
  1967: "The Role of the Azdite Muhallabid Family in Marw's Anti-Umayyad Power Struggle," *Arabica* 14: 191–207.
Masson, V.M.:
  1966: "I Monumenti Archeologici dell'Asia Centrale," in *La Persia e il Mondo Greco-Romano*, pp. 357–381 (Rome: Accademia Nazionale dei Lincei).
  1967: "Two Palmyrene Stelae from the Merv Oasis," *East and West* 17: 239–247.
May, J.M.:
  1961: "The Ecology of Malaria," in *Studies in Disease Ecology*, ed. J.M. May, pp. 161–229 (New York).
Meder, O.G.:

1979: *Klimaökologie und Siedlungsgang auf dem Hochland von Iran in Vor- und Frühgeschichtlicher Zeit* (Marburg/Lahn: Marburger Geographische Schriften 80).

Meissner, B.:

1925: *Babylonien und Assyrien*, I-II (Heidelberg).

Melville, C.:

1980: "Earthquakes in the History of Nishapur," *Iran* 18: 103–120.

1981: "Historical Monuments and Earthquakes in Tabriz," *Iran* 19: 159–177.

1984: "Meteorological Hazards and Disasters in Iran: a Preliminary Survey to 1950," *Iran* 22: 113–150.

Menasce, J.P.:

1966: "Textes pehlevi sur les qanats," in *Iranian Studies Presented to Kaj Barr*, ed. J.P. Asmussen and J. Læssøe, pp. 167–175 (Copenhagen).

Meyerhoff, M.:

1930: "The Book of Treasure: an Early Arabic Treatise on Medicine," *Isis* 14: 55–70.

1935: "Thirty-three Clinical Observations by Rhazes," *Isis* 23: 321–356.

1936: "The History of Trachoma Treatment in Antiquity and during the Arabic Middle Ages," *Bulletin of the Ophthalmological Society of Egypt* 29: 26–87.

Michel, A.A.:

1967: *The Indus River* (New Haven/London).

1972: "The Impact of Modern Irrigation in the Indus and Helmand Basins of Southwest Asia," in *The Careless Technology. Ecology and International Development*, ed. M. Taghi Farvar and J.P. Milton, pp. 257–275 (Garden City).

Miller, K.:

1916: *Itineraria Romana. Römische Reisewege an Hand der Tabula Peutingeriana dargestellt* (Stuttgart).

Minns, E.H.:

1915: "Parchments of the Parthian Period from Avroman," *Journal of Hellenic Studies* 35: 22–65.

Minorsky, V.:

1941: "A Civil and Military Review in Fars in 881/1476," *BSOS* 1: 141–178.

1955: "The Aq-qoyunlu and Land Reforms," *BSOAS* 27: 449–462.

Miquel, A.:

1975: *La géographie humaine du monde musulman jusqu'au milieu du 11e siècle*, I-II (Paris/Haag).

Morgan, D.:

1986: *The Mongols* (Oxford).

Moorey, P.R.S.:

1982: "Archaeology and Pre-Achaemenid Metalworking in Iran," *Iran* 20: 81–101.

Morony, M.G.:

1981: "Landholding in Seventh-Century Iraq," in *The Islamic Middle East, 700–1900*, ed. A.L. Udovitch, pp. 135–175 (Princeton).

1982: "Continuity and Change in the Administrative Geography of Late Sassanian and Early Islamic al-Iraq," *Iran* 20: 1–49.

1984a: "Landholding and Social Change: Lower al-Iraq in the Early Islamic Period," in *Land Tenure and Social Transformation in the Middle East*, ed. T. Khalidi, pp. 209–222 (Beirut).

1984b: *Iraq after the Muslim Conquest* (Princeton).

Morse, D.:

1967: "Tuberculosis," in *Diseases in Antiquity*, ed. D. Brothwell and A.T. Sandison, pp. 249–271 (Springfield Ill.).

Mottahedeh, R.:

1973: "Administration in Buyid Qazvin," in *Islamic Civilisation 950–1150*, ed. D.S. Richards, pp. 33–45 (Oxford).

Musallam, B.F.:

1981: "Birth Control and Middle Eastern History," in *The Islamic Middle East, 700–1900*, ed. A.L. Udovitch, pp. 429–453 (Princeton).

Myhrman, D.W.:
1902: "Die Labartu-Texte," *ZA* 16: 141–200.

Neely, J.A.:
1974: "Sassanian and Early Islamic Water-Control and Irrigation Systems on the Deh Luran Plain, Iran," in *Irrigation's Impact on Society*, ed. T. Downing and McGuire Gibson, pp. 21–42 (Tucson: Anthropological Papers of the University of Arizona 28).

Neusner, J.:
1966: *A History of the Jews in Babylonia*, I-V (Leyden).

Newman, J.:
1932: *The Agricultural Life of the Jews in Babylonia between the Years 200 C.E. and 500 C.E.* (London).

Nicol, M.B.:
1970: "Rescue Excavation near Dorudzan," *East and West* 20: 245–285.

Nisbet, R.A.:
1968: *Social Change and History. Aspects of the Western Theory of Development* (London).

Nissen, H.J.:
1975: "Geographie," *ZA* 20: 9–40.

Nodelman, S.A.:
1960: "A Preliminary History of Characene," *Berytus* 13: 83–121.

Noeldeke, A.:
1947: "Zur Hydrographie des Euphrat im Schwemmlande," *Die Welt des Orients*: 158–171.

Noeldeke, T.:
1874: "Griechische Namen Susiana's," *Nachrichten von der Königlichen Gesellschaft der Wissenschaften und der G.A. Universität zu Göttingen* 8, pp. 173–197.

Northedge, A.:
1987: "Karkh Fairuz at Samarra'," *Mesopotamia* 20: 251–262.

Nougayrol, J.:
1949: "Conjuration ancienne contre Samana," *Archiv Orientalni* 17: 213–226.

Oates, J.:
1972: "Prehistoric Settlement Patterns in Mesopotamia," in *Man, Settlement, and Urbanism*, ed. P.J. Ucko et al., pp. 299–310 (London).

Oates, D. and J. Oates:
1976: "Early Irrigation Agriculture in Mesopotamia," in *Problems in Economic and Social Archeology*, ed. G. Sieveking et al., pp. 109–135 (London).

Obermeyer, J.:
1929: *Die Landschaft Babylonien im Zeitalter des Talmuds und des Gaonats* (Frankfurt a.M.).

Oded, B.:
1979: *Mass Deportations and Deportees in the Neo-Assyrian Empire* (Wiesbaden).

O'Donovan, E.:
1882: *The Merv Oasis*, I-II (London).

Oelsner, J.:
1974: "Krisenerscheinigungen im Achaimenidenreich im 5. und 4. Jahrhundert v.u.Z.," in *Hellenische Poleis* II, ed. E.C. Welskopf, pp. 1041–1073 (Berlin).
1978: "Kontinuität und Wandel in Gesellschaft und Kultur Babyloniens in Hellenistischer Zeit," *Klio* 60: 101–116.

O'Leary, B.:
1989: *The Asiatic Mode of Production* (Oxford).

Oppenheim, A.L.:
1962: "Mesopotamian Medicine," *Bulletin of the History of Medicine* 36: 97–113.

1964: *Ancient Mesopotamia – Portrait of a Dead Civilization* (Chicago).

1967: "A New Look at the Structure of Mesopotamian Society," *JESHO* 10: 1–16.

1969: "Mesopotamia – Land of Many Cities," in *Middle Eastern Cities*, ed. I.M. Lapidus, pp. 3–18 (Berkeley/Los Angeles).

Paschoud, F.:

1978: "Le Naarmalcha: à propos du tracé d'un canal Mésopotamie moyenne," *Syria* 55: 345–359.

Pellat, Ch.:

1953: *Le milieu basrien et la formation de Gahiz* (Paris).

1957: "Les étapes de la décadence culturelle dans les pays arabes d'Orient," in *Classicisme et déclin culturel dans l'histoire d'Islam*, ed. R. Brunschvig and G. von Grunebaum, pp. 81–90 (Paris).

Perrot, J.:

1985: "Suse à la periode achéménide," *Paléorient* 11/2: 67–69.

Pigulevskaia, N.:

1956: *Les villes de l'état iranien aux époques parthe et sassanide* (Paris/Haag 1963).

Planhol, X. de:

1968: *Les fondements géographiques de l'histoire de l'Islam* (Paris).

Pollitzer, R. and K.F. Meyer:

1961: "The Ecology of Plague," in *Studies in Disease Ecology*, ed. J.M. May, pp. 433–501 (New York).

Ponzi, M. Negro:

1967: "The Excavations at Choche, Area 1," *Mesopotamia* 2: 41–48.

Poole, J.C.F. and A.J. Holladay:

1979: "Thucydides and the Plague of Athens," *Classical Quarterly* 29: 282–300.

Popovic, A.:

1976: *La révolte des esclaves en Iraq au III/IXe siècle* (Paris: Bibliothéque d'études islamiques 6).

Postgate, J.N.:

1984: "The Problem of Yields in Sumerian Texts," *Bulletin on Sumerian Agriculture* 1: 97–102 (Cambridge).

Powell, M.:

1985: "Salt, Seed, and Yields in Sumerian Agriculture," *ZA* 75: 7–38.

Prickett, M.E.:

1979: "Settlement and the Development of Agriculture in the Rud-i Gushk Drainage," *AMI* Ergänzungsband 6: 47–56.

Radermacher, H.:

1975: "Historische Bewässerungssysteme in Afghanistan-Sistan," *Zeitschrift für Kulturtechnik und Flurbereinigung* 16: 65–77.

Rawlinson, H.C.:

1873: "Notes on Seistan," *JRGS* 43: 272–294.

Redman, C.L.:

1978: *The Rise of Civilization. From Early Farmers to Urban Society in the Ancient Near East* (San Francisco).

Remler, Ph.:

1985: "New Light on Economic History from Ilkhanid Accounting Manuals," *Studia Iranica* 14: 157–177.

Répertoire géographique des textes cunéiformes:

2: D.O. Edzard and G. Farber: *Die Orts- und Gewässernamen der Zeit der 3. Dynasty von Ur* (Wiesbaden 1974: TAVO B.7).

3: B. Groneberg: *Die Orts- und Gewässernamen der Altbabylonischen Zeit* (Wiesbaden 1980: TAVO B.7.3).

5: Kh. Nashef: *Die Orts- und Gewässernamen der Mittelbabylonischen und Mittelassyrischen Zeit* (Wiesbaden 1982: TAVO B.7.5).

8: R. Zadok: *Geographical Names According to New- and Late-Babylonian Texts* (Wiesbaden 1985: TAVO B.7.8).

Ricciardi, R.V.:
1968: "Excavations at Choche," *Mesopotamia* 3–4: 57–68.
1980: "Survey in the Upper Atrek Valley," *Mesopotamia* 15: 51–72.

Robert, L.:
1949: "Inscriptions séleucides de Phrygie et d'Iran," *Hellenica* 7: 5–29.
1960: "Inscription hellénistique de l'Iran," *Hellenica* 11/12: 85–92.
1967: "Encore une inscription grecque de l'Iran," *Académie des Inscriptions et Belles-Lettres*: 281–296.

Roberts, J.M.M.:
1972 : *The Earliest Semitic Pantheon* (Baltimore).

Rodinson, M.:
1974: "The Western Image and Western Studies of Islam," in *The Legacy of Islam*, ed. J. Schacht and C.E. Bosworth, pp. 9–62 (Oxford: 2nd ed.).

Rogers, J.M.:
1970: "Samarra: a Study in Medieval Town-Planning," in *The Islamic City*, ed. A.H. Hourani and S.M. Stern, pp. 119–155 (Oxford).

Ronca, I.:
1971: *Ptolemaios Geographie 6.9–21* (Rome).

Rosenthal, F.:
1968: *A History of Muslim Historiography* (Leyden: 2nd ed.).

Rostovtzeff, M.:
1941: *The Social and Economic History of the Hellenistic World*, I–III (London).

Rotter, G.:
1982: *Die Umayyaden und der Zweite Bürgerkrieg* (Wiesbaden: Abhandlungen für die Kunde des Morgenlandes 45.3).
1984: "Natural Catastrophies and their Impact on Political and Economic Life During the Second *Fitna*," in *Land Tenure and Social Transformation in the Middle East*, ed. T. Khalidi, pp. 229–234 (Beirut).

Russell, J.C.:
1958: *Late Ancient and Medieval Populations*. Transactions of the American Philosophical Society 48.3.
1968: "That Earlier Plague," *Demography* 5: 174–184.

Sakharov, A.M.:
1958: "Les mongols et la civilisation russe," *Cahiers de Histoire Mondiale*: 77–97.

Said, E.W.:
1978: *Orientalism* (London).

Salmon, P.:
1974: *Population et dépopulation dans l'empire romain* (Bruxelles: Collection Latomus 137).

Sancisi-Weerdenburg, H.:
1987: "Decadence in the Empire or Decadence in the Sources?" in *Achaemenid History I: Sources, Structures and Synthesis*, ed. H. Sancisi-Weerdenburg, pp. 33–46 (Leyden).

Sauer, C.O.:
1956: "The Agency of Man on the Earth," in *Man's Role in Changing the Face of the Earth*, ed. W.L. Thomas, pp. 49–69 (Chicago).

Scerrato, U.:
1966: "Excavations at Dahan-i Ghulaman," *East and West* 16: 9–30.

Schinaja, P.:
1967: "A Coin Hoard from Choche," *Mesopotamia* 2: 105–133.

Schippmann, K.:
1980: *Grundzüge der Parthischen Geschichte* (Darmstadt).

Schlumberger, D.:
   1970: *L'Orient hellénisé* (Paris).
Schmitt, H.H.:
   1964: Untersuchungen zur Geschichte Antiochos des Grossen und seiner Zeit, *Historia*, Ein-zelschriften, Heft 6.
Schmieder, O.:
   1965: *Die Alte Welt I: Der Orient* (Wiesbaden: Bibliothek Geographischer Handbücher).
Scholz, F.:
   1972: "Die Physisch- und Sozialgeographischen Ursachen für die Aufgabe und den Erhalt der Kareze in Belutchistan," *Die Erde* 103: 302–315.
Schurmann, H.F.:
   1956: "Mongolian Tributary Practices," *Harvard Journal of Asiatic Studies* 19: 304–389.
Schwartz, B.:
   1938: "The Hittite and Luwian Ritual of Zarpiya of Kezzuwatna," *JAOS* 58: 334–353.
Schwarz, P.:
   Iran im Mittelalter nach den Arabischen Geographen, IIX (Leipzig: 1929–1935).
Seibert, J.:
   1983: "Heeresseuchen und Kriegsverlauf," *Historia*, Einzelschriften 40: 78–91.
Service, E.R.:
   1975: *The Origins of State and Civilization* (New York).
Shaban, M.A.:
   1970: *The Abbasid Revolution* (Cambridge).
   1971: *Islamic History. A New Interpretation*, I-II (Cambridge).
Sherwin-White, S.:
   1987: "Seleucid Babylonia," in *Hellenism in the East*, ed. A. Kuhrt and S. Sherwin-White, pp. 1–31 (London).
Siroux, M.:
   1971: *Anciennes voies et monuments routiers de la region d'Ispahan.* Mémoires publiés par les membres de l'Institut Francais d'Archéologie Orientale du Caire LXXXII (Cairo).
Smith, A.:
   1953: *Blind White Fish in Persia* (London).
Smith, J.M.:
   1969: "The Silver Currency of Mongol Iran," *JESHO* 12: 16–41.
   1970: *The History of the Sarbadar Dynasty* (Paris-Haag).
   1975: "Mongol Manpower and Persian Population," *JESHO* 18: 271–299.
   1978: "Turanian Nomadism and Iranian Politics," *Iranian Studies* 11: 57–81.
Smith, J.M. and S. Benin:
   1974: "In a Persian Market with Mongol Money" in *Near Eastern Numismatics, Iconography, Epigraphy and History: Studies in Honor of George C. Miles*, ed. D.K. Kouymjian, pp. 431–441 (Beirut).
Smith, N.:
   1971: *A History of Dams* (London).
Speck, J.R. van der:
   1987: "The Babylonian City," in *Hellenism in the East*, ed. A. Kuhrt and S. Sherwin-White, pp. 57–74 (London).
Spooner, B.:
   1974: "City and River in Iran: Urbanization and Irrigation of the Iranian Plateau," *Iranian Studies* 7: 681–712.
Sprenger, A.:
   1864: "Die Post- und Reiserouten des Orients." *Abhandlungen der Deutschen Morgenländischen Gesellschaft* 3.

Spuler, B.:
    1952: *Iran in Früh-Islamischer Zeit* (Wiesbaden).
    1955: *Die Mongolen in Iran* (Wiesbaden).
    1968: *History of the Mongols* (English ed. London 1972).

Steadman, J.M.:
    1969: *The Myth of Asia* (New York).

Stein, A.:
    1936: "An Archaeological Tour in the Ancient Persis," *Iraq* 3: 111–225.
    1937: *Archaeological Reconnaissances in North-Western India and South-Eastern Iran* (London).
    1940: *Old Routes of Western Iran* (London).

Steinkeller, P.:
    1982: "The Question of Marhasi," *ZA* 72: 237–265.

Steensgaard, N.:
    1984: "Set fra 1984. En model for nyere tids verdenshistorie," in *Tradition og Kritik: Festskrift til Svend Ellehøj*, pp. 413–435 (Copenhagen).

Steve, M.J.:
    1986: "La Fin de l'Élam: à propos d'une empreinte de sceaucylindre," *Studia Iranica* 15: 7–21.

Stewart, C.E.:
    1911: *Through Persia in Disguise* (London).

Sticker, G.:
    1908: *Abhandlungen aus der Seuchengeschichte und Seuchenlehre* (Giessen: 1908–1912).

Stolper, M.W.:
    1985: *Entrepreneurs and Empire. The Murasu Archive, the Murasu Firm, and Persian Rule in Babylonia* (Leyden: Uitgaven van het Nederlands Historisch-Archaeologisch Instituut te Istanbul 54).

Stone, E.C.:
    1981: "Texts, Architecture and Ethnographic Analogy: Patterns of Residence in Old-Babylonian Nippur," *Iraq* 43: 19–33.

Streck, M.:
    1917: "Seleucia und Ktesiphon," *Der Alte Orient* 16.

Stronach, D.:
    1969: "Excavations at Tepe Nush-i Jan," *Iran* 7: 1–20.

Sumner, W.M.:
    1974: "Excavations at Tall-i Malyan, 1971/72," *Iran* 12: 155–180.
    1985: "The Proto-Elamite City Wall at Tall-i Malyan," *Iran* 23: 153–161.
    1986: "Achaemenid Settlment in the Persepolis Plain," *American Journal of Archaeology* 90: 3–31.

Sykes, P.:
    1902: *Ten Thousand Miles in Persia* (London).

Tarn, W.W.:
    1938: *The Greeks in Bactria and India* (Cambridge. Ref. to 2nd ed. 1951).
    1948: *Alexander the Great*, I-II (Cambridge).

Tate, G.P.:
    1908: *The Frontiers of Baluchistan* (London).
    1910: *Seistan. A Memoir on the History, Topography, Ruins, and People of the Country*, I-II (Calcutta).

Teggart, F.J.:
    1941: *Theory and Processes of History* (Berkeley).

Thompson, R.C.:
    1910: *The Reports of the Magicians and Astrologers of Niniveh and Babylon*, I-II (London).

Tomaschek, W.:
    1883: "Zur Historischen Topographie von Persien I: Die Strassenzüge der Tabula Peutingeriana," *Sitzungsberichte der Philologisch-Historischen Classe der Kaiserlichen Akademie der Wissenschaften* 102: 145–231 (Wien).

1885: "Zur Historischen Topographie von Persien II: Die Wege durch die Persische Wüste," *Sitzungsbericht der Philologisch-Historischen Classe der Kaiserlichen Akademie der Wissenschaften* 108: 561–652 (Wien).

Tosi, M.:

1973: "Early Urban Evolution and Settlement Patterns in the Indo-Iranian Borderland," in *The Explanation of Culture Change: Models in Prehistory*, ed. C. Renfrew, pp. 429–446 (London).

Trinkaus, K.M.:

1983: "Pre-Islamic Settlement and Land Use in Damghan," *Iranica Antiqua* 18: 199–144.

1985: "Settlement of Highlands and Lowlands in Early Islamic Damghan," *Iran* 23: 129–141.

Troll, C.:

1972: "Die Qanat- oder Karez-bewässerung in der Alten und Neuen Welt als Problem der Universalgeschichte," in *Madrid. Die Wasserversorgung der Stadt durch Qanate im Laufe der Geschichte*, ed. C. Troll and C. Braun, pp. 529. Akademie der Wissenschaften und der Litteratur. Abhandlungen der Mathematisch-Naturwissenschaftlichen Klasse 5 (Wiesbaden).

Tscherikower, V.:

1927: "Die Hellenistische Städtegründungen von Alexander dem Grossen bis auf die Römerzeit," *Philologus*, Suppl. Band 19, Heft 1.

Ullmann, M.:

1970: Die Medizin im Islam. *Handbuch der Orientalistik*, 1. Abteilung, Ergänzungsband VI/1 (Leyden).

1972: Die Natur- und Geheimwissenschaften im Islam. *Handbuch der Orientalistik*, 1. Abteilung, Ergänzungsband VI/2 (Leyden).

Unger, E.:

1931: *Babylon. Die Heilige Stadt nach der Beschreibung der Babylonier* (Berlin).

Ungnad, A.:

1914: *Babylonische Briefe aus der Zeit der Hammurapi-Dynasti* (Leipzig).

Vallat, F.:

1985: "Éléments de géographie élamite," *Paléorient* 11/2: 49–54.

Vanden Berghe, L.:

1959: *Archéologie de l'Iran* (Leyden).

1961: "Récentes découvertes de monuments sassanides dans le Fars," *Iranica Antiqua* 1: 163–198.

1968: "Les ruines de Bihisht u Duzakh à Sultanabad," *Iranica Antiqua* 8: 94–105.

Vanstiphout, H.L.J.:

1974: "Was een Pestepidemie de Oorzaak van de Ondergang van het Nieuwsumerische Rijk?" *Phoenix − Ex Oriente Lux* 20: 351–370.

Vesel, Z.:

1986: "Les traités d'agriculture en Iran," *Studia Iranica* 15: 99–108.

Vogelsang, W.:

1985: "Early Historical Arachosia in South-East Afghanistan," *Iranica Antiqua* 20: 55–99.

Vries, J. de:

1976: *The Economy of Europe in an Age of Crisis, 1600–1750* (Cambridge).

Waardenburg, J.J.:

1962: *L'Islam dans le miroir de l'Occident* (Paris).

Wagstaff, J.M.:

1985: *The Evolution of Middle Eastern Landscapes* (London).

Waines, D.:

1977a: "The Third Century Internal Crisis of the Abbasids," *JESHO* 20: 282–306.

1977b: "The Pre-Buyid Amirate: Two Views from the Past," *IJMES* 8: 339–348.

Walters, S.D.:

1970: *Water for Larsa. An Old Babylonian Archive Dealing with Irrigation* (New Haven).

Watkins, S.C. and E. van de Walle:

1983: "Nutrition, Mortality, and Population Size: Malthus' Court of Last Resort," *Journal of Interdisciplinary History* 14: 205–226.

Watson, A.M.:

1967: "Back to Gold – and Silver," *Economic History Review* (2nd ser.) 20: 1–34.

1974: "The Arab Agricultural Revolution and Its Diffusion, 700–1100," *Journal of Economic History* 34: 8–35.

1981: "A Medieval Green Revolution: New Crops and Farming Techniques in the Early Islamic World," in *The Islamic Middle east, 700–1900*, ed. A.L. Udovitch, pp. 29–58 (Princeton).

1983: *Agricultural Innovation in the Early Islamic World* (Cambridge).

Weiner, E. von:

1971: Der Babylonische Gott Nergal. *Alter orient und Altes Testament* 11 (Neukirchen).

Wells, C.:

1964: *Bones, Bodies, and Disease. Evidence of Disease and Abnormality in Early Man* (London).

Wenke, R.J.:

1975: "Imperial Investments and Agricultural Development in Parthian and Sasanian Khuzistan: 150 B.C. to A.D. 640," *Mesopotamia* 10/11: 31–221.

1981: "Elymaeans, Parthians, and the Evolution of Empires in Southwestern Iran," *JAOS* 101: 303–315.

Whitcomb, D.S.:

1979: "The City of Istakhr and the Marvdasht Plain," *AMI* Ergänzungsband 6: 363–370.

1985a: *Before the Roses and Nightingales: Excavations at Qasri Abu Nasr* (New York).

1985b: "Islamic Archaeology at Susa," *Paléorient* 11/2: 85–90.

1987: "Bushire and the Angali Canal," *Mesopotamia* 22: 311–336.

Whitehouse, D.:

1974: "Excavations at Siraf," *Iran* 12: 1–30.

Whitehouse, D. and A. Williamson:

1973: "Sassanian Maritime Trade," *Iran* 11: 29–49.

Wickham, C.:

1984: "The Uniqueness of the East," *Journal of Peasant Studies* 12: 166–196.

Widengren, G.:

1971: "The Establishment of the Sasanian Dynasty in the Light of New Evidence," in *La Persia nel Medioevo*, pp. 711–782 (Rome: Accademia Nazionale dei Lincei).

Wilkinson, R.G.:

1973: *Poverty and Progress. An Ecological Model of Economic Development* (London).

Willcocks, W.:

1903: *The Restoration of the Ancient Irrigation Works on the Tigris*. Being a Lecture Delivered at a Meeting of the Khedivial Geographical Society, Cairo, 25th March, 1903 (Cairo).

Williams, R.:

1972: "Ideas of Nature," in *Ecology, the Shaping Enquiry*, ed. J. Benthall, pp. 146–164 (London).

Wills, C.J.:

1887: *Persia as It is* (London, 2nd ed.).

Wirth, E.:

1962: *Agrargeographie des Irak* (Hamburg: Hamburger Geographische Schriften 13).

Wolski, J.:

1967: "L'Aristocratie Parthe et les commencements de féodalisme en Iran," *Iranica Antiqua* 7: 133–144.

1985: "Dans l'attente d'une nouvelle histoire de l'Iran arsacide," *Iranica Antiqua* 20: 163–173.

Worster, D.:

1984: "History as Natural History: an Essay on Method," *Pacific Historical Review* 53: 1–19.

1990: "Transformation of the Earth: Toward an Agroecological Perspective in History," *Journal of American History* 76: 1087–1106.

Woods, J.E.:
   1976: *The Aqquyunlu. Clan, Confederation, Empire. A Study in 15th/9th Century Turco-Iranian Politics* (Minneapolis-Chicago).
   1987: "The Rise of Timurid Historiography," *JNES* 46: 81–108.
Wright, H.T.:
   1969: *The Administration of Rural Production in an Early Mesopotamian Town* (Ann Arbor: Museum of Anthropology, University of Michigan, Anthropological Papers 38).
Wrigley, E.A.:
   1978: "Parasite or Stimulus: the Town in a Pre-Industrial Economy," in *Towns in Societies*, ed. Ph. Abrams and E.A. Wrigley, pp. 295–309 (Cambridge).
Wüstenfeld, F.:
   1864: "Jacut's Reisen, aus seinem Geographischen Wörterbuch beschrieben," *ZDMG* 18: 397–493.
Wulff, H.E.:
   1966: *The Traditional Crafts of Persia* (Cambridge, Mass.).
Wylie, J.A.H. and H.W. Stubbs:
   1983: "The Plague of Athens," *Classical Quarterly* 33: 6–11.
Yaron, D. ed.:
   1981: *Salinity in Irrigation and Water Resources* (New York).
Yar-Shater, E.:
   1971: "Were the Sassanians Heirs to the Achaemenids?" in *La Persia nel Medioevo*, pp. 517–531 (Rome: Accademia Nazionale dei Lincei).
Young, T. Cuyler:
   1972: "Population Densities and Early Mesopotamian Urbanism," in *Man, Settlement, and Urbanism*, ed. P.J. Ucko et al., pp. 827–842 (London).
Zadok, R.:
   1977: "Iranians and Individuals Bearing Iranian Names in Achaemenian Babylonia," *Israel Oriental Studies* 7: 89–138.
   1978: "The Nippur Region During the Late Assyrian, Chaldean and Achaemenian Periods," *Israel Oriental Studies* 8: 266–332.
Zakaria, H.:
   1959: "Historical Study of Schistosoma Haematobium and Its Intermediate Host, Bulinus Truncatus, in Central Iraq," *Journal of the Faculty of Medicine of Baghdad*, N.S. 1: 1–10.
Zeist, W. van:
   1969: "Reflections on Prehistoric Environments in the Near East," in *The Domestication and Exploitation of Plants and Animals*, ed. P.J. Ucko et al., pp. 35–46.
Zimmern, H.:
   1917 "Das Nergallied," *ZA* 31: 111–121.

Notes

Notes to Introduction

1. A representative example of how this image still conditions our understanding of the historical processes in the Middle East may be found in Cahen (1968: 341f).
2. On themes and problems in this tendency, see Steensgaard (1984) and McNeill (1982a).
3. The most detailed studies of the formation and development of the European image of Islam/the Middle East are Daniel (1960 and 1966) and J. J. Waardenburg (1962). A concise summary can be found in Rodinson (1974).
4. E.g. A. Abdel-Malek (1963) and E.W. Said (1978). Said's book is formulated in an especially uncompromising tone.
5. E.g. Dols (1977).
6. See Williams (1972) and Worster (1984 and 1990).
7. The latter term refers to the idea of demographic growth as an independent variable which often lies behind explanations of change in pre-modern societies.

Notes to Chapter 1

1. Fraser (I: 205f, II: 6f).
2. Koçi Bey (tr.); B. Lewis: "Ottoman Observers of Ottoman Decline," *Islamic Studies* 1: 71–87 (1962); L.V. Thomas: *A Study of Naima*, chap. 2 (New York 1972). The European idea of decline was stated as early as 1603 in Richard Knolles' *A Generall Historie of the Ottoman Empire*.
3. On the history of the idea of progress, see Teggart (1941: chap. 8) and Nisbet (1968).
4. E. Huntington: *The Pulse of Asia* (Boston 1907) and subsequent works such as *Mainsprings of Civilization* (New York 1945).
5. E.g. Planhol (1968).
6. Cf. note 3 in the Introduction.
7. Von Grunebaum argued this at great length and in my view rather cryptically. See his *Medieval Islam* (1946) and *Classical Islam* (1973). Nonetheless, I believe I have restated the essence of his argument.
8. Summaries of the history of the idea of despotism can be found in P. Anderson, *Lineages of the Absolutist State* (London, 1974), pp. 397ff and 462–549; in Steadman (1969: 259–282); and in B. O'Leary (1989: 40–8l).
9. Cf. K. Butzer's summary in Brice (1978: 5–12).
10. See, for example, Cahen (1973).
11. See, for example, Cahen (1968, 1973). Also representative is D. Morgan, *The Mongols* (Oxford, 1986: 73–83). Within conventional Soviet research the notion of the Mongol invasions as a fatal catastrophe has not been revised, in spite of the fact that Barthold had already expressed his skepticism (Barthold, 1956 I: 43f). The explanation must be that the Mongols have traditionally constituted a central factor in Soviet explanations of Russia's own history. Because of the Mongols' destruction and the subsequent exhaustive wars with the Golden Horde and the

Khanates in Kazan, Astrakhan and the Crimea, Russia's development was "retarded" in relation to the rest of Europe. "Das Tatarenjoch war ein kolossales Übel, das den historischen Fortschritt hemmte," explains the *Geschichte der UdSSR* (Moscow, 1977 I: 56f). See also Petrushevsky in *CHIr* V and A.M. Sakharov's summary, "Les Mongols et la Civilisation Russe," *Cahiers de Histoire Mondiale* 1958: 77–97.

12. See note 4 in the Introduction.
13. Steadman (1969: 259).
14. Examples can be found in Service (1975: 273ff); see also the critiques in O'Leary (1989: 235–261).
15. See Jones (1981).

NOTES TO CHAPTER 2

1. Cf. the arguments in N.R. Keddie, "Is there a Middle East," *IJMES* vol. 4 (1973).
2. For example, Ibn Rusteh (tr.: 115); Mas'udi (*Tanbih*, tr.: 58); Mustawfi (*Nuzhat*: 18, 27f); Frye (1975: 8ff).
3. al-Baladhuri (tr., I: 465ff); Ibn al-Nadim (tr., II: 581f).
4. Frye (1975: 5).
5. al-Tanukhi (tr.: 229); Ibn Hawqal (tr., II: 251); Schwarz: 291.
6. al-Rudhrawari (tr.: 37); Nasir-é Khusraw (tr.: 7f); Marco Polo: 46; Barbaro (tr.: 82f).
7. P. Brown, *The World of Late Antiquity* (London, 1971), p. 12. In the first half of the 17th century, 140.000 tons of grain were shipped each year through the Sound (J. de Vries, *The Economy of Europe in an Age of Crisis, 1600–1750*, (Cambridge, 1976), p. 33; K. Glamann, "European Trade 1500–1700", in C.M. Cipolla (ed.), *The Fontana Economic History of Europe*, vol. 2 (Glasgow, 1974), p. 454ff.
8. For studies of local power structures see, for example, Bulliet (1973, 1978); R. Mottahedeh, "Administration in Buyid Qazwin", in D.S. Richards (ed.), *Islamic Civilisation, 950–1150* (Oxford, 1973), pp. 33–45.
9. Brice (1978); Van Zeist (1969); Butzer (1961). Any generalization about past climatic conditions in the Middle East must, however, be tentative. Obviously, pollen analyses are few and not representative. Regular measurements of rainfall and temperature have only begun in recent decades, and the results will to a certain degree be affected by the man-made changes which have influenced climate during this century, i.e. increasing infrared absorption as a result of the increased amount of carbon dioxide in the atmosphere, more dust particles due to pollution, etc. (see Flohn, 1973).
10. *CHIr* (I: 247ff); Kortum (1973: 180, note 2); English (1966: 9); Beaumont et al. (1976: 70, table 2.7).
11. Wirth (1962: 13–24).
12. *CHIr* (I: 571). Often these two forms of agriculture are combined: in years with sufficient rain extensive dry farming may be practiced in a "fan" beyond the "core" of irrigated land; in years with poor rainfall the "fan" will not be cultivated at all, but used for pasture.
13. Ibn Isfandiyar (tr.: 30).
14. Ya'qubi (tr.: 81); Ibn Isfandiyar (tr.: 118).

NOTES TO CHAPTER 3

1. On sources from Muslim times, see the relevant articles in *EI* and F. Rosenthal's *History of Muslim Historiography* (2nd ed., Leyden, 1968). Armenian sources are briefly discussed by R. W. Thomson in his introduction to the translation of Moses Khorenats'i. Syriac and other sources for Sassanian and early Muslim Mesopotamia are examined in Morony (1984b: 537–575). A summary, now rather outdated, of sources for the Sassanian period can be found in Christensen (1936).

2. These reports depict the Zagros region as divided into numerous small principalities. Several localities are named, including "towns," but most cannot be identified with any certainty (Levine, 1973). Also in earlier Mesopotamian sources we find references to unidentifiable political or territorial units in Fars and Djibal.

3. The most informative is Darius' inscriptions at Bisitun, Naqsh-é Rustam, and Persepolis which, beside Darius' official autobiography, contain brief enumerations of the peoples and territories which belonged to the Achaemenid Empire (Herrenschmidt, 1976).

4. Most of the tablets are written in Elamite. The small number which have been analyzed so far contain information about the payment of salaries to those craftsmen and workers who built the palace complex. They obviously shed some light on the way in which the Achaemenid kings mobilized the Empire's resources. Cf. G.G. Cameron, *Persepolis Treasury Tablets* (Chicago, 1948) and R.T. Hallock, *Persepolis Fortification Tablets* (Chicago, 1969).

5. Of the more than 2.000 ostraca from Nisa, some 200 have been analyzed more closely. They date from the 1st century B.C. and almost all of them concern the delivery of wine to a royal deposit (Chaumont, 1968). The Avroman documents, named after the site in Kurdistan where they were found, consist of three parchment texts, two written in Greek, one in Pahlavi. They date from the period between 100 B.C. to 100 A.D. and concern the sale of some vineyards (Minns, 1915).

6. Plutarch, *Moralia*, pp. 328–329 (Loeb ed.); Murray (1987).

7. Both Hecataeus and Herodotus had travelled in the western provinces of the Achaemenid Empire but not on the Plateau itself. It is not clear how they obtained information regarding the conditions here. In contrast, it is probable that the doctor Ctesias from Cnidos visited the Plateau, but his *Persica*, which contains paraphrases of an Achaemenid *stathmoi* handbook (itinerarium), exists only in fragments and is conventionally regarded as an unreliable source (cf. Ctesias, par. 64, p. 26). This verdict may be somewhat unjust, cf. H. Sancisi-Werdenburg (1987).

8. The reliability of both the extant secondary sources and the now lost primary sources has been disputed. Traditionally Arrian is considered the best source because he used contempory authors: Aristobulus and Ptolemy. Ptolemy is said to have possessed the official "diary" kept during the campaign (Hammond, 1981: 1–6). But Ptolemy had clear interests in promoting himself and may not be entirely trustworthy. Moreover, it seems that Arrian was careless in his use of the sources; so his authority may be no stronger than, say, that of Quintus Curtius (see A.B. Bosworth, 1976).

9. Pliny VI.49; Strabo XI.7.1.

10. Strabo XI.6.4 and XV.13; Pliny VI.141; Nodelman (1960: 107, note 160); further discussion in Tarn (1938: 43ff, 53ff); Herzfeld (1932: 4ff).

11. *CHIr* (III: 547ff, 738ff).

12. The evidence consists of two Palmyrene funeral stelae found in Marv. Even though their archaeological history is not completely clear, they must be considered a sure sign that at least some Palmyrene traders had travelled far to the east along the silk route, cf. M.E. Masson, "Two Palmyrene Stelae from the Merv Oasis", *East and West* 17: 239–247 (1967). To my knowledge no additional traces of Palmyrene activity have been found east of the Tigris. Perhaps some of the Palmyrene merchant families had particularly good connections to the Parthians and therefore obtained permission to travel on the Plateau. If so, they would have had little interest in transmitting information about what they saw. This is only speculation, however.

13. Pliny VI.139–140.

14. Strabo XI.13.3; Pliny VI.40.).
15. Ammianus XXIII.6.
16. Ptolemy VI.9–10 and 20–21. The maps preserved in the Ebner Manuscript reflect the same mistakes. Strabo (XI.6.1.), who had Patroclus as his source, also makes similar mistakes regarding the Oxus. However, it should be noted that the rivers in Central Asia have in fact changed their courses several times in pre-historic as well as in historical time. The Oxus (Amu Darya), for instance, both in pre-historic times and during the 14th–16th centuries partially flowed into the Sarikamish Depression southwest of the Aral Sea. The ancient bed of the Uzboy in the Karakum Desert is presumably the remains of a channel from the Sarikamish to the Caspian Sea, but by historical times this connection had long been interrupted. When the waters temporarily returned to the Sarikamish in the 14th century, they no longer flowed in the Uzboy bed, cf. Gerasimov (1978: 326ff). The possibility exists that Patroclus saw the remains of the mouth of the Uzboy and mistook it for the Oxus, but it is more probable that he and the classical authors simply confused the Oxus and the Ochus (Atrek). Classical Europe did not know that the Caspian and the Aral seas were two different bodies of water and therefore had the Djaxartes (Syr Darya) flowing into the Caspian Sea; see Barthold (1910: 8f); Kohl (1984: 29).
17. *TP* is a medieval copy (12th or 13th century?) of a Roman itinerary from the second half of the fourth century (Miller, 1916: xxix). It has the form of a map on which are entered towns and resting places and the distances between them. As concerns Iran, where distances seem to be rendered in *parasangs*, the map uses older sources, perhaps Isidore of Charax and/or a Seleucid-Parthian *stathmoi* book. Many of the names are illegible today, and several names and distances were apparently overlooked during copying.
18. Ptolemy VI.8.
19. Isidore (par. 9) states explicitly that Comisena (Kumis) contains no towns, only villages, which is impossible. All other sources locate Hecatompylus here.
20. See the relevant articles in *PW*.
21. As an example of a speculative identification we may cite *Yazd*. In modern times this enclave has housed a large group of Zoroastrians – some 4.000 households at the beginning of the 19th century (Kinneir: 113f; Abbott: 137ff). Apparently this has endowed the city with an aura of great age, as Tomaschek (1883: 165) calls it the "uralten Magiersitz Yazd." He does so partly on information provided by of Ptolemy and *TP*: Ptolemy (VI.6.), in connection with "Kirman's desert" (Dasht-é Kavir), states that the nomadic *Isatichae* had pastures in the southern part and this can be interpreted as a reference to the Yazd region. But the etymological link between the Isatichae and Yazd is questionable. Combinations with –*yazd*– were very common in pre-Muslim times, both in placenames and personal names. We have, for example, Yazd-é Khwast, a small town on the border between Djibal and Fars. Thus even though the Isatichae might have something to do with the *word yazd*, this does not necessarily point to the *town* Yazd. In any case Ptolemy says nothing of a settlement in the area. Tomaschek, however, finds it in *TP*'s *Cetrora,* a station on the road between Hamadan and "Aris" (Zarandj?). The name Cetrora to him resembles *Ketheh*, the old name of the Yazd enclave's principal urban center which (as was normal practice everywhere on the plateau) in daily usage was called by the enclave's name, i.e. (*shahr-é*) Yazd. The two names are not, to my mind at least, convincingly similar, and the distances given in *TP* indicate that Cetrora should be sought in Kirman, not in the Yazd region. Miller's conclusion (1916: 797) is that Cetrora must be identical with Khabis (now: Shahdab), a few hundred kilometers east of Yazd. *TP* does not indicate whether Cetrora was a town or simply a caravanserai. *TP*'s distances regarding Iran are so imprecise that I do not find the identification of Cetrora with Khabis very convincing either. Markwart (1895: 669) would on etymological grounds identify Yazd with Pliny's *Issatis* (Pliny VI.44,113), a suggestion which is unacceptable for several reasons. First, Pliny says that Issatis was on a cliff (*in rube*), while Yazd is situated on a plain at the edge of the desert. Second, Pliny locates Issatis in the country of Choara/Choarena, i.e.

north of the Dasht-é Kavir in what is now the Simnan area. In brief, the existence of the town Yazd can not be documented from classical sources. That it may in fact be very old cannot be ruled out, but there is simply nothing to prove it. A later local history, the *Tarikh-é Yazd* (15th century), states that the town was founded by the Sassanians as a military base (Bonine, 1980: 12, 21). This is at least plausible considering that the Sassanians founded other artifical oases on the edge of the desert, e.g. Veh-Ardashir in Kirman.

22. Schlumberger (1970: 12f).
23. Fragments of Babylonian chronicles from the late Achaemenid era indicate that other themes and traditions about Persian kings besides those popularized by the Greek authors circulated in the east (Kuhrt, 1987: 154).
24. The transmission of *Khuda-nameh* and the Persian historical tradition is discussed in Christensen (1925: 22f); Christensen (1936: 59ff); *CHIr* (III/2: 1279ff).
25. Tha'alibi (*Tar'rikh ghurar*: 14, 457f); Mas'udi (*Murudj* IV: 145); Mas'udi (*Tanbih*, tr.: 150).
26. Hamza (tr.: 6ff); Mas'udi (*Tanbih*, tr.: 149ff); Tha'alibi (*Ta'rikh ghurar*: 14); Ibn al-Nadim (tr., I: 260, II: 716, 737). Ibn al-Nadim was a bookseller in Baghdad at the end of the 10th century. His *Kitab al-Fihrist* was a systematic and partly annotated catalogue of books in Arabic, including translations from Persian and Greek.
27. Mas'udi (*Murudj*, II: 205ff); Mas'udi (*Tanbih*, tr.: 141); Ibn al-Nadim (tr., I: 276; II: 738ff).
28. Mas'udi (*Murudj*, II: 162, 223); Ibn al-Nadim (tr., I: 260,359, II: 589, 716); *Tarikh-é Sistan*: 8f.
29. Christensen (1936: 59ff).
30. Hamza (tr.: 47).
31. Noeldeke's theory, i.e. that the *Khuda-nameh* had been written by Zoroastrian priests and therefore represented the views of the clergy and the nobility, must be rejected for several reasons (see Noeldeke's commentaries to the Tabari translation: 21, 74f). Noeldeke built his argument on the fact that Yazdgird I, "The Sinner" (399–421) was practically the only king to be criticized in the *Khuda-nameh* as an unjust and bloodthirsty tyrant. Partly on the basis of Armenian sources Noeldeke assumed that Yazdgird had been friendly toward the Christians and for this reason drew the wrath of the clergy. As against this interpretation we can note the following:

First, it is hardly the case that Yazdgird was extraordinarily friendly toward the Christians. The majority of the inhabitants of Mesopotamia, the core of the Sassanian Empire, were Christian, and the Sassanian kings systematically sought to use the Christian churches, notably the Nestorian, as political and administrative tools, just as the Abbasids did later. For example, they selected candidates for episcopacies and sought to promote the formation of hierarchies within the churches, for instance by putting royal power behind the bishops' decisions. In other words, they made the church dignitaries' power dependent on their loyalty to the Empire. Many of the persecutions of Christians in which Syriac hagiography revels seem to have been attempts by the Sassanian state to regulate sectarian struggles within the Christian communities. Incidentally, these Mesopotamian Christian communities had among their members a significant number of Persian nobles. There is no reason to believe that the state forcibly sought to convert the subjects to some form of Zoroastrianism. Scholars have grown increasingly sceptical as to the existence, in Sassanian times, of a regular Zoroastrian "State Church", because the systematization and writing down of doctrines and regulations took place only in the 9th and 10th centuries (Morony, 1982b: 332ff; Frye, 1962: 222f).

Second, it is striking that Shah Narseh (293–303) is not condemned for his tolerance toward the unspeakable Manicheans. Kavadh I is certainly criticized for his long association with the religious (and perhaps also social) reformer Mazdak, but is otherwise consistently described as one of Iran's best kings. This hardly supports the view that the *Khuda-nameh* reflected the attitudes of the Zoroastrian clergy. Noeldeke seems to think that in a pre-industrial society like Iranshahr priests were needed to perform scribal work. But the Sassanians had at their disposal a large, professional and secular bureaucracy, the *dipiran* (cf. the description in Djahshiyari, tr.: 54ff).

Neither is it easy to identify a pro-nobility tendency in the *Khuda-nameh*. On the contrary, the account emphasizes the kings' absolute power, pretending, for example, that the succession of sons to the throne was an uncomplicated and recognized practice; Narseh's revolt (recorded in the Paikuli inscription) and conflicts over succession after Hormizd II's death are smoothed over (Tabari, Noeldeke tr.,: 46ff; Mas'udi, *Murudj*, II: 167). Kings with great personal authority could perhaps choose their heirs, but there is good evidence that the noble families normally exerted decisive influence as to which male members among the Sassanian royal family could succeed to the throne. On this point it seems that the Sassanian state did not differ from its Arsacid predecessor which the *Khuda-nameh* otherwise attempts to render as insignificant as possible. It may be added that Hormizd IV (579–591), who came into open conflict with the Mihrans and presumably also other powerful noble families, is praised as a just though strict ruler. Only Mas'udi (*Murudj*, II :.211) deviates from this by condemning Hormizd in strong terms, perhaps because he had as a source the romance about Bahram Chubin, the Mihran rebel.

32. Hamza Isfahani (tr.: 20, 24, 26).
33. Ammianus XX.6; Procopius II.14; Ps. Joshua Stylites (tr.,: 37, 41, 43); Ps. Sebeos (tr.: 63).
34. See i.e. Schwarz: 59, note 6.
35. Bosworth (1978).
36. Nizam al-Mulk (tr.: 10).
37. According to Yaqut, cited in H.F. Amedroz, "Three Years of Buwaihid Rule in Baghdad, A.H. 389–393," *JRAS* 1901: 502f.
38. Ibn al-Balkhi (tr.: 66); Nizam al-Mulk (tr.: 75).
39. Nizam al-Mulk (tr.: 18).
40. E.g. Ibn Khallikan (tr., IV: 322).
41. al-'Utbi (tr.: 397f).
42. E.g. the Armenian *ashkharhats'oyts'*, which consisted largely of revisions of Ptolemy; cf. Markwart (1901) and D.W. Thomson's introduction to the translation of Moses Khorenats'i.
43. On the origins and character of this group of sources, see primarily Miquel (1975).
44. Ibn Hawqal (tr., II: 322). Djayhani was a Samanid official who around 900 wrote an administrative handbook similar to Ibn Khurdadhbih's. It is not extant.
45. Ibn Battuta (tr., II: 299).
46. Ouseley (II: 11, 17, 25).
47. Waring: 33.
48. E.g. Ibn Hawqal (tr., II: 274); Ibn al-Balkhi (tr.: 37f); Miskawayh (tr., V: 443f); el-'Ali (1968: 428f) on brick-robbing from the famous "White Palace" of the Sassanians in al-Mada'in.
49. Oates (1972: 301).
50. Waring: 40.
51. J. Morier: *The Adventures of Hajji Baba of Ispahan* (World Classics ed., 1923: 5). Let me add from personal experience that I, too, was disappointed when I first visited Shiraz and saw its famous gardens.
52. Cf. p. 194
53. Ibn al-Faqih (tr.: 289); Yaqut (tr.: 605f); Mustawfi (*Nuzhat*, tr.: 75); Schwarz: 531; Petrushevskii (in *CHIr* V: 496).
54. Thus Mustawfi (*Nuzhat*: 51, tr.: 56–58) sometimes distinguishes between *dih* and *qariyeh* as belonging to different categories, apparently fiscally defined.
55. Krawulsky (1978: 74f); Lambton (1953: 4, note 2); Aubin (1967: 194f).
56. Peder Mortensen (oral communication) has assured me that pottery sequences in Mesopotamia, Khuzistan and on the western Plateau are now so well-known that non-archaeologists need not be skeptical about the dating. See also Adams (1970). Farther east, however, the dating continues to be a problem due to lack of comparable materials, cf. Korbel (1983).
57. The figures of *muqatila*, Muslim soldiers in, e.g. Basrah and Kufah in the seventh century, are not the result of a census, but only a recording of who had demands for certain forms of payments.

58. The credibility of the list in relation to the Persian epigraphic sources is discussed by Cameron (1973), who is followed by Cook (in *CHIr* II: 244ff); Herrenschmidt (1976); Kimball-Armager (1978); Callmeyer (1983).
59. Qudama (tr.: 180); al-Djahshiyari (tr.: 54); al-Baladhuri (tr., I: 465ff).
60. Newman (1932: chap. X-XI); Goodblatt (1979); Tabari (Noeldeke tr.: 241).
61. Tabari (Noeldeke tr.: 241f); Mas'udi (*Tanbih*, tr.: 62, 145); Hahn (1959).
62. Mas'udi loc.cit.; Lambton (1953: 15f, notes 2 and 3).
63. Tabari (Noeldeke tr.: 248); Bal'ami (tr., II: 223–233); Altheim (1957: 57–69).
64. Summary by Cahen (1968: 108ff); on the continuity from Sassanian times, see Morony (1984b: 511); cf. also Ibn Hawqal's description (tr., II: 297f) of local practices in Fars.
65. al-Baladhuri (tr., II: 260); Miskawayh (tr., IV: 254).
66. The figures given by Ya'qubi for the reign of Mu'awiyah (midseventh century) are not considered authentic (cf. von Kremer, 1889: 1 and note 1); they are therefore disregarded here.
67. *Dinar-é rayidj* was introduced in connection with the late Ilkhanid coinage standardization. In theory, this dinar weighed 12.96 grams and was divided into six dirhams of 2.16 grams each. When actually coined, however, the silverdinars proved to be somewhat lighter, and in Mustawfi's time they weighed as little as 8–9 grams (J.M. Smith, 1969).
68. Cahen (1968: 118).
69. Ehrenkreutz (1964).
70. Ibn Khurdadhbih (tr.: 31).
71. *Tarikh-é Sistan*: 157f; Ya'qubi (tr.: 138).
72. Miskawayh (tr., IV: 254).
73. Rotter (1982: 60f) holds a different view.
74. Qudama (tr.: 184); Ibn Hawqal (tr., II: 406).
75. Waines (1977a: 284).
76. el-'Ali (1971).
77. Definitions can be found in Lambton (1953: 86, note 2); Barthold (1956, II: 128, 155f); Spuler (1955: 309).
78. Von Kremer (1888: 313); al-Muqaddasi (tr.: 215).
79. E.g. the *Sa'adat-nameh* and the *Risaleh-é falakiyeh*. These handbooks and their value as sources for Ilkhanid history have most recently been discussed by Remler (1985).
80. E.g. Petrushevskii (*CHIr* V: 507f).
81. An exception is Tabriz, but even here the information is ambiguous. In one place (Pers. text: 80), Mustawfi says that *huquq* from the surrounding districts (*vilayet*) made up 275.000 *dinar-é rayidj*, to which should be added *tamgha* from the city, yielding a total of 1.150.000 dinars. Immediately above (p. 78), however, he says that the 875.000 dinars from the city consisted of both *huquq* and *tamgha*. He describes Isfahan in the same way (p. 50f): *huquq* from the surrounding districts made up 500.000 dinars, while *huquq* and *tamgha* from the city itself totalled 350.000. Remler (1985: 172) calculates on the basis of the *Risaleh-é falakiyeh* that agriculture contributed only 12% of the Tabriz region's total taxes of 3.3 million dinars. To support his statement Remler uses Mustawi's figures but, as pointed out, these are ambiguous.
82. Nasir al-Din Tusi (*Zidj-é Ilkhani*); Schurmann (1956).

NOTES TO PART II: INTRODUCTION AND CHAPTER 4

1. E.g. Ibn Rusteh (tr.: 115).).
2. Ibn Hawqal (tr., I: 226).
3. Newman (1932: 24f); al-Muqaddasi (tr.: 171, 201).
4. Initially we should clarify what is meant by the term "Mesopotamia". The floodplain has had many names: Asuristan, Sawad, al-Iraq, etc. It has also been delimited in various ways. Thus Ibn

Rusteh (tr.: 115) identifies the Sawad with Sassanian Asuristan, "from Mosul to Abadan." However, in Sassanian times Asuristan did not comprise the Mosul region, which was called Arbayestan (cf. Morony, 1982: 4f). Here we shall follow Ibn Hawqal (tr., I: 225), who delimits Mesopotamia as the actual floodplain south of the Takrit/al-Anbar line down to Abadan. Kaskar and Kuwar Didjla (Mayshan), which were sometimes administered separately, are thus included.

5. Jacobsen (1960); Adams (1981: 14f). More detailed descriptions of the physical conditions of the floodplain can be found in Buringh (1957), Wirth (1962), Oates (1976), Beaumont et al. (1976: 333f), Redman (1978: 27–33), Adams (1981: 1–26), Charles (1988).

6. Cf. "Farmer's Almanac" in Kramer (1963: 340f); Charles (1988); Hunt (1988).

7. Adams (1981: 6).

8. Kreeb (1964: 14).

9. On sediment deposition, see Charles (1988: chap. 3.2 and 7.3).

10. Adams (1981: 22).

11. Charles (1988: 8, 33f).

12. On salinization, its effects on plant growth, and the various countermeasures, see "Salinity Problems in the Arid Zone", *Arid Zone Research* 14, Paris: UNESCO, 1961; Bernstein (1962); Kreeb (1964: 95–117, 122ff); Ganssen (1968: 129–139); see Charles (1988) especially on conditions in Mesopotamia.

13. Buringh (1957); Wirth (1962: 140); Beaumont (1976: 342f); Charles (1988).

14. Michel (1967: 126).

15. Schmieder (1965: 76f, 314–26); Michel (1972); British "hydraulic imperialism" in India is surveyed by D.R. Headrick, *The Tentacles of Progress: Technology Transfer in the Age of Imperialism, 1850–1940*: 171–196 (Oxford, 1988); see also Michel (1967) and cf. note 12 above.

16. For earlier developments we chiefly refer to Robert Adams' studies of the changing settlement and canal patterns in the central floodplain and in the Diyala region. The results of Adams' archaeological surveys (Adams, 1965, 1981) may not be representative because the surveys do not include large areas to the south and southeast of al-Kut. Also, it may be that the survey method favors certain types of settlements: traces of very early settlements may today be entirely buried under sediments or may have disappeared through erosion and the expansion of modern cultivation (cf. Adams, 1981: 37–51). Of the pottery forming the basis for dating the remains of settlements and canals, a large part remains unpublished. Nevertheless I am not aware of any major criticisms of Adams' archaeological survey methods nor of his hypotheses regarding the general lines of the development.

17. Adams (1981: 27–46).

18. Hole (1966); Gibson (1972); Adams (1981: 54f).

19. Adams (1981: 60–94).

20. The hypothesis of early salinization in the south was originally suggested by Thorkild Jacobsen and generated a long debate on the productivity of Mesopotamian agriculture. Arguments for the hypothesis can be found in Jacobsen and Adams (1958), Jacobsen (1969), Jacobsen (1982), Helbaek (1960) and Maekawa (1984). Opposed to the hypothesis are Powell (1985), Butz and Schröder (1985, with comparative data). See also the summery in Postgate (1984).

21. Cf. Hunt (1988: 192f); the extent of summer cultivation in pre-Persian times is virtually unknown.

22. Walters (1970: 159f); Van Dijk (1965: line 50–55); *RGTC* (3: 285); *CAH* (I/2: 633).

23. Oppenheim: 175; Brinkman (1979: 237); precisely when this displacement occurred is not clear, cf. van Driel (1988: 124f).

24. *RGTC* (8: 362, 366, 389f); Wiseman (*Chronicle*: 9 and text p. 53, line 26); Unger (1931: 94f); summary and discussion in van Driel (1988, with map p. 151).

25. Against Wiseman (*Chronicle*: note p.79)) who assumes that the *Banitum* Canal, one of the eastward diversions in the Babylon region was transverse. As far as I can see there is no evidence for this; cf.

van Driel (1988: 151). Assyrian sources mention canals farther north and these have been designated as forerunners of the later Nahr 'IsaCanal (Luckenbill, *Ancient Records* I: sect. 408; Grayson, *Assyrian Royal Inscrip.* II: 101; *RGTC* (5: 312); *RGTC* (8: 395); Barnett, 1963). However, the evidence is not convincing. When, in 684 B.C., Sennacherib invaded Meso-potamia, the Assyrian army sailed down the Tigris to Upiya (at the moutn of the Diyala), and from here the ships were transported on sledges overland to *Arahtu* (the Euphrates). This does not point to the existence of transverse canals in the area. Of course, tactical considerations could have played a role, but for logistical reasons invading armies always followed and used as far as possible the canals and rivers (Luckenbill, *Annals*: 73, lines 60–78).

26. On the Nahr 'Isa and the Sarat branch which is said to be Sassanian, see further Ya'qubi (tr.: 12f, 34); Kazwini (tr.: 371, 373); the *Khuzistan Chronicle* (tr.: 36); Obermeyer (1928: 123). Wilcocks (1903: 14); Le Strange (1905: 51, 65) assumes that the Dudjayl Canal had originally been transverse (with its intake between Hit and al-Anbar), but around 900 the western section had silted up and later reconstructed as a diversion from the Tigris. This hypothesis seems improbable.

27. See further Adams (1965: 76f) and Wilcocks (1903: 10f).

28. Van Laere (1980: 49f).

29. Strabo XVI.1.9; Arrian VII.7.7.

30. Ibn Sarabiyun (tr.: 71).

31. Ibn Sarabiyun (tr.: 68). The structure is called *qantara*, i.e. "bridge." Weirs are generally referred to as *shadhurwan*, cf. Le Strange's commentary to Ibn Sarabiyun (tr.: 74).

32. Adams (1981: 188, 213).

NOTES TO CHAPTER 5

1. Herodotus I.193.

2. Xenophon (*Anabasis* I.7.15). The passage is usually rejected as a later interpolation because it mistakenly says that the canals run *from* the Tigris *to* the Euphrates. On the basis of Herodotus' information, however, there is no reason to doubt that Xenophon in fact saw transverse canals near the battlefield at Cunaxa, i.e. on the northern floodplain where we later find the Nahr 'Isa and the Nahr al-Malik; cf. Barnett (1963: 20f).

3. Herodotus I.193.

4. Van Laere (1980: 23–30; on the *shaduf* and other water lifting devices, see p. 30–40).

5. Hamza (tr.: 30); al-Kazwini (tr.: 377).

6. Polybius V.51.6. Dilleman (1962: 188) would identify Libba with Qal'at Chergat just north of the confluence of the Lesser Zab and the Tigris; he therefore assumes that this canal must be identical with the Dudjayl. However, Polybius' description clearly points to a transverse canal; it is even called "royal." So I believe Dilleman's hypothesis can be dismissed. Incidentally, mention of "royal canals" (Sumerian: *id lugal*, Akkadian: *nar śarri*) occurs all the way back to UR III times. Yet none of them can have had anything to do with the Nahr al-Malik of the 10th century. Cf. Goetze (1962) and *RGTC* (5: 130 under "Hudadu"). See also Van Driel (1987: 171); Van Driel (1988: 125–26).

7. Pliny V.90 and VI.120–122. Mesopotamian cuneiform sources from Achaemenid times mention several individuals with the name "Gubaru" = Gaubaruva = Gobryas/Gobares. Among them are two satraps, the first ruling in the time of Cyrus and Cambyses, the second from 421–417 B.C. Cf. Zadok (1977: 91, 97).

8. Ammianus XXIV.2.7.; Zosimus III.16.1. Isidore of Charax (par. 1) places the intake at "Neapo-lis"(?) and the mouth at Seleucia. Ptolemy (V.17), however, informs us that the "Royal River" passes by Seleucia, but flows into the Tigris at Apamia, south of Scaphae. The latter two localities are unknown. Adams (1965: 66) would identify Scaphae with the medieval Uskaf Bani Djunayd,

on the lower course of the Nahrawan. Ptolemy's information accords better with the course of the Nahr al-Malik in the 10th century, and may possibly reflect the fact that the original Naarmalchas had been enlarged in Parthian times. Ammianus' subsequent assertion that the mouth was at Seleucia may be explained by his ignorance of details regarding the canal branchings. See also Paschoud (1978) for an attempt to trace the course of the Naarmalchas.

9. The Murashu archive consists of about 750 clay tablets. The family ran a kind of banking business, branching into landleasing and subleasing. Similar, but smaller archives have been found in Ur and Uruk. See Stolper (1985: 37f); van Driel (1987); see also Kuhrt (1987).

10. Van Driel (1987: 179).

11. Adams (1981: 178ff) estimates that from New-Babylonian to Parthian times settlement on the central floodplain tripled. At the same time urbanization increased. By Parthian times settlement *east* of the Tigris had increased sixfold, but most of this expansion occurred in post-Achaemenid times (Adams, 1981: 191).

12. Xenophon (*Anabasis* II.4.).

13. Herodotus VI.20 and VI.119; Diodorus Siculus XVII.110.4; Olmstead (1948: 437).

14. Olmstead (1948: 293, 297ff); Oppenheim in *CHIr* (II: 585). The latter admits, however, (*CHIr*, II: 577–78, note 1) that significant innovations occurred precisely within the domain of irrigation technology. The idea of stagnation is also supported by Haerinck (1987). Critics can be found in Stolper (1985: 143f, 151), van Driel (1987) and Kuhrt (1987).

15. Quintus Curtius I.5; Arrian VII.8.21 and VII.19.3–4.

16. Pliny VI.117.

17. Libanius *Orat.* XI.101, cited by Cohen (1978: 89).

18. E.g. G. von Grunebaum, *Medieval Islam*: 322f (2nd ed., Chicago 1953).

19. Sherwin-White (1987); van der Speck (1987).

20. Sherwin-White (1987: 23f).

21. The character of Seleucid colonization is discussed in Briant (1978) and Cohen (1978). The older view that Seleucid policy consciously pursued "Hellenization" is represented by Tarn (1938) and Rostovtzeff (*CAH* VII). The latter, however, expresses skepticism of the results east of the Euphrates.

22. See the summary of the sources in Tscherikower (1927).

23. Van der Speck (1987).

24. The motives of Seleucus have been discussed by Funck (1976); McDowell (1972), and Sherwin-White (1987: 16f), among others. The latter points to the strategic location on the roads to the Iranian plateau and Bactria.

25. According to Pliny (VI.30) the city had in the 1st century no fewer than 600.000 inhabitants. This is a considerable exaggeration. The site covers approximately 400 ha which, according to the usual methods of calculation, would indicate a population of about 80.000 (Adams, 1965: 175, n.7). On the other hand, Seleucia should not be seen in isolation, but as part of a larger urban complex comprising an older settlement, Upiya (Opis, Akshak), as well as Parthian Ctesiphon. On recent excavations in the Seleucia area, see Invernizzi (1976) and G. Gullini, "Un contributo alla storia dell' urbanistica: Seleucia sul Tigri," *Mesopotamia* 2: 135–163.

26. E.g. Pliny VI.30; Strabo XVI.1.

27. Smith (*Babylonian Historical Texts*: 156, line 17); Oelsner (1978 110 and note 41); Sherwin-White (1987: 18f); Pliny VI.122.

28. Sherwin-White (1987: 18f).

29. Strabo XVI.1.5; Diodorus Siculus XXXIV.5.21 and LXVIII.30; Oelsner (1978: 114).

30. Pliny VI.117; Isidore: par. 2; Tscherikower (1927: 117); Tacitus (*Annales* VI.41), however, applies the designation "Parthian" to Artemita.

31. Adams (1965: 65).

32. Pliny VI.132. On the archaeological surveys see Adams (1981: 179). Xenophon (*Anabasis* II.4.13)

mentions Sittace as a "large and populated city", but at the same time situates it on the wrong side of the Tigris. Weissbach (*PW*,"Sittake") assumes that Xenophon had confused it with Upiya, but this indicates that Xenophon actually had heard of a town with the name Sittace. Barnett (1963: 22f) proposes that Sittace be identified with Humaniyah, which is not convincing considering that medieval Humaniyah lay far down the Tigris. On Apolloniatis see Strabo (XV.3.12; XI.13.6), Isidore (par. 2), Polybius (V.43.8) and Ptolemy (VI.1.). Ptolemy places Apollonia and Sittace next to each other, but his compilation of geographic names in the East is so uncritical that he might just as well be listing the same town twice.

33. Pliny VI.132. The Diyala seems to have been known by several names in Antiquity. This one is derived from Neo-Assyrian "Turnat" (Akkadian: "Turran"); cf. *RGCT* (5: 312f).

34. Pliny VI. 126, 132, 146.

35. Pliny VI.138–140. Charax has been identified with a major site *c.* 20 km south of al-Qurna. On the locating and the history of Charax, see Hansman (1967) and Nodelman (1960).

36. Cf. G. Downing, *A History of Antioch in Syria*: 82 (Princeton 1961).

37. Briant (1978).

38. Arrian VII.21.7; Strabo XVI.1.10. It is doubtful whether Alexander had any real understanding of Mesopotamian irrigation practices. Both Strabo (XVI.1.9) and Arrian (VII.7.7) expressly say that Alexander destroyed weirs on the Euphrates and the Tigris in the belief that they were defensive works intended to prevent troop movements down the rivers. In the case of the Euphrates the destruction may also be linked to Alexander's plans to expand the harbor of Babylon (Arrian VII.19.4).

39. Polybius IX.43.1–6.

40. According to Adams (1965: 63f; 1981: 178f, 194) settlement on the central plain doubled in Seleucid and Parthian times; on the Diyala plain, however, it increased ten-fold. Cf. Gibson (1972: 51, 59, 187). On the decline of Seleucia, see Keal (1975).

41. Mas'udi (*Tanbih*, tr.: 140f).

42. Strabo XVI.1.16; Pliny VI.122; Hamza (tr.: 30); Ammianus Marcellinus (XXIII.6.23) informs us that the city was founded by King Vardanes and subsequently enlarged by Pacorus (79–115).

43. Pliny VI.122; Ptolemy V.19; Maricq (1959); Keal (1975).

44. Pliny VI.122; Tacitus: *Annales* VI.42.

45. E.g. Pigulevskaia (1956: 85f). The explanation rests on the assumption that when the classical authors applied the designation *poleis* to oriental towns, they meant *poleis* in the juridical sense (e.g. Tarn, 1938: 21). In classical Greece the *polis* was a juridically defined settlement characterized by political self-government administered by a popular assembly of citizens. Oftimes the definition also included fortifications because the city wall served as a literal guarantee of autonomy. Ultimately, however, it was the formal juridical status and not the size, the number of inhabitants, or functions which distinguished a *polis* from other forms of settlement. Nevertheless Isidore and Strabo applied the designation *polis* to Parthaunisa, Zarandj, Ctesiphon, Niniveh, and Zadrakarta and other towns which under no circumstances were Greek foundings nor had Greek colonies. We must therefore conclude that they never meant to use *polis* in the narrow, juridical sense, but simply as a synonym for "town". See also van der Speck (1987).

46. Tscherikower (1927: 112f); Kreissig (1973).

47. McDowell (1972: 159f).

48. Hamza (tr.: 30); on the place of Shapur b. Ashk in the various versions of Arsacid chronology, see Lozinski (1984: 130).

NOTES TO CHAPTER 6

1. Adams (1981: 180f, 209).
2. Tabari (Noeldeke, tr.: 12, 16); Hamza (tr.: 33); see further the summary of sources in Fiey (1967) and al-'Ali (1968).
3. Invernizzi (1976); M. M. Negro Ponzi, "The Excavations at Choche, area 1," *Mesopotamia* II: 41–48 (1967); M. Carnevale Cavallero, "The Excavations at Choche, area 2," *Mesopotamia* II: 48–56 (1967); Gullini (1964); Schinaja (1967); Venco Ricciardi (1968).
4. Hamza (tr.: 57).
5. Yaqut (tr.: 518f); Fiey (1967: 28).
6. *SKZ*: line 10; Hamza (tr.: 35); Tabari (Noeldeke, tr.: 57); al-Baladhuri (tr., I: 433).
7. Zosimus III.18.6; Ammianus Marcellinus XXIV.2.9–22; the *Hoffmann* (tr.: 88); Bal'ami (tr., III: 336).
8. *Shahristan*: par. 14; according to Tabari (Noeldeke tr.: 24) the town dated from the time of Nebuchadnezzar. He probably picked up this information from the epic traditions of the Arabs concerning the genealogies and battles of the tribes, a tradition which was independent of the official Persian historiography. In these traditions the small town of al-Hira figures prominently and the Lakhmid princes appear almost as the equals of the Sassanian kings. Of course this is misleading, but being the part of the Sassanian machinery of power with which the Arabs had most contact, the Lakhmids must have made a quite an impression; see Kister (1968).
9. Ibn Rusteh (tr.: 120); al-Baladhuri (tr., I: 461); Le Strange (1905: 65).
10. Ammianus Marcellinus XXV.9; Tabari (Noeldeke tr.: 63).
11. Hamza (tr.: 35); Tabari (Noeldeke tr.: 19f); Ibn alFaqih (tr.: 243).
12. Hamza (tr.: 35); he adds that in Syriac Shad-Shapur was called *Vabha*; Tabari (Noeldeke tr.: 40); Tha'alibi (*Ta'rikh ghurar*, tr.: 494); the *Se'ert-Chronicle*: 221; on the establishment of Kaskar as a separate administrative unit, see Morony (1982: 30f).
13. Frye (1962: 291).
14. On Ruqbat Mada'in, see Finster and Scmidt (1976: 151f); on Djidr, see Adams (1981: 205, site 004).
15. al-Baladhuri (tr., I: 389); Ya'qubi (tr.: 165); al-Khatib al-Baghdadi (Salmon tr.: 90).
16. On the course of the Nahr Nars, see Adams (1981: 206).
17. Hamza (tr.: 35); Tabari (Noeldeke tr.: 57); Adams (1965: 76).
18. Northedge (1987).
19. Tabari (Noeldeke tr.: 157).
20. *SKZ*: line 34–36; Ammianus Marcellinus XX.6; Langlois (I: 247f, II: 150f); Tabari (Noeldeke tr.: 57f).
21. Altheim (1954: 134f); Altheim (1957: 60f); his arguments are accepted by Adams (1981: 201); see also Frye (1975: 8f); Altheim's suggestion that the fiscal reorganization also aimed at providing an economic basis for the professional military, the *dihqans*, seems plausible, however.
22. E.g. Lambton (1953: 14, note 8).
23. Adams (1981: 201).
24. Al-Kazwini (tr.: 375); Adams (1981: 211); Adams (1965: 76) notices that the Katul al-Kisrawi cuts across an older canal going from the right bank of the Diyala to 'Ukbara. This town was founded by either Shapur I or Shapur II and the older canal was probably dug in connection with the founding. This also points to a late-Sassanian date for the construction of the Katul (the Muslim conquest providing the *terminus ante quem)*.
25. Ibn al-Faqih (tr.: 255f); Ya'qubi (tr.: 164).
26. Hamza (tr.: 42); Tabari (Noeldeke tr.: 239); Procopius II.14.1; John of Ephesus III.6.6 (tr.: 385f) and III.6.19 (tr.: 415); Fiey (1967: 27); el-'Ali (1968: 429f).
27. Tabari (Noeldeke tr.: 16, 41, 239); *Shahristan*: 13; Ibn al-Faqih (tr.: 243f); Markwart (1901: 142);

on the administrative division of the floodplain in late Sassanian times, see Morony (1982); on the Zibliyat site, see Adams (1981: 259, site no. 700).

28. Ibn al-Faqih (tr.: 191, 243, 255); Hamza (tr.: 41); Schwarz: 487, 689f.
29. Watson (1983).
30. Whitehouse and Williamson (1973: 43f).
31. Strabo XV.1.18; Tabari (Noeldeke tr.: 244f).
32. *Chou Sou* (tr.: 15).
33. Wulff (1966: 242f); Watson (1983: 160).
34. al-Baladhuri (tr., I: 426f).
35. Newman (1932: 103); see further the article "Baumwolle" in *PW* and Ph. Talon, "Le Coton et la Soie en Mesopotamie," *Akkadica* 47: 75–77 (1986).

NOTES TO CHAPTER 7

1. Adams (1981: 205).
2. Ibn Sarabiyun (tr.: 299f); al-Baladhuri (tr., I: 453f); Mas'udi (*Murudj*, I: 224f); Ibn Rusteh (tr.: 104f); Wüstenfeld (1864: 412); Le Strange (1905: 26f, 43); Morony (1982: 31).
3. al-Baladhuri (tr., I: 453f); Mas'udi (*Tanbih*, tr.: 63f).
4. Gottfried (1983: 8).
5. Appleby (1980). Purely biological explanations for the differences in the frequency and virulence of the plague epidemics have in fact been advanced. One hypothesis has it that the highly contagious and lethal pneumonic strain disappeared from Europe as early as the 14th century but continued to ravage the Middle East (Musallam, 1971: 436; Bean, 1962: 426f). Apparently this idea was originally suggested by Fabian Hirst, *The Conquest of Plague* (Oxford, 1953). In view of the severe mortality in some of the later European outbreaks, the idea of widely different death rates fails to convince (cf. mortality figures in H. Kamen, *The Iron Century*: 29f, 2nd ed. 1976).
6. Cockburn (1963).
7. In the case of Egypt we have somewhat better information, thanks to the mummies. Thus the mummy of Ramses V (c. 1160 B.C.) shows marks of something which looks like smallpox (Cockburn, 1980: 32). The resemblance is most likely fortuitous. The signs and symptoms of disease are liable to change considerably over long time (Poole and Holladay, 1979). If, however, Ramses V had in fact died from smallpox or, rather, some ancestral infection, this would indicate that no later than by the 12th century B.C. a lethal smallpox-like disease had appeared in the Levant. Various widely accepted theories that smallpox had been disseminated westward from India in the 2nd and 3rd centuries A.D. would then become irrelevant.
8. Most texts have survived only in first millennium copies, but much of the information seems to date from the early 2nd millennium (Oppenheim, 1962). The oldest medical text, in Sumerian, dates from the late 3rd millennium. Unfortunately the part containing descriptions of symptoms has been broken (Kramer, 1961: 104–108). See further the texts collected by Labat, Geller, van Dijk et al., Oppenheim (1964: 292ff); Meissner (1925, II: 259); Ch. Virolleaud, "Présages tirés des eclipses de soleil," *ZA* 16: 215, 217 (1902); Thompson (II: no. 216, 231, 232); Contenau (1938: 104, 135); Grayson (1964).
9. Biggs (1969: 97). At the end of the 12th century B.C. Babylonian troops were infected when campaigning in Khuzistan (*CAH* II/2: 455). Further examples in Oppenheim: 63; Ungnad (1914: no. 97); Grayson (*Assyrian and Babylonian Chronicles*: 76, line 5); Luckenbill (II: sect. 791, 796); Smith (*Historical Texts*: 156 (line 14), 157 (line 20)).
10. The terminology is discussed by Labat: xxif.
11. E.g. Geller: line 549f; Nougayrol (1949); van Dijk: no. 73.
12. E.g. Goetze (1957); Myhrmann (1902: 141–200); van Dijk: no. 20, 86; Meissner (1925, I: 201; II: 390f).

13. Cockburn (1980: 84); Zakaria (1958); Malek (1961); Labat (XIV: 39); Meissner (1925, II: 303); Contenau (1938: 188).
14. May (1961); and summary in Grmek (1983).
15. Cf. Grmek (1983: 265).
16. Pritchard: 394f; Schwartz (1938).
17. McNeill (1976: 97, 112).
18. Cf. Gilliam (1961).
19. Thucydides II.47; Herodotus VIII.115; Diodorus Siculus XII.12.1–6, XII.14.2, XII.86.1–2, XIV.70.4–71, XV.24.4; Seibert (1983).
20. Aymard (1975); J.D. Haas and G.G. Harrison, "Nutrional Anthropology and Biological Adaption," *Annual Review of Anthropology* 6: 69–101 (1977).
21. Ellison (1981).
22. Butz and Schröder (1985: 171).
23. See summary in C. Tudge, *The Famine Business*: 70f (London, 1977, Penguin ed. 1979).
24. Malek (1961: 298f).
25. Appleby (1975).
26. Kass (1971).
27. E.C. Stone (1981).
28. Labat: XL; Zimmern (1917: line 20f); on Nergal as god of war, death, chaos, famine, and pestilence, see Weiner (1971) and discussion in J.M.M. Roberts (1972: 21f).
29. Data and hypotheses are summarized and discussed by Salmon (1974); see also Frier (1982).
30. It has been suggested that the fall of Ur III around 2000 B.C. was caused by a combination of drought, famine, and an early, hitherto unknown outbreak of plague (Vanstiphout, 1974). The argument is based on some passages in "The Lament for the Destruction of Ur" (see Pritchard: 612f), where it is said that the city was "struck" with the weapons of the gods, an expression which may mean "visited by pestilence." However, it may refer to other kinds of disasters as well. It is conceivable, of course, that Ur III was ravaged by a lethal epidemic, but it can hardly have been plague. As far as we know there were no plague foci anywhere near Mesopotamia at that time. The rodent communities of Kurdistan became carriers of the disease at a much later date (cf. Dols, 1979: 178 f and note 38; *CHIr* I: 296, 302).
31. Thucydides II.47. As it is the earliest thoroughly documented epidemic, "the Plague of Athens" has attracted a good deal of scholarly attention. The disease has not been identified. Smallpox, scarlet fever, measles, typhus fever, plague, influenza, even ergotism have been suggested. Recently it has been diagnosed as tularaemia, an acute bacterial infection also known as "rabbit fever" (Wylie and Stubbs, 1983). However, none of these diseases correspond to Thucydides' description. Most likely the "plague" was not a disease we know today. It may have been an ancestral form of a modern disease, but in that case very different from its descendant. Or it may simply have become extinct long ago (Poole and Holladay 1979).
32. Ammianus Marcellinus XXIII.6.24; *SHA*: Lucius Verus VIII and Marcus Aurelius XIII; Michael the Syrian (tr., I: 186).
33. Boak (1955); McNeill (1976); Wells (1964: 86); regarding the Parthians, see Bivar (1970).
34. Cassius Dio (71.2.4) only says that the troops of Verus and Avidius Cassius fell ill during their retreat to Syria. Later Dio (73.14.4) tells us that an epidemic in 189–190 in Rome was the worst he had witnessed or even heard of (cf. Herodian I.12.1–2).
35. The sources for the Plague of the Antonines, including the epigraphic material, have been analyzed by Gilliam (1961). I follow his conclusions.
36. Cyprian (*De Mortalitate*); Eusebius VII.22.
37. *SHA* (Gallieni Duo V.5–6); Zosimus I.26.2 and I.37.3; Michael the Syrian (tr., I: 193).
38. E.g. Newman (1932: 23f).
39. Ps.Stylites (tr.: 31–34).

40. Dols (1977: 13–35); Biraben and LeGoff (1969).
41. Procopius I.23.21; John of Ephesus (Brooks tr.: 212, 437, 531); Michael the Syrian (tr., II: 238f).
42. On the basis of Procopius' account it is sometimes assumed that the pneumonic plague strain rarely appeared in the first pandemic, e.g. Gottfried (1983: 12). In the Middle East spring and early summer were indeed the plague seasons (cf. Ibn Masawayh, tr.: 13), and pneumonic plague usually appears in fall and winter when temperatures drop and the infection moves into the lungs. However, some outbreaks did in fact occur in the winter (e.g. Dionysius of Tell-Mahré, tr.: 10). At all events, the accounts leave the impression that death rates were enormous by any standards.
43. The two oldest *Kitab al-tawa'in*, i.e. "Books of Plague," known to us were written by al-Asma'i (dead 828) and al-Mada'ini (dead 840). The former was transmitted through Ibn Qutayba's *Kitab al-ma'arif* (late 9th century), the latter through al-Nawawi's *Sharh muslim* from the second half of the 13th century. Al-Nawawi's version of the Basrah tradition served as source for the brief accounts of the first plague found in the books of plague written during the second pandemic. The transmission of the Basrah tradition is analyzed by Conrad (1981).
44. The original *Kitab al-tawa'in* distinguished carefully between *waba'*, i.e. lethal epidemic diseases in general, and *ta'un*, plague. Syriac sources likewise used a specific term for plague, *shar'uta* (Conrad, 1982). Later this terminological distinction was disregarded, at least in Persian sources, where terms alone do not allow any identification of the infections mentioned.
45. Michael the Syrian (tr., II: 268).
46. Michael the Syrian (tr., II: 373f).
47. Tabari (Noeldeke tr.: 385); Michael the Syrian (tr., II: 412); Ibn Qutayba and al-Mada'ini cited by Conrad (1981: 55, 62).
48. Ibn Qutayba and al-Mada'ini cited by Conrad (1981: 55, 62); Elias: 110; Michael the Syrian (tr., II: 431).
49. Tabari (Morony tr.: 87).
50. John Bar-Penkaye (Brock tr.: 68; Mingana tr.: 187f).
51. Ibn Qutayba and al-Mada'ini cited by Conrad (1981: 55, 62).
52. Dionysius of Tell-Mahré (tr.,: 10); Ibn Qutayba and al-Mada'ini cited by Conrad (1981: 55f, 62).
53. Ibn Qutayba cited by Conrad (1981: 56).
54. Ibn Qutayba cited by Conrad (1981: 56).
55. Dionysius of Tell-Mahré (tr.: 32f, 54); Tabari (Williams tr.: 121); Ibn Qutayba and al-Mada'ini cited by Conrad (1981: 57, 62).
56. Dionysius of Tell-Mahré (tr.: 178–186); Elias: 130–131.
57. Tha'alibi (*Lata'if*, tr.: 119); Conrad (1982: 273, 283).
58. Biraben and LeGoff (1969).
59. Russell (1968: 180).
60. Cf. table 6, p. Only Mas'udi (*Tanbih*, tr.: 62) dates the Sassanian figures later, to the reign of Khusraw I.
61. Morony (1984b: 119f, 584f), ignoring the plague, doubts that the difference reflects a real drop.
62. E.g. Dionysius of Tell-Mahré (tr.: 102f); Cahen (1954).
63. al-Baladhuri (tr., I: 450); A. L. Udovitch (ed.): *The islamic Middle East, 700–1900*: 62 (Princeton 1981).
64. On the American death rates, see Crosby (1976); Cook (1981); D. Joralemon, "New World Depopulation and the Case of Disease," *Journal of Anthropological Research* 38: 108–127 (1982).
65. Cook (1981: 134).
66. Eckholm (1976: 85–89).

Notes to Chapter 8

1. Mustawfi *(Nuzhat* tr.: 32f), says that as an official in the fiscal administration in Baghdad, he had seen an assessment of Mesopotamia – dating from the time of the caliph al-Nasir (1180–1225) – of not less than 30 million *dinar-é rayidj*, approximately the equivalent of 130 million Abbasid dirhams when converted according to silver weight. Considering the large areas which even at that time had gone out of production, the figure seems entirely improbable. It is presumably the result of an error in copying.
2. See Ibn Hawqal (tr., I: 226).
3. al-Muqaddasi (tr.: 47, 51, 171); Mas'udi, *Tanbih* (tr.: 64, 507).
4. al-Baladhuri (tr., I: 453f). In non-Muslim sources the memory of the destructive character of the Arab conquest appears even more clearly; e.g. Ps Sebeos (tr.: 99f, 104f, 108f); Michael the Syrian (tr., II: 413f).
5. al-Baladhuri (tr., II: 65f); Ibn al-Faqih (tr.: 202, 223ff).
6. Shaban (1971, I: 55). My understanding of the political instability in Mesopotamia in the decades after the conquest is largely based on Shaban's work.
7. Shaban (1971: 88f).
8. Ziyad began in 672/73 by sending 50.000 men with their families to Marv, the most important Arab base in the east. In 698/699 al-Hadjdjadj attempted to send 40.000 men to Sistan, but they revolted when they realized that they were not supposed to return. In 731/32 the caliph Hisham got rid of an additional 20.000 men. They were also sent to Marv (al-Baladhuri (tr., II: 171); Hamza Isfahani (tr.: 169); Shaban (1971, I: 88, 110f, 140).
9. al-Baladhuri (tr., I: 454ff); Ibn Sarabiyun (tr.: 299ff); Morony (1984a: 213f).
10. For example, Abu Yusuf al-Ansari (tr.: 106), Yahya b. Adam (tr.: 53).
11. In Muslim jurisprudence, *qati'a (qata'i)* denotes land which the state transferred to private persons for an indefinite period. They thereby incurred an obligation to bring the land under cultivation (Qudama, Ben Shemesh tr.: 31; Cahen 1968: 149f).
12. al-Baladhuri (tr., II: 78ff); Ibn al-Faqih (tr.: 229ff); Morony (1981 and 1984a). On Basrah's early history see also Pellat (1953: 1–48).
13. Ibn Sarabiyun (tr.: 303); al-Baladhuri (tr., I: 455f and II: 97ff).
14. The canal system is described in Ibn Sarabiyun (tr.: 303f (west). See also note 2, p. 305, and 307f (east); al-Baladhuri (tr., II: 78ff); Ibn Rusteh (tr.: 104f); Ibn Hawqal (tr., I: 228f).
15. Djahiz (tr.: 41).
16. al-Baladhuri (tr., II: 97f); Morony (1984a: 216).
17. al-Muqaddasi (tr.: 184, 208); on special, local infections see also Abu al-Hasan al-Tabari (tr: 137). Because of the brackish water, schistosomiasis was probably not widespread, however (cf. Malek 1961: 315).
18. al-Baladhuri (tr., I: 450); Ya'qubi (tr.: 165); Wüstenfeld (1864: 410); Le Strange (1905: 39f).
19. al-Baladhuri (tr., I: 450); Le Strange's note 5 to Ibn Sarabiyun (tr.: 260); Obermeyer (1928: 307); Adams (1981: 206, 277).
20. al-Baladhuri (tr., I: 455); Shaban (1971, I: 143).
21. Summary of the archeological material in Adams (1981: 218). See also Finster and Schmidt (1976: 164ff).
22. Ibn Battuta (tr., II: 321).
23. For example, Miskawayh (tr., V: 123f, 133ff).
24. Ibn Sarabiyun (tr.: 256).
25. al-Baladhuri (tr., I: 456); further examples of colonization activities in Umayyad and early Abbasid times are summarized in Morony (1984a). Maslamah, by the way, was involved in similar initiatives as far away as Bayt Balash in North Syria (Dionysius of Tell-Mahré, tr.: 24).
26. al-Tanukhi VIII/55 (tr. in *IC* 4, 1930: 233f).

27. Ibn Khallikan (tr., IV: 316). al-Tanukhi loc. cit.
28. Ibn Hawqal (tr., I: 231f); Wüstenfeld (1864: 409f, 412f).
29. Rashid al-Din (Quatremére tr.: 311); Krawulsky (1978: 479).
30. See table 7.
31. Ibn Battuta (tr., II: 272f).
32. al-Ghiyati (tr.: 101f, 107, 117f, 125f).
33. Abbé Carré (III: 849).
34. Le Strange (1905: 40).
35. Abbé Carré (III: 848).
36. Wüstenfeld (1864: 410); Fraser (II: 122).
37. Today, at any rate, the area around Wasit is salinated; cf. Beaumont (1975: 330).
38. Morony (1984a: 216f); Lapidus (1981: 187).
39. Popovic (1976: 52f, 64f).
40. The first viewpoint is asserted by Popovic (1976), the second by H. Halm (1967: 52).
41. Mas'udi *(Tanbih* tr.: 472).
42. Ibn Hawqal (tr., I: 228f).
43. Nasir-é Khusraw (tr.: 235f).
44. Ibn Hawqal (tr., I: 230).
45. Mustawfi *(Nuzhat* tr.: 45f); Ibn Battuta (tr., II: 275f).
46. E.g. Cesare Federico (1563) in Hakluyt (V: 371f).
47. Teixeira (28f).
48. Yaqut *(Mu'djam,* V: 847); Wüstenfeld (1864: 406ff); Le Strange (1905: 58).
49. Adams (1965: 99); his accompanying reflections on the decline as an expression of a difference between an agrarian Sassanian civilization and a more urban-mercantile Muslim culture are speculative; they are redundant as well, considering that the population loss during the plague provides a simpler explanation.
50. Al-Mada'in had apparently been damaged and partly abandoned during the Arab conquest, cf. al-Baladhuri (tr., I: 417); Michael the Syrian (tr., II: 424); The "Khuzistan Chronicle" (tr.: 34); Ps. Sebeos (tr.: 99). Bahurasir, i.e. Veh-Ardashir, continued, however, to exist as a small town, surrounded by extensive ruins which even in the 12th century drew amazement from travellers, cf. Ibn Djubayr (tr.: 225); Wüstenfeld (1864: 407).
51. See the summary and discussion in Lassner (1970: 157ff).
52. Wüstenfeld (1864: 428); Mas'udi *(Murudj* VII: 120ff) and *Tanbih* (tr.: 457f); Rogers (1970).
53. Ibn Hawqal (tr., I: 236).
54. Le Strange (1905: 58).
55. al-Suli (tr., I (al-Radi): 172f); Miskawayh (tr., IV: 439f).
56. al-Suli (tr., II (al-Muttaqi): 52).
57. Miskawayh (tr., V: 110, note).
58. Miskawayh (tr., V: 177); Ibn Hawqal (tr., I: 236).
59. Rudhrawari (tr.: 69f); Nizam al-Mulk (tr.: 75f).
60. Rudhrawari (tr.: 71).
61. Miskawayh (tr.: 100ff). In Muslim jurisprudence there appear several forms of *iqta'*. The core of the concept was a transfer of rights to demand taxes, wholly or partly, from a certain area over a restricted period of time. An *iqta'* allotment was thus an administrative measure which in principle had nothing to do with property relations. In pre-Buyid times *iqta'* forms of payment were chiefly used in areas which were assessed according to *'ushr/sadaqa* rates. During the 10th century they increasingly came to include land covered by *kharadj* taxation, and this in a very noticeably manner reduced the income directly available to the central power. The system was further diffused in Saldjuq times. Regarding the *iqta'* institution and its superficial similarities with the feudal fiefs of Western Europe, see Cahen (1953, 1960); Cahen (1968: 203f); and Lambton (1965).

62. Adams (1965: 104f); Le Strange (1905: 59f); Wüstenfeld (1864: 406).

63. Jacobsen (1982); Wüstenfeld (1864: 406ff); Ibn Djubayr (tr.: 239).

64. Le Strange (1905: 59); Ibn Djubayr (tr.: 239ff); Ibn Battuta (tr., II: 346); Mustawfi (*Nuzhat* tr.: 47); al-Ghiyati (tr.: 106, 113).

65. See table 7; Wassaf (tr.: 78f).

66. With al-Ghiyati as source we can list the following disasters after the fall of the Ilkhanid Empire: Timur-é Lenk sacked Baghdad in 1393. In 1401 he returned and massacred the inhabitants. Qara Yusuf Qara-qoyunlu plundered the town in 1404. Renewed pillaging took place in 1411, in 1446 (when 10.000 were supposed to have died), and in 1466. Furthermore, the Tariq-é Khurasan district was ravaged in 1433 and 1456. In 1465 it was the turn of the Tigris' east bank, and a few years later Uzun Hasan deported peasants from here to Diyarbakir. In 1478 Turkoman armies again pillaged the region.

67. Ibn Hawqal (tr., I: 234); Rudhrawari (tr.: 69); Ibn Djubayr (tr.: 226, 234ff).

68. Around 1470, i.e. immediately after the prolonged wars between the Qara-qoyunlu and the Aq-qoyunlu, the Venetian Barbaro was told that Baghdad was considerably damaged and hardly had more than 10.000 dwellings (Barbaro: 79). A hundred years later the descriptions are much more positive, cf. Cesare Federico and John Eldred in Hakluyt (V: 368f and VI: 5).

69. Teixeira: 60ff.

70. Part of the decline in settlement on the Diyala Plain seems to have taken place later, in the 18th and 19th centuries. See A. Invernizzi, "Excavations in the Yelkhi Area," *Mesopotamia*, vol. 15, 1980: 23f and note 7.

71. The surveys carried out by Adams on the central plain in 1956–1957 focused exclusively on the pre-Persian epochs, cf. Adams (1958). In recent decades agrarian re-expansion and state construction works has reduced the possibilities for conducting representative investigations in the north (Adams 1981: 209). The ancient Kish region, comprising parts of the countryside along the Nahr Kutha, was surveyed in the early 1970s (Gibson 1972); but we are unable to draw any major conclusions from this research, because the historical framework used by Gibson for interpreting his data is faulty (e.g. dating of the transverse canals to Muslim times; cf. Gibson 1974).

72. al-Khatib al-Baghdadi (Lassner tr.: 100); Le Strange's comment to Ibn Sarabiyun (tr.: 73ff).

73. Miskawayh (tr., IV: 200).

74. al-Suli (tr., I: 210f); Miskawayh (tr., V: 9). al-Suli (tr., I: 116) states that the *amir* Tuzun in 944 also made a futile attempt at repairing the breach.

75. al-Suli (tr., I: 166).

76. al-Suli (tr., I: 64).

77. Miskawayh (tr., V: 177).

78. Cf. Miskawayh's characterization of Mu'izz al-Dawleh (tr., V: 154).

79. Miskawayh (tr., V: 443–446); Rudhrawari (tr., I: 69).

80. al-Istakhri (tr.: 53); Ibn Hawqal (tr., I: 230ff).

81. Ibn Djubayr (tr.: 221f).

82. Ibn Battuta (tr., II: 324f). Notice that here – as elsewhere in his description of Mesopotamia – he uses Ibn Djubayr as source. The information can therefore be out of date, even though Ibn Battuta generally seems to have been careful in keeping his material up to date (cf. his description of Basrah).

83. Krawulsky (1978: 500, 505ff).

84. Maintenance and repair work must therefore still have been undertaken regularly. However, the Ilkhanids are not noted for any great efforts in this field, perhaps because the works they began were all too routine to attract the attention of the chroniclers. These instead focused on a number of canal works around the Shi'ite shrines. Abaqa thus spent 100.000 dinars on a new canal from the Euphrates to Nadjaf; Ghazan Khan, too, constructed canals all the way to Nadjaf and Karbalah and founded villages along them (Wassaf, tr.: 112; Krawulsky, 1978: 481).

85. Hakluyt (V: 366ff and VI: 3ff). Eldred travelled during the summer, after the harvest. Having spent two years in Baghdad, however, his knowledge of local conditions must have been sufficient that he would not have mistaken stubble fields for desert.

86. Teixeira: 74.

87. Abbé Carré (III: 863).

88. As late as the 19th and the beginning of the 20th centuries, remains of the old canals carried some water from the Euphrates into the central plain. During the interwar period they were repaired and extended by the British. It is not entirely clear how these canals relate to the great feeder canals of the early Middle Ages. Much depends on where one locates the village of Dimmima, which is mentioned in the descriptions from the 10th century. As a rule, the Nahr 'Isa is identified with the Saqlawiyah Canal, the Nahr Sarsar with the Nahr Abu Ghurayb, the Nahr al-Malik with the Radhwaniyah, and the Nahr Kutha with the Habl Ibrahim (Le Strange, 1905: 69; Wirth, 1962: 140). Krawulsky (1978: 476, 500, 506f), however, would identify the Nahr 'Isa with the Abu Ghurayb, the Sarsar with the Nahr Yusufiyah, and the Nahr al-Malik with the Nahr al-Latifiyah. The question remains, then, as to the origins of the Saqlawiyah canal, for the medieval sources leave no doubt that the Nahr 'Isa was the northernmost of the transverse canals. Nor does Krawulsky discuss the localition of the Nahr Kutha. In any case, identifications will be tentative because the canals have constantly changed their course due to floods, repairs, etc.

89. C. Niebuhr, *Reisebeschreibung nach Arabien und andern umliegenden Ländern*, II: 291f (Copenhagen, 1778).

90. Adams (1978: 387); Adams (1981: 210).

91. Beaumont et al. (1976: 183f and Table 5.5).

92. Barkan (1970: 171, table 4).

93. Mustawfi *(Nuzhat* tr.: 34).

94. Adams (1965: 106f); see also B. Lewis, "The Mongols and the Muslim Polity" in *Islam in History*, ed. B. Lewis (London, 1973).

95. Waines (1977a).

96. Elias (tr.: 131).

97. Hamza (tr.: 188f).

98. al-Baladhuri: *Ansab al-Ashraf*, cited in Conrad (1982: 273). Use of the term *ta'un* during this time cannot be taken as evidence of actual plague.

99. Tabari, cit. Conrad (1982: 283); Tha'alibi *(Kitab al-lata'if* tr.: 119).

100. al-Suli (tr., II: 69).

101. Hamza: 195; Miskawayh, II: 168 (tr., V: 180). A description of the symptoms of *mashara* can be found in Abu al-Hasan alTabari (tr.: 157f).

102. Elias (tr.: 150).

103. von Kremer (1880: 121f).

104. von Kremer (1880: 121).

105. von Kremer (1880: 124); Dols (1977: 32) asserts that this *may* have been plague.

106. von Kremer (1880: 129).

107. ibid.

108. von Kremer (1880: 130).

109. von Kremer (1880: 130ff).

110. There is no direct evidence for schistosomiasis, only the indications provided by, for instance, references to haematuria, e.g. in Thabit b. Sinan's medical handbook from the end of the 9th century (Meyerhof, 1930: 67). On trachoma, see Meyerhof (1936). On leprosy, see Dols (1983). For a general impression of what diseases and infections were usual in Baghdad at the beginning of the 10th century, consult the records of the famous doctor al-Razi (Meyerhof, 1935). See also Ibn Masawayh (tr.: 117, 129, 133).

111. Meyerhof (1930: 66); Mez (1922: 392).

112. Elias (tr.: 137).

113. Elias (tr.: 138).
114. Elias (tr.: 141).
115. Miskawayh (tr., V: 9); al-Suli (tr., II: 116).
116. Miskawayh (tr., V: 464); Elias (tr.: 145).
117. al-Suli (tr., II: 69).
118. Miskawayh (tr., V: 99).
119. Miskawayh (tr., V: 180).
120. Miskawayh (tr., V: 446).
121. Hilal al-Sabi' (tr.: 365).
122. Miskawayh (tr., V: 9, 177, 446).
123. Ashtor (1976: 220f); Ashtor (1968). In both studies Ashtor draws far-reaching conclusions on the basis of the hypothesis of chronic malnutrition.
124. Dols (1977: 45f, 310f).
125. al-Ghiyati (tr.: 122f).
126. See the summary in Sticker (1908 I/1: 237ff).
127. Dols (1977: 223); Dols (1981).

NOTES TO CHAPTER 9

1. The Achaemenids called the country *Shush*. From this the Greeks and Romans derived names like *Susis* and *Susiana*. Another name which appears in the classical sources is *Elymais*, presumably a distortion of *Elam*. The name *Khuzistan*, used by both Parthians and Sassanians (cf. SKZ line 1–35), and the corresponding Syriac name, *Beth Huzaye*, both seem to be derived from an ethnic name.

2. The identification of the territorial and political units in Elam, mentioned in Mesopotamian sources from the 3rd millennium B.C. and onward, is problematic indeed. However, there seems to be agreement that *Anshan*, the political center of Elam, is identical with the Marvdasht Plain in Fars (Hansman, 1972). As for the other units, the suggested localizations are conflicting. *Shimashki*, for instance, has been identified with three different regions: Isfahan (Hansman in *CHIr* II: 25–35), northeastern Kirman, i.e. Shahdab (Vallat 1985), and Nihawand-Kangavar-Burudjird in the Zagros (Stolper 1982; see also Hinz in *CAH* II/1). *Awan* has been interpreted as another name for Anshan (Hansman in *CHIr* II) as well as a locality somewhere in Kurdistan (Vallat, 1985). Finally *Marhashi* has been sought in Baluchistan (Vallat 1985), Fars, and western Kirman where Tepe Yahya would have been the center (Steinkeller 1982).

3. When and why this downcutting occurred is a problem. Apparently, in pre-historic times the river beds lay higher, which made irrigation easier but also increased the danger of flooding (Kirkby 1976: 280ff; Dollfus 1985). The construction of the great weirs in Sassanian times shows that by then the hydrological changes had taken place.

4. More detailed descriptions of the environment in Khuzistan can be found in Kirkby (1976); Ehlers (1975: 5–17); and Adams (1962).

5. Dollfus (1985); Carter and Stolper (1984).

6. In 1948 Donald McCown carried out an archaeological survey of the Ahwaz/Ram-Hormuz/Hendidjan region, concluding that significant settlement expansion first took place in Sassanian and early Muslim times. McCown never published his data, but recently they have been re-examined by Alizadeh who would date the expansion somewhat earlier, i.e. to the last centuries B.C. (Alizadeh 1985).

7. E.g. Tha'alibi *(Lata'if* tr.: 126).

8. See the articles on Khuzistan in *Paléorient* 11/2 1985.

9. The mixed-up and confused river-names of the classical sources are discussed by Le Rider (1965 chap. 4); Hansman (1967); and Kirkby (1976: 272ff).

10. Strabo XV.3.2–3 and XV.3.11.
11. Strabo loc. cit.; Arrian III.16.6.; Boucharlat (1985); Perrot (1985: 67ff).
12. Herodotus VI.20.
13. Arrian VIII.42.5.
14. E.g. Strabo XV.3.4. and Pliny VI.134. The relations between the tribes and the Achaemenid Empire are discussed by Briant (1982b: 67–94).
15. Briant (1978: 65); Briant (1982a: 84f).
16. Pliny VI. 135–136. Diodorus XIX.19.1. The identification of Hedyphon with the Djarrahi has been suggested by Le Rider (1965: 261ff, 354). The location of Seleucia-on-the Red Sea is discussed by Tscherikower (1927: 98) and Le Rider (1965: 270 and note 11). According to Strabo (XV.3.11) there were no ports on the Khuzistan coast, but as this information probably came from Nearchus it may well have been dated by Parthian times. In the 2nd cent. Ptolemy (VI.3) listed many villages and *poleis* in Susiana. Except for Susa, none of these can be identified or located.
17. Adams (1962: 116); Wenke (1975); Hansman (1978); Alizadeh (1985).
18. Strabo XV.1.18; Diodorus Siculus XIX.13.6.; Wenke (1975: 107f).
19. Pigulevskaia (1963: 82f); Boucharlat (1985: 76f); Wenke (1975: 60–80) believes on the basis of a revised dating of the archaeological data from the Susa-Diz area that the settlement maximum in Khuzistan was achieved under local rulers in late Parthian times. This hypothesis does not accord with the written sources' reports about Sassanian colonization activities, and Wenke's arguments that the gigantic weir- and city-founding schemes were never fully implemented is not convincing. *If* general changes in the settlement pattern – such as an increased urbanization and a decline in the number of villages – did occur in Sassanian times, the cause might as well be sought in changes in the organization of agricultural production, e.g. in the form of increased large-scale farming. In any case, I see no reason to doubt that cultivation did in fact reach a maximum extent in Sassanian times and that this largely was the result of the constructions carried out by the great kings.
20. Strabo XVI.1.8.
21. Tabari (Noeldeke tr.: 32ff); Hamza (tr.: 35); Tha'alibi, *Ta'rikh ghurar*: 527; Mas'udi, *Murudj* II: 184 (here, however, the credit goes to Shapur II). According to Yaqut (tr.: 534) Ardashir I dug the Mashruqan. As the construction of the Great Weir across the Karun must have involved a temporary diversion of the river's waters, it is possible that Ardashir did in fact begin the construction work. Hamza (tr.: 34f) has the more likely explanation that Shapur I built the canal and then named it after his father; see also Schwarz: 300f, and Smith (1971: 56f).
22. Schwarz: 303.
23. Le Strange (1905 :236f); Smith (1971: 59).
24. Ibn al-Faqih (tr.: 256); Mas'udi, *Murudj* II: 285; Yaqut (tr.: 218); Schwarz: 354.
25. E.g. Adams (1962: 116).
26. Cassius Dio LXVIII.28.
27. *SKZ* lines 25–26; Hamza (tr.: 35); Tabari (Noeldeke tr.: 41); Mustawfi (*Nuzhat*, tr.: 109); Schwarz: 303f.
28. Tabari (Noeldeke tr.: 57ff); Hamza (tr.: 38); Mas'udi, *Murudj* II: 185f; Tha'alibi, *Tar'rikh ghurar*: 529; Yaqut (tr.: 534); Ammian XX.6.7 and XX.7.15; the *Se'ert-Chronicle*: 78; Stein (1940,: 171f); Hansman (1967). According to the Muslim historians Shapur II actually founded two towns in the area: *Iran-Khurreh-Shapur* and *Iranshahr-Shapur*. Although confused, the towns were clearly not identical. The explanation is apparently that Old Susa (*Shush*) was damaged during a revolt, rebuilt, and then officially re-named *Iranshahr-Shapur Iran-Khurreh-Shapur* – the remains of which are today called *Ivan-é Karkh* – stood 25 km further north.
29. *SKZ*: line 5.
30. Tabari (Noeldeke tr: 13); Hamza (tr.: 33f); Ibn al-Faqih (tr.: 243, 256); Schwarz: 315f.
31. Schwarz: 297ff, 303, 310; Layard (846: 53); Kirkby (1976: 278).
32. Yaqut (tr.: 576f); Schwarz: 307ff.

33. Hansman (1978); Schwarz: 371f; Yaqut (tr.: 242) credits "Kavadh b. Dara" with the buildings.
34. Tabari (Noeldeke tr.: 46, 57); Hamza (tr.: 37); Mustawfi *(Nuzhat* tr.: 109); Krawulsky (1978: 352 and note 1).
35. Herodotus I.193; Diodorus Siculus XIX.13.6; Newman (1932 chap: VI).
36. The Babylonian Talmud cited in Newman (1932: 90f); Ibn Hawqal (tr. II: 251); Schwarz: 403.
37. Cf. p. 71 above.
38. Ibn Hawqal loc.cit; Schwarz: 337, 349, 422.
39. Ibn al-Faqih (tr.: 256); Mas'udi, *Murudj* II: 285; Yaqut (tr.: 218).
40. Schwarz: 471; Stein (1940): 44f, 48f, 56, 71f, 117, 122, 190, 193f, 229, 235.
41. Neely (1974); Kirkby (1976).
42. Kinneir: 85ff; Layard (1846 passim).
43. Ibn Khurdadhbih (tr.: 31); al-Tanukhi VIII/114 *IC* 3, 1929: 509.
44. Schwarz: 349, 386; Le Strange (1905: 238); Whitcomb (1985).
45. Hamza (tr.: 144, 150); Ibn al-Faqih (tr.: 281f); Schwarz: 319; Ibn Hawqal (tr. II: 254); al-Tanukhi loc.cit.
46. Cited in Lambton (1953: 95f).
47. Ibn Battuta (tr. II: 281, 283ff, 287f).
48. Benjamin of Tudela (tr.: 298).
49. al-Ghiyati (tr.: 126f). See also W. Caskel, "Ein Mahdi des 15. Jahrhunderts. Saijid Muhammad ibn Falah und seine Nachkommen," *Islamica* 4 1931: 48ff.
50. Teixeira: 26.
51. Krawulsky (1978: 350, note 2 and 352, note 3).
52. Ibid.; Kinneir: 85ff.
53. Layard (1846: 42, 44).
54. Newman (1932: 23f).
55. E.g. Tha'alibi *(Lata'if* tr.: 126, he relies on Djahiz) and Yaqut (tr.: 59f, 217).
56. Mas'udi, *Murudj* II: 233.
57. Cf. the description given by Layard (1846).

NOTES TO CHAPTER 10

1. Winter crops are sown in October-November and can be harvested, as a rule, in May-June. Spring crops are sown from the end of February until April and are harvested from the end of June (barley) to September (wheat).
2. Mustawfi *(Nuzhat* tr.: 154).
3. Abbott in *JRGS* 27, 1857: 154, 176, 180; Abbott: *Cities and Trade*: 122, 133, 161, 164f, 173, 183, 221.
4. Issawi (1971: chap. 5).
5. J. Malcolm, *Sketches of Persia*, vol. I: 12f (London 1828).
6. de Vries (1976: 35f); Braudel (1967: 78f).
7. E.g. the 40 million estimated by Chardin (Issawi, 1971: 28).
8. Cf. the article "Iran" in *The Middle East and North Africa 1988* (Europe Publications, London); data on the extent of fallow vary somewhat, cf. Beaumont et al. (1976: 446).
9. For further details on hydrological conditions, see Beaumont et al. (1976: 26f, 447ff); CHIr (I: 93ff, 574f).
10. Embanked fields is a technique applied in arid areas where precipitation frequently occurs as heavy downpours. At the end of the field a low earthen embankment is raised, which prevents the rainwater from running off. When the soil has absorbed the water, the field is plowed and sown. This technique for holding moisture is still used in Baluchistan-Makran. It is generally associated with extensive methods of subsistence. (Schmieder, 1965: 69).

11. Clevenger (1969); Smith (1971: 63f).
12. Bonine (1982); Goblot (1979); Beaumont et al. (1976: 88f); Troll (1972), with extensive bibliography; English (1966: 135–140, Appendix D); Wulff (1966: 249ff); Cressey (1958); Smith (1953).
13. Cressey (1958: 36); Wulff (1966: 249); Gentelle (1977: 253).
14. Stewart (1911: 341).
15. Smith (1953: 79).
16. English (1966: 139f); other estimates in Wulff (1966: 254) and Goblot (1979: 41f).
17. Bonine (1982).
18. Goblot (1979: 42).
19. Goblot (1979: 41f).
20. E.g. Ibn Rusteh (tr.: 177f).
21. Aubin (1970).
22. Yaqut (tr.: 274).
23. Ibn al-Balkhi (tr.: 39, 49, 53).
24. Ibn Rusteh (tr.: 175ff); Ya'qubi (tr.: 77f); Yaqut (tr.: 44, 195). On Nishapur and Shiraz, see pp. 194f and 168f.
25. Aubin (1970).
26. Ibn Hawqal (tr. II: 418, 423).
27. Ibn Hawqal (tr. II: 275f, 402f, 417f); al-Isfizari (tr.: 13).
28. Cf. p. 146f below.
29. Ibn Hawqal (tr. II: 437ff); Le Strange (1905: 285).
30. Mez (1922: 409).
31. al-'Utbi (tr.: 365f, 370f).

NOTES TO CHAPTER 11

1. Meder (1979: 23ff, 83ff and chap. 4); Redman (1978: 169ff); on the Kopet Dagh region, see Lisitsina (1969) and Kohl (1984: chap. 4).
2. I assume macro-climatic conditions to have been largely the same then as now.
3. Meder (1979: 23).
4. Stein (1936: 150, 157); Stein (1937: 136); Meder (1979: 129).
5. E.g. in the Rud-é Gushk Valley in southern Kirman (Prickett 1979).
6. Henrickson (1985).
7. Vallat (1985); Steinkeller (1982); cf. p. 107, note 2.
8. Sumner (1974); Sumner (1985); Sumner (1986); a summary of the archaeological material can be found in Carter and Stolper (1984) and Hansman (1972). The early state in the Kur area is discussed in *Current Anthropology* 23 (1982) and 24 (1983); see especially Sumner's comments in vol. 24 (1983: 531ff).
9. Cf. below p. 225f.
10. The results of Soviet archaeological investigations during the 1970s are summed up by Kohl (1984: chap. 13 and 18).
11. Kohl (1984: 30, 94, 137ff).
12. Kohl (1984: 91).
13. Ya'qubi (tr.: 86); Le Strange (1905: 396).
14. Kohl (1984: chap. 18).
15. Cf. Kortum (1976: 88f) on settlement remains along the Kuh-é Rahmat in the Nayriz Basin.
16. Ibn al-Balkhi (tr.: 24).
17. Ouseley, I: 187, 305.
18. Waring: 25.

19. Læssøe (1951); Troll (1972: 13); Goblot (1979: 60–69); Gentelle (1977: 250); Biscione (1977: 115); Soviet archaeologists date some *qanats* in the Kopet Dagh region (at Ulug Tepe) to Achaemenid times; but the basis for this dating is not entirely convincing (cf. Kohl 1984: 195).

20. Moorey (1982); apparently iron technologies were spread to Iran from Anatolia.

21. Arrian III.18.10; Quintus Curtius V.4.6–10; Diodorus Siculus XVIII.70–73 and XIX.21; Strabo XV.3.6.

22. Presumably at the end of the second millennium B.C., Hansman (1975: 294); Sumner (1986).

23. E.g. Quintus Curtius V.4.33 and V.6.10.

24. Nicol (1970); Kortum (1973: 13); Sumner (1986: 13) believes that the Band-é Dukhtar and the Burideh weir could originally be Achaemenid.

25. Sumner (1986: 13).

26. Quintus Curtius V.6.12–13 and V.6.17–19. According to P. de Miroschedi (*Paléorient* 11/2, 1985: 60) the settlement of Fars by sedentary farmers began with the formation of the Achaemenid state. Before that the inhabitants had lived largely as nomads.

27. Arrian VIII.39.1.; Strabo XV.3.3. Taoce stood farther up the coast than Hieratis, presumably at the mouth of the Shirin/Hilleh river. I am not sure that the identification with Tawwaz is entirely correct, as the latter lay inland (Schwarz: 66ff). Arrian also states that there was an Achaemenid palace 200 *stadia* (nearly 40 km) inland from Taoce. Perhaps this is identical with the remains of a large structure found at Borazdjan (*Iran* 9, 1973: 188f).

28. Whitcombe (1987); Steinkeller (1982: 243).

29. Arrian VIII.37–39.

30. Arrian III.19.2; Quintus Curtius V.13.8; Strabo XV.2.8; art. "Paraitakene" in PW.

31. Cf. art. "Aspadana" in *PW*. The name Paraetacena has been interpreted as "river-watered" or "river-embraced," cf. Markwardt (1895: 33).

32. Plutarch, *Eumenes* XV.3; Diodorus Siculus XIX.26.2, XIX.32.1, XIX.34.7.

33. Pliny VI.43; Polybius X.27; Isidore, sect. 6; Diodorus Siculus XIX.44.4.

34. Se Keall in *AMI* Ergänzungsbd. 6: 537–544 (1979); Arrian III.19.2; III.20.2; Quintus Curtius V.8.1; Isidore, sect.7.

35. Strabo XI.9.1.

36. Hansman and Stronach (1970); Hecatompylus' location has long been the object of controversy. Hansman (1968) proposes that it be identified with the ruins of Shahr-é Kumis, 20 km southwest of Damghan.

37. Isidore, sect. 9; Quintus Curtius VI.2.15; Diodorus Siculus XVII.75.1; *Shahristan*, sect. 18. There is no doubt of Hecatompylus' existence in Parthian times, but perhaps Isidore might be correct after all. The "terminal horizon" on one of the archaeological excavations at Shar-é Kumis has been C-14 dated to the beginning of the 1st century (the year 10 ± 35): see Bivar (1982). Ptolemy (VI.5.) mentions *Semina* among Parthia's "towns and villages"; the name certainly reminds one of present-day Simnan, cf. Tomaschek (1883: 223).

38. Strabo XI.7.2; Quintus Curtius VI.4.20; CHI (4, I: 247, Table 5); Planhol (1969).

39. Arrian III.23.6. and III.25.1; Quintus Curtius VI.5.22; Isidore mentions here no towns, only "11 villages"; Tomaschek (1883: 225) and the article "Hyrkania" in *PW*; Kiyani (1982b: 59); *Iran* 11: 196 (1973).

40. Polybius X.31.5–6; *Iran* 11: 141ff (1973); Kiyani (1982b: 48f) would identify Sirynx with the 338 hectare Parthian site Dasht-Qaleh, near Qunbad-é Kabus.

41. Strabo XI.7.2–3.

42. Arrian III.19.7. and III.24.1–3; Strabo XI.7.2. The country did produce mercenaries, however, and these of course formed a link to the outside world. Some Mardii and Cadusii (Gilanis) fought, for instance, at Gaugamela (Arrian III.8.5 and III.11.35).

43. Ricciardi (1980: 60ff).

44. According to Quintus Curtius VII.10.15. Arrian does not mention the oasis at all. Hamilton (1973: 100); article "Margiana" in *PW*.

45. Arrian III.25.1.
46. Arrian III.25.2–5; Quintus Curtius VI.6.33; Diodorus Siculus XVII.78.1.
47. Arrian III.25.4, see below.
48. Arrian III.28.1; Quintus Curtius VII.3.1–4.
49. Strabo XI.8.9; Pliny VI.92. calls the town in Arachosia "Cutis" or "Cutin", while Ptolemy (VI.20), besides Arachotus, mentions several towns and villages which cannot be identified. See also Bernard (1974); Davary (1975); Fussman (1966); Fischer (1967); Vogelsang (1985); Fraser (1979); Helms (1979); McNicoll (1978).
50. Arrian VI.23–28.
51. Arrian VI.24.3.
52. Yaqut (tr.: 539).
53. Arrian VI.22.5., VI.23.1. and VI.23.1; Strabo XV.2.7.
54. Strabo XV.2.14.
55. Pliny VI.107; Ptolemy VI.8; Ammian XXIII.6.49.
56. Lamberg-Karlovsky (1972).
57. E.g. Mustawfi (Nuzhat, tr.: 139f). Around Djiruft – which Tomaschek (1883: 179) would identify with the "Archiotis" of the Tabula Peutingeriana – there had been settlement in pre-historic times (Stein, 1937: 148ff). In the Middle Ages Bam was watered by both the river Tah-rud and extensive qanat systems (Yaqut, tr.: 15; Aubin, 1956: 383f, 460) which seems to speak against according the town any great age. However, forest clearance on the Djibal Bariz during historical times could have so worsened the hydrogralogical conditions in the area that it became necessary to supplement the supply of water from Tah-rud with qanats.
58. Arrian VIII.32.5 and 33.2; Stein (1937: 184).
59. al-Istakhri (tr.: 79).
60. Meder (1979: 79f).
61. Cf. Briant (1979) on the Kossae, Uxii, Mardii, and other transhumant pastoralists in the Zagros.
62. Vanden Berghe (1959: 19); Vanden Berghe (1961: 164).
63. Polybius X.28.
64. Xenophon, Oeconomicus, IV.4.25 and Cyropaedia III.2.18–23.
65. Frye (1962: 129).
66. Frye (1962: 140f); Schlumberger (1970); Bickerman (1966 and in CHIr III/1: 12f); Tarn, Hellenistic Civilisation, 3rd ed., 1952 (London).
67. I have relied here principally on Strabo and Pliny. Appian's long list of Seleucid foundings seems all too mythological.
68. Tscherikower (1927: 97ff); on Kandahar see Helms (1979) and on Nihawand see Robert (1960).
69. Arrian III.19.1 and III.20.2; Quintus Curtius V.8.1; Strabo XI.9.1; Isidore, sect.7; Tscherikower (1927: 66).
70. Strabo XI.10.1–2 and XI.13.6; Pliny VI.43, 47–48, 61, 93, 113.
71. Pliny V.115–116; Tscherikower (1927: 99) regards them as separate towns, but was unaware of the identification of Laodicia-in-Media with Nihawand.
72. Ptolemy VI.17; Tscherikower (1927: 102).
73. The figures are collected in Hammond (1981: 152ff). On the basis of Nearchus' information (Arrian VIII.19) Hammond estimates (p.203) that Alexander, at the close of the Pandjab campaign, commanded no less than 120.000 men, a figure which seems unrealistically high, even when transport and noncombatants are included. In any case, a large portion of the troops were no longer Greeks and Macedonians, but various local non–Hellenized mercenaries.
74. Arrian V.27; Diodorus Siculus XVII.99; Hammond (1981: 239).
75. Bickerman (1966: 109). The city's location is unknown. Bickerman would indentify it with Bushire, but it seems more probable that it stood in the Nayriz Basin in the center of Fars.
76. The extent of the Seleucid Empire is discussed in Schmitt (1964: 32–84), where, however, the

criteria for domination are unclear (e.g. regular transfer of tribute). The result is that Schmitt overestimates the extent of effective control.

77. Strabo XI.7.2.
78. Strabo XI.10.2; Pliny VI.49.
79. Polybius X and XI.
80. Polybius XXXI.9 The text's "Tabae in Persis" must be a simple transcription error of "Gabae" (Markwart, 1895: 32). The locating of Isfahan in Fars (and not in Media) is also found in Ptolemy VI.4.
81. Polybius X.31.11.
82. Robert (1960). The circumstances of the find are unclear. It is a quite ordinary document, a manumission, while all other known Seleucid inscriptions contain royal commands.
83. Helms (1979); Fraser (1979); McNicoll (1978); Isidore (sect. 18–19) refers to Alexandria-in-Sacastana and "nearby" Alexandropolis, "the metropolis of Arachosia." Ptolemy (VI.20) and Ammian (XXIII.6.72) mention only Alexandria-in-Arachosia, not Alexandropolis. No doubt Fraser (1979) is correct that Alexandria-in-Sacastana is identical with Alexandropolis/Alexandria-in-Arachosia. Other suggestions have been made by Tscherikower (1927: 103), Tarn (1938: 479f) and Hammond (1981: 186).
84. Aï Khanum, at the confluence of the rivers Kokcha and Oxus (Amu Darya), was discovered in 1964. During the excavations the French archaeologists found remains of monumental buildings which on stylistic and technical aspects would appear to of Greek origin. Some inscriptions were also found and from these it is evident that Aï Khanum had been established by one Kineas in the early part of the 3rd century B.C. It is presumably identical with the classical sources' Alexandria-in-Bactria or Alexandria Oxiana, if these two towns are not one and the same.

The excavations also show that the Greek town was founded in an existing enclave where a complex irrigation technology had evolved centuries before. Aï Khanum was thus a parallel to Kandahar, the difference being that Aï Khanum contained a physically separate Greek settlement.

Archaeologists believe that an agrarian expansion took place in Greek times (3rd-2nd centuries B.C.). If this is correct, it cannot be because the Greek colonists (whose number is unknown) had brought with them new and superior technology. The explanation must be, rather, that the increased urbanization increased the demand for surplus production. In addition, the role of the Greeks in the urbanization process in this part of the world cannot have been vital. In Khwarizm, i.e. the Oxus delta (outside Greek influence), the process was entirely autonomous. It should also be noted that when the Greek-Bactrian states collapsed in the 2nd century, no agrarian decline apparently occurred in the Aï Khanum enclave. See Bernard (1967); Gentelle (1977: 256 and map); Gentelle (1978: 85ff, 108f, 141).
85. For example, CHIr (III/1: 12ff, 17); Schlumberger (1970: 25ff). On the Gedrosians and the Greek tragedies see also Tarn (1948, II: 254ff).
86. Frumkin (1970: 123). A large site on the Oxus, some 10 km from present-day Tirmiz, is also mentioned as being Greek: the remains of either Alexandria Oxiana or a town founded by Demetrius I, one of the Greek-Bactrian princes (Tarn, 1938: 118f). The archaeological indices are uncertain, however, and more likely the ruins date from a later period ("Kushan"). In any case, settlement on this site goes back to the beginning of the 1st millennium B.C. (Frumkin, 1970: 110f). Soviet archaeologists date other Transoxanian cities such as Afrasiab (i.e. Samarkand), Bukhara, and Balkh to this period as well (Kohl, 1984: 184, 194).
87. Rostovtzeff (1941, I: 488, 518); see also the discussion in Briant (1978, 1982).
88. Polybius X.27.3.
89. Iustin XLI.5. According to the classical sources the original land of the Parthians consisted of Apavarcticena, Parthiena and Astauena. Parthiena seems to have been the northern part of the Kopet Dagh corridor around present-day Ashkhabad, while Apavarcticena was the southern

part, opposite the Tedzhen delta. Astauena must have been nearby, perhaps in the upper Atrak Valley (Tomaschek, 1883: 215f; *CHIr*, III/2: 768). Isidore cites no town called Dara here, but instead mentions *Asaak*, "where Arsaces was first proclaimed king", *Parthaunisa*, *Gathar*, *Siroc*, *Apavarktiké*, and *Ragau*. Apart from Parthaunisa (see below) none of these have been identified. Tomaschek (1883: 215f) proposed that Apavarktiké should be identified with Abiward, a site near the village of Kaakha. Perhaps Dara and Apavarktiké are simply one and the same (i.e. Dara might have been the *shahr-é Apavarcticena*) or perhaps Dara was a "forbidden city" like Parthaunisa, founded next to a pre-existing urban settlement.

90. Pliny VI.44 and VI.113; Hecatompylus served as capital for a period during the 2nd century B.C., prior to the conquest of Mesopotamia. See Strabo XI.9.1; Pliny VI.44; *Shahristan* (sect. 18); Hansman and Stronach (1970); Bivar (1980).

91. Isidore (sect. 7); tribes called Mardi or Amardi appeared in different places, e.g. in Mazandaran, Azarbaydjan, and Fars.

92. Pliny VI.47.

93. *Shahristan* (sect. 17).

94. *Shahristan* (sect. 41).

95. *Shahristan* (sect. 42); Ibn al-Balkhi (tr.: 31); Hamza (tr.: 28); Tha'alibi (*Ta'rikh ghurar.* 398); Noeldeke's commentaries to Tabari, p.6, note 7; Frye (1962: 204f); Stein (1936: 190); *CHIr* (III/1: 299f).

96. Frumkin (1970: 144ff).

97. *CHIr* (III/2: 1037ff); Noeldeke's commentaries to Tabari, p. 6, note 7. At least three Arsacid kings bore the name Mithradates, and the suffix "-*gird*/*kirt*" (Arabic: "-*djird*") is certainly post-Seleucid and perhaps specifically Parthian. It appears in numerous settlement-names on the Plateau.

98. Isidore (sect. 12).

99. Isidore (sect. 11); Ricciardi (1980: 62ff, 69).

100. E.g. Strabo XI.7.2–3; Isidore lists no towns here, only "11 villages". Among the larger sites are, e.g.: Dasht-Qaleh (338 ha), Qizil-Qaleh (100 ha), Qaleh Sultan 'Ali (60 ha) and Qaleh Qarabeh (56 ha). See Kiyani (1982b: 40, 43, 48ff, 53, 59).

101. The exact starting point cannot be determined precisely, because changes in the water level of the Caspian Sea, road construction, agricultural and other activities have covered up the remains. No doubt the wall reached all the way to the sea, as al-Baladhuri, among others, states (tr., II: 42).

102. Kiyani (1982a); Kiyani (1982b: 14ff).

103. Iustin XLII.1–2; Tabari (Noeldeke tr.: 123, 157, 160); *Shahristan* (sect. 18). Procopius (I.3.1–8) characterizes the Haytal as settled and civilized, "like the Romans and the Persians."

104. Frumkin (1970: 146f); Albaum and Brentjes (1972: 84f).

105. *Han Shu*: 175ff.

106. Trinkaus (1983: 141ff).

107. See preliminary reports in *Iran* 13: 192f (1975); *Iran* 14: 160f (1976); *Iran* 17: 156f (1979).

108. Whitcomb (1985: 216f); Kleiss (1972: 199f).

NOTES TO CHAPTER 12

1. The name *Media* was derived from Old Persian *Mad* or *Mah*: Frye (1975: 11).

2. Qudama (tr.: 185).

3. Similarly, Yaqut (tr.: 151). Shapur I also cleary used the name *Mad* (*Madene*) in the same wider sense in his victory inscription at Naqsh-é Rustam (*SKZ*: line 3).

4. Ibn Khurdadhbih (tr.: 38).

5. The identification of Isfahan and Hamadan is quite unproblematical. The third locality, *Goman* or *Gwdmin*, can be identified with Qum on the basis of Ya'qubi's information (tr.: 75) that one of the pre-Muslim settlements in the Qum region was called Kumundan or Kumindan. Cf. al-Baladhuri (tr., I: 485); Frye (1975: 11); Lambton (1947: 587).

6. Ibn al-Faqih (tr.: 336); Mustawfi (*Nuzhat*, tr.: 62ff, 67); Ya'qubi (tr.: 69f); Mustawfi (*Tarikh-é Guzideh*, summary: 227); Schwarz: 706ff, 726ff, 730.

7. Tabari (Noeldeke tr.: 123); Schwarz: 726f, 730.

8. Ibn al-Faqih (tr.: 253ff); Schwarz: 480f.

9. Hamza (tr.: 41); Ibn al-Faqih (tr.: 244) lists Shad-Kavadh as a district in Mayshan.

10. Sees are also reported in Shahrazur, Mihridjankadhak and Masabadhan, all located in the Zagros foothills close to the Mesopotamian (and predominantly Christian) heartland. *Synodicon*, see references in index.

11. Ibn al-Faqih (tr.: 338).

12. Thus the Igharayn district was detached from Isfahan in the 9th century, cf. Yaqut (tr.: 65); Schwarz: 576.

13. Ibn Hawqal (tr., II: 350, 363).

14. Ibn Rusteh (tr.: 177ff); cf. Lambton (1953: 213f) on conflicts in Qum over irrigation-water supplies.

15. al-Baladhuri (tr., I: 487); Yaqut (tr.: 43); Schwarz: 588, 629f.

16. Ibn Rusteh (tr.: 178); Browne (1901: 439f).

17. *Shahristan* (tr.: par. 53); Markwart (1901: 28f).

18. Langlois (I: 247f, II: 150f); J. Neusner, "The Jews in Pagan Armenia," *JAOS* 84: 230ff (1964); Obermeyer (1929: 296) is inclined not to trust these stories.

19. According to Ibn Hawqal (tr., II: 358) Yahudiyeh was founded by Jews deported from Syria by Nebukadnezzar. This of course is pure fiction. A variant of this story is given by Ibn al-Faqih (tr.: 215).

20. Hamza (tr.: 41); Browne (1901: 417f); Schwarz: 589.

21. Ibn Rusteh (tr.: 186f); Schwarz: 593, notes 2 and 3. Muhammad al-Ludda calculated the area as 2.000 *dihqan-djarib*. A frequently used variant of the surface measure *djarib* equalled 0.16 ha, but as al-Ludda expressly states that the circumference of the circular town was 1/2 *farsakh*, the particular *djarib*-measure used here must have been smaller, about 0.035 ha.

22. Ibn Khurdadhbih (tr.: 16).

23. Siroux (1971: 43f, 158f).

24. Ibn Hawqal (tr., II: 354); al-Baladhuri (tr., I: 488); Schwarz: 582ff; see also Golombek (1974).

25. Ibn Rusteh (tr.: 176).

26. Le Strange (1905: 204f).

27. Browne (1902: 599).

28. Nasir-é Khusraw: 93.

29. Yaqut (tr.: 45f); Ibn Battuta (tr., II: 294).

30. Browne (1901: 443); further references are gathered in Schwarz: 605, 610 and discussed by Golombek (1974).

31. Mustawfi (*Nuzhat*: 51, tr.: 56f).

32. See below p. 217f.

33. Browne (1902: 575).

34. Yaqut (tr.: 46); Mustawfi (*Nuzhat*, tr.: 56).

35. Bulliet (1979: 52ff, 59ff).)

36. Boyle (1979).

37. Ibn Arabshah (tr.: 44f).

38. al-Samarkandi (tr.: 127, 130f).

39. al-Ghiyati (tr.: 139); Barbaro (71f).

40. The references are gathered in the art. "Isfahan" (*EI/2*); Cartwrights decription can be found in *Purchas* (VIII: 510).
41. Malcolm (1829, II: 518ff).
42. Fraser (I: 6).
43. Issawi (1971: 281); on the growing economic ties between Iran and Russia, see M.L. Entner: *Russo-Persian Commercial Relations, 1828–1914* (Gainesville: University of Florida Monographs, Social Sciences 28, 1965).
44. Adamec (1976, I: 249–259).
45. Wills (1887: 253ff).
46. Cf. Keall in *AMI* Ergänzungsband 6: 537–544 (1979).
47. Ya'qubi (tr.: 79).
48. Polybius X.28; Strabo XI.9.1.
49. *Synodicon* (cf. the entries *Ray* and *Beit Raziqayé* in register); Göbl (1971: table XV).
50. Tabari (Noeldeke tr.: 123); Hamza Isfahani also mentions a founding in the Ray area by Firuz, but places Ram-Firuz "in India."
51. Yaqut (tr.: 277).
52. al-Baladhuri (tr., II: 6f); Ya'qubi (tr.: 79); Ibn al-Faqih (tr.: 322); Schwarz: 748, 752f.
53. Ibn Hawqal (tr., II: 363); Tha'alibi (*Lata'if* tr.: 129).
54. Schwarz: 763, 767 and note 11; 1.5 sq *farsakh* would roughly equal 5400 ha. With a standard population density of 200 per hectare, Ray would then have had a total population of close to 1 million. Such numbers are obviously improbable.
55. Mustawfi (*Nuzhat*, tr.: 59); Le Strange (1905: 216); Schwarz (775); Ahmad al-Razi's *Haft iqlim* is cited by Barbier de Meynard in Yaqut (tr.: 273f, note 1).
56. al-Nasawi (tr.: 240).
57. Djuwayni (tr., I: 147).
58. Yaqut (tr.: 274).
59. Strabo XI.9.1; Tabari (Saliba tr.: 14); Miskawayh (tr., II: 180); Melville (1981).
60. Mustawfi (*Nuzhat*, tr.: 59); Schwarz: 762, 770ff.
61. According to Ambraseys (1979) earthquakes were not entirely unknown in Isfahan, but the shocks were generally of a very low magnitude, as the epicenters were situated far away. The only large shock on record occurred in 1344 and caused no significant damage.
62. Mustawfi (*Nuzhat*, tr.: 59).
63. Mustawfi (*Nuzhat*, tr.: 61).
64. Clavijo (tr.: 98f).
65. Kinneir (119).
66. Estimates of Tehran's population in the 19th and early 20th centuries can be found in Issawi (1971: 26f).
67. Some sources make Shapur II the founder. The historical tradition often fails to distinguish clearly between these two kings. Kazwin is treated at some length (though from a rather traditional perspective) in the *EI/2*; I refer to the article therein.
68. Ibn al-Faqih (tr.: 336); Mustawfi (*Nuzhat*, tr.: 62f); Mustawfi (*Tarikh-é Guzideh*, Barbier de Meynard tr.: 259); Schwarz: 706f.
69. On pre-Sassanian settlement in the Kazwin-region see: H. Tala'i, "Late Bronze Age and Iron Age I Architecture in Sagzabad," *Iranica Antiqua* 18: 51–57 (1983). Sagzabad is situated *c.* 60 km south of Kazwin.
70. Mustawfi (*Tarikh-é Guzideh*, Barbier de Meynard tr.: 261f); Mustawfi (*Nuzhat* tr.: 64); al-Baladhuri (tr., II: 12); Ibn alFaqih (tr.: 337).
71. Mustawfi (*Tarikh-é Guzideh*, Barbier de Meynard tr.: 261, 265).
72. See summary of sources in Le Strange (1905: 218f).
73. Ya'qubi (tr.: 69f); Mustawfi (*Tarikh-é Guzideh*, Barbier de Meynard tr.: 266f).

74. Nasir-é Khusraw: 4; al-Istakhri (tr.: 94); Mustawfi (*Tarikh-é Guzideh*, Barbier de Meynard tr.: 268).

75. Mustawfi (*Tarikh-é Guzideh*, Barbier de Meynard tr.: 267ff).

76. Melville (1981).

77. Schwarz: 717ff.

78. Mustawfi (*Nuzhat*, tr.: 62ff); Barbaro (72).

79. See the article "Kazvin" in *EI/2*.

80. Mustawfi (*Nuzhat*, tr.: 72); al-Baladhuri (tr., I: 485ff); Schwarz: 568.

81. Le Strange (1905: 209); Mustawfi (*Nuzhat*, tr.: 72).

82. Ibn Hawqal (tr., II: 362); Schwarz: 558f, 568f.

83. Djuwayni (tr. II,: 437 note 46, 542).

84. Mustawfi (*Nuzhat*, tr.: 71f); al-Ghiyati (tr.: 156).

85. Barbaro (tr.: 72, 129f); Purchas (VIII: 509f).

86. Kinneir: 115.

87. Ibn al-Balkhi (tr.: 20); Mustawfi (*Nuzhat*, tr.: 77); Adamec (1976, I: 689–96).

88. Bonine (1980: 12, 21).

89. Ibn Hawqal (tr., II: 275f); Ibn al-Balkhi (tr.: 20); Schwarz: 19f.

90. Browne (1901: 432); Bonine (1980: 13f).

91. Polo: 46. Here cited after the Penguin edition (Harmondsworth 1958, p. 62).

92. Mustawfi (*Nuzhat*, tr.: 77).

93. Ibn Arabshah (tr.: 42f); al-Ghiyati (tr.: 163f); *CHIr* (V: 489; VI: 56, 61).

94. Barbaro (73f).

95. *CHIr* (VI: 320); Kinneir: 113.

96. Ibn al-Faqih (tr.: 296); Ya'qubi (tr.: 72f); Adamec (1976, I: 221f).

97. *SKZ* line: 64; *Synodicon*: 366; *Shahristan*: par. 23.

98. Schwarz: 519.

99. Ibn Hawqal (tr., II: 350); cf. art. "Hamadhan" in *EI/2*.

100. Schwarz: 523.

101. Nasawi (tr.: 121); Djuvayni (tr., I: 147).

102. Wassaf (tr.: 59).

103. Ibn al-Faqih (tr.: 289); Mustawfi (*Nuzhat*, tr.: 75); cf. p. 56 above.

104. Mustawfi (*Nuzhat*, tr.: 75).

105. al-Ghiyati (tr.: 176); see also the art. "Hamadhan" in *EI/2*; according to some studies, e.g. Bémont (1973, III: 194), Hamadan was razed by Timur. However, Ibn Arabshah (tr.: 56f) states that Timur was bought off. Cf. also Aubin (1968: 112).

106. Kinneir: 126f.

107. *SKZ*: line 62.

108. Ya'qubi (tr.: 75); al-Baladhuri (tr., I: 485); Ibn al-Faqih (tr.: 317f); Lambton (1947: 587).

109. Lambton (1953: 213f).

110. Ya'qubi (tr.: 76); al-Istakhri (tr.: 94f).

111. References gathered in Le Strange (1905: 209f); Schwarz: 559f.

112. Lambton (1947: 589); Schwarz: 564; Mustawfi (*Nuzhat*, tr.: 71); cf. also the art. "Kumm" in *EI/2*.

113. See art. "Kumm" in *EI/2*.

114. Kinneir: 116.

115. Ibn al-Faqih (tr.: 253ff); Schwarz: 480f.

116. Ibn Hawqal (tr., II: 354); Schwarz: 475ff; art. "Dinawar" in *EI/2*.

117. Schwarz: 481f.

118. Cf. art. "Kirmanshah" in *EI/2*.

119. Spuler (1955: 332ff); Blair (1986).

120. Mustawfi (*Nuzhat*, tr.: 61).

121. Clavijo (tr.: 92ff).

122. al-Samarkandi (tr.: 132).

123. Barbaro (68); Purchas (VIII: 505).

124. Ibn al-Balkhi (tr.: 23).

125. Aubin (1965: 164ff); on the routes in the 10th and 11th centuries, see Ibn al-Balkhi (tr.: 77f) and Schwarz: 180ff.

126. *Shahristan*: par. 18; Tabari (Noeldeke tr.: 123, 157, 160).

127. The *"Kirkuk-Chronicle"* (tr.: 50 and excursus 20, p. 277f); Langlois (II: 186); Hansman (1968); Hansman and Stronach (1970); Schwarz: 815f.

128. Yaqut (tr.: 223); Adle (1971: 73).

129. Trinkaus (1983).

130. al-Istakhri (tr.: 99); Mas'udi (*Tanbih*, tr.: 74); Le Strange (1905: 365); Schwarz: 812f.

131. See art. "Kumis" in *EI/2*.

132. Tabari (Noeldeke tr.: 123); Hamza (tr.: 41); Khiyani (1982b).

133. Procopius (I.4.10) states that the battle was fought at *Gorgo*, "on the far borders of Persia", while Priscus (frag. 33) mentions the town of *Gorga* as Firuz' base of operations. In the Muslim sources the geographic reference points are very vague: for instance, Bal'ami (tr. II: 139) states that the battle was fought somewhere on "the borders of Balkh and Tukharistan"; however, in all the accounts there figures a system of moats, perhaps a reference to the Sadd-é Iskandar.

134. Tabari (Noeldeke tr.: 158); Hamza (tr.: 41); Ibn al-Faqih (tr.: 260); Ibn Isfandiyar (tr.: 27); Grignaschi (tr.: 25); Bivar and Fehervari (1966).

135. The *"Kirkuk Chronicle"* (excursus 20, p. 278); *Synodicon*: 285; Yaqut (tr.: 156); Ibn Khudadhbih (tr.: 29) lists "Chul" as the title of the King of Gurgan.

136. Yaqut (tr.: 154); further references in Le Strange (1905: 376ff).

137. *Iran* 11: 196 (1976); Bulliet (1976: 89); Mustawfi (*Nuzhat*, tr.: 156).

138. Tha'alibi (*Lata'if*, tr.: 130f); al-Muqaddasi (tr.: 48).

139. Lambton (1953: 57); the art. "Ilat" in *EI/2*.

140. Mustawfi (*Nuzhat*, tr.: 156); *Iran* 11: 196 (1976).

141. Cf. preceeding note.

142. Aubin (1976: 38); Aubin (1965: 117); se also art. "Astarabadh" in *EI/2*.

143. Issawi (1972: 28).

144. Kohl (1984: chap. 18).

145. See references in Le Strange (1905: 379ff); Barthold (1956, III: 93f); the art. "Dihistan" in *EI/2*.

NOTES TO CHAPTER 13

1. Ibn al-Balkhi (tr.: 45f); Tabari (Noeldeke tr.: 12, 19f); Hamza (tr.: 33); Ibn al-Faqih (tr.: 243); Ibn Hawqal (tr., II: 274); *Shahristan*: 44; *Karnameh* (tr.: 22).

2. Tabari (Noeldeke tr.: 19; Hamza (tr.: 34. Ibn al-Balkhi (tr.: 62) in the 11th century locates a small town named Rishahr on the coast between Arradjan and Khuzistan, but at the same time he refers to the Rishahr district (p. 64) as lying inland from Siniz, another of the Gulf ports. Moses Khorenats'i (Markwart, 1901: 138) refers to a town, Reshir-é Pahrsan, from which came pearls and that certainly indicates a location on the Gulf. To complicate things even further, there exists farther south, at present-day Bushire, a large site also known as Rishahr. This is an old settlement (2nd millennium B.C.), perhaps identical with Nearchus' Hieratis. The site has extensive Sassanian remains (Whitcomb 1987), and Whitehouse and Williamson (1973) argue on this basis that this Rishahr must be identical with Ardashir's Rev-Ardashir. All information in the written sources, however, points to a location in the Arradjan area; Whitehouse's and Williamson's

compromise proposal, that there existed two towns with the same name, appears unconvincing. Most likely, Rishahr-at-Bushire in Sassanian times bore a name which has been lost. See further *Hudud* (tr.: 127); al-Baladhuri (tr., II: 128); Schwarz: 120; Gaube (1973: 32ff).

3. Hamza (tr.: 35); *SKZ* (line 25–26); *Shahristan*: par. 43; Ibn al-Balkhi (tr.: 50f, 55).
4. Tabari (Noeldeke tr.: 136, 138); Hamza (tr.: 42); Ibn al-Faqih (tr.: 243); Tha'alibi (*Ta'rikh ghurar*: 527, 594); Ibn al-Balkhi (tr.: 61); Ps.Stylites (tr.: 43); the *Se'ert Chronicle* (tr.: 41); Yaqut (tr.: 18f).
5. Ibn al-Faqih (tr.: 243); Tabari (Noeldeke tr.: 138); Ibn al-Balkhi (tr.: 61); Le Strange (1905: 254, 270).
6. Cf. p. 167f below.
7. Hansman (1975); Kleiss (1972: 194f); see also references in Le Strange (1905: 290).
8. See art. "Lar" in *EI/2* for further information on the climatic and hydrological conditions of the region.
9. Ibn al-Balkhi (tr.: 41, 48f).
10. Stein (1936: passim); Vanden Berghe (1959: 19); Vanden Berghe (1961).
11. Gropp (1970); Azarnoush (1983).
12. Ibn al-Balkhi (tr.: 34); al-Baladhuri (tr., II: 31).
13. Aubin (1955); Aubin (1965); Aubin (1969); Schwarz: 133.
14. See summary in Kortum (1975).
15. Ibn al-Balkhi (tr.: 29); Kortum (1976: 94–114).
16. Ibn al-Balkhi (tr.: 29, 65).
17. Ibn al-Balkhi (tr.: 66).
18. Whitcomb (1979: 369).
19. Ibn al-Balkhi (tr.: 66); Kortum (1976: 115f).
20. Tabari (Noeldeke tr.: 4f); Chaumont (1958); *Synodicon* (tr.: 285).
21. Whitcomb (1979: figure on p. 364).
22. Ibn al-Balkhi (tr.: 28, 83); al-Baladhuri (tr., II: 132f).
23. Whitcomb (1979).
24. Ibn al-Balkhi (tr.: 28).
25. Ibn al-Balkhi (tr.: 35f). On Qasr-é Abu Nasr, see Whitcomb (1985: 13f, 38f, 221f).
26. Ibn Khurdadhbih (tr.: 39).
27. Ibn al-Balkhi (tr.: 36–39); Yaqut (tr.: 365).
28. Ibn al-Balkhi (tr.: 38); Ibn Hawqal (tr., II: 276).
29. Ibn al-Balkhi (tr.: 37f). Shabankareh was the name of a federation of "Kurds", i.e. tribally organized nomads and agriculturalists. During the Buyid wars of succession in the 11th century one of the federation's leaders made himself master of most of Fars. This position he sought to make legitimate by asserting that his family previously had ruled as representatives of the Sassanian kings. The Saldjuks eventually curtailed the power of the federation, but during the break-up of the Saldjuk empire the Shabankareh princes re-emerged as local rulers in the Darabgird-Fasa-Lar region with their capital in the fortress of Shahr-e Idj. In Ilkhanid times their possessions were considered a separate province, known as Shabankareh and roughly equivalent to the Darabgird district (Mustawfi: *Nuzhat*, tr.: 124, 137; Krawulsky, 1978: 148f).
30. Ibn al-Balkhi passim.
31. Cf. the article "Fars" in *EI/2*.
32. Rashid al-Din (Boyle tr.: 307); Spuler (1955: 142f); Ibn Battuta (tr., II: 299f).
33. Ibn Arabshah (tr.: 42f); al-Ghiyati (tr.: 165f); *CHIr* (VI: 60).
34. Barbaro (tr.: 74f). The spelling has been slightly modernized.
35. Barbaro (tr.: 94f).
36. Fasa'i (tr.: 395f).
37. Christensen (1987: 8f).
38. Ouseley, II: 17; Kinneir: 62f.

39. Cf. Kortum (1976: 118–139) where indications and possible causes are discussed.
40. Ouseley, II: 178f; Kinneir: 77.
41. Tabari (Noeldeke tr.: 11f).
42. Yaqut (tr.: 174f).
43. Ibn al-Balkhi (tr.: 45f); Tabari (Noeldeke tr.: 12, 19f); Hamza (tr.: 33); Ibn al-Faqih (tr.: 243); Ibn Hawqal (tr., II: 274); *Shahristan*: par. 44; *Karnameh* (tr.: 22); Schwarz: 56f; *Iran* 11: 192f (1973). For both Veh-Ardashir and Firuzabad the model seems to have been the Parthian circular town of Darabgird.
44. *Synodicon* (tr.: 287, 322, 331).
45. Tabari (Noeldeke tr.: 111f); Vanden Berghe (1961: 181f).
46. Ibn Hawqal (tr., II: 277); Vanden Berghe (1959: 19); Vanden Berghe (1961: 171); Vanden Berghe (1968).
47. Tabari (Noeldeke tr.: 20); Hamza (tr.: 34); Whitehouse and Williamson (1973).
48. Ibn al-Balkhi (tr.: 46); Ibn Hawqal (tr., II: 274); Tha'alibi (*Lata'if*, tr.: 127).
49. Ibn Hawqal (tr., II: 275).
50. Waring: 106; Kinneir: 69.
51. Abbott (1857: 176).
52. *Synodicon* (tr.: 287, 352); Ibn Hawqal (tr., II: 273); Tha'alibi (*Lata'if*, tr.: 128); Yaqut (tr.: 20); Ibn al-Balkhi (tr.: 31).
53. Stein (1936: 166f, 173, 190f); Le Strange (1905: 289).
54. Kinneir: 75.
55. Abbott (1857: 158f); Fasa'i (tr.: 336, note 160).
56. Abbott (1857: 158f); see also Fryer II: 172.
57. Ibn Hawqal (tr., II: 277); Ibn al-Balkhi (tr.: 32); summary of sources in Schwarz: 97f.
58. Fasa'i (tr.: 83); Ouseley (II: 90); Abbott (1857: 152).
59. Kinneir: 75; Ouseley (II: 163f); on Nayriz in the 10th-11th centuries, see Ibn al-Balkhi (tr.: 29).
60. Cf. Kleiss in *AMI* 6: 72 (1973).
61. *Synodicon* (tr.: 276, 322f).
62. Ibn Khurdadhbih (tr.: 32); Le Strange (1905: 262); Schwarz: 32.
63. Ibn Hawqal (tr., II: 273); Ibn al-Balkhi (tr.: 51).
64. Ibn al-Balkhi (tr.: 51, 57).
65. Ibn al-Balkhi (tr.: 55); Yaqut (tr.: 472, note 1).
66. Ibn al-Balkhi (tr.: 55f); Ibn Hawqal (tr., II: 273); Ibn Battuta (tr., II: 319f); Schwarz: 33f.
67. Rashid al-Din (Boyle tr.: 307).
68. Ibn al-Balkhi (tr.: 61); Hamza (tr.: 42); Tabari (Noeldeke tr.: 136, 138); Tha'alibi (*Ta'rikh ghurar*: 527, 594); Ps.Stylites (tr.: 43); The *Se'ert-Chronicle*: 41; Ibn al-Faqih (tr.: 243); Yaqut (tr.: 18f); Schwarz: 111f; Stein (1940: 80f); Gaube (1973: 28f, 41f).
69. Ibn Hawqal (tr. II: 265, 299); Yaqut (tr.: 20); Schwarz: 111f, 114f; *CHIr* (IV: 282).
70. Nasir-é Khusraw (tr.: 249f).
71. Ibn al-Balkhi (tr.: 61); Gaube (1973: 75).
72. Early references to Bihbihan are gathered in Gaube (1973: 99f).
73. Kinneir: 72.
74. Gaube (1973: 35).
75. Ibn Hawqal (tr., II: 277); Schwarz: 59–62.
76. Schwarz: 59–62; Ibn al-Balkhi (tr.: 42); Aubin (1959).
77. Ibn al-Balkhi (tr.: 63); Yaqut (tr.: 166); Schwarz: 125f; Gaube (1973: 31f, 53, 80, 214).
78. Ibn al-Balkhi (tr.: 41, 81f); Yaqut (tr.: 142f); Schwarz: 66f; Le Strange (1905: 259f).
79. Yaqut (tr.: 337); Ibn al-Balkhi (63); Schwarz: 125f; Gaube (1973: 38, 68f, 92, 213).
80. Ibn al-Balkhi (tr.: 63f); Nasir-é Khusraw (tr.: 247f); Gaube (1973: 61f, 87f, 212).

81. Teixeira: 24; see also Abbé Carré's description of Nakhilu in the 17th century (vol. I: 102f; vol. III: 839).
82. See art. "Bushihr" in *EI/2*.
83. Kinneir: 69f; Issawi (1971: 82f).
84. Thus Aubin (1959).
85. Aubin (1969).
86. See the references gathered by Lambton in the art. "Ilat" in *EI/2*: 1096f; Lambton (1973: 122).
87. Aubin (1969).

Notes to Chapter 14

1. E.g., the Banu Ilyas (932–968), the Kirman Saldjuqs (1050–1200), the Qutlugh-khanids (1220–1300), the Muzaffarids (1340–1393); on the political history of the region see the article "Kirman" in *EI/2*.
2. Veh-Ardashir is not mentioned by Tabari in his version of the historical tradition. It is listed, however, by Hamza (tr.: 33), Mustawfi (*Nuzhat*, tr.: 139), *Shahristan*: sect. 18, and other sources. See also Schwarz: 220f.
3. See the summary of sources in Le Strange (1905: 303f).
4. The tradition is found in Vaziri's *Tarikh-é Kirman*, a compilation from the last century, here cited after English (1966: 22). That the town must have been in existence by early Muslim times is indicated by Ibn al-Faqih (tr.: 250).
5. Tabari (Noeldeke tr.: 57); Le Strange (1905: 286).
6. Yaqut (tr.: 285) calls Zarand an "old town", a designation which usually means pre-Muslim. From the distances given in the geographical literature Le Strange (1905: 286) would identify Rafsandjan, previously Bahramabad, with the medieval town of Unas (see also Schwarz: 224). It might also be a case of successive settlements. The name "Bahramabad" appears from the end of the 14th century (Samarkandi tr.,: 113f). Also Kuh-bunan (between Bafq and Ravar) is sometimes listed as a Sassanian founding (Tomaschek, 1883: 605).
7. Ibn al-Faqih (tr.: 249f).
8. Tabari (Noeldeke tr.: 157).
9. Ibn al-Faqih (tr.: 250) thus names Damindan, a district and a "large town" seven farsakh from Bardasir, which had various kinds of mines. Ravar, north of Bardasir, had rich copper deposits (Tomaschek, 1883: 602). See also Schwarz: 268.
10. *SKZ* (lines 4 and 55); Tabari (Noeldeke tr.: 10).
11. Tabari (Noeldeke tr.: 71); Ibn Khurdadhbih (tr.: 13).
12. Tabari (Noeldeke tr.: 71). *Shahristan*: sect. 39. Noeldeke suggests that this refers to Kirmanshahan, yet another small town on the edge of the desert between Yazd and Rafsandjan. Markwart notes a similarity in names to Bahramabad, but, as stated above, this name seems not to have appeared until much later. *Shahristan* points to Sirdjan which must certainly be older.
13. *Iran* 14: 176ff (1976); Prickett (1979).
14. Mustawfi (*Nuzhat* tr.: 140); Aubin (1956: 383, note 4).
15. Le Strange (1905: 300); Tabari (Noeldeke tr.: 10); *Shahristan*: sect. 39; Tomaschek (1883: 176) suggests that Sirdjan is the same as *Pantiene* of the Tabula Peutingeriana.
16. Ibn Hawqal (tr., II: 307); Yagut (tr.: 333); according to Ibn Khurdadhbih (tr.: 34) Sirdjan was certainly the administrative center, but smaller than Djiruft; see also Ibn al-Faqih (tr.: 250).
17. Ibn Hawqal (tr., II: 306); Schwarz: 240f.
18. Ibn Hawqal (tr., II: 306); Yaqut (tr.: 115); Schwarz 236f.
19. Schwarz: 228f.
20. Yaqut (tr.: 483).
21. Schwarz: 220, 231; Bosworth (1971: 122, note 23).

22. Aubin (1956: 393f); Le Strange (1905: 301f); Khundji (*Tarikh-é 'Alam-ara-yé Amini*, tr.: 43); see also the article "Kirman" in *EI/2*.
23. Houtsma (1885: 385, 389, 394); Krawulsky (1978: 139).
24. Polo: 48f.
25. According to Frye the town survived into Timurid times (cf. the article "Djiruft" in *EI/2*); the site of Shahr-é Daqiyanus, near the village Sabzavaran, is generally considered to be the remains of medieval Djiruft.
26. Houtsma (1885: 385); Aubin (1956: 461); Gaube (1978: 101).
27. On the Bam region at the beginning of the 15th century, see Aubin (1956: 405, note 2, 461, note 1).
28. Schwarz: 228; Mustawfi, in the 14th century, still cites Narmashir as a large town, but his information may not be up to date. The remains of Narmashir are usually identified with the site of Chukukabad (Krawulsky, 1978: 144).
29. Kinneir: 195f.
30. Le Strange (1905: 313); Kinneir: 195f; Sykes (1902: 215f, 220).
31. Kinneir: 196.
32. Gaube (1978: 100f).
33. Ibn Khurdadhbih (tr.: 34f). Incidentally he does not mention Bardasir; Ibn Hawqal (tr., II: 279f, 308); summary of additional sources in Le Strange (1905: 320f) and Schwarz: 186f, 190f, 276f.
34. Houtsma (1885: 372); Mustawfi (*Nuzhat*, tr.: 178f); Aubin (1959: 300).
35. Ibn Hawqal (tr., II: 302, 303).
36. Houtsma (1885: 389).
37. Houtsma (1885: 382, 396).
38. Djuzdjani (tr., II: 1118f); Rashid al-Din (Boyle tr.: 68, 305f).
39. al-Samarkandi (tr.: 208); Hafiz-é Abru cited by Aubin (1956: 407f, 422f); see also the article "Kirman" in *EI/2*.
40. Fasa'i (tr.: 61).
41. Kinneir: 198f; nevertheless, the number of inhabitants was still estimated at 20.000.
42. Sykes (1902: 69f, 199f).
43. Le Strange (1905: 308).
44. Cf. above p. 181, note 6.
45. Le Strange (1905: 308). Ghubayra stood at the confluence of two small rivers, the Chari and the Ghubayra, some 80 km south of Bardasir/Kirman. The settlement went back to the 3rd millennium B.C. Possibly in Sassanian times it was provided with extensive fortifications. The abandonment in Ilkhanid times is established through archaeological indicators (cf. *Iran* 10, 1972; 11, 1973; 12, 1974; 15, 1977 in the sections on excavation reports).
46. Polo: 48f.
47. Planhol (1968: 211).
48. Cf. A.K.S. Lambton's article "Ilat" in *EI/2* (p. 1098).
49. Lambton (1973: 124).
50. Houtsma (1885: 338).
51. Polo: 48f.
52. Vaziri, cit. by Busse (1972: 295).

NOTES TO CHAPTER 15

1. *Synodicon*: 285.
2. *Synodicon*: 366f, 432.
3. Marv al-Rud is said to have been founded by Bahram V Gur (421–439) during the Haytal wars (cf. *Shahristan*: sect. 11); Shapur I is credited with the founding of Pushang (Ghuriyan) on the road to Herat (*Shahristan*: sect. 13).
4. Cf. table 13; the most striking discrepancy is that *Balkh*, which at least until the mid-12th century was considered one of Khurasan's largest and richest towns, is assessed with such a low amount. There appears to be no immediate explanation for this.
5. *Synodicon*: 299 and note 2, 366f.
6. *CHIr* (III/1: 729f). The argument is that while *SKZ* (line 55), in the middle of the 3rd century, still refers to a "king" of Marv, the Muslim accounts of conquest tell of a *marzban* (governor): cf. al-Baladhuri (tr., II: 164); Ibn Khurdadhbih (tr.: 14). However, because of Marv's unique military importance this cannot be taken as proof of a general centralization in Sassanian times (as does the *CHIr*).
7. al-Baladhuri (tr., II: 169); Grignaschi: 24.
8. Figures for the tribute agreements in Khurasan are summarized in Shaban (1970: 19ff).
9. al-Baladhuri (tr., II: 171); Hamza (tr.: 169).
10. Shaban (1970: 46f, 95f).
11. Shaban (1970: 115ff).
12. Ibn Hawqal (tr., II: 420f).
13. Le Strange (1905: 399, 401); Yaqut (tr.: 260).
14. Ibn Hawqal (tr., II: 420ff); *Hudud* (tr.: 105); Tha'alibi (*Lata'if* tr.: 135); Yaqut (tr.: 529); Hafiz-é Abru (*Djugrafiya* tr.: 48f).
15. cf. Ibn Hawqal (tr., II: 421, 440); Ibn al-Faqih (tr.: 381); Yaqut (tr.: 259f); Le Strange (1905: 397f).
16. Ibn Hawqal loc. cit.; Bosworth (1963: 156).
17. Hafiz-é Abru (*Djughrafiya* tr.: 49).
18. Djahiz (*Kitab al-buhala*, tr.: 26f); Ibn Hawqal (tr., II: 420).
19. Mustawfi (*Nuzhat*, tr.: 154).
20. Mustawfi, loc. cit.; Yaqut (tr.: 529).
21. Hamza (tr.: 188).
22. Browne (1902: 851, 853f).
23. Yaqut (tr.: 526ff).
24. Djuwayni (tr., I: 142ff).
25. Djuwayni (tr., I: 154ff).
26. Djuwayni (tr., I: 161f, 318f); Nasawi (tr.: 114f); Wassaf (tr.: 135).
27. Ibn Battuta (tr., III: 574).
28. Mustawfi (*Nuzhat*, tr.: 154).
29. Hafiz-é Abru (*Djughrafiya*, tr.: 4f); al-Samarkandi (tr.: 90, 122); Barthold (1956, II: 14, 123, III: 21, 47).
30. Hafiz-é Abru (*Djughrafiya*, tr.: 46f); al-Samarkandi (tr.: 169); Isfizari cited by Krawulsky in Hafiz-é Abru (op.cit.: 177).
31. Hafiz-é Abru (*Djughrafiya*, tr.: 48f). Hafiz' suggestion that Bakhsh-ab is identical with al-Raziq is hardly justified and is presumably simply an attempt to make his own account agree with the older sources.
32. Kinneir: 179f; Mir Abd al-Karim al-Bukhari: *Tarikh-é Bukhara*, tr. Ch. Schefer: *Histoire de l''Asie Centrale* (Paris 1876), p. 142.
33. O'Donovan (1882, II: 499). O'Donovan's exaggerated estimate of the population and – by

implication – of the oasis' importance, is no doubt connected to his political purpose: namely, to warn British public opinion of the danger of a Russian occupation which in fact took place a few years later.

34. O'Donovan (1882, II: 175–194).
35. O'Donovan (1882, II: 197f).)
36. Ibn Hawqal (tr., II: 422); O'Donovan (1882, II: 324ff).
37. O'Donovan (1882, II: 120f, 162, 321f).
38. O'Donovan (1882, II: 312).
39. Tabari (Noeldeke, tr.: 59); Hamza (tr.: 35); *Shahristan*: sect. 15. Nishapur/Nev-Shapur was clearly the official name, while Abrashahr seems to be derived from the name of the region.
40. Cf. Vardapet Elishe and Lazar P'arpets'i in Langlois (tr., II: 186, 229, 306, 312); Ps. Sebeos (tr.: 48ff).
41. Bulliet (1976: 87).
42. *Synodicon*: 272f.
43. Shaban (1970: 20).
44. Ya'qubi (tr.: 85); Hamza (tr.: 169, 179); Ibn Hawqal (tr., II: 420); Bosworth (1963: 157).
45. Ibn Hawqal (tr., II: 418); 'Utbi (tr.: 483); on the aversion of the Khurasani towns to the Ghaznavids, see 'Utbi (tr.: 397f) and Bosworth (1963: 80–91).
46. Bosworth (1963: 157).
47. Bulliet (1972: 11); Bulliet (1976: 88f); Bosworth (1963: 160) suggests a much lower figure, from 30.000 to 40.000. Bulliet, however, argues that the size of the site supports his estimate.
48. Ibn Hawqal (tr., II: 437f); Ibn al-Faqih (tr.: 378); Bosworth (1963: 154).
49. Ibn Hawqal (tr., II: 419, 438); Tha'alibi (*Lata'if*, tr.: 131f).
50. On the struggle between the law schools, see Halm (1971); Bulliet (1972: 28f, 38f); Bulliet (1979: 58–63); Bosworth (1963: 171f); on the Karramiyeh, see Bosworth (1960) and Bosworth (1963: 185f).
51. Bulliet (1978: 48f).
52. Qudama (tr.: 161f); Mustawfi (*Tarikh-e guzideh*, tr. M.C. Barbier de Meynard in *Journal Asiatique* Series 5, vol. 10, p.294, 1857). The number and dating of earthquakes in Nishapur is uncertain, and I rely here and in the following on Melville (1980).
53. al-Rawandi: 180f.
54. Djuwayni (tr., I: 316); Bulliet (1972: 76f).
55. Ibn Hawqal (tr., II: 417); Hafiz-é Abru (*Djugrafiya*, tr.: 43).
56. On earthquakes, see Melville (1980); Yaqut (tr.: 580); Bulliet (1976: 89).
57. Djuwayni (tr., I: 177); al-Nasawi (tr.: 92); Yaqut (tr.: 580f).
58. Mustawfi (*Nuzhat*, tr.: 157); Hafiz-é Abru (*Djughrafiya*, tr.: 43); Melville (1980).
59. Hafiz-é Abru (*Djughrafiya*, tr.: 43); Ibn Battuta (tr., III: 583f).
60. Mustawfi (*Nuzhat*, tr.: 147); Bulliet (1976: 89) estimates the maximum extent of Nishapur in the 10th and 11th centuries at 1.680 hectares.
61. al-Isfizari (tr.: 121).
62. Clavijo (tr.: 107f).
63. Hafiz-é Abru (*Djughrafiya*, tr.: 44); Bulliet (1976: 69).
64. Kinneir: 185f; other descriptions from the 19th century are cited by Bulliet (1976: 89).
65. Ya'qubi (tr.: 83f); Ibn Hawqal (tr., II: 419).
66. Clavijo (tr.: 109).
67. On the growth of Mashhad in Ilkhanid and Timurid times, see Mustawfi (*Nuzhat*, tr.: 149); Ibn Battuta (tr., III: 582f); Hafiz-é Abru (*Djughrafiya*, tr.: 59).
68. Hafiz-é Abru (*Djughrafiya*, tr.: 62); Ruzbihan (*Mihman-nameh*, tr.: 312–17).
69. Kinneir: 175f.
70. *Shahristan* (sect. 13); al-Izfizari (tr.: 33). In *SKZ* (line 4) Shapur I also lists Herat among his possessions, but we need not take this at face value.

71. Tabari (Noeldeke tr.: 99ff); *Synodicon*: 285. I assume that the bishop was not just chosen for Herat, but that like his Sistani colleagues he actually took up his office.

72. Tabari (Noeldeke, tr.: 119f); Procopius I.4.35.

73. Tabari (Noeldeke, tr.: 156f, 167); Tha'alibi (*Ta'rikh ghurar*: 615); Grignaschi: 19; *Synodicon*: 366, 423.

74. Tabari (Noeldeke, tr.: 269f); Ps. Sebeos (tr.: 48f); al-Baladhuri (tr., II: 164).

75. Shaban (1970: 20); Tabari (cited by Shaban, 1970: 108) refers to a *dihqan* ruling in Herat as late as the 720s.

76. However, one of the Samanids is said to have spent four years in Herat in the 10th century, cf. *The Chahar Maqal of Nidhami-i Arudi-i Samarqandi*, ed. Muh. Qazwini: 34. GMS IX (London 1910).

77. al-Isfizari (tr.: 45, 47); Ya'qubi (tr.: 87); Ibn Rusteh (tr.: 200); al-Istakhri (tr.: 117); Ibn Hawqal (tr., II: 422f); Tha'alibi (*Lata'if*, tr.: 134f).

78. al-Isfizari (tr.: 53, 55, 58f, 78).

79. Mustawfi (*Nuzhat*, tr.: 151).

80. *CHIr* (V: 485–87); Hafiz-é Abru (*Djughrafiya*, tr.: 30); J.A. Boyle: "The Mongol Invasion of Eastern Persia, 1220–1223," *History Today* 13/9, 1965; Djuzdjani (tr.: 1036ff).

81. On the basis of al-Harawi's figures and Mustawfi's information about the number of houses in Ghurid times, Petrushevskii calculates that Herat and its hinterland had 1.9 million inhabitants in pre-Mongol times (*CHIr*, V: 485 and n.5). This estimate seems just as arbitrary as the figures on which it is based. It can be added that before the Soviet invasion in 1979 the Herat enclave had about one million inhabitants.

82. Ibn Battuta (tr., III: 574); on the building activities of the Kart kings, see al-Isfizari (tr.: 84, 108).

83. al-Isfizari (tr.: 12, 15f).

84. Aubin (1968: 112f).

85. al-Isfizari (tr.: 123f, 126f); Samarkandi (tr.: 20f).

86. al-Isfizari (tr.: 11f, 15f).

87. Hafiz-é Abru (*Djughrafiya*, tr.: 18, 30); Le Strange (1905: 408); al-Isfizari (tr.: 19f).

88. *Tarikh-é rashidi* (tr.: 195).

89. al-Isfizari (tr.: 274, 276f, 316).

90. al-Isfizari (tr.: 313).

91. Kinneir: 181f; Christie estimated the intramural area at four square miles which is impossible. British agents later in the 19th century estimated the area at 160 ha, while a German survey undertaken during World War I gave 240 ha (1.500 m by 1.600 m). These figures agree more or less with the measurements cited by Isfizari (Gaube, 1978: 32ff).

92. Krawulsky (1978: "Sarahs"); Djuwayni (tr., I: 152, 155, 158, 162ff); Ibn Battuta (tr., III: 583); Le Strange (1905: 396); Mustawfi may not have been fully abreast of events. More important is therefore Ibn Battuta who as a rule recorded the names of towns destroyed by the Mongols.

93. Aubin (1968: 113).

94. Yaqut (tr.: 13, 563f); Le Strange (1905: 394f).

95. Melville (1980: note 13); al-Nasawi (tr.: 87f).

96. Cf. B.J. Stawiskij, *Die Völker Mittelasiens*: 52 (Bonn, 1982).

97. See article "Abiward" in *EI/2* (by Vl. Minorsky). No date for the abandonment of settlement is given here, however.

98. Aubin (1971: 116f); both the Abivard and the Nisa districts appear in Safavid lists (cf. the *Tazkirat al-muluk*, tr.: 103).

99. Ricciardi (1980: 69); Ibn al-Faqih (tr.: 244).

100. Ricciardi (loc. cit.); Yaqut (tr.: 196).

101. Djuwayni (tr., II: 617); Hafiz-é Abru (*Djughrafiya*, tr.: 55); Le Strange (1905: 393); Clevenger (1969).

102. MacGregor (1879, II: 85).

103. Yaqut (tr.: 208); Melville (1980: note 13).

104. Le Strange (1905: 391); Aubin (1971: 128f); on the Sarbadars, see Aubin (1976b) with criticisms of J.M. Smith (1970).

105. Kinneir: 170f; MacGregor (1879, I: 271f; II: 83ff); O'Donovan (1882, II: 34ff); *Tazkirat al-muluk* (tr.: 103).

106. Nasir-é Khusraw (tr.: 259ff); Yaqut (tr.: 466); summary of sources in Le Strange (1905: 352–363).

107. Ambraseys and Melville (1977).

108. Djuwayni (tr., II: 615, 618ff); The Isma'ilis were a militant, messianic movement tinged by egalitarianism. Apparently it had its chief support among merchants and craftsmen in the towns. Between the 11th and 13th centuries the movement succeeded in establishing several small states scattered through the mountainous zones of Iranshahr (*CHIr* V: ch. 5).

109. Le Strange (1905: 355); Adamec (1976 II: 628).

110. Nasir-é Khusraw (tr.: 259): Yaqut (tr.: 126).

111. Ibn Battuta (tr., III: 580f); Sykes (1902: 29); a hundred years before Kinneir (p. 184) had estimated the population at 18.000.

112. Malcolm (1829 II: 224f); Goldsmid (1876: 373); MacGregor (1879 I: 161f, 171f); Sykes (1902: 407).

113. The strategic transferrings of tribal peoples to different places in Khurasan, practiced from Safavid times onwards, do not seem to have led to any marked extension of nomadic subsistence, because the greater part of these tribal peoples were either sedentary or quite rapidly became so (cf. article "Ilat" in *EI/2*).

NOTES TO CHAPTER 16

1. Cf. Ibn Khurdadhbih (tr.: 91f) and the 10th-century geographers. Next to nothing is known about the administrative borders in Sassanian and earlier times (see the summary in Frye, 1975: 12).

2. Le Strange (1905: 159).

3. Kroll (1984).

4. Kroll (1984); also Kleiss in *AMI* 9: 19–44 (1976).

5. *CAH* (III/1: 314–371).)

6. Cf. I.M. Diakonoff and S.M. Kashkai, "Geographical Names According to Urartian Texts," *RGTC* 9 (*TAVO* B 7/9), Wiesbaden 1981.

7. Levine (1973).

8. See article "Matiana" in *PW*; Strabo (XI.14.8) explicitly identifies Matiene with Urmiyeh.

9. Arrian IV.18.3; Strabo XI.13.1.

10. The locating of Ganzak is uncertain, but Minorsky's suggestion that it is identical with Laylan seems plausible (cf. art. "Adharbaydjan" in EI/2). The name "Ganzak" (alternatively Gazakon, Gazaka, or Gazae) appears in classical and Armenian sources, but not in the Muslim ones. Rather, the latter refer to a town called *al-Shiz*, with a famous fire-temple, Azar-Gushnasp, said to have had special ritual functions in relation to the Sassanian dynasty (see the summary in Schwarz: 1117f). Shiz is no doubt identical with Takht-é Sulayman, a complex of temple and palace ruins about 100 km southeast of Lake Urmiyeh. Rawlinson suggested a further identification of Shiz and Ganzak, stating that: Shiz = Ganzak = Takht-é Sulayman. However, there are arguments speaking against this identification. First, the German archaeologists who excavated Takht-é Sulayman have found no traces of civilian settlement which could justify calling the site a "town" (D. Huff in *Iran* 7: 192, 1969). Second, Strabo (XIII.11.3.), whose data came from participants in the Azarbaydjan campaign in 36 B.C., clearly states that "Gazaka" lay on a plain. Takht-é

Sulayman is situated in the mountains, where Strabo has a fortress, Ouera, while Cassius Dio here mentions Phraaspa (49.25.3). It may be added that Theophanes (tr.: 16f), in his description of Heraclius' campaign in Azarbaydjan in the 7th century, distinguishes between "Gazakon" and – farther east on the road to Media -Thebarmais with the fire-temple. This can only be a reference to Takht-é Sulayman.

11. Ibn Khurdadhbih (tr.: 13).
12. Ibn Khurdadhbih (tr.: 91).
13. Procopius I.10.4.-12; Menander Protector, fragments 11 and 32 (in Constantine Porphyrogenitus).
14. Tabari (Noeldeke tr.: 123); al-Baladhuri (tr., II: 19); Schwarz: 1026f.
15. Ibn al-Faqih (tr.: 343); Movses Dasxuranc'i, *The History of the Caucasian Albanians* (tr. C. Dowsett): 4, 25, 115 (London 1961).
16. Procopius I.10.12 and I.16.7; Ibn al-Faqih (tr.: 343); Tabari (Noeldeke tr.: 157f); Hamza Isfahani (tr.: 42).
17. *Synodicon*: 307; Arran had a bishop of its own (cf. p. 276); al-Baladhuri (tr., II: 19); Yaqut (tr.: 21).
18. al-Baladhuri (tr., II: 26); Ibn al-Faqih (tr.: 341); Schwarz: 1006f.
19. Shaban (1971, II: 26, 33f); al-Baladhuri (tr., II: 24); Schwarz: 1185f.
20. Shaban (1971, II: 121).
21. Miskawayh (tr., V: 242f).
22. See the summary in Schwarz: 1006 and onward; Le Strange (1905: chap. XI).
23. Ibn Hawqal (tr., II: 327f).
24. Yaqut (tr.: 315 (Salmas), 14 (Udjan), 39 (Ushnuyeh), 524 (Marand), 219 (Khunadj).
25. A.K.S. Lambton, art. "Ilat" (in *EI/2*); Lambton (1973).
26. J.M. Smith (1975); Lambton, art. "Ilat" (in *EI/2*).
27. Planhol (1968: 210) bases his argumentation on the following: the 10th-century geographers mention villages, inhabited by Zoroastrians, in Mughan. Al-Muqaddasi adds that the capital, (shahr-é) Mughan, was a large and important town. At the beginning of the 13th century Yaqut refers to Mughan as grazing land for Turkoman nomads, but adds that villages could also be found. Finally, "al-Kazwini in the 15th century" states that the plain had become pasture for the Tatars who had driven away the Turkomans. Planhol refers to the sources collected in Schwarz (pp.1086–1094). He apparently assumes that the al-Kazwini referred to is identical with Mustawfi al-Kazwini (writing in the 14th century); but the author is in fact Zakariyeh al-Kazwini who died in 1283 and whose geographic writings were based extensively on Yaqut's *Mudjam al-buldan*.

Planhol thus assumes that Mughan in the 10th century was identical with the Mughan steppe, i.e. the lowland area south of the lower branch of the Aras. Yet this is not so simple, for on closer examination the information on Mughan is quite imprecise. Ibn Hawqal (tr., II: 365, 377) places Mughan town direct on the Caspian Sea. Al-Muqaddasi, on the other hand, locates it between Ardabil and Gilan (see ref. in Schwarz, cited above), far from the steppe itself. Yaqut (tr.: 548) states that one passes by the Mughan area when travelling from Ardabil to Tabriz. Regardless of whether the road ran north or south of the Sabalan masssif this does not indicate a location in proximity of the steppe. Mustawfi al-Kazwini (*Nuzhat*, tr: 91) mentions Mughan as a province, extending from the Qareh Su to the bank of the Aras, and he adds that winter grazing here was poisonous to the cattle. He cites as provincial center the town of Badjarvan which Le Strange (1905: 175) would therefore identify with the Mughan of the earlier geographers. However, this conflicts with Mustawfi's information that Bardjarvan was located some 100 km north of Ardabil, a fair distance inland. By this time, says Mustawfi, Bardjarvan had declined, as had the other towns of Mughan: Pil-Suwar and Barzand. The latter also stood north of Ardabil. The land surrounding the towns, however, remained under cultivation. Ghazan Khan is said to have founded a new town, Mahmudabad – presumably an *ordu-bazar* – on the "Gavbari plain near the Caspian Sea". Thus Gavbari, in the 14th century, denotes the Mughan steppe proper, which again was part of a larger administrative unit known as Mughan. We can conclude that the name "Mughan" in the Middle Ages comprised a much larger area than just the Mughan steppe. The descriptions in the geographical literature are vague, but indicate that settlement and cultivation were in fact concentrated in the uplands south of the steppe. The fact that changing groups of nomads used the steppe for grazing therefore constitutes no proof of any process of "bedouinization".

28. al-Baladhuri (tr., II: 27); Ibn al-Faqih (tr.: 341); further references in Schwarz: 1056f.
29. Nasir-é Khusraw (5f, tr.: 17).
30. Ibn Hawqal (tr., II: 328); Yaqut (tr.: 132f, 521).
31. Polo: 39; see also Ibn Battuta (tr., II: 344).
32. Mustawfi (*Nuzhat*, tr.: chap. 8).
33. Mustawfi (*Nuzhat*, tr.: 78–83).
34. Barbaro (tr.: 165f).
35. Kroll (1984).
36. Dols (1977: 45); Hafiz-é Abru (*Bayat*, tr.: 147); Khundji (*Tarikh-é 'alam-ara*, tr.: 87); on the later outbreaks, see Fasa'i (tr.: 80) and Sticker (1908 I/1).
37. See summary in Melville (1981).
38. Article "Tabriz" in *EI/1*.
39. Kinneir: 151; on Khuy, Maragheh etc., see p. 154f.
40. Fraser (I: 8); also *Memoir of the Right Hon. Sir John McNeill and His Second Wife Elizabeth Wilson*: 132, 147 (London 1910).
41. "Report on Persia" (1867), cited by Issawi (1971: 27f). The number of inhabitants can hardly have been greater in earlier times and Chardin's guess of over 500.000 in the 17th century is in any case improbable (Issawi, 1971: 13).
42. See Christensen (1987) for a short description of this process.

NOTES TO CHAPTER 17

1. S.M.A. Djamalzadeh, *Sar va tah-é yek karbas*, II: 109 (1956).
2. Thomas of Marga (tr.: 510).)
3. Mas'udi (*Murudj*, V: 170).
4. *Tarikh-é Sistan*: 190.
5. Hamza: 188.
6. Ibn al-Athir, cited in Schwarz: 312.
7. Tabari, cited in Schwarz: 1190; Elias (tr.: 136).
8. Ibn al-Athir, cited in Schwarz: 606.
9. Miskawayh (tr., IV: 445).
10. Miskawayh, II: 161; Hamza: 195.
11. Mirkhwand, C.F. Defrémery (ed.), *Histoire des Samanides, A.D. 892–999 par Mirkhkond*: 57 (Paris, 1845).
12. *Tarikh-é Sistan*: 356.
13. Ibn al-Athir, cited in Schwarz: 606; von Kremer (1880: 124).
14. al-Isfizari (tr.: 55).
15. Ibn al-Athir, cited in von Kremer (1880: 124); Dols (1977: 32) believes that this may have been a genuine case of plague.
16. Browne (1902: 602).
17. Ibn al-Athir, cited in Kremer (1880: 130); Schwarz: 522, 607.
18. al-Ahri (facsim. ed.: 173) where the 1346/47 outbreak in Tabriz is called *waba'-é 'azim*; on the outbreaks in Astarabad in the 1350s, see Aubin (1976: 38).
19. al-Samarkandi (tr.: 127, 131).

20. al-Isfizari (tr.: 274f).
21. al-Isfizari (tr.: 316).
22. al-Khundji (*Tarikh-é 'alam-ara-yé amini*: 87).
23. Jean Aubin takes it for granted that the Black Death decimated the population of the Plateau (e.g. Aubin, 1986), but provides no documentation.
24. Gottfried (1983: 49, 74f).
25. Fasa'i (tr.: 166). This was almost certainly an epidemic of the first pandemic of cholera.
26. Dols (1977: 40, note 3).
27. Dols (1979: 178f and note 38); *CHIr* I: 296, 302.
28. Pollitzer (1961: 453).
29. al-Isfizari (tr.: 274–277).)
30. *CHIr*, I: 296, 302; Sticker (1908, I/1: 237f).
31. J. Fryer: *A New Account of East India and Persia, being Nine Years' Travels, 1672–1681,*vol. III: 99. Ed. W. Crooke, London 1909–15.

Notes to Chapter 18

1. More detailed surveys of the physical environment can be found in Fairservis (1961: 12–22); Brice (1978: 165–182); Meder (1979: 30–53).
2. E.g. Ibn Hawqal (tr., II: 406); Mas'udi (*Murudj*, II: 80).
3. E.g. Goldsmid (1876: 256f).
4. Goldsmid (1876: 259, 267, 271f, 287); Tate (1910, II: 334).
5. The first steps were already taken at the turn of the century by British intelligence officers such as G.P. Tate. The American Pumpelly expedition carried out several investigations, largely of a geographic character in 1903–1904. In 1916 the indefatigable Aurel Stein made a survey, and Herzfeld examined the ruins at Kuh-é Khwadja in 1925. Immediately after World War II the French archaeological mission in Afghanistan searched Sistan for pre-historic settlements and also began excavating Lashkar-é Bazar, the Ghaznavid garrison town at Bust. The American Museum of Natural History made two smaller surveys in 1949–1951, and in 1967 the Italian Institute for the Middle and Far East (ISMEO) began systematic excavations of the site of *Shahr-é Sukhteh*. Finally the University of Bonn carried out surveys in the Afghan part of Sistan during 1969–1971.
6. Biscione (1974); Biscione (1977); Brice (1978: 166–183); Fairservis (1961: 94–102); Meder (1979: 53–65). Whether the necessary irrigation technology had been invented independently or, as asserted by the excavators (Tosi, 1973), was the result of diffusion from earlier settlements in the Tedzhen Delta in Turkistan via Mundigak, is of little importance in the present context.
7. Meder (1979: 53–65); Brice (1978: 166–183); Biscione (1977).
8. Scerrato (1966); Fischer (1976); Ball (1982: no. 752).
9. Herrenschmidt (1970); Herzfeld (1932: par. 1); Herodotus III.93.
10. Strabo XV.2.10; Arrian III.25.4; Polybius XI.39.13.
11. Isidore: par. 17; *Tarikh-é Sistan*, hereafter cited as *TS*: 22; *Shahristan*: par. 38; Tomaschek (1888: 211f); Ibn al-Faqih (tr.: 252).
12. Isidore: par. 16; Tomaschek (1888: 213); Tarn (1951: 14 and note 4).
13. Herzfeld (1932); Tarn (1951: 79ff, 276ff); Frye (1962: 171ff). See also A.D.H. Bivar's summary in *Fischer Weltgeschichte* 16 (Ch. 2) and *CHIr* (III/1). Tarn's suggestion (1951: 223) that there was no massive Saka immigration, but just an arrival of smaller groups of Saka mercenaries who eventually gave Sistan its name, is equally speculative. Yet it is at least more plausible than the idea of gigantic movements of peoples through the impassable terrain of the Hindu Kush (cf. Herzfeld, 1932: 21, who speaks of "hundreds of thousands").
14. Isidore: par. 17–18.
15. *SKZ*: lines 4, 42, 48; Tabari (Noeldeke, tr.: 17).

16. Isidore: par. 17. According to Tomaschek (1888: 207f, 211f), "Parin" must be identical with the town which the Tabula Peutingeriana calls "Aris. Perhaps this name is yet another misspelling of "Zarin". Ptolemy (VI. 19) also lists a number of *poleis* and *kumai* in Drangiane, but none of the names can be identified with historically known settlements.

17. Isidore: par. 18. Ball (1982: no. 792) would identify Palacenti with the site of Palangi, by the Hilmand (south of Zarandj). The distances given by Isidore speak clearly against this, but his information may not be that precise either.

18. Etymology and especially the distances given make plausible the identification of Phra with Farah, and of Nie with Nih. Schoff's suggestion (commentary to Isidor: 32, par. 16) that Gari is the same as Girishk, however, seems improbable considering that Girishk is located far east of Farah. Cf. Isidore: par. 16.

19. Ball (1982: no. 824, 1006, 190).

20. Herzfeld's reconstruction (1932: 70f) of the history of Sistan in Parthian times is highly speculative and cannot form the basis of hypotheses about the actual development. He thus identifies the "Indo-Parthian" kings, known from epigraphic and numismatic material in Pandjab, with the Suren, one of the seven famous Parthian-Sassanian noble families. He does so on the basis of Tabari's story that the Suren, at one time in a mythical past, had been allotted Sistan as their homeland. However, considering that the local *Tarikh-é Sistan* does not even mention the Suren, the notion of a special relationship between this family and Sistan appears to be sheer fiction. That the head of the Suren, bringing his own army, was made general of the Carrhae campaign does not suggest that the family's power base should be sought several thousand kilometers farther east.

Notes to Chapter 19

1. *Shahristan*: par. 38; Mustawfi (*Nuzhat*, tr.: 141); Ibn Hawqal (tr., II: 405). Notice also that Rustam, one of the central figures of the epic legends, came from Sistan.

2. *SKZ*: lines 55–56; Tabari (Noeldeke, tr.: 17). Ardashir of Sakastan continued to strike money in his own name, cf. *CHIr* (III/1: 729).

3. *SKZ*: lines 42 and 48.)

4. Ammianus Marcellinus XVIII.6.22; XIX.2.3.

5. Tabari (Noeldeke, tr.: 49, 115); Hamza (tr.: 36f); Herzfeld (1932: 2); *CHIr* (III/1: 132f, 140) where it is stated erroneously that the title of Sakanshah was abolished in 326.

6. Tabari (Noeldeke, tr.: 127f); Langlois (II: 352).

7. *TS*: 8f, 81f.

8. *TS*: 329.

9. al-Baladhuri (tr., I: 141f) where the local ruler is called "Aparviz, satrap of Sistan."

10. Ya'qubi (tr.: 90); on Sistan in early Muslim times, see Bosworth (1968).

11. *TS*: 92; Shaban (1970: 67f).

12. Shaban (1970: 67f).

13. *TS*: 146; al-Baladhuri (tr., II: 153f).

14. *TS*: 190ff; Ya'qubi (tr.: 97).

15. *TS*: 18f, 130.

16. *TS*: 126f, 140, 151. The name "Kharidjite" (*khawaridj*) originally referred to the "third party" of the civil wars of the 7th century, i.e. the group who would recognize neither 'Ali nor Mu'awiyah as the rightful caliph. The group's political goal was gradually forged into a doctrine that only the most orthodox and righteous Muslim could become caliph, regardless of his social and ethnic background. All true Muslims were bound to elect precisely this person to be caliph – and to remove him if he sinned – and to fight against all unjust caliphs.

When Ziyad b. Abihi and al-Hadjdjadj drove the Kharidjites from Mesopotamia, Khuzistan, and Fars, the latter dispersed into small groups under different leaders throughout eastern Iranshahr, where they established several small states. Because of their small numbers and their numerical inferiority in relation to the forces of the Empire, they developed a style of guerilla warfare and, if we are to believe the opponents' historiographers, they also applied terror on a systematic basis. The movement rapidly underwent ideological splits, and eventually the word "Kharidjite" came to mean "rebel" in general (Bosworth, 1968: 37–42).

17. *TS*: 156ff, 159f.
18. *TS*: 157f, 176f.
19. *TS*: 179f, 188.
20. Cahen (1958).
21. E.g. *TS*: 303.
22. *TS*: 175, 179, 191f.
23. Barthold (1928: 214f).
24. Ibn Khallikan (tr., IV: 301); Ibn Hawqal (tr., II: 407). 'Amr is said to have been a mule driver. The obscure social background of the brothers partly explains why official Muslim historians generally regarded them with such animosity. The anonymous author of the *Tarikh-é Sistan* was painfully aware of this problem and therefore constructed a fictive genealogy making the brothers direct descendants of Ardashir I and – through him of the legendary heroes of the epic traditions (*TS*: 200f).
25. Fairservis (1961: 37f and table 5).
26. Fairservis (1961: table 5, site no. 60–104); Ball (1982: no. 957).
27. Fairservis (1961: 45); Ball (1982: no. 752).
28. Fischer (1973: 145f); Fischer (1976: map 3); Ball (1982: no. 648, 808, 883).
29. Ball (1982: no. 200–201, 375, 778, 1073); Fischer (1973: 142); Ball (1982: no. 300, 390, 558, 607, 824, 836).
30. The contents of the geographical sources are summarized by Le Strange (1905: 335–351).
31. Ya'qubi (tr.: 89f); Le Strange (1905: 335f).
32. al-Istakhri (cited by Rawlinson, 1873: 293); Ibn Hawqal (tr., II: 405f); Le Strange (1905: 339).
33. Radermacher (1975); Fischer (1976: 180–191 and map 7); Tate (1910, I: 145–152).
34. *TS*: 125; that Ibn Suwayd was in fact governor of Sistan is confirmed by Ya'qubi (tr.: 95).
35. Fischer (1976: 40, 48f).
36. al-Baladhuri (tr., II: 141f); Rawlinson (1873: 292).
37. *TS*: 30–33.
38. Ibn Hawqal (tr., II: 404).
39. E.g. *TS*: 277.
40. *TS*: 406.
41. *TS*: 265f, 314.
42. Cf. Ibn Hawqal (tr., II: 406–409); Mas'udi (*Murudj*, II: 80); Tate (1909: 224f); Tate (1910, II: 325f).
43. Abbott: 173.
44. Cf. note 42 above. Concerning the use of wind-power in production, see also *TS*: 12.
45. Tate (1910, II: 289).
46. *TS*: 303.

NOTES TO CHAPTER 20

1. *TS*: 277.
2. *TS*: 268; the story admittedly sounds apocryphal. Bosworth asserts (*CHIr*, IV: 127f) that the Layth brothers' military adventures and building activities at home in Sistan must have entailed exorbitant taxation. This is unlikely, however, considering that *TS* emphasizes the moderate tax burden. Despite all his campaigns, 'Amr is said to have amassed great wealth in the treasury (*TS*:

247, 277), subsequently squandered by Tahir b. Muhammad. The original popularity of the Saffarid family also speaks against Bosworth's assertion.

3. Rudhrawari (tr.: 199f).
4. Ibn Hawqal (tr., II: 404f, 412).
5. *TS*: 404.
6. E.g. Chigini (Ball, 1982: no. 200–201); Gul-é Safid (Ball, 1982: no. 390); Pishwaran (Ball, 1982: no. 810).
7. *TS*: 358, 365, 389.
8. E.g., failing water supplies caused famine in 835 (*TS*: 186).
9. *TS*: 357, 368f, 394.
10. Djuzdjani (tr., II: 198). It is inconceivable that this would not have received mention in the *Tarikh-é Sistan*, had it actually occurred.
11. *TS*: 376, 386, 389.
12. *TS*: 371.
13. *TS*: 404–408, 411.
14. Finster (1976); Aubin (1968: 116f).
15. Cited in Finster (1976: 212).
16. Samarkandi (tr: 143); another Timurid historian, Salmari, says nothing of the destruction of weirs in his account of Shah Rukh's Sistan campaign.
17. Cited in Finster (1976: 214); see also Samarkandi (tr.: 139f).
18. *Ihya al-Muluk* cited by Aubin (1968: 93); Tate (1910, I: 63).
19. Ball (1982: no. 1006).
20. Tate (1909: 251); Tate (1910, I: 159f). Tate would locate this weir at Rudbar. Fischer (1976: 182) doubts that any large weir could have been located here. Considering that settlement generally tended to contract toward the northern part of the delta, a hypothetical weir in the Rudbar area can only have been of strictly local importance.
21. Tate (1910, I: 90).
22. E.g. Nishk, Gul-é Safidka, Shawal, and Kordu; cf. Ball (1982: no. 778, 375, 1073, 648).
23. Tate (1910, I: 167).
24. Kinneir: 190f.
25. Goldsmid (1876: 259, 267f, 271f, 281f, 288).
26. Goldsmid (1876: 256); Tate (1909: 231).
27. Goldsmid (1876: 259, 261); Tate (1909: 114f, 123f, 215, 223f); Tate (1910, I: 142, II: 331).
28. E.g. Barthold (1956, III: 9f); Finster (1976); Fischer (1975).
29. Goldsmid (1876: 281f). Bandjar was a village situated a few kilometers northeast of Zabul.
30. Tate (1909: 224f).
31. Mustawfi (*Nuzhat*: 48).
32. *TS*: 190, 358.
33. *TS*: 411.
34. Sticker (1908).
35. Ibn Hawqal (tr., II: 404f, 412).
36. Kinneir: 190; Goldsmid (1876: 262); Fairservis (1961: 13); Fischer (1976: 165, 173f, 189); Brice (1978: 172f). The salt concentrations now occur in spots, because over the centuries the rain has washed out the salt and deposited it in hollows in the terrain.

NOTES TO CHAPTER 21

1. E.g. art. "Bevölkerung" in *Kleine Pauly*.
2. J. Gernet, *Le Monde Chinois*: 65f (Paris, 1972).
3. Barkan (1957).
4. Cook (1981).
5. R. Davis, *The Rise of the Atlantic Economies*: 91 (London, 1973).
6. This estimate rests on an extremely limited basis: to the 5–6 million people which Mesopotamia *may* have had in late Sassanian times before the plague (see above, p. 99) must be added the populations of Khuzistan, Sistan, and the Plateau's innumerable small enclaves. Today these areas form the modern Iranian state which according to the first census had 19 million in 1956. This figure thus refers to a time when the population explosion characteristic of the 20th century had already begun to affect Iran. All figures for pre-industrial times are pure speculation. British diplomats, who were as well informed as anyone else, estimated the population in the 1860s at 5 million. John Malcolm, in the beginning of the 19th century, had given the slightly higher estimate of 6 million. As both Khuzistan and Sistan undoubtedly had been more densely populated earlier, the total population of Iranshahr east of Mesopotamia may have exceeded 5–6 million in the early Middle Ages, but it can hardly at any time have been greater than 10 million (which was also the estimate for the population at the outbreak of World War I): Beaumont (1976: 183f); Malcolm (1829, II: 518f); Issawi (1971: 28f).
7. An expert in Middle Eastern seismology, N.N. Ambraseys, does not believe that earthquakes were a serious obstacle to economic development in Iran, pointing out that the destroyed towns were usually rapidly rebuilt (Ambraseys, 1979; see also Ambraseys in Brice, 1978: 208f). In contrast, E.L. Jones argues (1981: 24ff) that the *cumulative* weight of disasters, including earthquakes, has generally been a serious burden for the societies in Asia. Given the vulnerability of the *qanat* to earthquakes, Jones would seem to have a point: collapsed and ruined *qanats* certainly represented a huge loss of capital. The question, however, is whether, in the absence of earthquakes, the resources spent on repairs could have been used to expand and improve production and productivity. This seems unlikely. Earthquakes may explain individual case of decline, but not "stagnation" as such.
8. The diffusion of the vertical windmill on the eastern Plateau does not change the picture. The technological innovation taking place within certain branches of industry (paper, ceramic tiles, etc.) during the Middle Ages is not relevant here.
9. On development potential in pre-industrial wet-rice producing societies, see Bray (1983).
10. Although Herodotus and other classical authors describe the Achaemenid armies as a veritable *levée en masse*, it is clear that the Persian armies even in this period possessed a professional core, represented by the 10.000 "immortals" and especially by a considerable number of Greek mercenaries. Documents from Mesopotamia regarding the distribution of *bit* ("fiefs") also indicate a certain degree of professionalization (see M.A. Dandamayev, "On the Fiefs in Babylonia in the Early Achaemenid Period," *AMI* Ergänzungsband 10: 57ff, 1983). When Herodian (VI.5.3, VI.7.1) states that the Sassanian Army consisted of a *levée en masse* which occasionally even comprised women, he is taking creative license with the stereotyped image of the barbarians. One has only to read Ammianus Marcellinus or the *Strategicon* of Mauricius (XI.1) in order to get an impression of the highly professional character of the Sassanian Army.
11. W.T. Treadgold, *The Byzantine State Finances in the Eigth and Ninth Centuries*: 24–29, 37 (New York, 1982). East European Monographs 121.
12. D. Twitchett (ed.), *The Cambridge History of China* (III, Sui and T'ang China, part 1: 207f, 362f, 465f. Cambridge 1979).
13. E.g. Tabari (Saliba tr.: 143).

14. Yaqut, cited by Wüstenfeld (1864: 428). On the increasing problems of financing the army, see Miskawayh (tr., IV: 26f, 32f); Hamza (tr.: 155).
15. Shaban (1971, II: 43).
16. Bosworth (1963: 126f).
17. Bosworth (1961: 73); Bosworth (1963: 261–266).
18. Barthold (1928: 238).
19. al-Rawandi, cited by Browne (1902: 598); see also Lambton (1953: 73f).
20. The question has been touched on, however, by Smith (1978).
21. On Transoxania under Uzbek rule, see V. Fourniau, "Irrigation et nomadisme pastoral en Asie Centrale," *Central Asian Survey* 4(2): 1–39 (1985).
22. A specific example of how nomad leaders came to control a combination of different resources can be found in J.J. Reid, "The Qajar Uymaq in the Safavid Period," *Iranian Studies* 11: 117–143 (1978). See also K.M. Röhrborn: *Provinzen und Zentralgewalt Persiens im 16. und 17. Jahrhundert*, Berlin (1966); J.E. Woods (1976).
23. Cf. the comments of Minorsky to the *Tazkirat al-muluk*: 30f.

DANSK RESUMÉ

I det europæiske billede af verdenshistorien er Mellemøsten kendetegnet ved at have gennemgået et langvarigt forfald: engang for længe siden, i den muslimske civilisations guldalder (8. til 10. århundrede), skal området have oplevet en økonomisk og kulturel blomstring og ydede ved den lejlighed sit bidrag til den menneskelige civilisations fremmarch. Men siden indtrådte så et vedvarende, uafvendeligt forfald: befolkningstallet faldt, byerne skrumpede ind (eller blev helt forladt), og barbarisk nomadisme bredte sig på det civiliserede agerbrugs bekostning. Vidtstrakte ruin-landskaber i bl.a. Nordafrika, Mesopotamien, Sistan viser, at forestillingen ikke er grebet ud af luften, og at tilbagegangen for civiliseret, bofast agerbrug nogle steder har været af enormt omfang. Men var tilbagegangen virkelig så generel og så omfattende, at vi kan tale om "forfald" som et overordnet kendetegn for Mellemøsten? Og hvad kan forklaringen i givet fald være?

Undersøgelsen tager udgangspunkt i den antagelse, at vekselvirkningen mellem menneskene og naturen er et dynamisk, forandringsskabende felt, og at et økohistorisk perspektiv vil give nye oplysninger og dermed en ny forståelse af langtidsudviklingen.

I undersøgelsens første del gøres rede for arbejdsmetoden, definitioner og anvendte kilder. Kapitel 1 behandler den knæsatte forestilling om "forfaldet" og de forklaringer, der i tidens løb er blevet givet: klimaforandringer, Islams konservative natur, Mongolerstormen og de andre middelalderlige barbarinvasioner, det Orientalske Despoti. Der argumenteres for, at disse forklaringer enten er forkerte eller i hvert fald utilstrækkelige.

I kapitel 2 afgrænses undersøgelsens genstand til *Iranshahr*, d.v.s. landene mellem Eufrat i vest og Amu Darya (Oxus) i øst. Afgrænsningen er ønskelig, fordi "Mellemøsten" er vagt defineret og derfor vanskelig at håndtere som historisk analyseenhed. Iranshahr er derimod en overskuelig størrelse, en politisk defineret enhed, som eksisterede fra det 6. århundrede f.Kr. til det 16. århundrede e.Kr. Landbruget i Iranshahr hvilede i høj grad på kunstvanding, og i kapitlet argumenteres for, at kunstvandingens omfang, former og konsekvenser var centrale variable. I grove træk kan Iranshahr således deles i tre økologiske regioner: (1) de lavtliggende, flodvandede sletter i vest, d.v.s. Mesopotamien og Khuzistan; (2) de spredte oaser på det iranske plateau, hvor kunstvanding i vid udstrækning var baseret på *qanat*-konstruktionen, der tapper grundvand. Sistan-bækkenet længst mod øst hører teknisk set med til plateauet, men takket være Hilmand-floden udgjorde det i praksis en region for sig og havde i kunstvandingsteknologisk og økologisk henseende lighedspunkter med flodsletterne i vest. (3) Endelig udgjorde den smalle stribe land langs det Kaspiske Havs sydbred en region for sig. Forholdene her var radikalt forskellige fra de øvrige regioner, først og fremmest p.g.a. den rigelige nedbør, og indtil for nylig var landet ret isoleret og marginalt i forhold til resten af

Iranshahr. Afhandlingen er lagt komparativt an, idet den går ud fra, at en sammen-ligning af langtidsforløbet i de vigtigste regioner, flodsletterne i vest og plateauet, vil kaste lys over karakteren og omfanget af den materielle tilbagegang og antyde udslagsgivende variable.

I kapitel 3 diskuteres nogle af problemerne, der knytter sig til de anvendte kilder, herunder også det arkæologiske materiale. Særlig vægt lægges på de sparsomme kvantitative informationer, bl.a. de forskellige skattepåligninger fra det 9. til 14. århundrede. Det godtgøres, at disse informationer kun i et vist omfang kan bruges til at dokumentere et generelt forfald, og at de snarere afspejler forskydninger i de skiftende imperiers geografiske baser.

Afhandlingens anden del behandler langtidsudviklingen i "Iranshahrs Hjerte," d.v.s. Mesopotamien og Khuzistan, fra ca. 500 f.Kr. og frem til og med den anden pestpandemi. Kapitel 4 behandler kort de særlige klimatiske og hydrologiske for-hold på flodsletterne, hovedlinierne i kunstvandingsteknologiens udvikling, samt de farer i form af saltophobning og sedimentering som storstilet kunstvanding in-debærer.

I kapitel 5 argumenteres for, at det gigantiske system af kanaler, der beskrives i kilder fra det 9. og 10. århundrede, begyndte at blive anlagt allerede i Achaemeni-disk tid, og at udbygningen fortsatte i Seleukidisk og Parthisk tid, ledsaget af grundlæggelsen af nye byer.

I kapitel 6 behandles kunstvandingens kulmination under Sassanidisk herre-dømme (3. til 7. århundrede). Der argumenteres for, at ekspansionen i vid ud-strækning var et resultat af en systematisk statslig koloniseringspolitik, der omfattede både anlæggelsen af store kanaler (som f.eks. Nahrawan-komplekset), grundlæg-gelsen af talrige byer, samt storstilede deportationer og tvangsbosættelser.

I det 6. og 7. århundrede afløstes ekspansionen af en dramatisk tilbagegang, der skyldtes en kombination af flere faktorer: voksende økologisk ustabilitet som følge af kunstvandingens omfang, borgerkrige og invasioner, samt de katastrofale følger af den første pestpandemi (541- ca. 750). I kapitel 7 tillægges pestepidemierne af-gørende betydning, fordi de decimerede arbejdsstyrken og dermed forhindrede den nødvendige vedligeholdelse af de komplekse kanalsystemer. I kapitlet argumenteres yderligere for, at epidemiske infektionssygdomme mere systematisk inddrages i den historiske analyse.

Trods skiftende herskeres forsøg på at vende udviklingen gennem anlægs- og reparationsarbejder fortsatte tilbagegangen og affolkningen i Mesopotamien også efter pestens forsvinden i det 8. århundrede. Kapitel 8 behandler denne udvikling, og der argumenteres for, at forklaringen skal søges i den helt særlige kombination af økologiske omstændigheder, sygelighedsmønstre (herunder pestens tilbagevenden i det 14. århundrede) og politiske variable.

Kapitel 9 ridser hovedlinierne i Khuzistans historie op i samme periode. Også her indtrådte et historisk maximum i Sassanidisk tid, og storstilede kunstvandingsanlæg, bygrundlæggelser, samt deportationer var igen elementer i en systematisk kolonise-ringspolitik. Khuzistan blev også ramt af en markant affolkning i løbet af mid-delalderen, men p.g.a. det svage kildemateriale er de nærmere omstændigheder vanskelige at identificere. Både økologisk ustabilitet og sygelighed synes dog at have været centrale variable.

Afhandlingens tredje del behandler langtidsudviklingen på det iranske plateau, Iranshahrs anden økologiske hovedregion. De særegne fysiske forhold, bosættelsens spredte karakter, samt *qanat*-konstruktionens revolutionerende betydning disku-teres i kapitel 10.

Kapitel 11 forsøger i meget grove træk at tegne et billede af bosættelsens karakter i før-Sassanidisk tid. Der argumenteres for, at selv om der fandtes *qanat*-baserede bosættelser allerede i Achaemenidisk tid, synes teknologien ikke at være blevet taget i storstilet anvendelse før Parthisk og Sassanidisk tid. Følgelig havde det kortvarige græske herredømme næppe mærkbar indflydelse her (i modsætning til Meso-potamien).

I de følgende kapitler (12 til 16) gennemgås hovedlinierne i udviklingen i plateauets enkelte "lande": Djibal (med Kumis og Gurgan), Fars, Kirman, Khurasan (med Kuhistan) og Azarbaydjan. Som i Mesopotamien og Khuzistan iværksatte kongerne, frem for alt Sassaniderne, bygning af kunstvandingsanlæg og grundlæg-gelse af byer, og bosættelsen ekspanderede ind i selv de mest marginale og ugæst-milde områder, f.eks. det nordlige Kirman. Men i modsætning til Mesopotamien oplevede plateauet ikke nogen entydig tilbagegang. Trods krige, naturkatastrofer og epidemier forblev bosættelsen bemærkelsesværdig stabil. I det samlede billede ses konstante fluktuationer, men få dramatiske ændringer. I kapitel 17 diskuteres den slående historiske forskel mellem Iranshahrs regioner, og der argumenteres for, at de økologiske forskelle, herunder også et lavere sygelighedsniveau på plateauet, er nøglen til forklaringen.

For at udvide det komparative aspekt og underbygge argumentationen for de økologiske variables betydning, foretages i afhandlingens fjerde del en undersøgelse af Sistan-bækkenet, som netop i økologisk henseende ligner flodsletterne i vest (kapitel 18).

Sistans udvikling forekommer næsten helt parallel med Mesopotamiens, selv om der er mindre kronologiske forskelle. Kunstvandings- og bosættelsesmaximum indtrådte således først i tidlig muslimsk tid (8. til 9. århundrede) ledsaget af anlæg-gelsen af imponerende kanalsystemer. Der er dog stærke indicier for, at ekspansio-nen var begyndt allerede i Parthisk og Sassanidisk tid, og at de middelalderlige kanaler faktisk havde forløbere i før-muslimsk tid (kapitel 19). Under alle om-stændigheder vendte udviklingen tilsyneladende pludseligt mod slutningen af det 10. århundrede, og trods de lokale herskeres anstrengelser for at reparere vandings-anlæg og bremse sandflugten blev Sistan i løbet af middelalderen skueplads for en affolkning og tilbagegang, der overgik hvad der skete i Mesopotamien. Traditionelt lægges skylden på de ødelæggende krige, især under timuriderne, men det passer hverken med de arkæologiske data eller med de lokale skriftlige kilder. Der er næppe nogen enkel forklaring, men – som i Mesopotamien – synes voksende økologisk ustabilitet affødt af selve kunstvandingsekspansionen at have været en afgørende variabel. Argumenter herfor fremlægges i kapitel 20.

Forestillingen om et generelt forfald er således en misvisende forenkling af Iranshahrs historie. De store flodvandede enklaver, Mesopotamien i vest og Sistanbækkenet i øst, oplevede ganske vist i løbet af middelalderen en massiv deurbanisering og tilbagegang i landbrug og befolkningstal. Antagelig var de storstilede kunstvandingssystemer selvødelæggende i det lange løb. Under alle omstændigheder gjorde den voksende økologiske ustabilitet de store landbrugsenklaver sårbare over for forstyrrelser, og for i hvert fald Mesopotamiens vedkommende synes den demografiske katastrofe under den 1. pestpandemi at have været et vendepunkt.

Et andet mønster tegner sig i det iranske højland. De enkelte oaser og enklaver her gennemlevede fluktuationer forårsaget af både krige, epidemier og naturkatastrofer, men de fleste overlevede. Enkelte enklaver, først og fremmest Marv og Ray, blev forladt; i nogle områder, f.eks. i det sydlige Fars og Kirman, blev mange gamle byer forladt, og ekstensive subsistensformer vandt udbredelse på bekostning af bofast agerbrug. Men i andre områder, f.eks. Azarbaydjan, skete der samtidig en betydelig bosættelsesekspansion og urbanisering. I et langtidsperspektiv er kontinuiteten derfor slående, og afhandlingen argumenterer for, at de økologiske forskelle regionerne imellem må inddrages, ikke som forklaring i sig selv, men som et heuristisk redskab.

I et afsluttende kapital fremhæves de politiske konsekvenser af udviklingen. Sammenbruddet i de mest produktive regioner (Mesopotamien og Khuzistan) berøvede de skiftende statsdannelser i Iranshahr en stor del af deres ressourcegrundlag. Trods deres stabilitet kunne plateauets enklaver ikke kompensere for dette tab. Deres produktionskapacitet var begrænset af teknologiske og økologiske årsager, og staterne i Iranshahr, der i oldtiden og den tidlige middelalder havde været stormagter, sank ned til at blive andenrangs magter. Dette afspejles i den militære transformation, der fandt sted i løbet af middelalderen: de kostbare stående hære blev erstattet af billigere (men også upålidelige) opbud af nomadekrigere, og til sidst overtog nomadeledere kongemagten i Iranshahr. De favoriserede områderne med god græsning (f.eks. Azarbaydjan), hvilket forklarer, at Iranshahrs politiske og økonomiske tyngdepunkt begyndte at forskyde sig mod nordvest. Men det skal understreges, at denne udvikling ikke skyldtes nogen iboende militær overlegenhed hos nomaderne, men derimod at det økonomiske grundlag for at opretholde regulære hære forsvandt. Det historiske forløb i Iranshahr må ses i lyset af den særegne dynamik i landbruget, som udsprang af sammenstødet mellem de specifikke økologiske og teknologiske begrænsninger på den ene side og de politiske krav om merprodukt på den anden.

Index

Detailed references to certain regions (Mesopotamia, Khuzistan, Djibal, Fars, Sistan etc.) and dynasties (e.g. Achaemenids, Arsacids, Sassanians, Abbasids, Buyids) have been omitted because their number is so great as to have little use to the reader.